The India-China Relationship

A Joint Project of the Asia Society and the Woodrow Wilson International Center for Scholars

The India-China Relationship

What the United States Needs to Know

Francine R. Frankel and Harry Harding

Editors

Columbia University Press
New York

Editorial Offices

Woodrow Wilson Center Press
One Woodrow Wilson Plaza
1300 Pennsylvania Avenue, N.W.
Washington, D.C. 20004-3027
Telephone: (202) 691-4010
www.wilsoncenter.org

Order from

Columbia University Press
New York, Chichester, West Sussex
136 South Broadway
Irvington, N.Y. 10533 USA
(800) 944-8648 or (914) 591-9111
www.columbia.edu/cu/cup

Printed in the United States of America on acid-free paper ♾

2 4 6 8 9 7 5 3 1

Library of Congress Cataloging-in-Publication Data

The India-China relationship : what the United States needs to know / Francine R. Frankel and Harry Harding, editors.
p. cm.
ISBN 0-231-13236-0 (cloth : alk. paper) — ISBN 0-231-13237-9 (pbk. : alk. paper)
1. India—Foreign relations—China. 2. China—Foreign relations—India. 3. United States—Foreign relations—20th century. 4. World politics. I. Frankel, Francine R. II. Harding, Harry, 1946–

DS450.C61523 2004
327.51054—dc22 2003062712

ABOUT THE CENTER

The Center is the living memorial of the United States of America to the nation's twenty-eighth president, Woodrow Wilson. Congress established the Woodrow Wilson Center in 1968 as an international institute for advanced study, "symbolizing and strengthening the fruitful relationship between the world of learning and the world of public affairs." The Center opened in 1970 under its own board of trustees.

In all its activities the Woodrow Wilson Center is a nonprofit, nonpartisan organization, supported financially by annual appropriations from the Congress, and by the contributions of foundations, corporations, and individuals. Conclusions or opinions expressed in Center publications and programs are those of the authors and speakers and do not necessarily reflect the views of the Center staff, fellows, trustees, advisory groups, or any individuals or organizations that provide financial support to the Center.

Contents

Figures and Tables

Figures

Tables

Nicholas Platt, President

The Asia Society is America's leading institution dedicated to fostering understanding of Asia and communication between Americans and the peoples of Asia and the Pacific.

An international nonprofit, nonpartisan educational organization, the Society provides a forum for building awareness of the more than thirty countries broadly defined as the Asia-Pacific region—the area from Japan to Iran, and from Central Asia to New Zealand, Australia, and the Pacific Islands.

Through quality programs, including high-level conferences, symposia, international study missions, press briefings, publications, art exhibitions, and performing arts productions, the Society reaches out to a broad range of professionals and citizens interested in foreign affairs and culture.

Founded in 1956 by John D. Rockefeller 3rd, the Society reaches audiences around the United States through its headquarters in New York and regional centers in Houston, Los Angeles, Washington, D.C., and San Francisco. Asians from all walks of life also participate in the Society's work through its Hong Kong and AustralAsia Centers, representative offices in Shanghai and Manila, an International Council, and programs in Asia.

The Asia Society is supported by contributions from foundations, corporations, and individuals who believe in the mandate of the Society: to build bridges of understanding between Americans and Asians.

The Asia Society's family of websites includes: AsiaSociety.org (www.asiasociety.org), AskAsia® (www.askasia.org), and AsiaSource (www.asiasource.org).

Foreword

As we head into a new century, the two most populous nations on earth, India and China, continue a long and tangled relationship. With a contested border, sharp eyes on the balance of power in Asia, economic competition, nuclear weapons, and daunting internal problems, their interaction will deeply affect not only stability and prosperity in the region, but also vital U.S. interests. The dynamics of the India-China relationship are little known to or understood by Americans.

The Asia Society and the Woodrow Wilson International Center for Scholars are therefore pleased to present *The India-China Relationship: What the United States Needs to Know.* This book is the result of years of collaborative efforts and the hard work of many dedicated individuals. The project that resulted in this book was inspired by the belief that U.S. policy makers, the academic community, and the informed public require fresh thinking and greater attention to India-China relations, as both countries promise to be of strategic importance to the United States in the decades ahead.

India and China are wary neighbors who have fought border wars and still have unresolved border issues left unattended but certainly not forgotten. India watches China carefully and keeps close tabs on China's friendly relationship with Pakistan. China also has its own concerns—for example, India's hosting of the Tibetan government in exile. India and China pay careful attention to each other's military developments, whether nuclear capabilities, planned blue-water navies, missile tests, or the exercises of troops along their common border. Moreover, there is the growing competition between these two countries in any number of areas: for markets and foreign direct investment, for closer ties with Southeast Asia, and for improved relations with the United States.

Against this backdrop, there has been a remarkable sparseness of scholarly attention to this relationship and a general lack of interaction between China and India scholars. As the project began, there existed only two book-length studies of India-China relations authored by Americans in the last twenty-five years. South Asia watchers looked at the region in terms of an India-Pakistan binary, while the vision of China watchers never seemed to veer to the southwest of the Tibetan plateau. With such limited intercourse between these two, academic modes of inquiry in Asia as well as the institutions of policy formation have been severely handicapped.

It was our belief that if the United States is to lead effectively in the emergent post–Cold War world, it must better understand what drives national policies and the important dynamic between these two major and still emerging Asian powers. The September 11, 2001, terrorist attacks and subsequent war in Afghanistan served to underline this need.

In June 2003, Prime Minister Atal Behari Vajpayee spent six days in China, the first trip of an Indian prime minister to China in a decade. The visit is a welcome sign that India and China have reestablished channels of communication. These were put under great pressure following India's nuclear test in 1998. This said, few tangible agreements were reached during the Vajpayee visit, and much hard work remains to be done on the questions that this book addresses.

This volume takes a multidisciplinary approach. It brings together scholars from political science, history, economics, international relations, and security studies to add depth to the debate beyond security considerations. The book is divided into three sections. The first provides a historical overview of India-China relations. The second explores the various dimensions of the relationship. The third assesses the implications for the United States. Throughout, the contributors address three common issues: (1) the similarities and differences between the two countries' strategic cultures, domestic circumstances, and international environments; (2) the broader international contexts for their bilateral relations; and (3) the parallels and tensions between their national interests.

From the outset, we have benefited from a distinguished advisory committee to guide this project. We are deeply grateful to Harry Harding, Francine R. Frankel, the contributors to the volume, and the project advisers for their hard work on this complex, important enterprise. The chapter authors deserve our gratitude for their patience and diligence through many drafts and revisions. Marshall M. Bouton, at the time executive vice president of the Asia Society, played a seminal role in developing the project. On the Asia Society's staff, Rob Radtke, Alyssa Ayres, Mike Kulma, Sanjeev Sherchan, Hee Chung Kim, and Justin Sommers have all made significant contributions. We express our gratitude to Robert M. Hathaway and Liang Sun of the Woodrow Wilson International Center for

Scholars for their important role. Special thanks as well to the Woodrow Wilson Center Press and Columbia University Press for publishing this work and to their directors, Joseph Brinley and James D. Jordan, respectively, and copyeditor Suzanne Schaeffer who worked to bring this project to its published conclusion.

The Asia Society and the Woodrow Wilson Center also want to thank the Shanghai Center for International Studies, the China Institute of International Studies in Beijing, the Institute of Peace and Conflict Studies in New Delhi, and the Confederation of Indian Industries in Bangalore for hosting a delegation of our editors and authors during the summer of 2001. These meetings provided valuable insights in the evolution of chapters from drafts to final versions.

Finally, this book and the larger project would not have been possible without the generous support of the C.V. Starr Foundation, the Rockefeller Brothers Fund, the BGM Kumar Foundation, the GE Fund, and the Irfan Kathwari Foundation.

The centrality of the India-China relationship to the long-term future of peace and stability in the region cannot be overstated. We believe this book will add significantly to the field of study as well as sharpen the thinking of U.S. policy makers and academics about Asia.

Ambassador Winston Lord
Co-Chairman, International Rescue Committee, and former Ambassador to China

Ambassador Frank G. Wisner
Vice Chairman, External Affairs, AIG Inc., and former Ambassador to India

Part I

Historical Overview

1

Introduction

Francine R. Frankel

Security partnerships in Asia are entering an era of realignment amid considerable uncertainty about how new configurations will affect the national interests of the United States. The September 11, 2001, terrorist attacks on the World Trade Center and the Pentagon sent a savage message of rage against U.S. policies among fundamentalist Muslim groups in Afghanistan, Pakistan, and the Middle East. They also paved the way for the projection of American power into Central Asia, which is increasingly taking on the appearance of a long-term presence. The U.S.-led war on global terrorism, with its initial assault on Al Qaeda in Afghanistan, has involved the provision of long-term support for Pakistan to strengthen moderate Muslim leadership; sizable contributions to the international coalition of donor nations for rebuilding Afghanistan as a unified and stable state; and the establishment of American military bases in the former Soviet republics of Kyrgyzstan and Uzbekistan to protect core interests in the region. In addition, the doctrine of preemption adopted by the George W. Bush administration to justify its controversial attack on Iraq in March 2003, and to prevent potential threats from Iraq's program to develop weapons of mass destruction, will involve the United States in the reconstruction of Iraq and in the "remaking" of the Middle East for years to come.

The U.S. preoccupation with the war on international terrorism and with preventing the spread of weapons of mass destruction should not divert attention from underlying changes, well under way before the September 2001 attacks, that have the potential to affect the overall balance of power in the foreseeable future. Most important is the rise of China and India in Asia, both states with great-power ambitions. This is a period when old habits of suspicion and distrust could be shaken up by building on the mutual benefits of cooperation among the United States, China, and India against a common new danger. Alternatively, depending on how well U.S. strategy accommodates the security interests of China and India—which, as this volume demonstrates, are often conflicting—long-standing suspicions of U.S. intentions in this part of the world could be exacerbated.

The United States faces, on the one hand, an unprecedented threat for an indeterminate time, but, on the other hand, a set of unexpected opportunities. One example in the aftermath of the terrorist attacks is the effort of the United States and Russia to find a new framework of strategic relations. President Vladimir Putin's decision to open Russian airspace to U.S. military planes headed for bases in the Central Asian republics created new room for cooperative Russian-American relations, symbolized by the establishment of the NATO-Russia Council in May 2002 as a formal mechanism for consultation. Opportunities for political dialogue could ultimately result in agreements on cuts in stocks of nuclear warheads, greater economic ties, scientific collaboration on some aspects of an antiballistic missile system, and cooperation in developing the oil and gas resources of Central Asia and the Caspian.

Yet the cooperation of Russia, China, India, and—under U.S. pressure—the Pakistani government in the U.S.-led war on Islamist terrorism should not obscure the persistence of their significant concern about the purposes for which American power will be deployed. China, India, and Russia all have been uneasy with America's role as the sole superpower and the Bush administration's inclination toward unilateralism. All three countries have been searching for ways to create a multipolar or polycentric international system in which they can ensure their autonomy in making foreign policy.

China's concern about the inroads of fundamentalist Islamist groups in its vulnerable western border region of Xinjiang has, for the time being, produced general expressions of political support for the United States in the war on terrorism, although China opposed the Bush administration's decision to wage war on Iraq. In addition, bilateral differences over such important issues as the future of Taiwan, theater missile defense, non-proliferation, human rights, and, potentially, the new presence of the United States in neighboring Central Asia and Pakistan will be difficult to resolve.

India, the most vulnerable to Pakistani-trained *jehadis,* whose origins are in Pakistan or other Muslim countries but who constitute anywhere from 40 to 70 percent of the terrorists operating inside Kashmir, has even more reason to support the U.S. attack on Al Qaeda. In an unprecedented decision, India offered the use of its naval facilities and intelligence to American forces in support of U.S. operations against the Taliban in Afghanistan. At the same time, India is apprehensive about the U.S. strategy that makes Pakistan—India's enemy neighboring state and the source of training and support for *jehadi* groups operating in Kashmir—into a frontline ally, along with promising in June 2003 a multiyear program of $3 billion in economic and defense assistance as rewards for Pakistan's withdrawal of official support from the Taliban, fighting terrorism, and ensuring there is no nuclear proliferation.

The 13 December 2001 terrorist attack on India's Parliament by groups operating from Pakistan produced a turning point in national policy, generating a consensus among all Indian political parties that "cross-border terrorism" must be ended. This demand was not satisfied by the statement of Pakistan's President Pervez Musharraf on 17 January 2002, outlawing five Islamist groups and withdrawing support from terrorist groups based in Pakistan and Pakistan-administered Kashmir. India, which put its army on full alert, resulting in approximately one million troops massed on both sides of the Indo-Pakistani border, preferred to wait for clear evidence that infiltration had stopped on the ground. Only toward the end of October 2002 did India announce that it would begin a gradual pull-back of troops from the border, having carried out fair elections to Kashmir's state legislative assembly despite a boycott called by Islamist separatist groups and a reported step-up in Pakistan-supported infiltration. Although India's view is that the elections, with a voter turnout of close to 40 percent in very difficult conditions, will settle the international issue of India's legitimate integration of Jammu and Kashmir, it is hard to predict the future course of

Pakistan's reaction. The October 2002 elections called by President Musharraf to national and provincial legislatures produced a "shock" result, giving six religious parties under the umbrella Muttahida Majlis-e-Amal (MMA) more than 17 percent of the seats in Parliament. The MMA made its strongest showing and formed the governments in the two provincial assemblies of Baluchistan and North West Frontier province bordering Afghanistan, where Al Qaeda and Taliban activists are suspected to have found sanctuary.

So long as Russia remains militarily and economically weak, the United States has little reason to be concerned about the "strategic partnerships" struck by Moscow with both Beijing and New Delhi. Nevertheless, they indicate the interest of both China and India in establishing a security system in Asia that curtails U.S. "hegemonism." In particular, China and Russia share concerns about strategic pressure from the eastward expansion of NATO, the active American role in Central Asia, the reinforced U.S.-Japan Security Guidelines, U.S. intervention in countries on grounds of humanitarian concern, and the Bush administration's policies for developing national missile defense (NMD) and theater missile defense (TMD). On 16 July 2001, the Russian and Chinese Presidents, Vladimir Putin and Jiang Zemin, signed a twenty-year Treaty of Neighborliness, Friendship, and Cooperation, the first such agreement between their two countries since the breakdown of their Cold War alliance culminated in the border skirmishes of 1969. Although the treaty does not have the character of a military alliance and its focus is on economic and military-technological cooperation, it commits Russia to unqualified support for China's claim to Taiwan, offers China's support for Russia on Chechnya, and pledges both countries to create "multilateral" mechanisms of collaboration on questions of security in neighboring regions.[1] According to the signatories, the "utmost responsibility" for maintaining international peace and stability belongs to the UN Security Council, where each country enjoys veto power.

India has revived its close cooperation with Russia on military and defense issues. During the visit of Russian President Vladimir Putin to New Delhi 2–4 October 2000, India and Russia issued a "Declaration on Strategic Partnership" and agreed to establish an Inter-Governmental Commission on Military-Technical Cooperation to facilitate "defence and military-technical cooperation in a long-term perspective," including cooperation in the peaceful use of nuclear energy and outer space. The two countries closed deals for the sale of 310 T-90 Russian battle tanks, more than half of which will be coproduced in India, and for technology transfers to manufacture 140 Su-30 MKI fighters under license.[2]

During Prime Minister Atal Behari Vajpayee's return visit to Moscow in early November 2001, Russia agreed, over U.S. objections, to construct two 1,000-megawatt light-water pressurized reactors in southern India and to supply low-enriched uranium fuel for the light-water reactors at Tarapur. The Moscow Declaration signed by the two leaders during the visit echoed the language of the China-Russia treaty in reaffirming the "central role of the United Nations in the efforts of the international community in the struggle against terrorism."[3]

China has also hinted that it would be more receptive than it has in the past to the idea, floated by then Russian Prime Minister Yevgeny Primakov in 1999, of strengthened cooperation between Russia, China, and India on international issues about which they have similar concerns. In November 2001, Russian Foreign Minister Igor Ivanov revived the idea of Moscow, Beijing, and New Delhi working in tandem "to establish a system of security and stability" in Asia.[4] This idea of a strategic triangle will be difficult to pursue so long as India perceives greater benefit from advancing the qualitatively new level of bilateral U.S.-India ties that has followed Washington's decision in December 2001 to lift sanctions imposed after New Delhi's May 1998 nuclear tests. At the same time, the formal announcement, on 16 December 2001, by the United States of its unilateral withdrawal from the 1972 Antiballistic Missile Treaty to pursue the development of national missile defense not only stunned Russia but created a conundrum for India, which had offered conditional support for NMD as a defensive weapons system on the assumption that a mutual agreement could be worked out with Russia.

Subsequently, a meeting of the India-U.S. Defense Policy Group resulted in a pledge of significantly increased defense cooperation, including combined training exercises between U.S. and Indian military forces, joint small-group exercises in special operations, and the establishment of a separate Security Performance Group to speed up review of India's requirements for defense supply. The Bush administration, moreover, has cleared sales of the Israeli Phalcon system to India, allowing India to acquire a state-of-the-art Airborne Warning and Control System. Meanwhile, Pakistan, with help from China and North Korea, is emerging as a serious missile power.

American foreign policy makers, proud of U.S. military successes and caught up in the short-term compulsions of maintaining fragile antiterrorist coalitions to sustain support in the Muslim world, have paid little attention to efforts by China and India, in cooperation with Russia, to establish the groundwork for a multipolar international order. Yet the United States confronts serious pressure to formulate coherent policies for responding to the long-term changes in the distribution of power represented by the rise of both India and China in Asia. This will become an urgent concern even with respect to short-term goals as both rising powers seek to assure their own influence—including access to critical energy resources—in Central Asia, an area each considers part of its own geographical and historical sphere of influence.

Focusing on the Long Term

In the medium to long term, the consensus among major powers on defeating international terrorism will have less direct impact on the role that China and India can be expected to play as rising powers in the first decades of the twenty-first century. Just as the struggle against international terrorism is an unprecedented foreign policy challenge for the United States, so is the emergence of two states in Asia with potential as global powers, both of which, like Russia, seek to be treated as equal partners with the United States.

China and India, each having a population of more than one billion people, experiencing historically high rates of annual growth in gross domestic product (GDP), and developing increasingly sophisticated scientific and military capabilities, only recently began to claim the attention of American policy makers within the context of an integrated Asia policy. Until the last years of the Clinton administration, U.S. security policy addressed India and China on separate, segmented planes, mapping India within South Asia, on a par with Pakistan, and China as an emerging dominant power in East Asia.

Decision makers have yet to form a consensus about the implications of the shifting balance in Asia for U.S. interests. Formulations about the potential for U.S.-China relations have swung sharply between the Clinton administration's goal of a "strategic partnership" and the characterization of China as a "strategic competitor," first introduced by President Bush during his 2000 election campaign. Subsequently, a positive but more cautious formula was adopted by both President Bush and President Jiang Zemin after the Asia-Pacific Economic Cooperation (APEC) meeting on 19

October 2001 at Shanghai: that of a "cooperative" and "constructive" relationship.

A similar indeterminacy characterizes the relationship of the United States and India, described by both countries late in the Clinton presidency as one of "natural allies." This formulation was warmly embraced during the early months of the Bush presidency, but the phrase was omitted after September 11 as senior administration officials emphasized the need to "balance" American pressure on Pakistan and India to resolve differences over Kashmir that threatened to escalate into war between the two nuclear-capable states. Instead, in the press conference held with Prime Minister Atal Behari Vajpayee in Washington on 9 November 2001, President Bush spoke of "developing a fundamentally different relationship with India—one based upon trust, one based upon mutual values."[5] The text of the congressional resolution welcoming the prime minister on his visit to the United States did describe the "world's two largest democracies" as "natural allies," but that alliance was "based on their shared values and common interests in building a stable, peaceful and prosperous world in the twenty-first century."[6] So long as President Bush feels constrained to use similar language to describe the bilateral U.S.-Pakistan relationship, characterizing it as "built on the shared interests and values of the American and Pakistani peoples," it will be difficult to spell out the specific policy content of the concept that India and the United States are natural allies.[7]

Most of all, a wide range of complex interactions between India and China that directly impact U.S. concerns, including defense and nuclear nonproliferation, have not been part of policy analysis on strategic issues in Asia. A continuing lack of focus on those interactions could seriously limit the ability of the United States to devise effective policies to stabilize its bilateral relationships with both China and India during a period in which interstate relations in Asia are "layered, complex and potentially subject to change."[8]

The dynamics of these complicated and potentially changing relations between India and China are closely analyzed by the contributors to this volume. In chapter 2, "Perception and China Policy in India," Steven Hoffmann contrasts India's great-power worldview with its modest role in international security affairs, but argues that India is entering a new phase as a rising power in which strategic autonomy will remain the basic principle of its foreign policy, and "polycentrism"—including India as an equal to the UN Permanent Five powers—its desired world power structure. Hoffmann asserts that within this worldview, India's strategic community remains wary about the possibility of an aggressive Chinese foreign policy over the long term. Such apprehensions arise from the scarring experience of India's defeat by China in the 1962 border war; the extremely slow progress of bilateral negotiations to establish the Line of Actual Control (LAC); and China's close alliance with Pakistan involving the transfer of nuclear and missile technologies, which has confined India's role within the South Asia region. Nevertheless, after the events of September 11 many mainstream strategists hold out hope of building a positive working relationship between the two countries to advance their common interest in curbing "hegemonic trends" in world affairs. Susan Shirk, in her counterpart chapter 3, "One-Sided Rivalry: China's Perceptions and Policies toward India," points to the marked asymmetry in China's view of India even after the May 1998 nuclear tests, which is that India does not merit special attention as a security threat. Shirk argues that since 1979 China has sought to improve relations with India to create a peaceful environment for the implementation of economic reforms, its highest priority in achieving great-power status. This has involved some distancing from Pakistan's position on Kashmir and a policy congenial to India of recommending bilateral negotiations. Although progress has been exceedingly slow, New Delhi and Beijing have been engaged in a strategic dialogue since 1993 aimed at keeping peace on the LAC.

Other contributors find reasons to be more pessimistic about the prospects of real improvement in the bilateral relationship. Sumit Ganguly's analysis in chapter 4, "India and China: Border Issues, Integration, and International Security," traces the obstacles to a better relationship as viewed from both the Indian and the Chinese perspectives. Ganguly argues that long-standing differences across several issue areas ensure that Sino-Indian relations, despite temporary improvements, will remain competitive over the long term. The "troubled relationship" goes beyond the glacial pace of progress on settling the border dispute. It also includes China's unwillingness to officially recognize India's 1975 annexation of Sikkim, India's concern about the growing Chinese military presence in Myanmar, the long-standing Chinese suspicion of Indian support for political activities of Tibetan exiles, the Chinese military's unhappiness with India's nuclear program, and India's conviction that the nuclear threat from Pakistan has been indirectly fostered by the transfer of nuclear weapons and missile delivery systems from China. Ashley Tellis, in chapter 5, "China and India in Asia," writes that the two countries found themselves "enmeshed in competition almost from the moment of their creation as modern states." Tellis argues that as their power and political capabilities grow, the structural context of Chinese-Indian interactions in Asia will sharpen competition between them in the subregions of South Asia, Central Asia, the Persian Gulf, and Southeast Asia, either to secure access to critical resources or to prevent the other from acquiring a preponderant position that could eventually constrain their foreign policy choices. At the same time, the multifaceted dimensions of the Sino-Indian competition will also require both countries to simultaneously reassure and befriend each other to avoid a "malignantly rivalrous" competition, and this outcome will be facilitated by their still subordinate position (to the United States) in the international order.

A critical element in the outcome of this competition is certain to be the two states' comparative performance in sustaining high levels of economic growth. As T. N. Srinivasan points out in chapter 7, "Economic Reforms and Global Integration," both countries emerged as "star growth achievers" in the two decades since 1980. Nevertheless, China's growth rate was about 4 percent higher than that of India, and China also outperformed India in exports, in attracting foreign direct investment, and in implementing prereform investment in physical and social infrastructure. Srinivasan suggests that China's dictatorship provided freedom to the reformers from pressure groups that stood to lose from the reforms, and also insulated them from press criticism. Yet he questions whether China's strategy of reducing social costs by keeping inefficient state-owned enterprises (SOEs) dominant, while trying to create new employment opportunities, will work as well once the economy is subjected to much greater international competition after entry into the World Trade Organization.

George Perkovich, in chapter 6, analyzes the reasons for another aspect of the gap in strategic strength between India and China in a comprehensive overview of the comparative development of their nuclear and missile programs and policies. Just as China began economic reforms much earlier than did India, in 1977 compared with 1991, so China decided on a crash nuclear weapon building program as early as 1955, testing its first nuclear weapon in 1964; India, by contrast, "ambivalently and haltingly" moved from a "peaceful" nuclear explosion in 1974 to a nuclear weapon test in 1998. Perkovich argues that the drivers for each country's nuclear and ballistic missile programs were quite different. Chinese leaders initially were motivated to prevent the United States from threatening the use of nuclear weapons in a crisis. Indian leaders and scientists were more concerned with signaling the United States, China, and the Soviet Union that they could not limit India's strategic autonomy through nuclear blackmail.

Even so, China's nuclear superiority at present confers no plausible war-fighting advantage against India because of India's conventional defensive advantage in the Himalayan border terrain.

India, which is relatively weaker than China, may be willing to accept America's global leadership so long as it is recognized as an equal partner, and to play an informal role with the United States in ensuring the Asian balance. However, Mark Frazier, in his overview of the future of Sino-Indian relations, chapter 9, anticipates complex challenges to the United States as both countries expand their power and influence outside their South Asia and East Asia neighborhoods. He considers the likelihood that India will pursue a realistic nuclear deterrent capability against China, involving more tests and missile launches, and the possible linkages between China's participation in various international nonproliferation regimes and U.S. pursuit of NMD, the latter of which could undermine India's security by encouraging Chinese transfers of advanced technologies to Pakistan. These dynamics are, of course, apart from the factors affecting structural reforms and economic growth in both countries, the impact of generational changes and institutional reforms, and contingencies ranging from an India-Pakistan war to unrest in Xinjiang or Tibet.

The U.S. stake in a stable security environment in Asia will be vitally affected by the ways in which the potentialities for conflict, competition, and cooperation in China-India relations develop. Many of the factors influencing the outcome will be outside the control of the United States. One dramatic example is North Korea's admission in late October 2002 of the existence of its secret nuclear weapon program, which American intelligence officials have concluded was based on uranium enrichment technology supplied by Pakistan in return for North Korea's Nodong missiles (called Ghauri in Pakistan), acquired to neutralize India's missile capabilities.[9] Nevertheless, Indian policy and Chinese policy can no longer be formulated without taking into account the linkages that will be perceived by each country as it measures its relative position with respect to the other. In the first decade of the twenty-first century, the United States confronts a challenge of the highest order. Decision makers will have to formulate U.S. policies toward India and China without exacerbating conflicts between the two countries and without forcing a choice between friendship and enmity with either of two rising powers striving to achieve their major-power destiny within a foreseeable future. The other path open to U.S. policy makers, and elected by the Bush administration in waging war against Iraq despite opposition by all members of the Security Council except Great

Britain, is even less attractive: the pursuit of unilateralist policies in Asia and the Middle East. That approach would confer some credibility on the potential evolution of a Russia, India, China strategic triangle.

An important signal of warming relations between India and China was the week-long visit of Prime Minister Atal Behari Vajpayee to China in June 2003. A joint statement signed by Prime Minister Vajpayee and Prime Minister Wen Jiabao was hailed as a breakthrough by both countries. India recognized Tibet is part of Chinese territory and agreed not to permit "anti-China activities" by Tibetan exiles living in India. China, in turn, recognized India's administrative control over the state of Sikkim, in the following wording incorporated in the statement: "The Indian side agrees to designate Changgu of Sikkim state as the venue for a border trade market."[10]

China and India in Historical Context: Origins of Overlapping Claims to Greatness

The relations between China and India in the twenty-first century would seem to have little relevance to the ancient past. Yet leaders in both states since the 1950s, a time when as "developing countries" they were among the most backward economies in the world, have been convinced of the historic destiny of their own nations to achieve great-power status. Such convictions are best understood by giving serious attention to the frequent invocations by each of geopolitical and cultural superiority over thousands of years as the dominant centers of civilization in overlapping regions of Asia.

This certitude in the case of China is embedded in historical memories of military and/or cultural preeminence over large areas of Asia by powerful dynastic states. The first unified Chinese state, dating from the short-lived Qin dynasty (221–206 B.C.E.) established in present-day northern China, paved the way for a long process of territorial expansion to the south, east, and southwest. It took more than a thousand years, marked by several "periods of division," to consolidate a well-defined heartland region. The Han dynasty, with two central poles first in the west and then in the east during the period from 206 B.C.E. to 220 C.E., gave way to multiple dynasties and kingdoms along an east-west axis, followed by an era of north-south divisions. The Sui dynasty (581–618) and the Tang dynasty (618–907) reunified most of the heartland to the southern and eastern coastal boundaries of the South China Sea, East China Sea, and Yellow Sea but had command of less territory than did the early Han in the north and southwest.

Nevertheless, the early Tang, like the early Han, manifested what became China's historical urge to control "the periphery" in order to protect the heartland. In the early dynastic period, this was accomplished by establishing military protectorates in Central Asia that went as far as the Khyber Pass, Kabul, Herat, Turkestan, Samarkand, and Tashkent. Side by side with the use of force in protecting China's strategic interests, basic precepts of Confucianism were adapted to emphasize the moral legitimacy and cultural superiority of China relative to surrounding states. Confucian teachings linking a harmonious cosmic order with rules of propriety based on hierarchical deference relations in the family, the society, and the state placed the emperor at the pinnacle of power as the Son of Heaven and China as the Middle Kingdom at the apex of a hierarchical international order.

These dual elements—the use of coercive power to expand territorial boundaries and the assertion of moral self-righteousness to legitimize China's claims to deference—coexisted from the earliest period of state formation. The Chinese used military force, usually at the beginning of a dynasty when they were strongest, to secure the Central Asian and northwest periphery. At the same time, they sought to establish notions of Chinese cultural superiority through symbolic and ritually prescribed tributary relationships with those weaker kingdoms in East Asia and Southeast Asia that were more sinicized in their cultural and political arrangements. The substance of such relations often consisted of no more than a protocol for trade relations, including a language of obeisance, presentation of gifts to the Chinese emperor (which were reciprocated), and performance of the kowtow. The tributary system also allowed China to keep potential rival coalitions divided, sowing competition by bestowing differential favors upon the various countries received at the imperial court, and in some cases facilitated China's internal political interference, e.g., in Vietnam and Silla (part of contemporary Korea).[11]

China's historical impulse to domination encountered serious setbacks, both from internal rebellion and from external conquest. According to Swaine and Tellis, China was "embroiled in domestic conflict, divided between Chinese and non-Chinese regimes or entirely ruled by non-Han Chinese invaders" for approximately half the period from the end of the Han dynasty in 220 B.C.E.[12] The conquering Mongols and their foreign Yuan dynasty (1271–1368) swept across Central Asia, including the Karakoram, Samarkand, and the Aral Sea, and sent expeditions against

Burma, Siam (Thailand), Annam (north Vietnam), and Champa (south Vietnam). The Ming dynasty (1368–1644) reestablished Han Chinese rule, but as John Fairbank points out, the Ming remained "transfixed by the Mongol menace."[13] During this period China adopted defensive policies in foreign relations. These policies included building the Great Wall against northern invaders, paying subsidies to the Mongols to check their raids into Chinese territory, and using the tributary system "as a form of defense" to limit involvement with foreigners by restricting trade.

Paradoxically, however, the conquests made by foreign dynasties were converted in historical memory to areas of legitimate Chinese influence. Indeed, the greatest transformations that led to the establishment of the boundaries of modern China were the result of invaders from the north. The Manchus established the sinicized Qing dynasty (1644–1911) and, although beset with internal rebellions and external struggles for almost all of their period in power, nevertheless used military force to extend China's control over a larger area than the limits of any previous dynastic regime. The Qing conquered Taiwan in 1682; defeated the Zunghar warriors in Mongolia, loyal to the Dalai Lama in Tibet, in 1696; installed a new Dalai Lama loyal to China in 1720; and conquered the western Mongols in the 1750s. Finally, after repeated failed attempts to defeat the Uighur kingdom in eastern Turkestan, the Qing succeeded, with the financial help of Great Britain, in annexing the area, renamed Xinjiang (or "new territory") in 1884. It was these conquests that provided the basis for Chinese claims to sovereignty over non-Han populations and territories in Manchuria, Mongolia, Taiwan, Tibet, and Xinjiang. The conquered regions did not become part of the Han Chinese "heartland" until the areas were formally annexed by the Nationalist Chinese government that overthrew the dynastic system in 1911 and ended the Confucian era.

Swaine and Tellis suggest that the rise of security threats to the heartland from distant and powerful modern nation-states pushed China to adopt direct methods of control as protection from external attack, in contrast to domination through suzerainty relations.[14] Yet the Chinese conquests for the most part preceded the "century of humiliation" that began with the Opium Wars in 1839, which forced China to conduct trade relations with Europeans as equals. More painful were the unequal treaties imposed by Great Britain, Germany, France, Italy, Japan, and Russia, which brought with them treatment of Chinese as inferiors in their own Middle Kingdom. The inability of the Qing to understand the transformation in warfare brought about by the revolution in sea power can perhaps be attributed to their experience of success, using traditional armies, in expanding Chinese power in East Asia, Central Asia, and Southeast Asia. This lack of comprehension led to greater humiliation for China during the Sino-French War of 1885, when the Chinese were forced to renounce their traditional tributary relationship with Vietnam and to recognize Vietnam's independence; and during the Sino-Japanese war of 1894–95, which led to their recognition of Korean independence. As John Garver points out, it was the British desire to maintain Chinese suzerainty over Tibet as a way of excluding the Russians that preserved a modest Chinese administrative and military presence in Tibet, while introducing a high level of Tibetan autonomy and British-Indian influence.[15] By contrast, in 1945 the USSR, supported by the United States, exerted strong pressure on China to recognize the full independence of Mongolia.

The Qing, nevertheless, had laid the groundwork for territorial claims that, after the victory of the Chinese Communist Party (CCP) over the Nationalist Guomindang in 1949 and the entry of the People's Liberation Army (PLA) into Tibet in 1951, significantly enlarged the Chinese "heartland." The vast area newly under Chinese control had a relatively small, non–ethnic Han population but was strategically located to neutralize any threat from India in the west or from the Soviet Union in the north. Tibet alone constituted almost 13 percent of the total land area of the People's Republic of China (PRC) and 40 percent of all its mineral resources.[16]

Adapting China's traditional formulation of strategic security—that of protecting the heartland by controlling the periphery—to the contemporary period, the Chinese are concerned about great-power influence in Central Asia, including that of Russia and the United States; about India's claim to dominance in South Asia and its "Look East" policy in Southeast Asia; and most of all about U.S. preeminence in South Korea, Taiwan, and Japan in East Asia. Adding to China's anxiety about being "contained" in its Far East backyard are the volatile situations within Tibet and Xinjiang, where the local populations have been in open opposition or actual rebellion against Chinese rule over more than five decades. Although the strong dictatorship of the CCP has so far contained any serious threat to central control from the annexed "periphery," the first concern of any ruling group that aspires to major-power status remains the preservation of internal social order. China's great advantage—the historical political consciousness of the majority Han population of China as a great state—remains.

The more extraordinary claim to destiny as a great power is that of India, which was never unified as a single state even during periods of great empires on the subcontinent. During roughly the same era in which a unified Chinese state started to evolve within the Han heartland, the rulers of the greatest and most powerful Indian empire, the Mauryas, (313–226 B.C.E.), spread out from their capital at Pataliputra in the middle Ganges valley northward to parts of Afghanistan and ruled most of the subcontinent through a system of district administration backed up by large military forces and sustained by a share of the value of all crops grown throughout the domain. Nevertheless, the last ruler of the dynasty, Ashoka, called by Basham the "greatest and noblest ruler India has known and indeed one of the great kings of the world,"[17] left a legacy influenced by Buddhism that had a universal moral appeal transcending territorial boundaries. Ashoka's edicts, preserved on rocks and pillars placed all over India, were addressed to his officers and subjects; they recount his feelings of pity and grief when hundreds of thousands of persons were killed or taken captive to conquer "an unconquered country." The edicts instruct that "the greatest of all victories is the victory of Righteousness, here and on all borders." As Basham interprets this message renouncing aggressive war, "Ashoka believed that, by setting an example of enlightened government, he might convince his neighbors of the merit of the new policy and thus gain the moral leadership of the whole civilized world."[18]

Ashoka left no centralized empire. The governors of the greatest provinces established the provinces' independence, and his descendants controlled only the area around the capital for about fifty years. Subsequent efforts of the Guptas (320–550) to rebuild imperial power, also from the Gangetic heartland of Pataliputra, extended dynastic rule on the Gangetic Plain from Punjab on the west to Bengal in the east, Kashmir in the north, and the Deccan in the south. This period, known as the classical age of Sanskrit culture, was one of patronage to artists, sculptors, dramatists, and architects of the Brahmanical, Buddhist, and Jain faiths. It was also an era of sea trade with China, Ceylon, and Southeast Asia, as well as the time of the overland camel caravans along the northern silk routes of Central Asia to China. The Guptan empire, organized roughly along the same lines as that of the Mauryas, had declined by the middle of the sixth century, drained of resources by efforts to ward off assaults by the Huns from the northwest. The third attempt to unify north India, by the remarkable warrior-king Harsha from his Gangetic kingdom at Kanauj, which also supported Buddhism, did not outlast his reign (606–47). Other great warrior-rulers asserted their authority in southern India; there, the dominance of the seafaring Pallava-Chola spilled over to Southeast Asia from roughly 600 to 1200.

What is striking, by contrast with China, is the missing impulse to create a territorial heartland and then to protect it against attacks from the periphery, in turn pushing the boundaries of the heartland to incorporate parts of the periphery and repeating the cycle to consolidate a territorial state. Jaswant Singh, who served as India's minister of external affairs before moving over to the Finance Ministry in 2002, wrote in 1999 that "a territorial consciousness, and a strategic sense about the protection of the territory" was absent until the period of British rule:

> Adversaries were confronted but only after invasion, then too, on a ground of the former's choosing; they were never, of course, pursued, and threats were not recognized until they actually occurred; they were neither anticipated nor neutralized beyond the territory, before they could actually materialize. . . . This absence of a sense of geographical territory persisted from ancient India down the ages, to the medieval period and even later. Of none of these periods does there exist even a suggestion of a reliable map, even though there are descriptions, but with only the unmistakable landmarks being fixed—say, of rivers, the mountains or the oceans.[19]

Contemporary scholars have referred to "ideas" of India that emerged out of plural notions of the nationalist elite, but these included no single, clear definition of India as a unified political community. As Khilnani put it, "the possibility that India could be united into a single political community was the wager of India's modern, educated urban elite . . . on an idea: the idea of India."[20]

Yet much more than such a wager underpins the nationalist narrative of India's great-power destiny. At its core, this conviction rests on beliefs about India's unbroken civilizational unity as the carrier of a superior ancient culture, one in which Ashoka's precept that the moral leadership of the world can be gained by setting an example of enlightened behavior has retained its resonance for a wide spectrum of the educated classes.

India did not become a political fact until independence in 1947. By contrast, the idea of India as a civilizational entity had its origins in the Vedic Sanskrit religious and literary texts composed over long periods, the precise dates of which are still matters of debate, but going back at least to 1500–500 B.C.E.[21] Vedic ideas about the origin of the universe, the ritual powers of Brahmans in maintaining cosmic order, the differentiation of society into the varna hierarchy, and associated notions of karma and reincarnation became the foundational ideas of Brahmanical religious beliefs and also penetrated Buddhism and Jainism. Historically, the structure of society built upon these religious beliefs and values, as they were adapted to varying regional patterns of social stratification, constituted India's civilizational identity. It is argued elsewhere that this same set of beliefs was the source of Brahmanical or sacral legitimacy for localized dominant warrior and landed groups, making it unnecessary to have a state in order to preserve social order.[22] The ritual hierarchy based on notions of purity and pollution coincided with the hierarchy of wealth and occupation, especially at the lower levels. The force needed to uphold this dual stratification system was exercised by the warrior-chief/king, and the use of force was legitimized by the Brahmans.

Control over a defined territory was of only secondary importance in the Hindu conception of kingship. Under the Brahmanical tradition, the king's primary role of upholding dharma and the hierarchical social order sanctified by the gods gave greater importance to ritual incorporation of conquered local kings and territories. Long after the time of the Mauryas, the Chola state, which established its sway over the southern half of peninsular India (1000–1200), never wielded direct political power outside its core domain around the Kaveri basin. Yet the founder of the dynasty is extolled by scholars much in the manner of Ashoka—that is, for establishing a ritual, dharmic hegemony over the intermediate and peripheral zones of his realm. Foremost among the accomplishments attributed to Rajaraja I are his support for Brahmanical institutions, the construction of great temples, and the adoption of the royal Siva cult. Indeed, the "genius of Rajaraja" is defined precisely in his ability to rule using sacral symbols of incorporation in the absence of a centralized and bureaucratic state. A similar assessment is made of the Vijayanagara state based to the north of the Kaveri in the Tungabhadra core region, whose mission was to protect Hindu culture against Muslim expansion. Outside the imperial center, the kings were linked to localities "neither by resource flows nor commands" but by ritual incorporation through support of Brahmanical institutions and temples.[23]

During the first millennium, especially during the period when Buddhism spread from central India, India's influence beyond the subcontinent was exerted not through aggressive war but by "exporting" religious ideas, cultural forms, and knowledge. Twentieth-century scholarship that "look[ed] over the fence . . . so as to restore in the world of the imagination the continuity of the real world" rediscovered the strong religious and cultural influences exerted by India on China and Southeast Asia, amounting to the "Indianization" of these societies. Wales refers to claims of "extreme Indianists" that the states of Southeast Asia had been Indianized in almost every aspect of their civilization to the point that they became Indian "cultural colonies." He stops short of endorsing this view, observing that if those claims were true it would be impossible to consider China "on the same plane as 'Greater India.'"[24] Yet it is striking that Jawaharlal Nehru, writing *The Discovery of India* from the Ahmadnagar Fort Prison between 1942 and 1945 while jailed by the British for leading the Quit India movement, quotes Wales's earlier account of the "marvelous flowering of Indian art and culture in Java and Cambodia." Nehru writes about his excitement when he first read detailed accounts of "waves of colonization" from India through the many countries of Southeast Asia, "sometimes referred to as Greater India," and throughout refers to "Indian colonies" and culture in Southeast Asia.[25]

The full extent of India's cultural influence on China does not appear to have been appreciated until well after independence, when scholarship in English became available on the spread of Buddhist teachings in Sanskrit texts by traders, missionaries, and monks who sojourned at monasteries in urban centers across the overland routes of northern India and Central Asia to China (the Silk Road).[26] Indian translators and teachers of Buddhist texts traveled to China at various times, in the fourth century though Kashmir and in the seventh century through Tibet, after it was united as an independent kingdom. Buddhist studies flourished at Nalanda university in Magadha, central Bihar, under the patronage of the King of Kanauj, from the fifth century until the early eleventh century. Chinese monks were among the many scholars from foreign countries who came to study with Indian teachers, obtain Buddhist texts, visit sacred Buddhist sites, and carry back Buddhist relics.

Many features of the Buddhism adopted in China by the time of the Tang dynasty contained elements of Sanskritic Brahmanical culture: the belief in Buddha as a deity with supernatural power; the performance of sacral rites and religious ceremonies imbued with magical power; the belief in the existence of heavenly worlds presided over by Vedic deities as way stations to the final destination of nirvana; the concept of the eternal Buddha beyond human understanding; historical manifestations of numerous Buddhas as sacred figures to whom precious gifts such as gold, silver, precious stones, and jewels could be made to accumulate religious merit; notions linking worship and donations to reincarnation and the prospect for a better birth in future life cycles and also prosperity in this life; and finally the concept of bodhisattvas, or religious apprentices, as candidates for Buddhahood who, when worshipped and offered donations of luxurious gifts, could provide laymen with vehicles of salvation to heavenly lands of bliss on the way to nirvana.[27] In China, from the time of the mid-seventh century Buddhist monks were believed to enjoy miraculous powers over the souls of the dead and to be able to transfer merit to determine the future lives of the living. Buddhists were appointed as spiritual preceptors at court, and in 648 Emperor Taizong, in failing health and seeking spiritual merit, began the process of issuing edicts to ordain thousands of monks and nuns and to lavishly endow Buddhist monasteries.[28] Tansen Sen reports that Chinese literature designated India as the "Western Heaven," signifying that India occupied a special place in the Chinese world order.[29]

Brahmanical teaching or sastras were also translated from Sanskrit into Chinese by the time of the Sui dynasty (581–618), including those on astronomy, mathematics, and medicine, and Indian astronomers or astrologers were advisers at the Chinese capital during the Tang dynasty (618–907), and also at the courts of Southeast Asian rulers. In Southeast Asia, Indian influences represented a mix of Buddhism and Hinduism spread mainly by way of an all-sea route from western ports through the Strait of Malacca. Indians played a significant role as advisers to local rulers, intermarrying and transmitting the Brahmanical sastras in areas that are now parts of Indochina, Cambodia, Thailand, Indonesia, and Myanmar (Burma). The borrowed concepts showed considerable staying power in court circles, and efforts to proscribe Buddhism in China as a "foreign" religion in the ninth century were abandoned because of the strong roots it had struck, particularly among the poorer classes.

Nevertheless, in the second millennium direct religious, cultural, and commercial links between India and China were virtually severed as each struggled to resist attempts by northern nomadic tribes to loot and conquer urban centers and annex border provinces. During the Mongol invasion of China, entire tribes of Turkish nomads were pushed into Afghanistan and Persia, which became the base for a series of invasions of northern India by Turko-Afghan Muslims, attended by looting of gold and jewels, rape of women, and destruction of Hindu and Buddhist temples. By 1202, "India's major center of Buddhism, including the great university at Nalanda, where more than ten thousand monks lived and studied, was sacked . . . driving thousands of Buddhists forward to Nepal and Tibet. . . . The severity of Turko-Afghan persecution directed against centers of Buddhist monasticism was so unrelenting that the religion of Buddha was now sent into exile from the land of its birth never to return again in any significant numbers."[30] The Central Asian invaders, who also destroyed Chinese Buddhist monasteries and caused many of the trade routes to be closed off, ensured that the Chinese were "no longer open to Indian and Central Asian influence."[31] By the fourteenth century, with the restoration of the Ming dynasty, a Han cultural resurgence of neo-Confucianism and religious Taoism, reflecting the "local genius" of the pre-Indianized civilization, "domesticated" and "appropriated" Indian influences. Subsequently, a kind of "forgetting" occurred about the origin of the Buddhist concepts that were incorporated in religious and philosophical thinking.[32] This paved the way for the revival of traditional notions of the legitimacy of the Chinese emperor as the Son of Heaven and imperial rule in accordance with the mandate of Heaven.

India, by contrast, never consolidated a strong national political identity that could be rallied to expel the series of Turko-Afghan Muslim sultanates that ruled in Delhi and the Gangetic Plain from 1206 to 1526. The Delhi Sultanate, which reached its peak of power in the early fourteenth century, defeated many Rajput chiefs in the Deccan and Gujarat, pushed back the Mongols, and brought the Muslim faith to peninsular India. But the sultanate also "Indianized" its dynasties by assigning grants of revenue from landed areas not only to Turkish military bureaucrats, but also to local Hindu chiefs and petty rajas who were left in control of their domains.

India was again vulnerable to Central Asian armies once the Delhi Sultanate declined at the end of the fourteenth century. Timur swept down the northwestern passes to plunder Delhi and the Punjab, leaving a "trail of blood and torture." It was Timur's great-grandson Babur, the king of Kabul (descended on his mother's side from the great Mongol, Genghis Khan), who founded the Mughal dynasty in 1526.

Even the rule of the Great Mughals (1605–1707) did little to shake the ingrained notion of the superiority of Indian culture. Muslim cultural syncretism, which attracted Persian artists, poets, architects, and musicians to the lavish "Mughlai" lifestyle of the imperial and provincial capitals, drew on "the best of maharaja traditions," while alliances between Mughal emperors and princes and Rajput kings and other Hindu chiefs "Indianized" Muslim culture. It is a tragic irony of history that the last Great Mughal, Aurangzeb, an orthodox Muslim committed to preserving a pure Islam in India, vanquished his elder brother Dara Shikoh in part because Dara became absorbed in the quest for religious enlightenment, and spent more time before his death immersed in the teachings of the Hindu classics translated from Sanskrit to Persian than in conspiring to save his throne. It is said that Rajput nobles in the thousands died for Dara Shikoh in the final battle with Aurangzeb, whose victory marked the end of religious tolerance and of the equal treatment of Hindus by Muslim rulers.[33]

Subsequently, Mughal power came under increasing strain from struggles over succession, factional rivalries at court, reassertion of independence by viceroys in South India, renewed attacks by Afghan invaders, and, in 1738, the devastating destruction of Delhi by the Persian armies of Nadir Shah. The Marathas moved out of their base in the western Deccan to undermine Mughal power in much of the north, east, and south during the eighteenth century, making effective use of sacral symbolism to rally Hindu chiefs against Muslim rule. But the Marathas also relied on deals with disaffected local Rajput and Jat landholders and chiefs, even while colluding with ambitious Mughal governors to form an elaborate but weak alliance system.

The main beneficiary of the breakdown in imperial power was the British East India Company, whose sepoy regiments, recruited primarily from peasant warrior castes and three hundred thousand strong, underpinned British territorial expansion in the subcontinent. The company not only defeated disunited Muslim, Maratha, and Rajput rulers, but also disarmed the local chieftains who served as their intermediaries. For the first time in India's history, the ground was cleared for establishing a centralized administration reaching down to the districts and in some areas to the subdistrict (tehsil or taluka) level. In 1857, British rule in India passed to the Crown. The Indian Civil Service, whose officers served as collectors and magistrates in the districts, was supported by a civil police force and a military contingent in cantonment towns.

The British Raj did not lead to the downfall of any dynastic system and, in its effort to preserve stability, as a matter of policy tried not to interfere with the existing hierarchical social order in the vast rural areas. Nevertheless, it was perhaps as destructive of Brahmanism in India as the century of humiliation had been of the Confucian belief system in China. Unwittingly in many ways, it created conditions for the emergence of a centralized state whose authoritative basis in law was normatively independent of Brahmanical legitimization.[34] In so doing, it established a separate sphere in which educated individuals, coming in principle from all castes high and low, and eventually with government assistance in the form of "reservations," could aspire to status and power based on accomplishment rather than birth.

Above all, the British Raj could not be Indianized. On the contrary, it produced and patronized English and European Sanskritists who marveled at the "wonder that was India" but dismissed contemporary Indian society as riddled with caste superstitions, steeped in ignorance, and economically and scientifically backward. The British turned the tables on Brahmanism, unequivocally asserting the superiority of Western civilization. This judgment was institutionalized in the adoption of English as the medium of instruction in all government schools as well as those of the Christian missionaries, who included in the curriculum a critique of the Brahmanical teachings as man-made tools of tyranny to keep the lower castes ignorant and suppressed.

The enormous changes unleashed finally ignited the flame of nationalism among the educated classes, albeit with only modest disruption of ancient cultural continuities in the localities. Unlike China, whose intellectuals attacked the outmoded principles of Confucianism as the cause of their humiliation, India, under the leadership of Mahatma Gandhi and the Indian National Congress, reached into its own cultural heritage to transform the principle of nonviolence into an effective political instrument of noncooperation with colonial rule.

Legacies of History in India-China Relations

The definition of India's territorial boundaries, never before considered important, became a first priority for the British, who sought to protect India from foreign invasion as the cornerstone of its empire from the Persian Gulf to the Indian Ocean. Their preoccupation focused almost entirely on Russia's advances in Central Asia, especially toward Afghanistan and the sea routes from Iran (Persia). Yet it was China that had historically carried on a lively trade with India along the silk routes, established protectorates in Central Asia, asserted control in Kabul and in the Khyber Pass, and shared the longest border of more than 2,500 miles (4,000 kilometers) with India. None of this history was considered relevant in an imperial age when China could no longer assert its power.

The mountainous barriers in the north provided the British with a strategy for protecting the heartland that shared much with the concepts that guided China at the times of its greatest expansion. The "inner ring" of the Himalayan kingdoms of Nepal, Bhutan, and Sikkim (separating China from India), as well as the tribal areas in northern and northeastern Assam on China's southern border and the tribal areas in the west bordering on

Afghanistan and Kashmir, were all to become British protectorates or be integrated into India. The British defeated an expanding Gurkha Kingdom in Nepal as early as 1814–15 and secured an agreement to appoint a British resident as well as to recruit Gurkhas for the army in India. That agreement was replaced by a treaty of peace and friendship in 1925, which formally recognized Nepal's independence but allowed the British, and subsequently India, to recruit Gurkha troops. Sikkim was a British protectorate in the 1860s, giving Britain exclusive control over its internal administration and foreign relations. Independent India went further and incorporated Sikkim as an Indian state in 1975. Bhutan was made a British protectorate in 1910 and remained an Indian protectorate after independence.

Beginning in 1911, the British Indian government embarked on a "forward policy" in the northeast, bringing tribal territories under loose political control and annexing the Tawang Tract, a salient of territory extending into northeast India that had been previously recognized as part of China. The Chinese refused to agree to a British proposal to divide Tibet into two zones, inner and outer Tibet, with China having no administrative rights in outer Tibet, thus creating a buffer between India and China. The British and the Tibetans, however, entered into a secret agreement about the Tibet-Assam (northeast) boundary that provided the basis for the northeastern border drawn by Sir Henry McMahon on British maps, known as the McMahon Line. China, which had not been consulted, later asserted that it did not accept the McMahon Line as the legal border. Nevertheless, the line was shown on British maps, and subsequently on Indian maps, as the northeast border. Shortly after Chinese armies marched into Tibet in 1951, the first Indian prime minister, Jawaharlal Nehru, presumably in an effort to forestall further Chinese claims, asserted that the northeast border was recognized as delimited by custom and treaty and was fixed by the McMahon Line.

Another area whose status became a matter of dispute was that of Ladakh. Ladakh was part of Tibet up to the tenth century, subsequently an independent kingdom, and a tributary state of the Mughal empire in the sixteenth century; in the nineteenth century it was again regarded as part of Tibet. The rulers of Kashmir attempted, but failed, to conquer Ladakh. The Chinese government, in 1846, refused to enter into negotiations with the British to fix the boundary between Kashmir and Ladakh, pronouncing that "these territories have sufficiently and distinctively been fixed, so it will be best to adhere to their ancient arrangement."[35] The British, undeterred, drew a boundary in 1846–47 between the Pangong Lake and the Karakoram Pass, which included the totally uninhabited "desolate plateau" of Aksai Chin (desert of white stones) within Kashmir. This boundary was published in an official British atlas in 1868. In the 1880s, China challenged the line, put its own boundary marker in the Karakoram, and in the mid-1890s claimed Aksai Chin. But Aksai Chin remained on British maps as part of Kashmir and as such was subsequently claimed by India.

India and China, the two giants of an awakening Asia, fought their prolonged battles against imperial rule and economic penetration over a similar time span roughly from the beginning of the twentieth century. Yet they confronted very different challenges and responded with equally divergent methods consistent with their respective strategic cultures—that of nonviolent noncooperation in the first case and of mobilization of the armed peasantry in the second, first by the Guomindang and then by the CCP in a movement of revolutionary nationalism. The nationalist leaders of each country were so immersed in the demands of their own struggle that they had minimal contact with each other. Nehru visited Chongqing in 1939, and Chiang Kai-shek traveled to India in 1942, where he had a not very successful meeting with Mahatma Gandhi. It does not appear that Nehru met either Mao Zedong or Zhou Enlai until after the CCP came to power.

India's leaders were convinced that their country's geostrategic position and size would make it an important actor in Asia and that India would exert major influence in world affairs. In 1946, Nehru confidently asserted, "[India] is potentially a Great Power. Undoubtedly, in the future she will have to play a very great part in security problems of Asia and the Indian Ocean, more especially of the Middle East and South-East Asia. Indeed, India is the pivot round which these problems will have to be considered . . . the importance of India to any scheme of Asian security is vital."[36] And in a similar vein, "India can no longer take up an attitude other than that demanded by her geographical position, by her great potential and by the fact that she is the pivot round which the defence problems of the Middle East, the Indian Ocean and South-East Asia revolve. Even in the course of the last war, this dominant position of India was obvious."[37]

From this perspective, the emergence of a strong Chinese communist government, based on nationalist sentiment against imperialist domination, was greeted with sympathy as the most important development of the postwar period in the rise of Asian nationalism. Nehru was inclined to believe that India's potential resources were more varied and extensive than those of China and that India would develop as the center of political and economic activity in the Indian Ocean area, in Southeast Asia, and up to the Middle East. This viewpoint was conditioned by the notion of India's historical sphere of cultural influence in Southeast Asia, as well as its modern role as the geostrategic linchpin of the British Empire astride the Indian Ocean. Such advantages strengthened his conviction that the new states just emerging from colonialism would follow India's example and not join any bloc. Within this worldview, China also, although it entered into an alliance with the USSR in 1949, was too big a country, and too nationalistic to subordinate its foreign policy to any third country for more than a brief period.

By the time that India became independent in 1947 and China was unified by the CCP in 1949, the two countries, except for their anti-imperialist sentiments, had developed virtually mirror-opposite "nationalist narratives" of their rightful place in Asia. Garver neatly summarizes this juxtaposition by superimposing a 1954 Chinese map on one constructed by India for the March–April 1947 Asian Relations Conference. The Chinese map, based on the widest extent of its traditional tributary system as well as more recently conquered territories, is drawn to show Mongolia, part of southern Russia, North and South Korea, Taiwan, northern Malaysia, Vietnam, Cambodia, Thailand, Myanmar (Burma), Bhutan, Nepal, Xinjiang, Tibet, and the Himalayan-Karakoram region, including Hunza and Gilgit in northern Kashmir, as part of the Chinese historic sphere.[38] Apart from the claims to Mongolia and in East Asia, the areas of Southeast Asia, Tibet, Nepal, the Himalayan kingdoms, and the whole of Kashmir, including Hunza and Gilgit, overlapped with India's perceived areas of cultural influence—and actual control over Bhutan and Sikkim and political influence in Nepal. From China's point of view, as revealed in authoritative and classified studies in the 1990s, Nehru's ideas of cultural influence and potential dominance of Southeast Asia and the Indian Ocean region appeared as a reassertion of the British imperialist mentality and of an ambition to establish a "greater Indian empire" by dominating neighboring states.[39]

In the late 1940s, neither country possessed anything approaching the great-power capabilities required to act on such grandiose visions. Moreover, India suffered a blow in 1947 that in retrospect curbed its long-term prospects of achieving a superior position relative to China, but without causing India's leaders to relinquish belief in their country's great-power destiny. By July 1947, the British government, weakened by World War II, fearing violence between Hindus and Muslims, and unwilling and unable to commit more resources to India to maintain order, made the formal decision to concede the demand of the Muslim League, based on the "two nation" theory, for partition of the subcontinent. On 14 and 15 August 1947, two Dominions, that of Pakistan as a homeland for Muslims and that of India as a secular state, became independent. The Government of India, in law, was the direct successor state of the British Government of India; from India's point of view, Pakistan, accounting for 17.5 percent of Indian territory, consisted of areas that had seceded from India. At the time, neither the Government of India nor the British believed that Pakistan, concentrated in two "wings" in the west and in the east, separated by a thousand miles of Indian territory and without strategic depth or access to industries in the Indian hinterland as markets for its raw materials, could survive without external support.

Yet partition had a serious impact both on India's immediate military strength and on its pivotal geostrategic position. Division of the assets of British India above all destroyed one of the best fighting forces in the world, leaving India with an unevenly equipped standing army further weakened by a truncated and depleted command structure. Partition, moreover, immediately involved India in a (still unresolved) conflict with Pakistan over Kashmir that threatened to drain her reduced forces in a full-scale war. By contrast, the CCP, swept to power by the People's Liberation Army of approximately one million men, took control of a unified country. Moreover, China's claim of sovereignty, as opposed to suzerainty, over Tibet, according to India's home minister, Sardar Patel, was likely to call into question the northern boundary between China and India known as the McMahon Line, which had been drawn under agreements with the Tibetan government. Sardar Patel even envisaged a possible alignment between China and Pakistan that could subject India to threats from both the west and the northeast.

Most damaging, although it was not fully recognized at that time, the creation of Pakistan robbed India of the advantages of its own geostrategic position. Overnight, India literally lost its location on the southern border of Afghanistan, with western flanks adjacent to the Persian Gulf and the Middle East, and eastern boundaries abutting Southeast Asia. Pakistan now occupied these positions.

Partition occurred at the same time that the Cold War was overwhelming all other foreign policy concerns of the United States and its allies. As the United States reacted to India's nonaligned policy, it found in Pakistan's offer of a military alliance the prospect of a foothold in the strategic area adjacent to the Middle East, the Persian Gulf, and Southeast Asia. The 1954 military assistance agreement between the United States and Pakistan was perceived by India's leaders as the beginning of the "building up" of allied Pakistan and the "building down" of nonaligned India.

In this situation, Nehru's foreign policy relied on cultivating an India-China friendship as the fulcrum of a rising Asia that could exclude the superpowers from the region. In the context of both India's military limitations and its political culture of leading by example rather than by force, Nehru pursued a "friendly approach" to China. This policy has been termed "appeasement" by Garver,[40] but that characterization does not capture Nehru's deeply ingrained sense of India's magnanimity toward China. Certainly Nehru was aware that neither India nor the other newly independent countries of Southeast Asia could prevail in a military confrontation with China, and he rejected all suggestions that could arouse China's fears of encirclement, including a regional security pact led by India (and proposed by Burma), open resistance to China's assertion of sovereignty over Tibet, and even discussions with the United States about the possibility of U.S. recognition of China, but with India instead of China becoming a permanent member of the Security Council.

Nehru's actions toward China, when it was most isolated in international forums by the refusal of the United States to grant recognition to the PRC as its legal representative, were motivated by feelings of moral righteousness and the conviction that by virtue of the example set by India's behavior, Chinese cooperation could be won for India's goal of constructing an Asian balance that would limit the influence of the Western (imperialist) powers, particularly the United States, in Asia. India's concessions on Tibet, which eliminated the western buffer between India and China; India's advocacy of China's admission to the United Nations; and its sympathetic attitude toward China in negotiations after the Korean War—all have to be seen in this larger context. Even more, Nehru assumed the role of "elder brother" to Zhou Enlai, introducing China's leaders and advancing their position among the heads of newly independent nations in Asia.

Yet, from the perspective of China's leaders, Nehru's implicit assumption of superiority, reflected in his positioning of China as the "younger brother," was interpreted as an assertion of India's hegemony. When, after a series of fruitless negotiations, China attacked India's forward posts and

Chinese troops poured over the contested northeast border in 1962, Nehru's overwhelming reaction was one of betrayal. He was unable to believe that the Chinese leaders could so brutally repudiate his friendly and righteous approach. When Nehru died less than two years later, it was often said that he had succumbed to a broken heart. Nehru's daughter, Indira Gandhi, prime minister for most of the period from 1966 to 1984, was never able to trust the Chinese. She blamed Zhou Enlai for hastening her father's death.

India's first generation of nationalist leaders applied the diplomatic, legal, and moral teachings of the traditional political culture based on leading by example to the practice of contemporary statecraft. Within the constraints of their idea of India, and in a situation of strategic vulnerability and military weakness, it was perhaps impossible to do otherwise. In the ancient world, China had been open to learning about religious, philosophical, and practical subjects from India. After India's defeat by China in 1962, its successive leaders learned to think about Indo-Chinese relations from the military perspective of realist (and Chinese) premises. During the 1980s and 1990s, as the economic gap between China and India grew, it became clear that India's claim to great-power destiny would also have to be demonstrated in material terms apart from the beliefs, many of which persist, in the nation's classical cultural superiority.

Notes

1. A discussion of the treaty and its provisions can be found in Subash Kapila, "Implications of the Sino-Russian Friendship Treaty," Institute of Peace and Conflict Studies, article no. 559, 4 September 2001.

2. Wade Boese, "Russian-Indian Summit Firms Up Conventional Arms Deal," *Arms Control Today,* November 2000.

3. Moscow Declaration, 6 November 2001.

4. Rainer Apel and Paul Gallagher, "China-Russia-India: A New Step for 'Survivors Club,'" *Executive Intelligence Review,* 27 July 2001.

5. David Stout, "Bush and India's Leader Pledge Cooperation in War on Terror," *New York Times International,* 9 November 2001.

6. House Concurrent Resolution 264, 9 November 2001.

7. The text of the joint statement issued after the meeting of President Bush and President Musharraf on 13 November 2001 is published in *Dawn,* 13 November 2001.

8. Richard J. Ellings and Aaron L. Friedberg, eds., *Strategic Asia 2001–02: Power and Purpose* (Seattle: National Bureau of Asian Research, 2001), 21.

9. "U.S. Says Pakistan Gave Technology to North Korea, *New York Times,* 18 October 2002.

10. "China and India Agree on Border Concessions," *Financial Times,* 24 June 2003.

11. See Michael Swaine and Ashley J. Tellis, *Interpreting China's Grand Strategy: Past, Present and Future* (Santa Monica, Calif.: RAND, 2000), chapter 3.
12. Ibid., 13.
13. John Fairbank, *China: A New History* (Cambridge, Mass.: Harvard University Press, 1992), 139.
14. Fairbank, *China,* 73.
15. John W. Garver, *Protracted Contest: Sino-Indian Rivalry in the Twentieth Century* (Seattle: University of Washington Press, 2001), 35.
16. Ibid., 37.
17. A. L. Basham, *The Wonder That Was India* (New York: Grove Press, 1954), 53.
18. Ibid., 54.
19. Jaswant Singh, *Defending India* (New Delhi: Macmillan, 1999), 16–19.
20. Sunil Khilnani, *The Idea of India* (New York: Farrar, Straus and Giroux, 1999), 5.
21. For problems involved in dating ancient literacy sources, see Rajesh Kochhar, *The Vedic People: Their History and Geography* (New Delhi: Orient Longman, 2000), chapters 3 and 6.
22. See Francine R. Frankel, introduction to *Dominance and State Power: Decline of a Social Order,* ed. Francine R. Frankel and M. S. A. Rao (New Delhi: Oxford University Press, 1989), 2–7.
23. Burton Stein, *Peasant, State, and Society in Medieval South India* (Cambridge: Oxford University Press, 1980), 340, 367.
24. H. G. Quartich Wales, *The Indianization of China and of Southeast Asia* (London: Bernard Quartich Ltd., 1967), xi.
25. Jawaharlal Nehru, *The Discovery of India* (New York: John Day Company, 1946), 194–204. Nehru's citation of Dr. H. G. Quartich Wales on pages 195 and 203 refers to his book *Towards Angkor* (London: Harrap, 1937).
26. Xinru Liu, *Ancient India and Ancient China: Trade and Religious Exchanges, A.D. 1–600* (Cambridge: Oxford University Press, 1988).
27. Ibid., chapter 4.
28. Tansen Sen, "In Search of Longevity and Good Karma: Chinese Diplomatic Missions to Middle India in the Seventh Century," *Journal of World History* 12, no. 1 (2001).
29. Ibid., 23. See also Hu Shih, *The Indianization of China: A Case Study in Cultural Borrowing* (Cambridge, Mass.: Harvard University Press, 1937), 223.
30. Stanley Wolpert, *A New History of India,* Third Edition (Cambridge: Oxford University Press, 1989), 108.
31. Valerie Hansen, *The Open Empire: A History of China to 1600* (New York: W. W. Norton, 2000), 258.
32. Hu Shih, *Indianization of China,* 231; Wales, *Indianization,* chapter 6.
33. Wolpert, *New History of India,* chapter 11.
34. Frankel and Rao, *Dominance and State Power* 1: 7–12.
35. Rajesh Kadian, *Tibet, India, and China: Critical Choices* (Delhi: Vision, 1999), 52.
36. "The United Nations," 16 September 1946, in *Selected Works of Jawaharlal Nehru,* ed. S. Gopal, second series, vol. 1 (New Delhi: Jawaharlal Nehru Memorial Fund, 1984), 439.

37. “India and the Membership of the Security Council,” 30 October 1946, in Gopal, *Selected Works,* 464.

38. Garver, *Protracted Contest,* 14–15.

39. Ibid., 18–19.

40. Ibid., 29.

2

Perception and China Policy in India

Steven A. Hoffmann

Some Indian self-perceptions and strategic beliefs do much to frame and elucidate the perceptions of China held by India's foreign policy–making elite. A crucial self-perception is that India is a state of major potential and future international importance. It possesses a great power's worldview, even if its role in international security affairs has been modest. India is entering a new phase in terms of its world role as its power-related resources increase. India is surely a rising power and should already be entitled to a major power's international prominence. Resistance by the top-tier, nuclear-have nations of the world (China among them) to greater acceptance of India, both as a major state and as a legitimate nuclear-weapons state, must be addressed actively via Indian diplomacy.

An additional self-perception predicts that Indian interests and values will be best served by a multipolar or polycentric world order in the future. Multipolarity/polycentrism in the world power structure therefore is to be preferred (or so a closely related argument goes) over the unipolar order that has prevailed for most (if not all) of the period since the Cold War ended. But the heart of the argument is that true multipolarity/polycentrism must and will include India, and it should not be confined to the Permanent Five (nuclear) powers (including China) that now dominate the United Nations Security Council.

Another self-perception, no less important, is that India has had to alter its relationships with the world's widely recognized major powers, most importantly the United States and China, since the Cold War ended and international bipolarity collapsed. But an element in what might be called Indian grand-strategic thinking is the belief that India must still maintain a value (or principle) that lay at the heart of its famous former policy of international nonalignment, namely, that of strategic autonomy. The policy of nonalignment between the Cold War blocs, or so it is recalled, did not preclude an Indian tilt toward Moscow when the United States, Pakistan, and China had reached a "*de facto* strategic consensus" around the beginning of the 1970s, a consensus detrimental to Indian interests. In equal measure, according to the Indian grand-strategic perspective, the strategic autonomy principle requires India to adjust to post–Cold War relationships in such a way as to maximize its security, safety, and freedom of action.[1]

The main purpose of this chapter is to describe and explain, on an admittedly impressionistic but intensively researched basis, the major perceptions of China found within an Indian elite that perceives its own country in the way just described. The focus is on those perceptions of China that interact with Indian governmental policy.

The primary method will be to highlight the views of Indian strategic analysts who are free to express their personal opinions at length in public. These people operate mostly outside the formal parameters of government, but a number of them have had and still have various connections with government personnel. Moreover, India's Ministry of External Affairs maintains a regularized if informal process of interaction with them. The Ministry of Defense, the National Security Council, and some politicians as well, also actively interrelate with such nongovernmental strategists in various ways.[2]

These are people who populate think-tanks, academic institutions, newspaper columns and journals, and television programs, as well as the seminars and informal discussions to be found mainly in New Delhi. Among them are some publicly prominent personalities. Such people may be referred to collectively as the Indian strategic community, a term that has come into vogue over the last decade or so as the group has constituted itself. *The term can also be taken to include, as shall be the practice here, the currently serving government officials and politicians with whom the extragovernmental analysts interact.*

The more responsible and nonextremist nongovernmental participants in the Indian strategic community can be said to "both mirror government thinking and influence it." Members of this group "both shape government thinking and represent or communicate that thinking to the larger public and to the international community."[3] One government source has said (privately and not for attribution) that there is an "osmosis" between people inside the government and intellectuals (and others) outside. The osmosis flows both ways, and the government is trying to achieve a consensus.

A consensus can be largely (but not completely) achieved. Partly because nonofficials generally do not have careers that rotate them in and out of government, as is the case with counterparts in the United States, the linkage between specific ideas they may champion and detailed policy decisions is murky. But a considerable congruence between government policy and nongovernmental perceptions can be created as the governmental and extragovernmental portions of the strategic community share ideas in their own fashion.

Such consensus creation is also made possible by the fact that the Indian strategic community contains a substantial number of former foreign office and defense officials as well as retired military officers. Not only does their background lend weight to their views, but their written and spoken output can provide an indication of what their views were while still in government service, and of what they probably left behind in the government's copious files.[4] Journalists, who think and write independently, can help to shape a consensus too. Journalists (and especially columnists and editors) count as members of the strategic community, and some have close government links. Some U.S. State Department officials even perceive certain journalists as having a respectable degree of influence on the government.[5]

Yet, strangely enough, India's strategic community does not necessarily think or write in a monolithic fashion, especially on the subject of China. Accordingly, to be discussed in depth in this chapter are the several distinctive perceptual positions (or what will be simply called "positions") with respect to China that could recently be found within the strategic community's body of thought. The relationship of the Chinese positions with Indian grand-strategic thought, and with Indian domestic political thinking, will be covered as well, if only briefly.

Some coverage will also be given, toward the end of the chapter, to a "working cluster" or "operational cluster" of Indian perceptions and policy prescriptions relating to China, held primarily by those members of the strategic community still in government service in 2001. Such a cluster will exist at any given time, and will be more sensitive to the then-prevailing circumstances in India-China relations than the established perceptual positions tend to be.

The reader should note that in the remainder of this chapter all the perceptions of China that are represented, as well as any items of related strategic thought and domestic political thought that are covered, should be considered those of Indian analysts, officials, and leaders, and not those of this writer. This is so even though in this type of essay the words must generally be those of the author, and even though the Indian views are sometimes described in broad or general terms that pull together a number of specific thoughts that may come from more than one person. Expressions of the author's own opinions will be rare and will be made quite explicit.

Historical Note: Evolution of the Core Indian Governmental Perspectives and Policies on China

Some crucial items of historical information must first be emphasized if present-day perspectives of the Indian strategic community on China are to be properly understood. First, it should be noted that an important cause of one of the world's major unresolved border disputes, i.e., the dispute between India and China, was a certain historical view that still persists in India. It is a view of an India whose borderlines are not merely the creations of the British officials of the colonial period. To India's foundational prime minister and foreign minister, Jawaharlal Nehru (and to the Indian government acting in its formal capacity ever since), border creation was not just a matter of policy set forth by British proconsuls; they rejected the Western imperialist idea that nothing of India's precolonial history, natural geography, and other non-British influences should enter into the determination of its modern borders.[6]

As India's dominant political figure and main foreign policy decision maker from 1947 to 1964, Nehru projected his own historical views onto historical evidence, geographic evidence, and what can be called "custom and usage" evidence concerning parts of the India-China frontier. This huge body of evidence was thought by him, and his government, to make a strong case for the existence of border alignments reflective "of tradition, custom, and administration stretching over centuries."[7] The British were seen as having done more to explore, discover, debate about, and possibly confirm these alignments (although not always) than to create them. Moreover, because British policies and choices in the realm of border development were not always thought to be the right ones, some Indian decisions were needed after independence and were made by Mr. Nehru and his officials.

Scholarly defenders and critics of independent India's border policies, writing from India and from abroad, have discussed at length those decisions and the Indian reasoning behind them. They have left no doubt as to the great importance of the Nehru-led border formulation exercise, undertaken after the British had departed, in the larger process through which the India-China border dispute emerged.[8] Nehruvian border-setting policies, border-defense policies, and border-related diplomatic policies all involved much more than just the use of historical evidence to set border claims. But the insistence that India should possess "historical" borders (shown to be such by Indian-developed documentary and other evidence) and not just "British" borders was a vital part of the Nehru-directed process of policy creation that ultimately contributed to the onset of the India-China boundary dispute.

From the time of the 1962 war onward, India's overall policy toward China centered on the border dispute, continuing to do so for decades despite such actions as the restoration of ambassador-level diplomatic relations between the two countries in 1976. The government of Indira Gandhi (Nehru's daughter) was responsible for that constructive action, from the Indian side, and there was at least one other, but "India's governments basically continued the policy established in Nehru's time of treating the border dispute as the core obstacle to normalization" of the India-China governmental relationship.[9] Mrs. Gandhi herself reportedly saw the Chinese as having betrayed her father, and she tended to cast personal blame on China's Zhou Enlai for the breakdown of China's relationship with Nehru and for the 1962 war. Although she did have what one observer called "occasional impulses toward conciliation" with China, her "basic animus . . . appears to have run deeper."[10] Reportedly she "carried the burden of memories of her father's . . . vision of a Sino-Indian détente being the cornerstone of Asian solidarity," but had also "witnessed this 'cornerstone' being destroyed in 1962."[11] The broad outlines of that negative outlook were widely shared in India after the 1962 war.

By the time of Rajiv Gandhi's prime ministership in the 1980s, however, Pakistan had taken the place of China as the "driving security and psychological threat animating India's interest in nuclear weapons," even if India could not allow itself to lower its "guard against China."[12] Such thinking was part of the picture as that government eventually came to conclude, reportedly for other reasons, that a policy change was in order. A basic Nehruvian policy was abandoned; no longer would resolution of the border dispute be held up by the Indian side as a precondition for bilateral normalization.[13]

Although the official Indian policy toward what constitutes the proper border had (at least until early 2003) not deviated from that of Mr. Nehru, the immediate focus of border-related Indian diplomatic activity in recent years has been the Line of Actual Control (LAC) established by the 1962 war. A prime objective of the Indian government is to overcome some current issues and have the location of the LAC made entirely clear and agreed upon by both sides, thereby becoming even more stable. In this fashion, in the Indian governmental view, a good basis can be laid for the two countries to engage in border settlement negotiations. (See the update that appears at the end of this chapter.)

India's historical border case is still seen by the government, and much of the strategic community, as being far stronger on the whole than that of China. But there is now, at the governmental level, a perceived need to balance that case against what can be considered feasible and desirable from a strategic and pragmatic standpoint.[14] This perception exists even though no Indian government has tried to refashion the Indian public's thinking about the China border itself, largely because of political, legal, and psychological residues from the 1962 border war.

India's China policy, according to reports from Indian strategic community members closely associated with the government, is heavily based on the perceived need to negotiate with China in a fashion that goes beyond the boundaries per se and deals with the kind of overall security environment India and China would like to have. More specifically, the location of the boundary must be treated by both sides in the context of how these two countries, both having substantial military power, will establish a security relationship that encompasses not only secure borders but other matters as well. Among those other matters are Pakistan (and China's relationship with Pakistan), the global security environment, the American factor, Indian and Chinese reactions to globalization, and bilateral commercial relations.[15] It seems safe to say that the issue of the proper historical border is perceived at the Indian governmental level as an older India-China issue, to be discussed with the Chinese while other immediately important bilateral imperatives receive equal, if not more, attention.

The Contemporary Indian Perceptual Positions on China

The Indian strategic community's several positions, or perspectives, on China, outlined in the pages to follow, are actually ideal types. As such they are constructs, or models, formulated for analytical purposes, and in each of them a number of Indian perceptions are clustered together. Inevitably, some of the components of an ideal-type construction must be described in a somewhat simplified fashion, one that leaves out variation and nuance. A certain logical coherence among these components must also be demonstrated.

Some persons familiar with the range of Indian perceptions and related strategic thinking about China may feel that this analytical exercise inserts artificial dividing lines into what is really a continuum. But support from Indian informants has left this writer with the powerful impression that the ideal-typical perspectives on China described here are useful descriptive and analytical devices and can be said to represent Indian thinking accurately—if (as a particular New Delhi informant has warned) the ideal types are not taken to be "hard categories," divided by absolutely fixed and rigid boundaries.

Additionally, no position, or perspective, should be taken as representing the outlook on China held by any one person in India. Each contains individual ideas offered by many people. Since there are several China positions, the reader must bear in mind that an individual thinker here identified (usually in an endnote) as contributing an idea to one such perspective can simultaneously be providing ideas to, and accepting ideas from, other positions too. Alternatively, someone can himself or herself be a bridge between positions, or shift from one position to another over time.

The Mainstream Indian Perceptual Position on China

In the years between 1998 and early 2003, an identifiable Indian perspective, or position, on China was found in the Indian strategic community, and that position has influenced governmental policy more than any other. One of its core perceptions has been that China does not constitute a clear-cut, direct military threat to India in the near term, but that the longer term is uncertain. From this perspective China has been viewed as a *potential* threat or challenge to Indian interests in the long run, because India needs to anticipate the possible emergence of a much more assertive China. One possible precondition for such assertiveness would be China's having reached the levels of national strength it is presently seeking.

A second core perception has held that China's worldview converges in some important ways with that of India, but that certain features of China's strategic interest calculation differ from India's, and that the mismatch contributes to real Indian security problems. The border dispute, and a Sino-Pakistani arms transfer nexus whereby Chinese weapons of mass destruction (WMD) technology has already gone to Pakistan, are among the most important of these problems. An additional mainstream core perception has been that China may well be unwilling to acquiesce to the rise of India as a power having a reach beyond South Asia and ultimately becoming one of the world powers. But a fourth core perception has been that the possibility exists for India and China to avert major future problems through diplomacy and other forms of appropriate action.

A further aspect of the mainstream position has been the perception that China has motives inclining it toward responsible and sober policies regarding India. These motives have included China's concentration on internal modernization, and a consequent desire to have "peaceful and stable relations" with its neighbors.[16] But sober and responsible Chinese activity may be likely to continue only for a limited time. It has been alleged that China has what can be called a "time frame" within which it has no desire to let anything interfere in a major way with its own economic development.[17] The question asked has been: Will all of this continue over the longer term? Serious "uncertainties mark any assessment of China's policies in [the] future," one analyst has remarked. While China "is not a 'threat' in the traditional sense," and there "exists a 'window of opportunity' through which China's evolution may be vectored in a cooperative framework," it would nevertheless "be imprudent" for India "not to institute adequate precautionary measures to cater for a possible reversal of China's policies toward an assertive and even aggressive stance in [the] future."[18]

Mainstream thinking has certainly emphasized what India shares with China. Both India and China have been thought to share a preference for multipolarity or polycentrism in the world, and neither simply accepts the idea that a U.S.-dominated world order must persist indefinitely. Both countries are determined to maintain their sovereign autonomy. China has also been perceived as a kind of role model, and not just within the mainstream Indian position alone. It has been "lionized by sections within virtually the whole spectrum of public opinion in India: from the extreme Left to the extreme Right . . . [for its] ability to take hard internal decisions as well as to face up to pressure from the West." China's economic and military rise, via timely economic reform carried out without compromising its national security posture, can be viewed "with awe and admiration." In the realm of strategic doctrine, analysts "compare India's [alleged] adhocism to China's systematic strategic planning."[19]

But factors like the seeming intractability of the border and territorial dispute, China's long-lasting friendship with Pakistan, and the nuclear and missile cooperation in which China and Pakistan have engaged, have been seen as precluding a truly close India-China relationship. Chinese "proliferation activity," carried on "with the [alleged] permissiveness of the U.S.," is even thought to pose "an indirect threat to India."[20] Additionally, China has been seen as trying to counterbalance India in the subcontinent by using Pakistan. China can even be seen as practicing a so-called Sun Tzu strategy. Via that strategy Beijing can be friendly with New Delhi and not constitute a direct near-term (or medium-term) military threat, while simultaneously locking India in a "nuclear standoff with Pakistan," and treating "Pakistan and India in the same category as regional powers, not in the same class as China, which is a global player."[21]

Another mainstream issue has been China's apparent resistance to greater international acceptance of India as a nuclear weapon state. As of 1999, at least, China's seeming determination to prevent political acceptance by the West of India "as a nuclear weapon power" was causing "deep resentment in New Delhi." Moreover, China's "past record on transgressing . . . non-proliferation principles by assistance to Pakistan's nuclear and missile programs" meant that what could be called "China's fulmination on non-proliferation" was given little credibility in India.[22] That last statement reflects a strong suspicion (indeed, within Indian analysis of China generally, a real conviction) that China's having signed the international nuclear Nonproliferation Treaty (NPT) in 1992 did not bring China's nuclear proliferation in South Asia to an end. One can also encounter skepticism within the Indian strategic community about China's absolving itself of any responsibility for the WMD-related links between Pakistan and North Korea.

The mainstream position on China has implicitly contained the following argument: if China has concluded that its nuclear arsenal is needed to end the nuclear monopoly of certain countries, prevent nuclear blackmail, deter any possible nuclear attack, and provide for a peaceful environment in which domestic economic construction can take place, India has similar reasons for possessing its own nuclear weapon capacity. Indeed, India itself needs those weapons to counter nuclear blackmail, from whatever quarter it might come.[23] One of those quarters is China itself. Mainstream opinion has argued, too, that a credible minimum Indian nuclear deterrent is needed to make sure that the country "does not become vulnerable to . . . nuclear coercion . . . either from the Chinese mainland" or as a result of the Chinese WMD relationship with Pakistan.[24]

Some mainstream opinion has gone so far as to argue that there is a direct potential threat to India from China's nuclear arsenal, which is "serious"; in this view China is thought "to have deployed nuclear missiles in Tibet" that target India. "Admittedly, Chinese inter-continental ballistic missiles elsewhere could also target India," one source has conceded, "but the potential political and psychological impact . . . [of the missiles thought to be in Tibet]—literally a few miles from India's border—during a future conflict cannot be under-estimated."[25]

In mainstream thinking, there is little fear of China staging a first strike against India even if the Chinese nuclear and missile arsenal is significantly greater than India's. An important strategic analyst's reasoning can be used to support this estimate, since he judges China, a relatively small nuclear power in the world setting, to be lacking "an interest in legitimizing the use of nuclear weapons." Moreover, the Chinese are not likely to employ much of "their arsenal [against India]," since this activity would weaken them vis-à-vis their more important rivals.[26] But, according to some thinking on the Indian side, China could use nuclear weapons within the disputed border territories if fighting were to take place there.

Indeed, people whose broad orientation is "mainstream" on China, as well as those who argue for other China positions (discussed in the following sections), could allude to the fact that China has a no-first-use doctrine applicable to nonnuclear powers. But some of these people will add that this can provide little comfort to India for several reasons. One is that Chinese strategists have openly indicated that "use of nuclear weapons in their own territory" would not violate the doctrine. So, a key question has been: Does China consider claimed areas on the Indian frontier to be its own territory in this context? Moreover, as a close observer of China has pointed out, even as early as 1992, when China formally signed the NPT, the Chinese were stating that countries staying outside the NPT were not covered by China's no-first-use pledge. Indian analysts can well ask: Wouldn't the exemption surely apply to India since the 1998 Pokhran tests?[27]

Additional ideas could be said to have figured in the mainstream Indian position on China. One is that China, having won the 1962 war, seems to be territorially nonaggressive toward India, for the present. Yes, the India-China boundary is undemarcated, and China still maintains frontier claims, including one to the so-called Eastern Sector (effectively this refers to Arunachal Pradesh, now a state in the Indian federal union) where much of the 1962 fighting took place. But the Chinese have not acted on this claim via substantial military activity in recent years (i.e., since 1986–87).

A disquieting inferential point that mainstream Indian analysis could draw from the border situation, however, is that China has left open for itself the options of threatening or starting border hostilities if it should ever desire to do so. A related point has been that China could initiate this kind of activity to demonstrate power rather than to gain more territory. A number of motivating scenarios could be imagined in which the Chinese would want to demonstrate their power in this fashion, such as China's government feeling a need to make a show of capability and willpower in the face of disaffection in Tibet, or elsewhere in China, or China desiring to make India behave like a strategic subordinate and encountering Indian refusal.[28]

Further mainstream thoughts have been included in the writings of a former foreign secretary. In one text he favored India and China building up a positive working relationship, not only as a contribution to Asian stability but more importantly to "counter discriminatory and hegemonic trends in world affairs" (i.e., trends coming from the United States and the West). But he also expressed hope that China will not reacquire what he calls its "'Middle Kingdom' complex." Additionally, he alluded to the Chinese having a "professed superiority vis-à-vis India," which he would not want them to be "smug" about.[29]

In another text, this publicly active former official took note of Chinese sensitivities about Tibet and of the connection the matter has to China's relations with India, Nepal, and Bhutan. Apparently he was not alarmed by China's ties to India's neighbors, unlike other Indian strategists who worry about China seeming to encircle India. But he said, too, that there is "logical" apprehension, further outward, in Southeast Asia, over China's military strength and China's "traditional collective nationalistic and assertive mindset" with regard to peoples and territories believed by Beijing to be "integral to the Chinese collective identity." Moreover, China considers itself destined for a predominant power position in Asia, and it views South Asia (along with Southeast Asia) as a potential zone of Chinese influence. His opinion was that India is not thought by the Chinese to be a challenger to its desired Asian role, but China is aware that it should maintain itself in a position of greater political influence as well as higher strategic, military, and technological capacity.[30]

This American outsider, observing mainstream Indian thinking about China over the last few years, can perhaps be forgiven for pointing out that even if India may lack a credible anti-China nuclear deterrent now, the general desire within the Indian strategic community (and not just within the mainstream China perspective) for this kind of deterrent capability will probably achieve results over time. That conclusion rests both on observations of the strength of conviction in mainstream Indian reasoning about China and on India's past technological record. Such a capability seems likely to be developed on at least a minimum level, as is now required by government policy. This American outsider can also assume, from being privy to some Indian diplomatic behavior (on the so-called "Track II" level where Indian think-tank scholars, academics, retired officials and officers, and a few serving officials and officers engage with appropriate persons from other countries), that the mainstream China position may well include a belief that India should engage in sustained strategic dialogue with China's other neighbors as part of an effort to compete with the Chinese for influence in Asia.[31]

The "China Is Not Hostile" Perceptual Position

Other significant Indian positions or perspectives on China are presently found within the Indian strategic community. Persons allegedly associated with the one discussed in this segment have been accused of being "apologists for China," while holders of a starkly contrasting position (discussed in the next segment) can be called "China-baiters."[32] But neither of these alternative perspectives lies entirely outside the realm of what is considered respectable China-related thought and discourse within the Indian strategic community, and neither should be dismissed by outside observers as necessarily radical or even extreme.

The first of these alternative positions perceives China as rather pragmatic, peaceful, and rational, and thus might well be called the "China is not hostile" view (or the nonhostile-China position, for short). A crucial feature of this perceptual outlook is the contention that China ought not to be assigned the sole blame for everything negative that has happened in India-China relations. Yet this position does include an awareness that China has done, and still does, things that are inimical to Indian interests and to India-China relations.

That the 1962 India-China war, still widely regarded in India as a betrayal by China, must be reconceived is an important notion found within the nonhostile-China perspective. The war was a product of mistakes, misperceptions, and misjudgments on both the Indian and Chinese sides.[33] In one prominent newspaper columnist's version of this perception, the Chinese can be blamed for resorting to arms, but India deserves blame for being politically intransigent earlier on, for refusing to recognize that the Chinese possessed genuine and legitimate territorial counterclaims, and for refusing to search for a "reasonable solution well beyond the imperially drawn boundaries of the colonial past."[34] In New Delhi, one can also hear the argument that immense changes in the India-China relationship have taken place since 1962, and that therefore people should not repeat the old mantras. This is not an idea unique to persons who tend to see China as nonhostile.

The nonhostile-China position is optimistic that China's positive attitudes toward its neighbors and China's effort to have a stable and peaceful neighborhood will become permanent features of Chinese foreign policy. The China it depicts is basically desirous of good India-China relations, having learned the proper lessons from the past. China is likely to remain so in the long term, not just the medium and short terms. But, for this to happen, the Sino-Indian relationship must be handled unprovocatively by both sides. As for the so-called China threat, it sees that threat as having been greatly "overblown" in India, partly because of insufficiently careful analysis.

A sinologist holding this last view once argued (to this author) that to refuse to be suspicious of the Chinese does not mean that one is un-Indian or naive, despite accusations to the contrary. But, he added, the Chinese themselves have to do a better job of convincing Indians that they are not a nuclear threat.[35]

It can be noted, from an outsider's analytical perspective, that the subject on which the nonhostile-China position must run into severe difficulty in the Indian strategic community is that of China's WMD nexus with Pakistan. The Sino-Indian border dispute and the 1962 war can prove amenable to explanation and accommodation via historical revisionism, given the new historical material that often emerges. But the Pakistan matter is more difficult to deal with. The fact that India's unmistakable enemy, Pakistan, is also China's de facto ally and the recipient of a truly unusual arms transfer package, requires those who believe in a nonhostile China to handle the Pakistan matter with great care.

One way to do so, as demonstrated by a recent book on India-China relations written by former Indian officials, is to treat the Sino-Pakistani nexus as a special case of Chinese behavior, i.e., as behavior predicated on Chinese appreciation of a reliable and loyal past and present ally that shared (at least in the past) China's "strategic perspective on India." Attention can also be drawn to pressure that the Pakistanis may have effectively placed on China in the past to ensure Pakistan's security against India. Moreover, much can be made of the idea that China's policies toward Pakistan have been based pragmatically and nonideologically on various aspects of Chinese national self-interest, such as the need to counter the Soviet Union (at one time) and the desire to make diplomatic gains from the fact that Pakistan is a Muslim state.[36]

A cautious version of the nonhostile-China perspective is obviously being presented here, one that overlaps the mainstream perspective. Like mainstream thinking, it holds that China does want to have Pakistan as a card available to be played against India. It further points out that China is presently caught in a strategic dilemma. China does not want a serious military conflict between India and Pakistan, and does not want to be forced into a choice between Pakistan and India, with which China has been engaged in a process of normalizing relations. Moreover, China will show care and caution in the future (according to this view) when faced with Pakistani requests for nuclear and missile assistance, even though Beijing will not want to see the balance of nuclear power on the Indian subcontinent tilted too heavily in favor of India either.

Another version of the nonhostile-China position includes the perception that India too faces something of a strategic dilemma. It is not in India's interest to have China-Pakistan collusion and China-U.S. collusion taking place.[37]

There are, in fact, a number of versions of the nonhostile-China position, each containing a definite sense of realpolitik; all may have areas of overlap with the mainstream position. But the nonhostile-China position in general may be losing influence over the long term, if the judgment of its defenders offered by a sinologist of a younger generation is any guide. He said that he respected the people holding this position or perspective on China, and that some of them had been his teachers. But he could not accept what he took to be their optimism about the China-India relationship, an optimism he himself emphatically lacked.[38]

The "China Is Hostile" Perceptual Position

The last of the positions or perspectives on China that have been considered respectable within the Indian strategic community might be called the "China is hostile" position. At its core it sees India and China already being rivals in something like a Cold War sense.[39] China allegedly exhibits hostility or belligerence toward India via its actions. Even though China in this view is not an immediate threat in either the conventional military sense or the nuclear sense, because it is not poised to attack India right away, China is definitely practicing strategic encirclement of India in Asia and enabling Pakistan to threaten India. Therefore, India-China relations cannot be conducted as an exercise in conflict prevention, according to a belief fundamental to this position, but must be treated as a form of conflict management, a realpolitik approach in which Indian security is protected properly, both militarily and diplomatically.

One leading contributor of ideas to this perspective (let us call it the hostile-China position, in brief) has shared the mainstream perspective in perceiving that China has an interest in Pakistan possessing "countervailing nuclear and missile capabilities against India." He has also perceived China as clearly intent upon having the unchallenged top power position in a unipolar Asia, even though China decries unipolarity at the global level. He has believed that wrongheaded Indian policy moves have allowed China simultaneously "to engage and contain" India, but felt that "Beijing should know that India can play the [containment] game" as well. India would do so by "forging strategic ties with Vietnam and Taiwan on the Sino-Pakistan model."

He has said, too, that the "flow of [Chinese] assistance" to Pakistan up to the time of India's 1998 and 1999 bomb and missile tests, was "calibrated to match every Indian advance," and that no other nation besides China "has engaged in such extensive and sustained transfers of weapons of mass destruction and their delivery vehicles." This commentator has not found satisfactory, as Indian strategic analysts generally have not (whatever their other perceptions of China), the Chinese arguments that such transfers "are part of regular, sovereign, state-to-state relations" and that China has a "normal relationship" with Pakistan "just as India has with many other countries." Instead, he has depicted China as wanting to have the freedom to keep India contained, intimidate Taiwan, split the Association of Southeast Asian Nations (ASEAN), "and make use of roguish Pakistan and North Korea." He has even indicated agreement with a U.S. Pentagon report in which China is said to desire such a degree of regional preeminence that no other international power would act in Asia in a major way without "first . . . considering Chinese interests."[40]

Commenting on China's negotiating stance concerning the Sino-Indian border, the same writer reveals his perception of quite sinister meaning: "By not keeping their promise to define the [post–1962 war] line of control, the Chinese are not only helping Pakistan by tying up large numbers of Indian troops along the Himalayas, they also retain the option to mount direct military pressure on India through border incidents if it attempted to play the Tibet card." The Chinese diplomatic position that the border dispute "can be resolved" when "conditions are ripe" means that resolution will occur only when "the balance of power has shifted in China's favor as it did vis-à-vis a weak Russia and Central Asia. China drops atmosphere building and becomes business-oriented with declining states, not rising powers."[41] Beijing did come to border settlement agreements that resolved most issues with Russia, and all issues with Vietnam, Kyrgyzstan, Kazakhstan, and Tajikistan, but the Central Asian states "accepted the bulk of the Chinese claims."[42]

Those whose opinions on China tend toward the hostile-China position also tend to see themselves as being ultrarealistic in several ways. They feel that they operate without illusions and without deference to anyone. For example, the writer whose views have just been described has criticized his own government for being too polite, restrained, and even obeisant in dealing with a recalcitrant China. He has done so, in part, by commenting on the existence of a pattern in which visits by high-level Chinese and Indian representatives to each other's country produce agreements to expedite negotiations concerning the border but ultimately produce little, if any, truly meaningful progress. He has added that the longest continuing frontier talks between any two countries since the end of the Second World War are those between India and China, saying that they started in 1981. What is more, the Line of Actual Control still remains undefined, undelineated, and undemarcated. No such lack of definition exists, he says (probably accurately), along a line of control between any other two countries. He has urged India to ask itself "why its nuclear shield," made overt in 1998, "is inspiring stronger Chinese containment of India" and not instilling "greater responsibility and caution in Beijing." And he has asked: "Is it because India has not tried to assert itself or exploit available strategic options?"[43]

Writing in a similar vein, another strategist accused the Indian government, at least once, of having had a "deep down fear of China" lasting up to the end of the I. K. Gujral prime ministership in 1998, a fear that to some degree continued to "color the views" in Indian "ruling circles" even after India's 1998 nuclear tests. An attitude of "genuflection" to China was related to an Indian governmental tendency, in the two decades after India's first nuclear test in 1974, to be fixated on the perception that Pakistan was the threat but not to undertake a realistic threat assessment. The "Indian Government's barely concealed fright in calling a spade a shovel, threat-wise, was . . . centrally responsible for the absence of serious or detailed studies on nuclear force planning."[44]

Criticism of this kind does not mean there have not been elements of overlap between the mainstream and China-is-hostile positions. Opinions can certainly coincide, even if the language of the hostile-China viewpoint is more brash. Adherents of both of these distinct perceptual positions have shown apprehension over what those with the hostile-China viewpoint will most readily take to be China's strategic encirclement of India. The hostile-China view, although very concerned about the present indirect threat seemingly posed by China via Pakistan and other Indian neighbors, has shared with the mainstream position an even greater concern about China over the long term, regarding the long-term threat as both known and dangerous. Both positions support India's taking significant countermeasures if necessary. A view that the United States shares the blame for China's transfer of WMD technology to Pakistan, based on the allegation that Washington has given higher priority to other matters in dealing with both China and Pakistan in the past, could be found in both the mainstream and hostile-China positions, and in at least one version of the nonhostile-China position too.[45] Although certain past and present Washingtonians would strongly contest this accusation, all of this common Indian reasoning can be considered part of a "realist" (as opposed to "idealist") direction being taken by Indian strategic thinking about China in particular and about the world in general.[46]

Correlations between the China Positions, Indian Grand-Strategic Reasoning, and Indian Domestic Political Thinking

Correlations with Indian Grand-Strategic Reasoning

It should already be evident that the various positions on China have been inevitably tied to Indian strategic thinking pitched at what might be called the "grand (Indian) strategy" level (table 2.1). This is not to say that Indian perceptions of China originate from grand-strategic thinking. Instead, China perceptions and grand-strategic views influence each other. Nor should the correlations described here be considered anything other than simplified propositions of the kind associated with model building. Additional factors shape perceptions of China, such as scholarly expertise, personal experience, and the many varieties and degrees of Indian nationalism. Three grand strategy outlooks have become prominent within the Indian strategic community since the 1998 round of nuclear testing, and these can be considered rough correlates of the three China perspectives already discussed. Like those perspectives, the grand strategy outlooks should be considered ideal-type models.

The mainstream position on China has tied in with the grand strategy outlook that might be called *moderate-realist* (to coin another phrase). It may be recalled that the heart of the mainstream thinking about China has been the perception that no short-term China threat exists, but that the long term is uncertain. Moderate realism in Indian grand-strategic thought perceives multipolarity or polycentrism as tending to emerge naturally and autonomously, without having to be forced by India. It holds that India can become a major international power (i.e., the possibility definitely exists, while China is in the same position). Whether India and China will be cooperative or conflictual powers is something to be determined by future developments.

Part of the reasoning found in such Indian realism holds that India can accept the U.S.-led international order, extant since the end of the Cold War, for the time being, and does not have to be a "revisionist" international actor in the sense of trying to rival the United States, despite its having become an overt nuclear power in 1998. India is revisionist in the sense of trying to improve its standing in international politics, but China may try to become a rival of the United States as China grows ever stronger. Another piece of this reasoning is that India does not oppose those international nonproliferation agreements, helping to make up the current world order, that do not discriminate against India.

This grand-strategic perspective foresees India achieving its future elevated status by working with, not against, the great powers of today. Because the great powers are not in fundamental Cold War–style conflict, India need not try to mediate between them. To follow a policy of constantly resisting them would be pointless and counterproductive. In order to become a great power, India needs to raise its rates of economic growth, and it is from the great powers that India can secure the necessary technol-

Table 2.1 *Indian Perceptual Positions on China and Their Grand Strategy and Domestic Political Correlates*

Mainstream Position	China-Is-Not-Hostile Position	China-Is-Hostile Position
Basics: No short-term China threat, but long term uncertain. In future, economically and militarily powerful China potentially a threat or challenge to Indian security. Chinese worldview similar to India's, but certain Chinese strategic interest calculations (regarding Pakistan and border) different and problematical. China is perhaps unwilling to acquiesce to rise of India as world power. India-China diplomacy can possibly avert major future problems.	Basics: China not hostile to India, basically pragmatic and rational, desirous of good relations over the long term. The 1962 war a result of both Indian and Chinese mistakes. One version of this position: Sino-Pakistani collusion is special case of atypical but still non-malevolent-minded Chinese behavior, although China does favor having a Pakistan "card" to play against India. China is caught in a strategic dilemma between its ties with Pakistan and its desire for better relations with India.	Basics: A hostile China is already a Cold War–style rival of India and a short- and long-term threat. Chinese are definitely practicing strategic encirclement of India. China is seeking top power and status position in Asia. China merits open diplomatic assertiveness by India, backed by the requisite military power, and not genuflection or obsequiousness.
Correlated Indian Grand-Strategic Ideas	**Correlated Grand-Strategic Ideas**	**Correlated Grand-Strategic Ideas**
Basics: India and China can become major powers. Whether they will be cooperative or conflictual powers is yet to be determined. Multipolar or polycentric world order can emerge naturally, and structuring of it, or of regional arrangements, to place limits on China would not be unwelcome to India. No Indian rivalry with U.S. is needed, while China may well become a rival to U.S. Having polarizing actors in Asia, e.g., possibly China and possibly the U.S., not desirable.	Basics: India should play moral, nonaligned, mediating role in world affairs. India should foster progressivism and equality in the world. The American-led world order and U.S. international hegemony should be resisted, and China and India hold similar views on this matter.	Basics: India should forcefully assert its right to be a recognized great power. International relations, for India, is basically a matter of conflict management among power-pursuing states. India needs highly robust nuclear arsenal. India should be willing to make anti-China security arrangements with other countries.
Correlated Indian Domestic Political Ideas	**Correlated Domestic Political Ideas**	**Correlated Domestic Political Ideas**
Basics: Best to relate Indian foreign policy to goal of accelerating growth of Indian economy via foreign investment and trade. Socialist governmental regulation of Indian economy should be eased. Close ties with the great powers important for furthering Indian economic development.	Basics: Commitment to egalitarianism and other progressive values applicable domestically too. Economic development in India should be socially just, equitable, and self-reliant.	Basics: Order and stability in both external and internal affairs to be maintained via governmental strength. Hindu nationalism is opposed to its own interpretation of the "soft state" concept. Acquisition of military power for India should be a prime internal political and economic objective.

ogy, trade, and finance. In fact, India "must, in effect, cut a deal with the great powers—pragmatically and with dignity."[47] The world order ought to increasingly accommodate the rise of India and discriminate less against Indian security and economic interests.

This particular strategic position, which emphasizes a search for converging interests between nations, is cautious, watchful, and somewhat optimistic about the natural evolution of international affairs. It therefore goes along easily with a position on China that is cautious and reserved as well as open-minded, if not trustful. Both moderate realism and mainstream perceptions of China can jointly lead to the conclusion that India needs (in terms reminiscent of American phraseology) a "hedge," i.e., "an insurance policy—against the possibility of a belligerent China in an uncertain anarchic world."[48]

Not surprisingly, this strategic position includes additional ideas that would have the effect of placing limitations on China, whether in the context of a worldwide power structure (i.e., via multipolarity or polycentrism), or in the context of an Asian setting in which both China and the United States participate. In dealing with India's immediate neighborhood, one analysis has called for relinquishing a long-standing "Monroe Doctrine" type of policy whereby India seeks to exclude or limit the influence of external powers (particularly China and the United States) in India's region. Its replacement would be a policy of improving India's relations with both the United States and China.[49]

A compatible view is that the rise of Chinese power, and the uncertainty about the uses to which it will be put in the future, mean that

> most Asian countries tend to agree that U.S. presence in Asia is a positive factor of stability. . . . India, which used to be deeply disturbed about the U.S. military presence in the Indian Ocean (essentially because it brought the Cold War to its shores), is more relaxed about this presence now that the Cold War is no more and Indo-U.S. relations are on the upswing.

But the person expressing this view has issued a warning. It is that the policies of the United States have tended to "undermine the capabilities of some countries like India to ensure a more equitable polycentric strategic balance in Asia." Another warning is that any "polarization" in Asia and the world caused by either U.S. or Chinese policies "will lead to difficult choices for others."[50]

For one leading Indian strategic commentator, "polycentrism" is a better concept than multipolarity because it accommodates the presence of states of unequal power, with some states gaining in strength. It also avoids the notion of polarization and conflict, which would be bad for India, especially if both the United States and China strive to be "poles" and to attract other nations as supporters.[51] A like-minded thinker has indicated that, in the polycentric world setup and the regional structure he would prefer, both cooperation and rivalry could exist, and "exclusive spheres of influence" or "balance of power wars" need not come into being. He has pointed to six possible future world poles or centers: the United States, European Union, China, Russia, Japan, and India. Four of them would be in Asia, and the United States, with its naval presence, troop deployment, and Asian alliances, is "an Asian power in the military sense."[52]

Turning to the nonhostile-China position in India, its correlation with Indian grand strategy ideas lies with a second major trend or direction in grand-strategic thought: the *idealist* one. Indian idealism would have the Indian nation-state continue to play something of a moral, nonaligned, and mediating role in world affairs, even though some contributors to it argue that India was right to become a state that openly possesses a minimum deterrent capable of deterring China as well as Pakistan.

"Idealism" can arguably be called "Nehruvian" too, since much of it did come from Mr. Nehru. But idealism also draws ideas from thinking that is more to the political left than that which Nehru himself tended to express publicly. Nehruvian "idealism," says an American political analyst,

> stressed the paramount role of public opinion and principle in constraining the exercise of power and viewed foreign policy as essentially a quest to build a more just world. Nehruvianism, as it came to be called, also had a strong sympathy for the world's "progressive" forces, including the USSR, and a visceral suspicion of the Western nations that had long exercised imperial dominion over the non-white world. Toward the United States Nehru combined the ideological prejudices of the British Labor Party with the cultural distaste for American vulgarity of the English aristocracy. This approach was shaken by the 1962 war and was often paralleled by hardheaded practical policies, but until the 1990s it was never reevaluated at a fundamental—that is, philosophical—level.[53]

As he also indicates, the correlation between Indian idealism, "antipathy to the West," and the matter of China is not simple. But, generally speaking, idealists "tend to be concerned with Western domination and exploitation and to be sympathetic to Chinese calls for Indian-Chinese cooperation to counter these evils."[54] The idealist grand strategy position, especially concerned as it is with limiting the political economic role of the United States in the world, recognizes that China has held similar views in the past and thinks somewhat similarly now, despite the ideological changes undergone by the Chinese leadership over time. Indian idealism logically favors the creation of a trusting India-China relationship, something that still does not exist now.

But it should be recalled that a certain version of Nehruvian idealism, which dominated Indian strategic thinking from the 1962 war to the late 1980s, was not at all trusting of China. What an acute American observer of Indian strategic thought has called "militant" Nehruvianism "rejected Nehru's 'softness' toward Pakistan and China." For contributors to this sort of Indian idealism, "best exemplified by Mrs. Indira Gandhi," the world was a threatening arena for India, and actions taken by China, and by the Americans, Pakistanis, or even smaller states in South Asia, were "'anti-Indian' in intent." America had allied itself with China "in the 1970s and 1980s." For its part, "China had humiliated India in 1962" and was determined to keep India "from emerging as an Asian equal."[55] Surely "militant" Nehruvianism, so described, has not entirely vanished from the Indian strategic community (or from the Congress Party Mrs. Gandhi once led) despite the events of the last decade or so. In modified or reworked form, it would correlate more closely with the mainstream and hostile-China perspectives on China than with the nonhostile-China position.

There is a third present-day grand-strategic tendency in India, and it is closely linked to the argument that the Chinese state tends to be basically hostile toward India. What can be called Indian *ultrarealism* urges the Indian nation-state to become a world power by forcefully asserting its right to be one, and expects that India should either already be considered a member of the great-power club or should make itself a member, whether or not that step is welcomed or liked by the club's other members. The ultrarealist strain in Indian thinking further argues that, for a rising power like India, international relations is a matter of states engaged in the pursuit of power, and that the movement toward a multipolar world order should be forced via assertive diplomacy backed by the requisite military strength.[56]

One advocate of ultrarealist ideas (and hostile-China views as well) has made the proposal that India aspire to having some rough equivalent of the number of nuclear weapons/warheads that he thinks China has (i.e., India should have 300 plus if China has 400 plus, and India can go to 400 plus if the Chinese figure goes to 500 plus, and so on). But the ultrarealist position is tolerant of smaller numbers too, and ultrarealism also stresses the overall robustness and wide range of capabilities that the Indian nuclear deterrent should possess. By way of contrast, the other major strategic positions found in India are more inclined to stress the virtues of minimalism in India's deterrence posture.[57] Indeed, the idealist position can even tolerate the argument that India need not have a nuclear deterrent.

The ultrarealist strategic outlook and the hostile-China position do not invariably agree with the Indian government's traditional allergy to thinking in terms of making anti-China security arrangements with other countries. A "meshing" of the interests of India with those of certain states—the ASEAN members, Vietnam (now an ASEAN member), and Israel have been mentioned—can lead to linking them with India in some sort of "cooperative security system," which would (as one of its functions) practice containment against China. The assistance of both Russia and the United States would be useful, even if the new coalition must be geared for autonomy and self-sustenance.[58] In comments made after the 1998 nuclear tests had taken place, a prominent Indian strategist holding such views even indicated that he could see the United States cooperating with India in some fashion against China, especially if the Republican Party acquired control of the White House. The Republicans, he said, had more "do-able objectives" regarding China than did the Democrats—objectives with which India could work. But more recently he has written of "the inconstancy of the United States as a 'natural ally' coupled with Washington's insisting on having things its own way." He has also argued that, historically speaking, a great power's interests and those of a "would-be great power" have converged only temporarily and that such convergence cannot be "the basis for a permanent *modus vivendi*." While China stands as the more principal and immediate threat to India, in his view, the United States is a "latent threat."[59]

Correlations with Domestic Indian Political Thought

Neither the main Indian perceptual positions on China, nor the grand strategy positions to which they can be loosely linked, have operated apart from Indian domestic politics.[60]

It is possible to say that an ideal-typical (i.e., model) internal Indian political counterpart of what has been the mainstream Indian position on

China, and of what has been the moderate-realist grand strategy position, is a political outlook that calls, among other things, for less governmental regulation of the Indian economy and for greater movement away from Indian socialist practices in the economic sphere. This internal political standpoint gives top priority to speeding up Indian industrialization, modernization, and general economic growth—not by maximizing autarky as idealists would prefer, but by securing foreign trade and investment—and is willing to relate foreign policy to that imperative. It further argues that closer relations with the great powers are therefore important for the purpose of furthering Indian economic development. The moderate realist position, including this view of the relationship between internal and external policy, is apparently being favored (at least in part) by certain government leaders from the ruling Bharatiya Janata Party (BJP), but not necessarily by the party as a whole, especially given the element in the party that is strongly Hindu nationalist. It also seems to have a following within the main opposition party, the Congress Party, but is only one among the several strategic views apparently represented there.

One definitely BJP-affiliated domestic viewpoint, which can be viewed as a subsection of the ultrarealist grand strategy position and is tied to the hostile-China perspective (to some degree), is what can be called the ideal-typical Hindu nationalist stream of consciousness. It favors strongly projecting to the domestic Indian population, and to the outside world, an image of India as a Hindu nation, bound together and tied to its region by its unique cultural heritage.

A more secular-minded line of thought that constitutes a subsection of ultrarealism, and is linked to the conclusion that China is hostile, could once have been expected to be associated with the BJP, a party that has advocated a strong and powerful nation-state asserting itself in international affairs. But this version of ultrarealism is being pursued partly or wholly independently of the party, since certain ultrarealist policy recommendations have not been accepted by the top BJP governmental leadership.

Ultrarealism in general is consistent in believing that Indian governmental strength is needed in both external and internal affairs. The government should take prompt and forceful actions internally in order to promote lawful and effective Indian behavior. A Hindu nationalist theme is that India should not be a "soft state" as Hindu nationalism defines that term. Ultrarealism, overall, further argues that acquisition of military power for India should be a prime internal political and economic objective.

The nonhostile view of China, along with the grand strategy idealism to which it is linked, can also be related to a certain model of identifiable domestic political thought and activity, especially concerning values. Social justice, egalitarianism, and antihegemonism are among those values, and a concern that they be vital parts of the international order is matched by a concern, at least on the theoretical level, that they figure strongly in Indian domestic political life and economic development. What one source has called the left-liberal part of the Indian political spectrum (although it also includes the far left) is in play here, and it seems to still include a segment of the Congress Party.

The Indian Working Cluster of Perceptions

A group of perceptions lie beyond the differing China positions, grand-strategic directions, and domestic policy orientations already discussed in these pages. They are the ones that were immediately related to Indian policy at the time when the bulk of the research for this chapter was done (summer to early autumn 2001), as indicated by the fact that they were especially prominent in the (not for attribution) discourse of persons privy to Indian governmental thinking. That discourse was occasioned by the presentations and discussions of the chapter's earlier drafts, in India and elsewhere, in 2001. What the entire research exercise made clear was that a broad working consensus on China did exist in the Indian strategic community, consisting of what this chapter has identified as the mainstream perspective and those parts of the nonhostile-China and hostile-China perspectives that overlapped with it. But made equally clear was the reality that certain parts of that consensus were evoked, emphasized, and expressed at different times, according to the prevailing circumstances of the moment. It is these parts that can be called a "working cluster" of perceptions (yet another ideal-type construction or model) and given special treatment.

Especially in the summer of 2001, a key circumstantial premise mentioned by Indian government sources was that Sino-Indian diplomatic dealings were recovering, or had recovered, from the downturn that had immediately followed India's 1998 nuclear tests. Apparently, another influential circumstance was the obvious existence of certain trends in India-U.S. and U.S.-China relations. A sustained improvement in Indo-U.S. ties had coincided with a time of heightened sensitivity in Washington-Beijing dealings.

India's strategic community as a whole seemed (at least to this writer) to be interested in making clear that India was not coming together with America in some anti-Chinese fashion.

What was emphasized in the perceptual working cluster was China's role as the giant neighbor with whom India has important present and potential convergences of worldview and national interest. India and China were said to have their historical and civilizational ties, even though India was not thought to have a history as a "middle kingdom" like China does. They were also said to have nearly identical problems of development that allow them to share and profit from common experiences. Made salient was the ability of India and China to make common and cooperative cause with each other on matters of international economics. Being emphasized, too, were the strong similarities between the two countries' worldviews, which include maximization of strategic autonomy for themselves in the world order. These positive elements were presented as if they outweighed India-China differences.

Although the major China-related security problems for India were certainly thought to still exist, no significant threatening situations were anticipated in the short and medium term. The longer term was still considered a matter of uncertainty, but India-China conflict was not considered inevitable. Said to be very likely (according to one source even "inevitable") was that India and China would continue to have a relationship featuring both friendliness and rivalry. A consensus was that greater diversification of political and economic ties would be sought, at least by the Indian side, but without any diminution of the importance assigned by New Delhi to India's real security concerns.

According to the 2001 working set of perceptions, India-China relations will not hinge on the border dispute, an expectation that the Chinese were thought to have accepted too. The 1962 war may have left a deep imprint on the Indian psyche, but Indian and Chinese diplomatic efforts were thought to have been rather successful in maintaining frontier peace and tranquility in recent years. The Indian government, for its part, was described by one knowledgeable commentator as being certain that neither side wants a confrontation along the LAC. His reasoning was that New Delhi wants to move quickly to settle differences on where the LAC is really located, particularly since such an interim settlement will minimize the chance of border incidents, and then proceed to the true border negotiations, which are expected to take a long time. Other parts of this line of thought were: the Sino-Indian negotiations on the LAC will proceed, even if that happens at the pace the Chinese want, rather than the faster one India wants; and long-term Indian engagement and normalization of relations with China are processes that can help produce a final border settlement someday.

The working cluster of perceptions included an awareness that China has, at least formally, adopted a more neutral stance in recent years with regard to India versus Pakistan on the Kashmir issue. A government-favored Indian analysis of Chinese motivation, in this context, reportedly was that China does not want an Indo-Pakistani war over Kashmir and is aware that direct conflict between India and Pakistan would bring other countries into the picture, something not wanted by Beijing. According to this analysis, the Chinese also have concerns about religious extremism linked to Pakistan, especially in light of their sensitivity about their own frontier region of Xinjiang and their concern about the impact that trouble there could have on other Chinese minority nationalities, such as the Tibetans.

As has already been noted, one of the working perceptions in 2001 was that China is a nation with which Indian ties ought to be diversified, i.e., extended beyond the traditional diplomatic issues into realms like economics and business. But another was that the relationship has already gone significantly beyond the old issues. Both governmental and nongovernmental Indian strategists were quite aware that Indian businesspeople were in regular contact with India's government concerning China, and that they were seeking more governmental help in dealing with China-related matters. The Chinese example was certainly thought to be something that Indian political decision makers (such as parliamentarians and the chief ministers of Indian states) should see in order to find out what is economically possible and practical in India and in order to learn what must indeed be done better by India in the near future. Chinese economic development, in this Indian perceptual framework, was described as something to be welcomed and studied rather than just feared.[61]

The rise of a China that is both prosperous and peaceful was perceived (within the "working cluster") as being good for India in some ways. But the growth of Chinese comprehensive power was still regarded as a reason for caution in Indian thinking about foreign policy and defense. As one informant pointed out (to this writer) in 2001, it is easy to emphasize the common India-China ideological opposition to "imperialism," and to other things, when China does not have much power, but different thinking is needed as China's power grows. India cannot count on a powerful China acting as it does now, even if the Chinese do say that their policy of peaceful and stable relations toward their neighbors will remain unchanged. Included in the working cluster was an awareness of signs that China still has a hierarchical view of the world, although one Indian analyst pointed to the existence of much Chinese literature on Indian comprehensive national power, a literature that does not reach a definite conclusion about what India will eventually achieve.

Both China and India were known by Indian strategic community members in 2001 to be unhappy with the international status quo, which they find restrictive. Both were also described as having a desire to improve their international standing and gain more autonomy or freedom in the realm of foreign policy decision making and action. But an expressed Indian hope was that both India and China would recognize a need to give each other maximal strategic "space." One Indian commentator observed, rather succinctly, that India and China do not necessarily agree on *how* to produce greater multipolarity or polycentrism in the world order.

India was not portrayed in the working cluster as a "revisionist" power, in the sense of seeking to oppose and counterbalance the United States as the world "hegemon." But China was seen as wanting to "stand up" to the United States. A relevant comment was that India wants a democratic multipolar world and not a new bipolar world. At least as of mid-2001, the Chinese were also thought to be worried about the United States and India coming together against China.

The events triggered by the September 11, 2001, terrorist attacks on the United States, such as the U.S. decision to lead a war in Afghanistan and improve ties with Pakistan, had not substantially altered this Indian working cluster of perceptions as of November 2001 (when this author discussed it again with knowledgeable Indian informants). It still gave every appearance of being focused on long-term trends, even though both India and China were obviously having to take into account the initiation of new U.S. policies toward Pakistan, Afghanistan, and Central Asia. New Delhi was reportedly aware that, among other things, the Chinese had become concerned about a U.S. presence coming right to their doorstep.[62] The Indian government and the Indian strategic community, in general, were less concerned about the new U.S. presence in Asia, while perceiving both possible opportunities and problems (particularly with regard to Kashmir) in the evolving situation.

Part of the post–September 11 working cluster was an Indian perception that China does not face a terrorism problem to the extent that both India and the United States do. Therefore, India and the United States were seen (from this Indian perspective) as needing to work together on terrorism, while China (whatever it may say or do in relation to Central Asia and elsewhere) remained largely out of this picture. According to this reasoning, the Chinese supposedly know that they have not been targeted by the Taliban and Osama bin Laden to the same degree as have the United States and India. China does have its own terrorism concerns, internally and externally, but they are manageable and the Chinese can control them better than the Indians and Americans can control theirs. China's bigger concern is the United States, and India simply does not have precisely the same concern.

But increased closeness between India and China was described as possibly coming about if the United States were to mismanage its current military and diplomatic operations with respect to Afghanistan, Pakistan, and India. India was thought to be prepared to show dexterity in its relations with both China and the United States, motivated by a wide internal consensus about the need for India to achieve great-power status and to deal with the United States in the context of Indian interests rather than ideology or empathy. During a visit to India in January 2003, a few discussions with knowledgeable individuals indicated that the Indian working consensus had shifted somewhat in a direction favorable to China, but this author could not discern a fundamental change in the working consensus, yet.

Conclusions and Implications

A study of the India-China relationship, published while successive drafts of this chapter were being written, raises an issue that cannot be ignored by any serious discussion of Indian policy-related perceptions of China. Put briefly, it is whether a fundamental geopolitical and security conflict between India and China, one that has arguably been a structural reality in Asian affairs for some fifty years, is often disguised or put aside by Indian and Chinese rhetoric.

A number of trenchant observations about such rhetoric are made. One is that a "rhetoric of Chinese-Indian friendship" exists. It "often decorates bilateral interactions between the two countries," and is "an exercise in wish fulfillment . . . to a considerable extent." The hope of "well-intentioned people," on both sides, is that by "making statements about Sino-Indian friendship," the relationship "will become so." Such rhetoric is also "instrumental" in that it is used, by Indian leaders and other persons directly responsible for Sino-Indian dealings, to "create a positive atmosphere" or "climate" that is "conducive to better relations" and that at other times will be employed to "cover up deeper tensions."[63]

Such a set of propositions, undoubtedly accurate, could conceivably serve as an interpretation of much of the kind of rhetoric reported in this chapter, unless other sources of that rhetoric are noted too. Propositions of this sort are also likely to produce an Indian and Chinese response similar to one offered when earlier drafts of this volume's chapters were discussed in Delhi, Shanghai, and Beijing during July 2001. There, a particular attitude was, Aren't "you" Americans overstressing the negative dimension of India-China dealings? In China, there was also an undertone of suspicion that our U.S. delegation might, for political reasons, be underplaying areas of India-China agreement and cooperation, in keeping with a (supposed) U.S. governmental interest in pitting China and India against each other.

That suspicion is surely not justified in the case of most American scholars, including this one, who function independently in academia and elsewhere. But it sometimes seems to this American observer that current Indian and Chinese strategic discourses overemphasize the promising future potentials in the India-China relationship and de-emphasize troublesome past and present realities. Some other observers might also contend—perhaps because of U.S. cultural biases—that Indian interlocutors, in particular, are doing too much theorizing or intellectualizing when they either weight equally the positive and negative in Sino-Indian relations or stress whatever is positive.

A case can certainly be made, and indeed has recently been put forward very ably by an American scholar, for the proposition that the divide between India and China is of a fundamental geopolitical and international-structural nature. At least one unapologetic Indian ultrarealist and holder of hostile-China views says that too. Indeed, he feels that the Chinese would be a real threat to India even if they had not armed Pakistan, given the size of the two countries, their geographic proximity, and other factors such as the basically conflictual nature of international affairs.[64] His willingness to criticize U.S. foreign policies can readily be documented, and so can his fierce protectiveness of Indian strategic autonomy. So, no particular pro-American bias and no U.S. governmental impetus need be suspected as the source of this sort of negativity about the India-China relationship.

Nevertheless, most of the positive or even-handed Indian perceptions of China (and of Sino-Indian ties) that have been noted here seem not to have been expressed primarily for decorative or instrumental reasons. They generally come from the extragovernmental portion of Indian strategic community and give all the appearance of representing genuine conviction, whatever instrumental-political function they may also serve. Moreover, whatever their source, the passion with which perceptions of China often are expressed within the Indian strategic community, the long time devotion of many Indian strategic analysts to those perceptions and/or to their own related larger strategic visions, and the personal career choices and consequences that may have helped to create and may have (at least partly) resulted from those visions, are all quite impressive. So is the conviction, easily sensed on the part of Indian colleagues, that Americans possess no special wisdom about the basic nature of the India-China relationship and surely understand it no better than Indian and Chinese strategic thinkers do themselves.

Concerning the subjects of whether positive future potentials are being given greater weight than they deserve in the overall Indian strategic discourse, and whether Indian analyses of China may be unduly affected by what American diplomats and others can say is an Indian penchant for over-intellectualization, ample evidence to the contrary can be adduced. The key piece of it, already provided by this chapter, is that the Indian mainstream perspective on China has been friendly but wary. It has treated both China and the India-China relationship as items about which a wait-and-see posture should be taken. Positive potentials have not been stressed by mainstream thinking any more than negative potentials and current negative problems. The situation-sensitive working cluster of perceptions probably does, at any given time, contain some statements that are instrumental and even wishful. But the rhetorical and intellectual content of all three of the Indian strategic community's basic China positions (including the nonhostile-China one) has probably contained very little instrumentalism and wishful thinking, as well as much rigorous observation and analysis of a country (China) and a relationship (India-China) about which opinions can quite legitimately differ and overlap.

That is one reason why India's several perceptual positions on China and Sino-Indian affairs should be treated seriously by strategists in both China and the United States. Americans have shown in the past that they can be dismissive of elements in Indian strategic thought that run counter to their own views. A form of dismissiveness of certain Indian concerns about China, on the part of some individual Chinese observers, was also clearly evident when this writer was in China in July 2001.

The national interests of both China and India might be better served if the Chinese strategic elite would treat Indian perceptions of China with unvarying seriousness. That elite might achieve much that is of value, too, by addressing what Indians can easily see as gaps between Chinese rhetoric, on the one hand, and the policies and actions constituting China's "body language,"[65] on the other, just as they can easily see gaps between U.S. rhetoric and U.S. policy-related activity. Strategic dialogue between the Indian and Chinese governments, devoted to these tasks among others, is a true necessity. So is continuation of the equivalent dialogues under way between the governments (and strategic communities) of India and the United States and of the United States and China.

Epilogue

By the end of June 2003 the possibility of a future attenuation or even a future breakup of the Indian working consensus on China (whatever its content in early June 2003) became evident. Indeed, at the end of the month it seemed that (what at least this outside observer would call) a new working consensus could form eventually, although with difficulty and with people having serious reservations about it. The causes of it all were signs of a change in the policy direction of the Indian government. The six-day state visit of Prime Minister Vajpayee to China in late June produced a certain governmental rhetoric. Included in it was a statement that the quality of the India-China relationship had been transformed by the two governments' joint process, over several years, of developing "all round" bilateral cooperation, while the differences between the two countries were being addressed simultaneously.

Vajpayee personally told a press conference that during his June meetings in Beijing a "path" to resolution of the boundary dispute had been found, and that, perhaps, the "kind of boundary talks" in which he had just participated had "never taken place before." At least in part he was referring to a decision of the two sides to appoint special senior representatives (one from each government) to begin rapid work on exploring the framework of an eventual boundary settlement, and do so from the "political perspective" of the overall India-China relationship. One implication of this phraseology was that technical and historical considerations would no longer be permitted to stall the advance toward reaching a boundary settlement.

Expressing great satisfaction with the results of his talks with China's leadership, the Indian prime minister (on another occasion) focused on the new importance of economic ties between China and India, with bilateral trade having surged recently and bilateral investments having picked up. He further suggested the formation of a natural alliance between the Indian and Chinese information technology industries, based on the core competence of India in computer software and that of China in hardware. Close cooperation by India and China on matters involving the World Trade Organization was also expected by the Indian government, and other economics-related measures were agreed upon by the two governments.

The Indian foreign minister, Yashwant Sinha, publicly cited a list of accords and understandings just concluded in Beijing (with regard to China starting a process of recognizing the accession of Sikkim to India, revived Tibet-India trade across the Sikkim border, and a reformulated statement of recognition by India of Tibet's status as a part of China) as constituting a "win-win situation" for both sides. The bilateral decision on the political upgrading of the border talks was described by Sinha as a "very big development." He also indicated that his government expected better relations with China to induce the Chinese to limit what they were prepared to do for Pakistan in the future. Whatever they (the Chinese) have done "in terms of military co-operation with Pakistan in the past is a done deal," he argued. He noted, "We feel that if we [India and China] manage to come closer together then the proclivity of China to do something that is not in India's interests will decline."[66]

Some published and privately expressed opinion in India attached the label "hype" to such rhetoric. The Vajpayee visit, or so a newspaper column reported, was also dismissively called a "grand show," an "extravaganza," and a "big picnic."[67] But analysis by Indian strategists of the 2003 Beijing summit, as well as the information being revealed about not just the visit but also the governmental process leading up to it, encompassed a number of shared conclusions about current Indian governmental perceptions of China and of the India-China relationship.[68] One is that the India-China economic relationship has improved so markedly in recent years and months, and now shows such promise for the near future, that great Indian and Chinese governmental emphasis can be placed on it. Another is that bilateral difficulties in the strategic or security area can be viewed by both sides in the context of successful economic relations, so that diplomatic progress can thereby (it is hoped) be better enabled.

Furthermore, from the Indian governmental viewpoint, an important component of diplomacy can and should be "political" in the sense of having the India-China border discussions go beyond consideration of the LAC and toward a final border agreement, even if reaching such an agreement takes time. The LAC must still be clarified, but obstacles in that process need not halt progress toward the kind of border settlement that is based heavily on political considerations. Government thinking may be that those considerations can and should include the advisability and feasibility (domestic political feasibility in India and China, as well as bilateral diplomatic feasibility) of trading India's notional claim to the really unrecoverable Aksai Chin (in the Western Sector of the frontier) for basic Chinese acquiescence to Indian possession of what is now Arunachal Pradesh.

To judge from both press-based material and personal conversations with Indian strategic analysts, there was (as of 30 June 2003) substantial agreement between the government and the ideal-type constructs or models that this chapter has presumed to call the mainstream China position and the moderate-realist strategic position. This was discernible even though the government seemed to be moving beyond the mainstream China position that was evolving over time between 1998 and early 2003. While political difficulties may well be experienced by the government, support for what may be its new China border policy should eventually be forthcoming, on the basis of an amended "mainstream" set of China perceptions, along with possible future political developments.[69]

Among these developments should be a gathering of support for the Vajpayee government's China initiatives from those strategists and political activists who usually support the government. The Indian left could have little choice but to provide at least general support on the China matter given its own well-established China and grand-strategic positions. The government has actually moved in the direction of, and has matched at least some of the optimism of, the so-called China-is-not-hostile perceptual position constructed in this chapter. Opposition coming from what have been identified as the hostile-China and ultrarealist positions could be expected, but Hindu nationalist opposition could be temporary. There is uncertainty as to what the Congress Party stand would be, but its past political stands and statements give reason to believe that it would ultimately be generally supportive of a governmental gamble or exploration with the Chinese. Yet the government may have to deal with the sensitivity of some Indian strategic idealist thinking and certain Hindu nationalist thought toward possible further damage to Tibet and Tibetans.

To judge even further from press articles and conversations with Indian strategic thinkers, certain fundamental elements and important implications of two of the models drawn up in these pages (i.e., the ideal-type Indian "mainstream" position on China and the moderate-realist grand-strategic correlate of it) do not seem to have been affected by the 2003 Beijing event and Indian anticipation of its further outcomes. Whether or not China will pose a strategic and security problem for India in the long term, especially as China becomes a great power, is still considered a matter of uncertainty. An Indian deterrent (i.e., a nuclear and missile hedge) against China is still thought to be needed, and should indeed include an adequate arsenal of missiles having the range to reach deeply into China. Although no warfare with China is expected in the foreseeable future, the Indian deterrent gives India protection for the long term. But added to moderate grand-strategic reasoning now is the perception that the 1998 nuclear tests have made India more confident in dealing with China and in seeking a more normal relationship with China.

Current problems, such as the Chinese all-weather friendship and military linkage to Pakistan, still place limitations on how close the India-China relationship can become. Anxiety still exists in India about what can be called Chinese encirclement. There has been much governmental reference to breaking away from past India-China mistrust, but a new era of trust has not dawned yet. India-China competition is still anticipated, along with cooperation, although it can be hoped that no divisive rivalry will take place. It is also thought possible that the border problem may still remain unresolved, and consigned to a low-priority position in India-China diplomacy, notwithstanding the current attention and activity being devoted to it. But government rhetoric has taken a core idea of the mainstream China perspective, i.e., that the possibility exists for China and India to avert future problems through diplomacy and related action, and added to it much more optimism and commitment.

Despite the disappointment and disagreement over the relationship with the United States that has been experienced by contributors to what this chapter has called the Indian moderate-realist outlook, they seem to see no reason to have the government apologize to China for the overall improvement in the Indo-American relationship. In fact, China's concern about American ties to India, a concern that is perceived on the Indian side, can be viewed (from this perspective) as aiding the Indian government in its present and future effort to have the kind of relationship with China that moderate-realist Indian thinking desires (a desire it shares with the other grand-strategic positions). It is a relationship that enhances India's maneuverability (or "space") in international affairs as well as India's position and status in the world order. But the moderate-realist view is that while diplomacy should be used toward this end, and in the process should establish as much India and China cooperation and warmth as may be possible as quickly as possible, India should still keep its proverbial guard "up" and have the China-directed military capabilities it fundamentally needs.

Notes

1. The first Indian self-perception in these paragraphs is drawn from Sujit Dutta, "India and the Global Order," in *Asian Security in the 21st Century,* ed. Jasjit Singh (New Delhi: Institute for Defense Studies and Analyses, 1999), 43, 51; and from Stephen P. Cohen, *India: Emerging Power* (Washington, D.C.: Brookings Institution Press, 2001), 54. The remark about true multipolarity in the world having to go beyond the Permanent Five to include India is one that Mr. Dutta, a sinologist who has been consulted by the government, frequently made in private conversations, 1997–2000. The "*de facto* strategic consensus" point and quotation is from C. Raja Mohan, "India's Relations with the Great Powers: Need for Reorientation," in Singh, *Asian Security,* 83–84. Mr. Raja Mohan, a journalist and editor for *The Hindu* newspaper, has been said by quite a number of knowledgeable people, both in India and in the United States, to have good access to Indian government thinking and to shape it to some small degree.

2. These points were made to the author by Indian strategists, serving and retired government officials, journalists, and American observers between 1997 and 2001 in New Delhi and elsewhere. Special thanks are owed to Professor Sumit Ganguly for his efforts to enable me to work constructively with such persons.

3. Kanti Bajpai, "India's Nuclear Posture after Pokhran II," *International Studies* 37, no. 4 (2000): 268, 277. In his article, Professor Bajpai defines the "strategic community" as lying mostly outside the government, and as containing those persons "who are supportive of government policy on nuclear matters" (Web version available at www.ceri-sciencespo.com/archive/jan01/pokhran.pdf, p. 9). The definition used in this chapter is more inclusive, but Bajpai's words are applied in a way that is accurate for all practical purposes. On the Vajpayee government not yet having forged a national consensus on its overall foreign policy direction, see C. Raja Mohan, *Crossing the Rubicon* (New Delhi: Viking-Penguin, 2003), 263–68.

4. The "files" reference is a conclusion drawn from an interview with a former foreign secretary, New Delhi, 2000. For an example of apparent continuity between in-service views and expressions made after a former official joins the strategic community, see J. N. Dixit, *My South Block Years: Memoirs of a Foreign Secretary* (New Delhi: USB Publishers, 1996), passim.

5. Interview with State Department official, Washington D.C., 16 May 2001.

6. For an expression of this viewpoint by a former government official who was highly involved in formulating the case for India's so-called "historical" borders at a

crucial time, see Sarvepalli Gopal, *Jawaharlal Nehru: A Biography,* vol. 3 (Cambridge: Harvard University Press, 1984), 303–6.

7. The most important published presentation of the "evidence" is the *Report of the Officials of the Governments of India and the People's Republic of China on the Boundary Question* (New Delhi: Government of India, Ministry of External Affairs, 1961). Quotation is from Gopal, *Nehru,* 306.

8. The literature attesting to these points is sizable and very extensively researched. Some important items in it are: G. N. Rao (Indian government official), *The India-China Border: A Reappraisal* (New York: Asia Publishing House, 1968); and the British historian Alastair Lamb's series of books, *The China-India Border* (London: Oxford University Press, 1964), *The McMahon Line* (London: Routledge and Keegan Paul, 1966), *The Sino-Indian Border in Ladakh* (Columbia: University of South Carolina Press, 1975), *Tibet, China, and India, 1914–1950* (Hertfordshire, U.K.: Roxford Books, 1989), and *Kashmir: A Disputed Legacy* (Hertfordshire, U.K.: Roxford Books, 1991), especially pp. 69–75. Important too are Karunakar Gupta, *The Hidden History of the Sino-Indian Frontier* (Calcutta: Minverva Associates Pvt. Ltd., 1971); and Neville Maxwell, *India's China War* (New York: Pantheon, 1970), 39–64, 73–74, 83–85. See also the Indian government's *Report of the Officials;* Steven A. Hoffmann, *India and the China Crisis* (Berkeley: University of California Press, 1990), 9–30; and Xuecheng Liu, *The Sino-Indian Border Dispute and Sino-Indian Relations* (Lanham, Md.: University Press of America, 1994), 47–78. The point about the British policies and formulations not always having been the right ones was brought to my attention by S. Gopal, former head of the Indian foreign ministry's historical division, a major force in compiling the historical case for India's borders and Nehru's official biographer, during conversations held in New Delhi, London, and Madras between 1983 and 1986.

9. John Garver, *Protracted Contest: Sino-Indian Rivalry in the Twentieth Century* (Seattle: University of Washington Press, 2001), 220.

10. Shashi Tharoor, *Reasons of State* (New Delhi: Vikas, 1982), 86–87.

11. Dixit, *South Block Years,* 230.

12. George Perkovich, *India's Nuclear Bomb* (Berkeley: University of California Press, 1999), 299, 289–290. Those this author calls "nuclear hawks" were using the "China argument" by the late 1980s nevertheless (p. 290).

13. Garver, *Protracted Contest,* 220–21.

14. Telephone interview with Sujit Dutta, Saratoga–New Delhi, 6 October 2002. Mr. Dutta heads the China and Eastern Asia Cluster of scholars at the government-affiliated and supported Institute for Defense Studies and Analyses in New Delhi (IDSA) and is a member of the so-called India-China "eminent persons" group, which has some Indian government participation and which discusses and makes suggestions on India-China issues.

15. Ibid., and interviews not for attribution.

16. Dixit, *South Block Years,* 231–22. Mr. Dixit was writing of his views while still in government some time ago. But his words are still indicative of mainstream thinking on China now. For updated versions see Verghese Koithara (vice admiral, ret.), *Society, State, and Security: The Indian Experience* (New Delhi: Sage, 1999), 173–76.

17. Interview with a sinologist at the IDSA, 14 January 2000.

18. Above quotations from Jasjit Singh, "Strategic Uncertainty and Defense Planning," in Singh, *Asian Security,* 238–39.

19. Amitabh Mattoo, "Imagining China," in *The Peacock and the Dragon,* ed. K. Bajpai and A. Mattoo (New Delhi: Har-Anand, 2000), 20–21.

20. K. Subrahmanyam, "Understanding China, Sun Tzu and Shakti," *Times of India,* 5 June 1998.

21. Ibid. Mr. Subrahmanyam is the doyen of Indian strategic thinkers, a former official, a former director of the IDSA (the think-tank financed by the Ministry of Defense and, to a small extent, by the Ministry of External Affairs), and someone widely known to be consulted by the Indian government. He has also been the head (i.e., "convener") of the government-created National Security Advisory Board (NSAB) and led an investigating committee concerning the Kargil affair. A contributor of opinion articles to the *Times of India,* he is involved, too, in the editorial writing process for same leading national publication.

22. Mohan, "India's Relations with the Great Powers," 92–93.

23. The matter of nuclear blackmail is often discussed by K. Subrahmanyam. See his "Understanding China."

24. The quotation (only) is from Swaran Singh, "China's Nuclear Weapons and Doctrine," in *Nuclear India,* ed. Jasjit Singh (New Delhi: IDSA, 1998), 154. Swaran Singh was an IDSA sinologist, who later left to join Jawaharlal Nehru University.

25. Amitabh Mattoo, "India's Nuclear Policy in an Anarchic World," in *India's Nuclear Deterrent,* ed. Amitabh Mattoo (New Delhi: Har-Anand, 1999), 23. Dr. Mattoo has been a professor and administrator at Jawaharlal Nehru University in New Delhi and a member of the NSAB.

26. Bajpai, "India's Nuclear Posture," 285–87. K. Subrahmanyam is quoted and cited there.

27. Quotation on China is from Swaran Singh, "China's Nuclear Weapons," 152–53. The close observer mentioned here is Sujit Dutta, interviewed in New Delhi, 13 January 2003.

28. Most of this paragraph, and the preceding one, are based on Koithara, *Society, State, and Security,* 255–57.

29. Dixit, *South Block Years,* 250–51.

30. J. N. Dixit, *Across Borders: Fifty Years of Indian Foreign Policy* (New Delhi: Picus Books, 1998), 412–18.

31. Mattoo, "India's Nuclear Policy," 23, and from my own personal participation in two of the three IDSA-sponsored and -managed "Annual Asian Security Conferences" held in New Delhi between 1999 and 2001.

32. Those names can be found in Mattoo, "India's Nuclear Policy," 19.

33. My own notes from a seminar to introduce the Ranganathan-Khanna book (see note 35), India International Center, New Delhi, 24 January 2000.

34. Achin Vanaik, "Dealing with China," *Hindu,* 27 January 2001.

35. These statements and quotations are from a lengthy conversation with Giri Deshingkar, of the Institute for Chinese Studies (see below) and the Institute for the Study of Developing Societies, in Delhi, 5–6 January 2000. I owe much of my continuing interest in India-China affairs to my twenty-five-year friendship with the late Mr. Deshingkar, one of India's foremost longtime sinologists.

36. See C. V. Ranganathan and Vinod C. Khanna, *India and China: The Way Ahead after "Mao's India War"* (New Delhi: Har-Anand, 2000), 137–47. Mr. Ranganathan is a former Indian ambassador to China, and he has twice been appointed as the head (i.e., "convener") of the NSAB. For the point that China wished to use Pakistan to counter the

Soviet Union at one time, see Ranganathan and Khanna, *India and China,* 137, 140. For agreement on this point, see Mira Sinha Bhattacharjea, *China, the World, and India* (New Delhi: Samskriti, 2001), 433–34. Mrs. Bhattacharjea, a senior, highly experienced sinologist, is affiliated with the Institute of Chinese Studies (ICS) in Delhi.

37. See Mira Sinha Bhattacharjea, "After the Beijing Summit," *Frontline,* 18–31 July 1998.

38. Interview with M. V. Rappai, sinologist, IDSA, New Delhi, 14 January 2000.

39. From a telephone conversation with Ashley Tellis, 22 May 2001. Dr. Tellis has been a senior analyst for the Rand Corporation and a personal adviser, in New Delhi, to the U.S. ambassador to India, Robert Blackwill.

40. See Brahma Chellaney, "Nuclear Deterrent Posture," in *Securing India's Future in the New Millennium,* ed. Brahma Chellaney (New Delhi: Orient Longman, 1999), 187 (source of the "countervailing" quote). At the time that this was written, at least, the author held the view that American and Chinese interests converged on this matter. Ibid., 149 (source of "calibrated . . . advance" quote). Brahma Chellaney, "Allied in Stealth," *Hindustan Times,* 12 July 2000 (source of "roguish Pakistan" quote); "The Regional Strategic Triangle," in *Securing India's Future,* 336 (source of quotes on containment "game" and Vietnam and Taiwan); "Rhetoric Fails to Mask Sino-Indian Realities," *Hindustan Times,* 24 July 2000 (source of "sustained transfers," "state to state," and "normal relationship" quotes); and "Regional Strategic Triangle," 330 (source of "engage and contain" quote). The "state to state" and "normal relationship" quotes are direct from Tang Jiaxuan, foreign minister of China at the time. The points about China and unipolarity and the mention of the Pentagon report are in Chellaney, "Allied in Stealth." The report is quoted directly.

41. Brahma Chellaney, "Two-Timing China: India Should Adopt a More Pragmatic Policy Towards Its Neighbor," *Hindustan Times,* 14 June 2000 (source of "Tibet card," "conditions are ripe," and "balance of power" quotes). The "conditions are ripe" quotation is a Chinese phrase that originated in the early phase of the border dispute, and Chellaney may be mentioning it partly as a reminder of China's alleged duplicity in the past.

42. Chellaney, "Rhetoric Fails."

43. Chellaney, "Allied in Stealth" (quotations), and see "Two-Timing China" and "Rhetoric Fails."

44. Bharat Karnad, "A Thermonuclear Deterrent," in Mattoo, *India's Nuclear Deterrent,* 133–34.

45. For the opinion that the United States shares responsibility for the China-Pakistan arms link, given in a hostile-China context, see Gurmeet Kanwal, *Nuclear Defence: Shaping the Arsenal* (New Delhi: Knowledge World and Institute for Defence Studies and Analyses, 2001), 8.

46. For a somewhat different view of Indian "realism," see Garver, *Protracted Contest,* 387–88.

47. Much of the material on Indian grand strategy presented here comes from the pioneering work of Kanti Bajpai. But the references to China and to much else involved in Indian "realism" (and the other directions in Indian strategic thinking) are drawn from lectures by members of the strategic community, author interviews and conversations within that community, and many newspaper columns, between 1997 and 2003.

Professor Bajpai designates the three grand-strategic postures noted in this chapter as schools of thought, which he calls "modernist," "neo-Nehruvian," and "hyper-nationalist/hyper-realist." Professor Bajpai was formally interviewed in New Delhi on 3 January 2000 and on 27 July 2001. See his "Nuclear Policy, Grand Strategy, and Political Values in India," Seventeenth P. C. Lal Memorial Lecture, 18 February 2000 (available at www.ceri-sciences-po.org/archive/jan01/nuclear.pdf), which is the source of the "cut a deal" quotation. I have also benefited greatly from conversations with him.

48. Mattoo, "India's Nuclear Policy," 18–19, and see his note 27 on p. 19.

49. C. Raja Mohan, "Burying the Indira Doctrine," *Hindu,* 24 May 2001, "India's New Neighbor," *Hindu,* 28 March 2001, and "Beyond India's Monroe Doctrine," *Hindu,* 2 January 2003; and Cohen, *India: Emerging Power,* 137–38.

50. Jasjit Singh, "Strategic Uncertainty," 239–41.

51. Jasjit Singh, conversation, New Delhi, 23 July 2001. See his "Introduction: Toward A New Asia," in *Reshaping Asian Security,* ed. Jasjit Singh (New Delhi: Knowledge World and Institute for Defense Studies and Analyses, 2001), ix–xix. He was longtime director of the IDSA and was, while director, a well-known consultant to the government. According to the Defense Ministry's 2000–2001 Web site, numerous "institutions, including the defence establishments, in India and abroad continued [in 2000] to draw upon the experience and expertise of the Institute to support their training, research and orientation programs." The Web site also indicated that both the external affairs and Defense Ministry "take active interest in supporting the activities of the Institute" (http://mod.nic.in/ainstitutions/welcome.html). A leading American specialist on South Asia has called the IDSA "India's official think tank"; see Cohen, *India: Emerging Power,* 165.

52. K. Subrahmanyam, "Asia's Security Concerns in the 21st Century," in Singh, *Asian Security,* 11–23.

53. Garver, *Protracted Contest,* 387.

54. Ibid., 388; see also Bajpai, "Nuclear Policy, Grand Strategy," where he points out that idealism would build India up to the great-power level via economic self-reliance.

55. Cohen, *India: Emerging Power,* 41–43.

56. From Kanti Bajpai, interview, New Delhi, 3 January 2000, his lecture "Nuclear Policy, Grand Strategy," and interview, 27 July 2001; and from an informal conversation with a leading ultrarealist, New Delhi, 24 July 2001.

57. My summary is based on Bajpai, "India's Nuclear Posture," Web version, 19, 14, and "Nuclear Policy, Grand Strategy"; interviews with Bharat Karnad, 3 January 2003, and with Bajpai, 27 July 2001; and Karnad, "Thermonuclear Deterrent," 128, and *Nuclear Weapons and Indian Security* (Delhi: Macmillan, 2002), 621, and see also xviii.

58. Bharat Karnad, ed., *Future Imperiled* (New Delhi: Penguin-Viking, 1994), 8, 45–47, 50, 53; and see his more recent publication, "India's Place in the World . . . ," in *Democratic Peace: The Foreign Policy Implications,* ed. M. L. Sondhi (New Delhi: Har-Anand, 2001), passim. Mr. Karnad, of the New Delhi think-tank known as the Center for Policy Research (CPR), and Brahma Chellaney, presently at the CPR as well, have both served on the National Security Advisory Board and were active in producing that body's drafted document on a nuclear doctrine for India.

59. Bharat Karnad, interview, New Delhi, 26 January 1999, and *Nuclear Weapons and Indian Security,* xvii, xxxv, 458–59.

60. This section is basically drawn from conversations with Professor G. P. Deshpande of Jawaharlal Nehru University, Kanti Bajpai, and the political leader and maga-

zine columnist Jairam Ramesh, all in New Delhi during July 2001, as well as from Bajpai, "Nuclear Policy, Grand Strategy." An earlier (19 January 2000) conversation with Ramesh was drawn upon as well. More recent sources have been brief discussions with Bharat Karnad and C. Raja Mohan in January 2003 (New Delhi). The references to Indian political parties reflect my efforts to put the information these sources have offered together with my own political observations over the years. The term "left-liberal" used in this section comes from Bajpai, "Nuclear Policy, Grand Strategy." For a discussion of the "soft state" idea also mentioned here, see L. K. Advani, "Far-Reaching Reforms on the Anvil," *Hindu,* 22 November 1999. I am also indebted to Stephen P. Cohen, telephone conversation, Saratoga, N.Y.–Washington, D.C., March 2003.

61. The economic dimension of the India-China relationship was prominent in interviews with Jairam Ramesh and with Mr. Gurpal Singh, senior director, Confederation of Indian Industry, New Delhi, July 2001, and in not-for-attribution comments made by other Indian informants that same month.

62. The points presented here about post–September 11 Indian thinking on relations with China come from telephone discussions with informed Indian sources, including C. Raja Mohan, of *The Hindu,* and a leading IDSA scholar, October 2001.

63. Garver, *Protracted Contest,* 9.

64. Ibid., pp. 3–8, and from the same conversation with the ultrarealist cited in note 56.

65. This phrase was used by Colonel Gurmeet Kanwal of the IDSA and the Indian army in a conversation with the author in New Delhi, 23 July 2001. The phrase originally seems to have come from Douglas Paal, president of the Asia-Pacific Policy Center; see Gurmeet Kanwal, "China's Long March to World Power Status: Strategic Challenge for India," *Strategic Analysis* (IDSA) 2, no. 11 (1999): 1713.

66. Manoj Joshi, "PM Happy with Outcome of Talks with China," *Times of India,* 25 June 2003; Amit Baruah, "Quality of Ties with China Has Changed, Says Vajpayee," *Hindu,* 25 June 2003; Reuters, "Sino-Indian Ties Transformed: Vajpayee," *Times of India,* 25 June 2003; Amit Baruah, "India, China Have Found a Path to Resolve Border Row," *Hindu,* 28 June 2003; Manoj Joshi, "PM Calls for India-China IT Alliance," *Times of India,* 26 June 2003; Manoj Joshi, "Sikkim, Tibet Pacts Boost India-China Ties," *Times of India,* 25 June 2003; Anil Joseph (Press Trust of India), "Atal Suggests Sino-Indian Alliance on IT Sector," *Hindustan Times,* 26 June 2003; Press Trust of India, "Win-Win Situation for India, China: Sinha," *Hindustan Times,* 25 June 2003; Vir Sanghvi, "India Hopeful of Speedy Border Settlement," *Hindustan Times,* 26 June 2003.

67. Dileep Padgaonkar, "Churlish at Best," *Times of India,* 30 June 2003.

68. Contributing ideas to the sentences and paragraphs that follow have been: K. Subrahmanyam, telephone interview, Saratoga–Delhi, 29 June 2003; M.V. Rappai, now with the Institute of Chinese Studies, telephone interview, Saratoga–Delhi, 27 June 2003; C. Raja Mohan, telephone interviews, 28–29 June 2003; and C. Uday Bhaskar, deputy director of the IDSA, telephone interview, Saratoga–Delhi, 30 June 2003. The responsibility for the synthesis contained here is, however, entirely mine. Contributing to the synthesis, too, has been a close reading of the Indian press before, during, and after the Beijing summit. See particularly Brahma Chellaney, "Beware of the Dragon," *Hindustan Times,* 1 June 2003, and his "Vajpayee's Triple Kowtow in Beijing," *Hindustan Times,* 26 June 2003; as well as Jasjit Singh, "Line of Actual Gain," *Indian Express,* 14 June 2003; and "A Hindi-China Road Map" (editorial), *Indian Express,* 26

June 2003. See also C. Raja Mohan, "Vajpayee Cracks the Two Front Problem," *Hindu,* 27 June 2003; Manoj Joshi, "New Leadership in China Key to Ties," *Times of India,* 29 June 2003; P. R. Suryanarayana, "Sino-Indian Dialogue Catches the World's Eye," *Hindu,* 28 June 2003; Jyoti Malhotra, "For India's Tibet Turn, China to Amend Its Sikkim Map," *Indian Express,* 25 June 2003; "Trade Winds" (editorial), *Times of India,* 26 June 2003; Inder Malhotra, "A Quantum Leap?" *Hindu,* 26 June 2003; and Special Correspondent, "Focus on Improving Ties with China, Says Natwar Singh," *Hindu,* 24 June 2003. The sensitivity to Tibet of some idealist thinking is mentioned in Garver, *Protracted Contest,* 388; and for some perspective on Hindu nationalism and the Tibetan issue, see "RSS Accuses China of Terrorism in Tibet," *Pioneer,* 14 January 2002.

69. Important milestones on the way to the present India-China rhetorical normalization of relations include Atal Bihari Vajpayee's official visit to China as foreign minister in 1979 and the visit of Indian defense minister George Fernandes to China in April 2003. The Rajiv Gandhi-Deng Xiaoping diplomatic breakthrough in 1988 should also be recalled.

3

One-Sided Rivalry: China's Perceptions and Policies toward India

Susan L. Shirk

There is a marked asymmetry in the mutual perceptions of India and China. For India, China looms large as an economic and political rival and as security threat, as Steven Hoffmann makes clear in chapter 2. But for China, India merits little attention and, even after India's May 1998 nuclear tests, is not taken seriously as a security threat. As the India scholar Stephen Cohen notes, China does not consider India one of the important states in the world; India is simply not on China's "radar screen."[1] China's smug attitude toward India is not just a pose adopted in official statements for international effect; it is reflected domestically as well. India has many more experts on China than China has experts on India. Indian journalists, intellectuals, businesspeople, and the informed public are avid China-watchers, while their Chinese counterparts follow developments in Taiwan, Japan, and the United States with much greater interest than developments in India. Indian policies toward China are broadly debated and handled at the highest level of the political leadership, in contrast to Chinese policies toward India, which are ignored by the public and managed by the foreign affairs and military bureaucracies. China's indifference to India, and its disdainful, patronizing attitude toward India, infuriate the Indians.

China's evolving policies toward India have reflected its own domestic priorities and its reactions not just to Indian aspirations on the subcontinent, but also to actions taken by the United States and the Soviet Union vis-à-vis India and Pakistan. Anti-imperialism bound the new Chinese and Indian governments together during their first decade of existence in the 1950s. During the 1960s and 1970s, however, the two countries were locked in a hostile standoff structured by the Cold War global contest between the Soviet Union and the United States and by the Sino-Soviet split. India and the USSR stood on one side of the Cold War divide, and China, the United States, and Pakistan on the other. Beginning in 1979, Beijing undertook a major initiative to improve relations with India, an effort that has continued up to the present time, with only a short hiatus after India's 1998 nuclear tests.

After a brief survey of China's policies toward India during earlier periods, this chapter will focus on China's post-1979 drive to establish more friendly relations with India, an effort motivated primarily by China's economic reforms and by the disappearance of the Soviet threat. A case study of China's response to India's May 1998 nuclear tests shows that the tests altered neither China's view that India is not a threat nor its efforts to engage India. The chapter goes on to review China's contemporary assessments of India's capabilities, and it concludes with some thoughts on how China might react to an American attempt to form an anti-China bloc with India.

The Evolution of China's Worldview and Perceptions

The first decade of relations between the People's Republic of China and the newly independent Indian government was peaceful and harmonious. Under Prime Minister Jawaharlal Nehru, India pursued a policy of accommodation toward China, and China responded positively. India recognized China's sovereignty over Tibet, a traditional buffer between the two countries; the skirmishes over the contested border were manageable; and both sides played up the spiritual kinship between the two great civilizations that had just come to assert their national independence after suffering foreign domination for a century or more.[2] United by their anti-imperialist perspective, the two countries cooperated well. Nehru believed that Indian-Chinese cooperation was vital to the success of the global nonaligned movement and that by cultivating a friendship with China—e.g., by advocating its entry to the United Nations and acquiescing to Chinese military presence and political rule in Tibet—he would mitigate its potential to threaten India. He also believed that an India-China détente "would stabilize Asia and keep the superpowers at bay."[3] The preamble of the 1954 India-China agreement on Tibet articulated the "Five Principles of Peaceful Coexistence," which China even today promotes as its international relations credo. Indian critics have noted that Nehru gave more than he got from Beijing,[4] reflecting China's greater ability and willingness to impose its will on Tibet and India's desire not to antagonize China.

Beginning in 1959, however, relations between the two countries soured as China was beleaguered by a combination of internal and external challenges.[5] Mao Zedong's misguided mass campaign, the Great Leap Forward, produced widespread famine and political disaffection and provoked a high-level leadership challenge to Mao in mid-1959. A revolt erupted in Tibet in March 1959 that the Chinese Communist Party (CCP) leaders believed was instigated by the U.S. Central Intelligence Agency (CIA) and supported by India, which allowed the Dalai Lama to flee there. In 1960, Sino-Soviet relations deteriorated sharply and led Soviet President Nikita Khrushchev to terminate Soviet technical assistance to China. The year 1961–62 was the trough of economic decline; People's Liberation Army (PLA) reports document malnutrition and illness within the army. China pressed India to accept its claim of the territory of the Aksai Chin road that it had built from Xinjiang to Tibet beginning in 1956, which China considered of prime strategic importance to facilitate troop movements between these two remote and potentially dissident regions. In October and November 1962, after a series of diplomatic protests including pleas for negotiations that were subsequently published in the *People's Daily,* the PLA forced a military showdown. After pushing back Indian forces, China called for a cease-fire and withdrew its forces twenty kilometers from what it claimed was the Line of Actual Control (LAC).[6]

After the 1962 war, Sino-Indian relations were cold and hostile for almost two decades. In John Garver's view, this hostility reflected an underlying geopolitical rivalry between China and India, both nations seeking to restore their traditional great-power status and with overlapping traditional spheres of influence. Garver sees this rivalry and mutual perceptions of military threat as constant features of Sino-Indian relations.[7] He notes, for example, Chinese analyses that identify the root cause of the 1962 war as

India's imperialist mentality, learned from the British, and its aspiration to dominate Southeast Asia to the Middle East.[8]

Garver characterizes China's special "entente cordiale" relationship with Pakistan, in the 1960s and today, as motivated by Beijing's desire to balance India and prevent it from dominating the subcontinent.[9] Indeed, China's relationship with Pakistan is the closest thing China has to a real alliance and is China's most durable bilateral relationship.[10] And it is no doubt true that especially after China and India clashed militarily in 1959 and 1962, China viewed its relations with Pakistan as a way to check India's dominance of South Asia.[11] The close military ties between them, however, were developed after the 1962 war in the context of the Cold War, as much to counter moves by the United States and the Soviet Union as to check India itself.

Chinese policies toward India, and toward Pakistan, during the 1960s and 1970s were strongly influenced not only by regional threat perceptions, but also by the Cold War context of global competition between the United States and the Soviet Union.[12] Beijing's specific actions during the Cold War often were reactive to American and Soviet maneuverings. For example, China did not respond positively to Pakistan's efforts to form an entente until the Americans started to supply arms to India just weeks after the 1962 war.[13] Searching for allies against communist China, the United States provided military aid and sold military equipment to India for several years in the 1960s.[14] China supported Pakistan in its 1965 war with India because it saw India as a "neocolonialist regime being built up by U.S. imperialism and the Soviet revisionists as a way of encircling China."[15] During the 1965 war, the United States suspended military aid and sales to both India and Pakistan. Pakistan then turned to China to provide weaponry during this period when the Americans had embargoed it and the Soviets were reluctant to alienate India by arming Pakistan.

The blending of China's anti-Soviet and anti-Indian motivations was also apparent in 1971 when Beijing strengthened its support of Islamabad. Pakistan had used repressive methods to crack down on the Awami League's resistance to Pakistan's authority in East Pakistan. Zhou Enlai, like U.S. National Security Adviser Henry Kissinger, was genuinely worried that India, having cut off Pakistan's east wing, would try to destroy West Pakistan. Yet Chinese support of Pakistan was minimal until the signing of an Indian-Soviet Mutual Assistance Treaty on 9 August 1971.[16] (The formation of a quasi alliance between the USSR and India was itself a response to the dramatic improvement in Sino-American relations when

Kissinger traveled to Beijing by way of Pakistan to arrange the visit of President Richard Nixon to China.[17]) According to Ashley Tellis, the Chinese nuclear assistance to Pakistan did not begin until 1981, after the Soviet invasion of Afghanistan. The Chinese had signed a nuclear agreement with Pakistani Prime Minister Zulfikar Ali Bhutto in 1976, after the 1974 Indian test, but did not act upon it until 1981.

From the Indian perspective, China's support of Pakistan during the 1965 and 1971 India-Pakistan wars reflected China's effort to contain India and prevent it from dominating the subcontinent. Although sorting out anti-Indian and anti-Soviet elements in China's motivation is difficult, Chinese leaders at that time generally described India more as a client of the Soviet Union in a global contest against the United States and China than as an autonomous rival. For example, in the December 1971 conversation between Huang Hua, the permanent representative to the United Nations for the People's Republic of China (PRC), and Nixon's national security adviser, Henry Kissinger, Kissinger, in an effort to make common cause with Beijing, said that President Nixon would not object if China intervened on the subcontinent with "measures to protect its security." He also told Huang that a U.S. carrier battle group was sailing to the Bay of Bengal as a signal of opposition to Soviet-Indian actions. Huang's response emphasized the threat of an India allied with the Soviet Union: "If India, with the aid of the Soviet Union, would be able to have its own way in the subcontinent then there would be no more security to speak of for a lot of other countries, and no peace to speak of. . . . The Soviet Union and India now are progressing along an extremely dangerous track in the subcontinent. And as we have already pointed out this is a step to encircle China."[18]

In a 1974 poem, Mao Zedong described India disdainfully as a "cow" on whose back rides the Russian "bear." A Chinese commentary, quoted by John Garver, explains that a cow "is only food or for people to raise and for pulling carts; it has no particular talents. The cow would starve to death if its master did not give it grass to eat. . . . Even though this cow may have great ambitions, they are futile."[19]

Post-1979 Rapprochement

For the last twenty-odd years China has sought to improve relations with India. China explains its shift toward India as driven mainly by the end of the Cold War. Foreign Minister Qian Qichen, in his discussions of regional foreign policy issues held with U.S. Secretary of State Madeleine Albright during 1997–98, raised the issue of South Asia and noted that during the Cold War, because the Soviet Union made India its ally, both China and the United States were left with Pakistan. His point was that now that the Cold War was over, both China and the United States had new opportunities to achieve balanced relationships with India and Pakistan.

China's efforts to warm its relationship with India, however, began in 1979, ten years before the end of the Cold War. As the timing indicates, these diplomatic initiatives were motivated primarily by China's domestic reform drive, not by changes in the international situation, although they were reinforced by the collapse of the Soviet Union in 1989.[20]

In 1976, Mao Zedong died, and in 1979, Deng Xiaoping initiated an ambitious new policy of economic reform and opening. Deng recognized that to concentrate on economic modernization, China needed a peaceful, stable environment, which in turn would require a reorientation of China's foreign policies. For the first time in China's modern history, the country developed a coherent, integrated Asia regional policy, consisting of pragmatic relations with the two superpowers and improved ties with all the countries on its periphery.[21] This regional policy was omnidirectional, and over the 1980s and 1990s China restored or established diplomatic relations with Indonesia (1990), Singapore (1990), Brunei (1991), and South Korea (1992); elevated relations with India and the Philippines; normalized relations with Russia (1989), Mongolia (1989), and Vietnam (1991); began to build bilateral and multilateral ties with Kazakhstan, Tajikistan, Kyrgyzstan, Uzbekistan, and Turkmenistan (1992); and began to participate actively in regional multilateral organizations like the Association of Southeast Asian Nations (ASEAN) Post-Ministerial Talks, the ASEAN Regional Forum (ARF), and the Asia-Pacific Economic Cooperation (APEC) forum.

In 1979 and 1981, the Chinese and Indian foreign ministers exchanged visits, and between 1981 and 1987 China and India held eight rounds of negotiations on their boundary dispute but failed to produce a solution. Border frictions persisted, and became heated during 1986–87, but were kept in check by the two sides. India dropped its insistence that a border agreement had to precede the restoration of bilateral relations.

During Foreign Minister Atal Behari Vajpayee's February 1979 visit, he was embarrassed by China's poorly timed invasion of Vietnam, but he brought home Deng Xiaoping's commitment to cease support for insurgencies in India's northeast. That support, begun after the 1962 war, was perhaps intended to pressure India to restrain insurgents in Tibet, as Garver suggests,[22] or else was part of the broader revolutionary foreign policy pursued by Mao in many Asian and African countries.

The relationship got a major boost from the 1988 visit of Rajiv Gandhi, the Indian prime minister, to Beijing. Deng Xiaoping told Gandhi, "Let both sides forget the unpleasant period in our past relations, and let us treat everything with an eye on the future."[23] As a result of the visit, New Delhi agreed to restrain anti-China activities by Tibetans in India,[24] and the two sides de-linked the development of bilateral relations from the border dispute.[25] Visits followed by India's president in 1992 and by its prime minister in 1993. The two countries signed an Agreement on the Maintenance of Peace and Tranquility along the Line of Actual Control in 1993. The agreement included provisions that the two sides would resolve border issues peacefully through consultations, observe the LAC pending a final resolution, reduce military forces along the LAC, and work out confidence-building measures along the LAC.[26]

Sino-Indian rapprochement was further solidified by President Jiang Zemin's visit to New Delhi in late 1996. During the visit, the two sides signed another important agreement, the Agreement on Confidence-Building Measures in the Military Field along the LAC. The two militaries committed to limit the number of field-army troops, border-defense forces, paramilitary forces, and major categories of armaments along the LAC; to avoid holding large-scale military exercises near the LAC and to notify the other side of exercises involving one brigade (five thousand troops) or more; not to discharge firearms, cause biodegradation, use hazardous chemicals, set off explosives, or hunt with firearms within 2 kilometers of the LAC; to hold regular meetings of border representatives; and to set up hot-line telecommunication links between local military headquarters along the LAC.[27]

In its most significant gesture to promote rapprochement, Beijing unilaterally adjusted its position on Kashmir. Beginning in 1980, it gradually moved away from the Pakistan-preferred position—i.e., "the hope that the Kashmir dispute would be resolved in accord with the wishes of the people of Kashmir as pledged to them by the people of India and Pakistan"—to take the more neutral position that the Kashmir issue was a bilateral dispute between India and Pakistan that should be solved peacefully by the two sides.[28] China also refrained from criticizing India's intervention in Sri Lanka or India's nuclear and missile programs.

The Chinese diplomatic campaign toward India continued right to the spring of 1998 with the 27–30 April visit by PLA Senior General Fu Quanyou, the first by a PLA chief of the general staff.[29] Ten days before General Fu's embarkation, George Fernandes, the Indian defense minister, had publicly alleged that China was continuing to carry out border incursions. The Chinese foreign ministry spokesman responded to the charges, calling them "unfounded and extremely irresponsible," but Beijing decided to go ahead with the visit nonetheless.[30] General Fu had meetings with newly appointed Prime Minister Atal Behari Vajpayee and Defense Minister Fernandes, as well as with his military counterparts. He visited military bases and observed exercises. Both sides took the occasion to highlight publicly the positive trends in Sino-Indian relations, the Chinese playing up the two-thousand-year history of the relationship between their ancient nations and their more recent history of cooperation in the cause of anti-imperialism, including their shared authorship of the "world famous five principles of peaceful coexistence."[31] But no sooner had General Fu's airplane lifted off for other destinations than Defense Minister Fernandes was again lambasting China, accusing it of being the number-one threat to Indian security, greater even than Pakistan.[32] The May 11 and 13 Indian nuclear tests followed, occurring even before General Fu returned to Beijing on 18 May.[33] The timing undoubtedly humiliated General Fu and intensified the outrage of the Chinese government, the military in particular.[34] According to one Chinese informant, the Indian tests were timed to pay back the Chinese for the embarrassment they had caused then-Foreign Minister Vajpayee when they had attacked Vietnam during his 1979 visit to China, forcing him to cut his trip short.[35]

From Beijing's perspective, it had worked for almost two decades to offer its hand in friendship to New Delhi, only to have it slapped by the Indians.[36] Given this context, Beijing might have been expected to react strongly, even violently, to the Indian nuclear tests, or at least to make a strategic reassessment and abandon its efforts to engage India. In fact, the tests produced only a brief hiatus, and no fundamental adjustment, in China's engagement policies toward India.

China's Response to the Indian Nuclear Tests

China's initial reaction to the Indian nuclear tests was very mild. On 12 May, the day after the first round of tests, the Ministry of Foreign Affairs (MFA) spokesman expressed the PRC government's "grave concern" because the tests ran against the international trend of nuclear disarmament and were detrimental to the peace and stability of South Asia.[37] Such restraint might have continued—after all, Chinese reaction to Pokhran I, the earliest Indian test in 1974, had been mild to neutral—had the Indian government not deflected responsibility for the recent tests onto the China threat.[38] On 13 May, the *New York Times* published a letter from Prime Minister Vajpayee to President Bill Clinton, leaked in the United States, which blamed China for India's decision to test:[39]

> I have been deeply concerned at the deteriorating security environment, especially the nuclear environment, faced by India for some years past. We have an overt nuclear weapon state on our borders, a state which committed armed aggression against India in 1962. Although our relations with that country have improved in the last decade or so, an atmosphere of distrust persists mainly due to the unresolved border problem. To add to the distrust that country has materially helped another neighbor of ours to become a covert nuclear weapons state. At the hands of this bitter neighbor we have suffered three aggressions in the last 50 years.[40]

The Chinese always place as much weight on words as on actions, and in this case, they seemed even more offended by the Indians' words than by the tests themselves. The MFA issued a formal statement on 14 May, ratcheting up its reaction to "strong condemnation." Much of the statement was devoted to defending China's record against the "malicious accusation that China posed a nuclear threat to India." It stated, "This gratuitous accusation by India against China is solely for the purpose of finding an excuse for the development of its nuclear weapons."[41]

In the following weeks, Chinese officials emphatically reiterated their outrage against what they regarded as the Indians' groundless accusations against China. Vice Premier Qian Qichen (he had recently handed his Foreign Ministry portfolio to Tang Jiaxuan) said that "the most unacceptable thing was that India dare say that it is conducting nuclear testing in response to China's threat to India."[42] The English-language *China Daily* took an ominous tone on 20 May 1998:

> India's improper move of attributing its nuclear tests at Pokhran to potential threat from China has made the international community realize that the new Indian Government is not only irresponsible, but also immoral. This is the first time in history that a nuclear country has denied its own responsibility for its nuclear tests and shifted the blame to others. To

justify its series of nuclear tests, India uses the political tactic of making India-China ties tense. China had been taking a reserved attitude towards provocative statements from India in order to push forward Sino-Indian ties. However, India took China's forbearance as weakness.[43]

Instead of acting alone to punish India, however, China joined with the United States and the other major powers in a rapid, concerted response to defend the international nuclear arms control and nonproliferation regime against the Indian violation. This approach was designed to enhance China's own international reputation and improve its relations with the United States. In a series of telephone calls during the days following the Indian tests, Secretary Albright and Foreign Minister Tang decided to call a meeting of the permanent members of the United Nations Security Council in Geneva, not only to condemn the Indian tests but also to come up with a strategy for preventing a nuclear arms race in South Asia.[44] China, serving as president of the Security Council, took the lead, but as a positive gesture toward the United States, asked Secretary Albright to chair the 4 June 1998 Geneva meeting. Senior officials in Beijing and Washington also coordinated their efforts to persuade Pakistan not to make its own nuclear test in a tit-for-tat manner; despite those efforts, the Pakistanis held tests on 28 and 30 May.

The South Asian nuclear tests occurred during the preparations for President Clinton's historic visit to the PRC in June 1998. China and the United States found a silver lining in the South Asian tests, using them as an opportunity to demonstrate Sino-American strategic cooperation. The UN Permanent Five joint communiqué of 4 June, which laid out five benchmarks that India and Pakistan must meet to prevent a nuclear arms race and preserve the international nonproliferation regime, and which was endorsed by UN Security Council Resolution 1172, was a tangible result of such cooperation. On the eve of the Clinton visit, President Jiang gave an interview to *Newsweek* journalist Lally Weymouth in which he described how, because of his good memories of the friendly welcome he had received during his 1996 trip to India, he was surprised at the Indian nuclear tests and even more surprised that the Indians cited China as the reason to test. Yet Jiang emphasized his balanced perspective toward the subcontinent, stating that "no matter whether India or Pakistan, conducting nuclear tests is against world trends," and he urged both countries to "keep calm, show restraint, and reopen dialogue," and to sign unconditionally the nuclear Nonproliferation Treaty and the Comprehensive Test Ban Treaty.[45] In this interview, he also promised not to sell missile technology to Pakistan: "we don't plan to sell missiles."[46]

During the Clinton visit, the two presidents issued a joint statement on South Asia, condemning the tests, declaring support for the Permanent Five communiqué benchmarks and the international nonproliferation regime, and pledging that neither China nor the United States would provide nuclear weapons or delivery systems capable of delivering nuclear weapons to India or Pakistan. Washington viewed the statement as one of the most significant "deliverables" of the summit because in it Jiang hardened his pledge, made a few days earlier to the *Newsweek* journalist, that China would not sell missile technology to Pakistan. Beijing appreciated the opportunity to showcase its common stance with the United States even though it recognized that the statement would infuriate the Indians. In fact, the subtext of all China's cooperation with other Permanent Five countries in reacting to the Indian tests was "We're a global power, and you're not."[47]

Back to Engagement

The impact of the May 1998 nuclear tests on Beijing's threat perceptions and policies toward New Delhi was remarkably limited. Only a few months later, Beijing resumed its efforts to engage India diplomatically, and there was no sign that China had adjusted its view that India does not present a security threat. The meeting of the Joint Working Group on the Boundary Question (JWG), scheduled for October 1998, was postponed until April 1999, but a June 1998 bilateral meeting of military experts went ahead,[48] and consultations in preparation for the JWG were held in February 1999. Foreign Minister Tang met the Indian prime minister's special representative, Jaswant Singh, at the ASEAN Regional Forum meeting in Manila in July 1998. The Indian government, especially after Mr. Singh became foreign minister in December 1998, sent signals that it wanted to mend fences; the Chinese "welcomed" these signals and said that China "always attached importance to the growth of its good neighborly, friendly and cooperative ties with India" and that "normalization of Sino-Indian relations complies with the fundamental interests of the people of both countries."[49] After the tests, one talking point of American officials urged China to resume dialogue with India; by the end of 1998, the point had been dropped as no longer necessary. In June 1999, Foreign Minister Singh met

Foreign Minister Tang in China, and the two sides agreed that neither side regarded the other as a threat, the prerequisite for the resumption of relations insisted upon by the Chinese side. On 18 February 2000, India and China concluded their bilateral agreement for China's accession to the World Trade Organization; in March 2000, the two countries held their first security dialogue in Beijing; in May 2000, Indian President K. R. Narayanan visited China to mark fifty years of diplomatic relations; and in January 2001, National People's Congress Standing Committee Chairman Li Peng visited India and revived the notion of a "constructive cooperative partnership between the two countries."[50]

The engagement imperative dictated China's continued accommodation on Kashmir, an issue critical to India. Shortly after the tests, China had floated the idea of a multilateral meeting to help resolve the Kashmir dispute. A month later, however, it reverted to the more equidistant stance of recommending bilateral negotiations, and during Foreign Minister Tang's July 2000 visit to South Asia he continued to urge the bilateral approach to the issue.[51]

The most vocal spokesperson for China's conciliatory approach to India was its ambassador to New Delhi, Zhou Gang. In a 25 July 1998 speech at the India International Center, he emphasized that China had never hoped to see an abnormal state of Sino-Indian relations; that China would never be a threat to India; and that China had refuted the charges against China by some people in India only to protect the friendship between China and India.[52]

Meanwhile, however, some official statements took a tougher line—for example, a series of official commentaries after the tests. The 15 May 1998 *People's Daily* commentator's article, "Plot to Dominate South Asia," said, "The Indian Government has disregarded the fundamental interests of the vast numbers of its people and desperately developed nuclear weapons in defiance of world opinion. The reason for this is nothing less than a desire to threaten neighboring countries and dominate South Asia."[53] The 19 May 1998 *People's Daily* commentator's article, "History Shall Not Be Denied, Facts Speak Louder than Words," took an even more strident, polemical tone in condemning India's words and actions:

> The whole world has strongly condemned India and sternly protested against it for suddenly carrying out five nuclear tests within 48 hours. . . . Prime Minister Vajpayee's recent brazen announcement that India would not sign the Comprehensive Test Ban Treaty has even evoked the

> wrath of the whole world. Because of the Indian authorities' perverse deeds, India is now in a state of unprecedented isolation. . . . [They] say that India was developing its nuclear weapons because of China's threat. However, nobody believes such preposterous logic and the so-called "China threat" lies.[54]

Interview data help illuminate the bureaucratic sources of these mixed messages. The divergence reflects the different perspectives of the nonproliferation specialists and the regional specialists within the Chinese Ministry of Foreign Affairs, a split that can be found in every foreign ministry, including the U.S. Department of State. The nonproliferation specialists pushed a harder line on the tests than the regional specialists, who were eager to resume their engagement efforts with India.

After the May tests, the Arms Control and Nonproliferation Department of the MFA moved quickly to take the lead in crafting China's response. This department, established in 1997, has close ties to the PLA and until 2000 was headed by Sha Zukang, an intelligent, highly articulate diplomat and arms control negotiator whose wife was serving in the Chinese embassy in New Delhi. Sha, China's negotiator of the Comprehensive Test Ban Treaty (CTBT), appeared to be the architect of the tough response line, although some Indian and Chinese officials believe that he was reflecting the PLA perspective.

Sha also articulated China's criticism of what it viewed as a wobbly U.S. attitude toward India's nuclear program, a refrain that was included in the talking points of meetings with senior U.S. officials during 1999–2000. The Clinton administration had undertaken an intensive effort to persuade India and Pakistan to sign the CTBT and commit to the other Permanent Five communiqué benchmarks: Deputy Secretary of State Strobe Talbott met thirteen times with Indian Special Representative and then Foreign Minister Jaswant Singh and approximately six times with Shamshad Ahmad, the foreign secretary of Pakistan; he also debriefed the PRC ambassador in Washington following most of these encounters. The Americans also imposed economic sanctions on India and Pakistan, which the Chinese never even considered. At the same time, however, the administration did not abandon its diplomatic efforts to strengthen ties with India. President Clinton's long-planned visit, although postponed, occurred in March 2000. And whereas China took the purist line that India and Pakistan should both immediately adhere to the Nonproliferation Treaty as nonnuclear states, the U.S. position was that although that was a worthy long-term goal—and the

United States would never concede that India and Pakistan had established themselves as nuclear weapon states under the NPT—the United States was "not simply going to give India and Pakistan the cold shoulder until they take that step." Instead the United States was concentrating on "practical steps," such as CTBT signing and ratification; a fissile material moratorium; constraints on the development, flight testing, and storage of missiles; export controls on sensitive materials and technologies that could be used to build weapons of mass destruction; and Indo-Pakistani dialogue.[55]

Sha's criticisms of American policies toward South Asia appeared to be designed more to score points against the United States than to constrain India's nuclear program. In a widely reported speech, "Some Thoughts on Non-Proliferation," at the January 1999 Carnegie Endowment International Non-Proliferation Conference, Sha took up the issue of the Indian and Pakistani tests as the number-one threat to the nuclear nonproliferation regime. The speech, without mentioning the United States by name, implied that it was acquiescing to "India's so-called minimum nuclear deterrence capability" in order to obtain "unilateral short-term political, economic or strategic benefits at the expense of the other countries and the international solidarity" and was thereby undermining the international nonproliferation regime.[56]

The divergent arms-control and regional perspectives within the MFA bureaucracy shaped China's response to the Indian nuclear tests because the issue was treated as "normal" foreign policy, not as a crisis. According to interview accounts, following the second tests and the publication of the Vajpayee accusations against China, the Foreign Policy Leading Small Group (FPLSG) met to determine China's response. Whereas policies toward the United States, Taiwan, or Japan sometimes merit consideration by the Politburo Standing Committee (PBSC), in this case, no PBSC meeting was called. Jiang Zemin was the chairman of the FPLSG, which also included a military representative (usually General Xiong Guangkai), Vice Premier Qian Qichen, Foreign Minister Tang Jiaxuan, CCP Foreign Affairs Office head Liu Huaqiu, the minister of state security, and the head of Xinhua News Agency. Apparently emerging from this meeting were the decisions to issue an MFA statement defending China's record against India's "gratuitous accusation" and to join with the United States and other powers to condemn India and lock it out of legitimate nuclear power status. In subsequent months, however, either the FPLSG did not take up policies toward India, or the group blessed the bifurcated approach of taking a tough official position on India's nuclear status (and needling the United States for being too soft) while at the same time resuming diplomatic engagement of India.

Most Chinese diplomats were just as eager as their American counterparts to rekindle relations with India. Neither the MFA nor the State Department was willing to give India the "cold shoulder" to pressure it to roll back its nuclear program. The tough arms-control line remained only a subtheme in Chinese policies toward India. According to interview accounts, the Asia Department retook control over India policies from the Arms Control and Nonproliferation Department by the end of 1998. From the perspective of the regional specialists, the 1998 tests said nothing new about India's capabilities—Beijing had recognized India as a nuclear-capable country ever since the 1974 tests—and India's slanderous accusations against the China threat were simply an argument for more active efforts at diplomatic reassurance. Therefore, they saw no reason to let the tests derail their engagement policies toward India.

That China was just as eager as the United States, or even more so, to improve relations with India can be seen by comparing the two countries' state visits with India during the spring of 2000. During President Clinton's March visit to India, the Indian nuclear program was the main agenda item of the high-level discussions, and Clinton's criticism of the nuclear program was met by a vehement defense from Indian officials, including President Narayanan.[57] But when President Narayanan visited China in May, the two major themes of discussion were the desirability of resolving the border dispute and commercial ties.[58] According to interview accounts, President Jiang's talking points for the meeting with Narayanan included the nuclear issue, but he did not raise it; the nuclear question was addressed only in the vice foreign ministers' meeting.

China's Military Posture toward India

India's nuclear tests and its hostile rhetoric toward China did not provoke any serious rethinking of Chinese military posture toward its neighbor; China continued to accord the Indian threat low priority. Security scholar Ming Zhang asserted that a new military posture toward India was under active consideration at military institutes when he conducted interviews in Beijing in the fall of 1998, and he suggested that China was likely to move nuclear weapons to Tibet or enhance its launch sites in Gansu, Qinghai, and Yunnan and to develop tactical nuclear weapons and a missile defense system to defend against the increased Indian threat. He also stated that there was a consensus within the military that the Indian threat is real and that China should build up its nuclear forces to respond.[59]

My own interviewing indicates that China has done none of these things and that Chinese military posture continues to be focused overwhelmingly on Taiwan and the United States, not India. Other experts in Chinese security policy draw the same conclusion based on their own interviews with military analysts and officials in Beijing.[60] True, some military analysts are paying more attention to India as a potential security threat than they were before May 1998,[61] but their ideas do not appear to have had much impact on Chinese military planning or policy. A comparison of the defense white papers issued by China's State Council Information Office for 1998 and 2000 confirms this preliminary view: the 1998 document devoted a paragraph to condemning the tests, whereas the 2000 paper gives only passing mention to the fact that Pakistan and India have not signed the CTBT.[62]

Chinese military planners see little need to change their posture because they had already factored in India's capability to produce nuclear weapons. As Leo Rose put it, China has "considered India as a 'quiet' nuclear power for over two decades . . . since India's first 'peaceful nuclear explosion' in 1974."[63] The 1998 tests did not alter Beijing's "indifference to nuclear developments in India," which, according to one Chinese expert, is based on three factors: conventional weapons better serve the cause of security given the limited nature of disagreements between China and India; China sees the risk of war with India to be small; and China enjoys an advantage in nuclear capability over India, both in warheads and in delivery systems.[64] An indication that China has not made planning for a nuclear war with India a high priority is that in 1995 it cancelled the development of the DF-25, an intermediate-range missile with 1,700-kilometer range that could cover most of the India strategic forces. The focus of its nuclear force development, according to Hu Weixing, is "to retain a credible second-strike strategic capability against major nuclear powers, not to nuclearize any regional conflicts on its periphery."[65]

Although there have been some assertions on the part of the Tibetan exile and Indian intelligence communities that China has deployed nuclear weapons in Tibet, other foreign analysts are skeptical. They point out that it would be too costly and risky to maintain such capabilities, and that China has sufficient coverage from other parts of southwestern China.[66] In any case, there is no requirement to redeploy strategic systems or design new ones configured to a postulated Indian threat when retargeting by changing computer codes would be sufficient.

This context suggests that even additional Indian tests would be unlikely to have a significant impact on Chinese strategic plans or deployments. Should India, however, proceed to weaponize and actually deploy nuclear weapons, Chinese defense planners would certainly react. But until then, they see no need to elevate the priority of an Indian threat. As a Chinese diplomat observed, China's military posture reflects the fact that the country has always faced more strategic pressure from the east (i.e., the United States, Japan, Taiwan), than from the west.[67]

Beijing's lack of concern about the Indian nuclear program helps explain why it rejected the United States proposal for a moratorium on fissile material production among the five recognized nuclear powers. India had indicated that it would cut off production if the other nuclear powers did. The Clinton administration promoted the idea because it would cap India's nuclear program and provide an impetus for the negotiation of a global fissile material cut off treaty. A moratorium would simply recognize the reality that all of the five nuclear powers, including China, had ceased production of fissile material. When asked why China would not sign on to such a moratorium, a Chinese official said, "Of course it was clearly in China's interests to limit India's program, but people are just not yet very worried about India."

China Adjusts Its Relationship with Pakistan

China's efforts to improve relations with India over the past two decades have been accompanied by some adjustment in its relations with Pakistan, but not enough to satisfy the Indians. As noted earlier, China's relationship with Pakistan is the closest thing China has to a real alliance. Military ties between the two countries are close, and China has transferred nuclear and missile technology to Pakistan.

During the 1990s, China began to disinvest from its military relationship with Pakistan. As John Garver notes, "China distanced itself from Pakistan during the process of Sino-Indian rapprochement" by no longer threatening to intervene militarily on Pakistan's side during periods of conflict with India over Kashmir.[68] In a 1997 agreement with the United States, China also pledged to cut off all assistance to nonsafeguarded nuclear facilities in Pakistan. In the context of the 1998 Clinton visit, it committed not to transfer missile technology to Pakistan, a pledge that it made more explicit in a November 2000 agreement with the United States. Despite these commitments, however, China's actual assistance to Pakistan's missile program reportedly continues. Various explanations have been offered for these continuing transfers: Beijing may be unable to discipline missile export companies; it may be trying to accumulate leverage against U.S. arms sales to Taiwan; or it may simply find it difficult to cut off completely a longtime ally that feels threatened. The Indians believe that the transfers are motivated by Beijing's determination to balance against India.

Chinese willingness to reduce somewhat its military assistance to Pakistan stems not only from its desire to improve relations with India and the United States; China also has genuine worries about Pakistan's internal weakness and fears that it could become a "failed state." Its greatest concern is Pakistan's inability to control Islamic extremist terrorist organizations that threaten China's western provinces, a concern that was intensified by the September 11, 2001, terrorist attacks on the United States. Al Qaeda terrorist organizations have recruited Uighurs from Xinjiang for training in camps in Afghanistan. Uighur separatist organizations already have claimed responsibility for several bombings in Xinjiang, and even in Beijing. Chinese officials discuss with Indian diplomats their doubts about Pakistan's ability to control terrorism, a fact that reflects a certain political distancing from their ally. Yet, as one Indian diplomat observed, their terrorism problem also motivates the Chinese to sustain an ongoing relationship with Pakistan: China does not want to foreclose any way of managing its terrorism problem, including working with Pakistan.

China also has established a multilateral regional process for Central Asia consisting of China, Russia, Kazakhstan, Tajikistan, Kyrgyzstan, and now Uzbekistan, formerly known as the Shanghai Five and now called the Shanghai Cooperation Organization (SCO). Originating as a mechanism for resolving border disputes, the SCO has become a mechanism for managing the threat of Islamist extremist terrorism. Chinese associated with the SCO talk about someday having both India and Pakistan become members of the organization, another example of China's increasingly equidistant approach to the two South Asian countries, but one that may be impractical given the continuing antagonism between the two.[69]

As noted earlier, China's distancing from Pakistan is also reflected in its international positions on Kashmir, which now are closer to India's than to Pakistan's. China also has rejected Pakistani efforts to have the Kashmir issue discussed at the United Nations.[70] A senior Indian official observed that during the Kargil conflict in 1999, China's public statements were almost as even-handed as the Group of Eight's. Implicitly criticizing Pakistan's actions, China urged dialogue between India and Pakistan for the peaceful settlement of the Kashmir issue based on the line of control. Yet the Indian official observed that Chinese domestic media, in particular the People's Liberation Army publications, are still hawkishly pro-Pakistan.

When Premier Zhu Rongji visited India in January 2002, he was the epitome of even-handedness: He condemned the terrorist shooting incident that had taken place at India's Parliament building in December 2001, which has been attributed to Pakistani Muslim extremists. He said, "Pakistani President Musharraf's 12 January speech indicated Pakistan's determination in rebuffing terrorism and India has responded to the speech. We applaud the two countries' positive attitudes . . . [and] hope the two countries will settle their differences peacefully through talks."[71]

Although China has been willing to reduce its assistance to Pakistan, Chinese officials make clear that they have no intention of cutting off Pakistan and that it remains a valued ally. (The PLA may be particularly insistent on this point.) Beijing asks Indian officials to decouple Sino-Indian and Sino-Pakistani relations and, as a gesture of reassurance, briefs them about the substance of its relations with Pakistan.

China's Assessment of India's Capabilities

Chinese efforts to cultivate better relations with India since 1979 are part of its omnidirectional regional diplomacy and do not reflect any increased respect for India's capabilities. China continues to give very low priority to India in its foreign policy. Indians continue to complain that they pay much more attention to China than the Chinese do to them. And the Indians strongly resent China's condescending attitude toward their country.

It is instructive to compare China's attitude toward India with its attitude toward the other major power in Asia, Japan. There are some similarities: China would like to keep both India and Japan in a secondary status in Asia. It does not actively support United Nations Security Council membership for either of them. But whereas it respects Japan's capabilities, even during recessions, and sees Japan as a serious competitor in Asia, it simply does not take India seriously. China's pragmatic response to the Indian nuclear tests that New Delhi blamed on the China threat was in marked contrast to its reactions to Japanese slights. Beijing takes advantage of every opening, particularly those related to questions of history, to keep Japan on the defensive. Because it views India as a much less powerful competitor, it can afford to turn the other cheek to India.[72]

Underlying China's relaxed attitude toward India is its confidence, verging on arrogance, about Chinese capabilities and its low opinion of Indian capabilities. The Chinese take pride in their economic reforms and the dramatic growth they have produced, and look down on the Indians for their slower growth and continuing economic problems. Chinese experts and officials do not attribute the economic growth gap between China and India to the advantages of authoritarianism. They have a more nuanced explanation: According to one Chinese official, the root cause of India's poorer economic performance is its "immature democracy" with too many parties representing particular regions or languages, competing on the basis not of government policies, but of communal interests. He also explained that the Indian central government had spent too lavishly on the military and that its strength was diverted by internal conflicts and secessionist threats.

The one exception to the disdain the Chinese hold for India is the dynamic Indian software industry. The Chinese computer industry has concentrated on hardware and is now seeking to build software capabilities as well. Chinese respect for Indian capabilities in software has led one Chinese company (Huawei) to open a facility in Bangalore with three hundred Chinese and three hundred Indian software engineers (National People's Congress head Li Peng presided at the opening during his visit to India). Even while expressing admiration for the Indian software industry, some Chinese officials hasten to add that it is almost entirely export-oriented because India's domestic economy is still so backward.

India's aspirations to play a more active role in East Asia are not encouraged by China; the latter prefers that India remain in South Asia, although it pays lip service to the notion that India should be a major player in global affairs. The Chinese, however, believe that India's own inadequacies will limit its influence in East Asia.[73] Despite recent movements by the Indian navy in the South China Sea, the Chinese do not believe that the Indian navy has what it takes to be a serious factor in East Asia. They also point out that Vietnam is the only country in Southeast Asia to have much of a relationship with India.

Conclusion: The Evolution of China's Perceptions of India

Despite the recent international interest in the strategic rivalry between Asia's two giants, China and India, China does not regard India as a serious rival. It seeks a friendly relationship with India because it wants to avoid conflict with its neighbors, not because it believes India could be a dangerous enemy.

Should we expect Beijing to continue to take this amicable but condescending attitude toward New Delhi in the future? What would cause the Chinese to treat India as a real challenge to its interests? Were India finally to undertake a genuine liberalization of its economic system, including its policy toward foreign investment, or China to encounter serious economic problems, China would start to see India as a worthy economic competitor and possibly, but not necessarily, a strategic rival. If India deployed nuclear weapons against Chinese targets, China might adjust its strategic posture to provide more deterrence against India, but would not necessarily abandon its efforts to engage India. If, however, a future Indian government provided support to a younger generation of Tibetan freedom fighters willing to use violence to achieve independence, Beijing would react strongly and quite possibly retaliate against India.

Yet another scenario would involve India's relationship with powers outside of Asia. The United States, by playing India off against China, could dramatically transform China's attitude toward India. What soured Beijing–New Delhi relations during the 1960s and 1970s was India's alliance with the Soviet Union. One of the sources of Chinese antagonism toward Japan is its alliance with the United States. If the United States were to adopt a policy of containment against China and embrace India as its "natural ally," the result would be a hostile relationship between China and India as well as between China and the United States. Although it makes sense for the United States to pay more attention to India after years of neglect, a crude real-political approach that gives favors to India to pressure China would backfire against American interests, as well as Indian ones. Early Bush administration movements in this direction were noticed in Beijing, but did not ring alarm bells. Most Chinese experts were skeptical that the Indians would allow themselves to be drawn into an alliance with the United States against China.[74] The September 11 terrorist attacks deflected American attentions from India and required Washington to strengthen its relations with Islamabad. If the United States and India do not form a close collaboration aimed against China, then the so-called Sino-Indian rivalry is likely to continue to be one-sided.

Notes

1. Stephen P. Cohen, *India: Emerging Power* (Washington, D.C.: Brookings Institution Press, 2001), 1, 26.

2. Steven A. Hoffmann, *India and the China Crisis* (Berkeley: University of California Press, 1990), 57.

3. Cohen, *India: Emerging Power,* 56.

4. John W. Garver, *Protracted Contest: Sino-Indian Rivalry in the Twentieth Century* (Seattle: University of Washington Press, 2001), 52.

5. This paragraph is based on Allen S. Whiting, *The Chinese Calculus of Deterrence: India and Indochina* (Ann Arbor: University of Michigan Press, 1975).

6. India defined the LAC differently.

7. In Garver's own words, his "entire book is an elucidation of the Indian worldview embodied in Vajpayee's letter to Clinton" (p. 10).

8. Garver, *Protracted Contest,* 19.

9. Ibid., 187–215.

10. Ibid., 187.

11. Harry Harding, "China's Cooperative Behavior," in *Chinese Foreign Policy: Theory and Practice,* ed. Thomas W. Robinson and David Shambaugh (Oxford: Clarendon Press, 1994), 386.

12. According to Harold C. Hinton ("China as an Asian Power," in Robinson and Shambaugh, *Chinese Foreign Policy,* 353), by 1959 Beijing saw New Delhi and Moscow as being "drawn together by their territorial quarrels with China."

13. Garver, *Protracted Contest,* 193.

14. Ibid., 192–96. China also stepped in to sell arms to Pakistan when the United States suspended sales in 1990.

15. Garver, *Protracted Contest,* 199. Garver adds that "China's firm support of Pakistan was a rebut to the superpowers, which it saw as colluding to use India to contain China."

16. Ibid., 209.

17. Hinton, "China as an Asian Power," 358.

18. William Burr, ed., *The Kissinger Transcripts: The Top-Secret Talks with Beijing and Moscow* (New York: New Press, 1998), 53.

19. "Mao Tse-tung's 'Trimetrical Classic,'" *Chinese Law and Government* 9, nos. 1–2 (Spring–Summer 1976), 7–11, quoted in Garver, *Protracted Contest,* 113.

20. China pursued détente with India even as the Soviet Union was transferring massive amounts of modern military hardware, making India the world's largest arms importer during the 1980s (Cohen, *India: Emerging Power,* 142).

21. Bin Yu, "China and Its Asian Neighbors: Implications for Sino-U.S. Relations," in *In the Eyes of the Dragon: China Views the World,* ed. Yong Deng and Fei-Ling Wang (Lanham, Md.: Rowman and Littlefield, 1999), 186.

22. Garver, *Protracted Contest,* 95.

23. Xinhua, 22 December 1988, quoted in Hu Weixing, "India's Nuclear Bomb and Future Sino-Indian Relations," *East Asia: An International Quarterly* 17, no. 1 (Spring 1999).

24. India allows the Tibetan government-in-exile to travel abroad to build international support, but not to engage in anti-Chinese political activities such as demonstrations or meetings between the Dalai Lama and high-level U.S. officials on Indian soil.

25. The disputed border situation affords a "certain equilibrium from the perspective of stability," as Ashley Tellis explains: China claims about ninety thousand square kilometers of Indian territory in the eastern sector and occupies parts of the Aksai Chin in the western sector. The most valuable area in the east claimed by China is effectively under Indian control. China's control over part of Aksai Chin claimed by India is vital to Beijing because of the critical landline of communication between Xinjiang and Tibet that runs through it. So each side already occupies the territory it defines as important for security, although it will not give up its claims to the other territory. "Neither state has any real incentives either to give up the areas each currently occupies or to usurp control over the areas currently held by the other." "India's Emerging Nuclear Doctrine: Exemplifying the Lessons of the Nuclear Revolution," *NBR Analysis* 12, no. 2 (May 2001): 30.

26. Sony Devabhaktuni, Matthew C. J. Rudolph, and Amit Sevak, "Key Developments in the Sino-Indian CBM Process" (Washington D.C.: Stimson Center, 1998), 201–4.

27. Ibid., 203–4.

28. Garver, *Protracted Contest,* 228.

29. Xinhua, 28 April 1998.

30. Agence France Presse, 18 April 1998.

31. Xinhua, 27 April 1998.

32. Agence France Presse, 5 May 1998; Fernandes subsequently claimed that his observation, made to a private television channel, had been distorted.

33. Xinhua, 18 May 1998.

34. "A few days before the nuclear tests, Defense Minister George Fernandes spouted out nonsense that China is India's 'No. 1 potential threat,' a statement that provoked strong criticism from China; other Indian officials also disagreed and dismissed his remarks as nonsense. After the nuclear tests, it became clear that Fernandes' comment was a premeditated effort to mold public opinion for the tests and to deceive the Indian people. . . . Less than a month [before], Fernandes himself said smilingly to visiting Chinese guests that India was satisfied with the peace and stability in the Indian-Chinese border region. Now he has suddenly turned hostile, spouting the 'China threat theory.'" Zhongguo Tongxun She (Hong Kong), 16 May 1998.

35. In 1992, China held a nuclear test during the visit of Indian President R. Venkataraman.

36. An interesting question is whether China could have done more to mitigate the security dilemma that its growing economic and military power, combined with its nuclear capability, created for India. See Ashley Tellis, *Changing Grand Strategies in South Asia,* RAND Studies in Public Policy (Cambridge: Cambridge University Press, 2000).

37. Xinhua, 12 May 1998.

38. In an August 1998 interview with the Indian magazine *The Hindu* (12–25

September 1998), Chinese MFA spokesman Zhu Bangzao highlighted the fact that after India's first tests, "Chinese exercised restraint in exercising its position," but after the second round and publication of Prime Minister Vajpayee's letter alleging that China posed a threat, "China issued a statement of the MFA which we hadn't done for many years."

39. It was particularly striking that the Indians made no mention of Pakistan's April 1998 tests of the Ghauri medium-range ballistic missile in justifying their nuclear tests the following month.

40. *New York Times,* 13 May 1998, 4.

41. Xinhua, 14 May 1998.

42. Xinhua, 19 May 1998.

43. *China Daily,* 20 May 1998.

44. The telephone calls are reported by the Chinese side in Beijing China Radio International, in Hindi, 14 May 1998, FBIS-CHI-98-135. Secretary Albright made the calls from Europe where she was attending a Group of Eight meeting. Her original idea, worked out with European allies, was to convene an enlarged G-8 meeting for this purpose. But when the Chinese, who are not members of the G-8, told her that they were not keen on the idea, she suggested the Permanent Five approach instead.

45. In China's official reaction to the Pakistani tests, it made clear that India was the instigator and most to blame by "strongly condemning" India's tests and "expressing deep regret" over Pakistan's (Xinhua, 2 June 1998).

46. *Newsweek,* 29 June 1998.

47. President Jiang's effort to obtain a joint statement with Russia condemning the tests during his November 1998 visit to Moscow was less successful than the American one because Russia refused to mention its friend India in the statement.

48. The group talked about "the current situation of bilateral relations" instead of border issues. (Hu Weixing, "India's Nuclear Bomb").

49. B. Raman, "Sino-Indian Relations: A Chronology," South Asia Analysis Group Papers, 23 April 1999, available at www.saag.org/papers/paper49.html.

50. *Taaza News,* 18 January 2001.

51. Satu P. Limaye, "India–East Asia Relations: India's Latest Asian Incarnation," *Comparative Connections* (Pacific Forum CSIS, Third Quarter 2000).

52. Xinhua, 27 July 1998; also see Xinhua, 10 July 1998.

53. *Renmin ribao,* 15 May 1998.

54. *Renmin ribao,* 19 May 1998. This tougher line was echoed by Hong Kong communist media. For example, see "Nuclear Tests Reveal India's Hegemonist Ambition in South Asia," Zhongguo Tongxun She (Hong Kong), 16 May 1998, and "India's Nuclear Tests Threaten World Peace," *Ta Kung Pao* (Hong Kong), 20 May 1998.

55. Strobe Talbott, "U.S. Diplomacy in South Asia: A Progress Report," speech delivered at the Brookings Institution, 12 November 1998. Mark W. Frazier says that "China has taken a stronger posture than the United States on India's nuclear weapons program," and that the United States "appears to have accepted India's pursuit of a minimal deterrent as a fact of life and now seeks to limit India's ability to conduct further tests." He also states that the U.S. strategy "has largely proven successful." "China-India Relations since Pokhran II: Assessing Sources of Conflict and Cooperation," *AccessAsia Review* 3, no. 2 (July 2000).

56. Sha Zukang, "Some Thoughts on Non-Proliferation," speech delivered at the Carnegie Endowment for International Peace, 11–12 January 1999.

57. Frazier, "China-India Relations," 17.

58. Ibid., 15.

59. Ming Zhang, *China's Changing Nuclear Posture: Reactions to the South Asian Nuclear Tests* (Washington D.C.: Carnegie Endowment for International Peace, 1999).

60. Informal communication with Tai Ming Cheung, Avery Goldstein, and Jonathan Pollack.

61. Yuan Jing-dong, "India's Rise after Pokhran II: Chinese Analyses and Assessments," *Asian Survey* 41, no. 2 (November–December 2001): 978–1001; Zou Yunhua, "Chinese Perspectives on the South Asian Nuclear Tests," working paper, Center for International Security and Cooperation, Stanford University, January 1999.

62. State Council Information Office white papers, "China's National Defense, 1998," and "China's National Defense in 2000," Beijing. In a personal correspondence, John Garver has suggested to me an alternative instrumental interpretation, i.e., the white papers show China's effort to play down the military dimension of its relations with India in order to expand multidimensional cooperative relations with all the countries of South Asia. Then, if India objects to China's strengthening ties with Myanmar, Pakistan, Nepal, and Bangladesh, it is revealing its own hegemonistic intentions on the subcontinent.

63. Leo Rose, "India and China: Forging a New Relationship in the Subcontinent," in *The Asia-Pacific in the New Millennium: Geopolitics, Security, and Foreign Policy,* ed. Shalendra Sharma (Berkeley, Calif.: Institute of East Asian Studies, 1999), quoted in Neil Joeck, "Nuclear Developments in India and Pakistan," *AccessAsia Review* 2, no. 2 (July 1999): 18.

64. Hua Han, "Sino-Indian Relations and Nuclear Arms Control," in *Nuclear Weapons and Arms Control in South Asia after the Test Ban,* ed. Eric Arnett (Oxford: Oxford University Press for the Stockholm International Peace Research Institute, 1998), 47, quoted in Joeck, "Nuclear Developments," 18.

65. Hu Weixing, "India's Nuclear Bomb."

66. China reportedly has a ballistic missile base headquartered in Xining, Qinghai province, located about 1,000 kilometers from India's northeast border and 2,000 kilometers from New Delhi. The Xining base was established about fifteen to twenty years ago and has three brigades, one of which has DF-3 medium-range ballistic missiles (MRBMs) with a 2,800-kilometer range. China also has a missile base in Yunnan province with one brigade of DF-21 MRBMs with a range of 1,800 kilometers. These two areas are sometimes called "historical Tibet," but they lie outside the Tibet Autonomous Region (Ken Allen, "Nuclear Weapons and Sino-Indian Relations," news advisory, Henry L. Stimson Center, Washington, D.C., June 1998).

67. The Tibet scholar Dawa Norbu suggests that one reason China worries more about threats from the east than from the west is that with the takeover of Tibet and the nurturing of relations with Nepal and Bhutan, it has shut "the backdoor to China." "India, China, and Tibet," in *The Peacock and the Dragon: India-China Relations in the 21st Century,* ed. Kanti Bajpai and Amitabh Mattoo (New Delhi: Har-Anand, 2000), 282–83.

68. Ibid., 231–32.

69. A Chinese expert noted that the readjustment of China's relationships with India and Pakistan was symbolized by the fact that in paying visits to the region, Chinese leaders now visit India first, before Pakistan.

70. Garver, *Protracted Contest,* 231.

71. Xinhua, 14 January 1992.

72. Chinese diplomacy toward Korea and Southeast Asian countries bears greater resemblance to its manner of dealing with India than to its manner of dealing with Japan.

73. India's entry to the ASEAN Regional Forum was engineered by the United States and Singapore.

74. Thus, Beijing's response to the Indian government's support of American plans for national missile defense was much milder than its response to the Australian government's support.

Part II

Dimensions of the India-China Relationship

4

India and China: Border Issues, Domestic Integration, and International Security

Sumit Ganguly

A Troubled Relationship

Despite fitful improvements during the 1980s, Sino-Indian relations today remain fraught with tension. The two nuclear-armed countries eye each other with distrust based on a long history of discord and conflict stemming primarily from disputes over the border that separates the two, sections of which have remained unsettled since India's founding in 1947. Efforts to resolve the dispute have repeatedly foundered. Since the Sino-Indian border war of 1962, India has expressed some willingness to settle the dispute; China, however, has not yet shown any inclination to negotiate the conflict to a close.

Numerous differences—some long-standing, others of more recent vintage—hobble the prospect of improvement in the bilateral relationship. From the Indian standpoint, these long-standing differences focus on the border dispute, China's concomitant unwillingness to accept India's incorporation of Sikkim, and China's supply of advanced military and nuclear technology to Pakistan. In recent years decision makers in New Delhi have also become quite concerned about China's growing military presence in Burma (Myanmar).[1]

From the Chinese perspective the relationship is also problematic. Chinese decision makers have long been vexed by the unresolved border question and by the presence and putative political activities of more than a hundred thousand Tibetans and their spiritual and temporal leader, the Dalai Lama, in India.[2] More recently, the Chinese leadership has become concerned about the growth of Indian nuclear and ballistic missile capabilities, especially after the Indian nuclear tests of May 1998.[3] Finally, the Chinese remain intent upon preventing India from asserting what they deem to be "hegemony" in South Asia.[4] Nevertheless, it should be underscored that, although in Indian eyes the long-term Chinese threat is the most serious that India faces, for China the magnitude of the threat from India is relatively smaller. The Chinese do not consider the outstanding disputes with India, including the border question, to be of the same order as other, more compelling security concerns and irredentist claims, such as the Taiwan question.[5]

Since some acrimonious exchanges in the aftermath of the Indian nuclear tests in 1998, the two sides have attempted to repair their relations. In 1999, in an attempt to mollify bruised Chinese sensibilities, the Indian foreign minister, Jaswant Singh, visited Beijing. Although no substantive agreements were reached during his visit, the harsh rhetoric emanating from Beijing subsided significantly. More recently, the former Chinese Prime Minister Li Peng visited New Delhi as part of the ongoing effort to improve relations.[6]

Will these two Asian giants be able overcome their troubled legacy and their more recent discord to forge a normal bilateral relationship? If a Sino-Indian rapprochement does take place, what will be the likely implications for the United States? Could the Indians and the Chinese form a common front with, say, Russia to oppose the United States on major global issues such as international climate change, humanitarian intervention, human rights, and trade liberalization?[7]

The discord between India and China is so deep-seated, and the memory of the 1962 war between the two so searing on the Indian side, that any dramatic improvement in the bilateral relationship is unlikely.[8] Improvements in Sino-Indian relations will be, at best, incremental, and the specter of sustained triangular Chinese-Indian-Russian cooperation will not materialize. Thus, the United States need not be overly concerned about the seeming amelioration of relations that has taken place between India and China, for it is unlikely to adversely affect U.S. relations with either state. Nor does the United States need to fear the emergence of a coalition against its strategic interests in Asia. India, China, and Russia do not have sufficient common interests to bandwagon against the United States. Indeed, the competing Chinese and Indian aspirations for leadership in Asia significantly limit the prospects of bilateral or trilateral cooperation.

Tracing the Sources of Discord

Finding the sources of the tensions in the Sino-Indian relationship does not require much searching. Both experienced some degree of imperial control in the nineteenth century.[9] The Indian nationalist movement and the Chinese communist movement drew specific conclusions from the experience of European imperial expansion in and domination of Asia. India came to accept many of the precepts of Western conceptions of statehood and the obligations of international society.[10] As the principal inheritor of the British imperium in the subcontinent, India also zealously adhered to the legacy of colonially bequeathed borders.[11]

For India's first prime minister and the principal architect of its foreign policy, Jawaharlal Nehru, the borders of British India merely gave corporeal form to the idea of an India that had long existed in the collective historical imagination of the region's populace.[12] This perspective, however, did not accord well with the outlook of the Chinese communist leadership under Mao Zedong. The Chinese communist worldview was infused as much with a particular version of anticolonial nationalism as it was with Marxist-Leninist ideas.[13] This variant of nationalism portrayed China as the hapless victim of nineteenth-century Western machinations that subjected the Chinese to various "unequal treaties." Thus, after the British departure from the subcontinent, the revolutionary Chinese leadership sought to recover the territory "lost" to the Western colonizers.

The communist precepts held by the leaders in Beijing put them at odds with Nehru's commitment to liberal democracy. More to the point, Nehru's uncritical acceptance of inherited colonial borders propelled the two countries down a path of confrontation as China sought to question the legitimacy of British colonial expansion to the outer reaches of China in the Himalayas. The fallout from the Chinese annexation of Tibet brought the underlying tension to the surface, and the next border dispute erupted into war.

The specific dimensions of the border dispute and the Tibetan question will only be summarized here.[14] Among India's inheritance from the British colonial empire were the results of a set of colonial border policies. The northern frontiers of India, especially as they related to China and Tibet, had been formulated as a consequence of the interplay of cartography and imperial concerns about warding off potential expansionist threats from imperial (and then Bolshevik) Russia.[15] Out of three possible alignments proposed by colonial administrators and cartographers for the western sector of the northern Himalayan border, the most expansive was the Ardagh-Johnson line, fashioned between 1865 and 1867 (figure 4.1). This border labeled the region of Aksai Chin, which is adjacent to Tibet, as part and parcel of British colonial territory under the nominal tutelage of the maharaja of Kashmir. The second proposed alignment, the Macartney-MacDonald line, placed portions of the Aksai Chin in China's Xinjiang region. Finally, the Trelawney Saunders survey placed the boundaries along the Karakoram mountain range. Based on the evidence in the public domain, it appears that the national government of independent India chose the most expansive alignment, the Ardagh-Johnson line, as its interpretation of the frontier with China in the west. The decision to seize upon this particular formulation does not appear to have been arbitrary. Instead, it seems to have been chosen on the basis of the body of cartographic, administrative, and revenue-collection records left behind by the British.[16]

Key political and strategic choices, which in retrospect appear fundamentally flawed, sparked the tensions between India and China within a decade of the former's emergence as an independent state and the latter's emergence as a communist one.[17] The political context in which these choices were made is crucial to understanding the genesis of the tensions. In the aftermath of India's independence, Prime Minister Jawaharlal Nehru was primus inter pares in the new government on matters concerning India's foreign and defense policies. Nehru was acutely concerned about maintaining materially weak India's freedom and autonomy in the realm of foreign policy. Consequently, he seized upon a moral and normative vision that he believed would enhance India's ability to play a significant yet independent role in global affairs. The quest for this moral mission of world order, of course, was also based on a shrewd calculation of India's national interests.[18] Passionately opposed to high levels of military spending and fearing the militarization of Indian society, Nehru sought to steer India

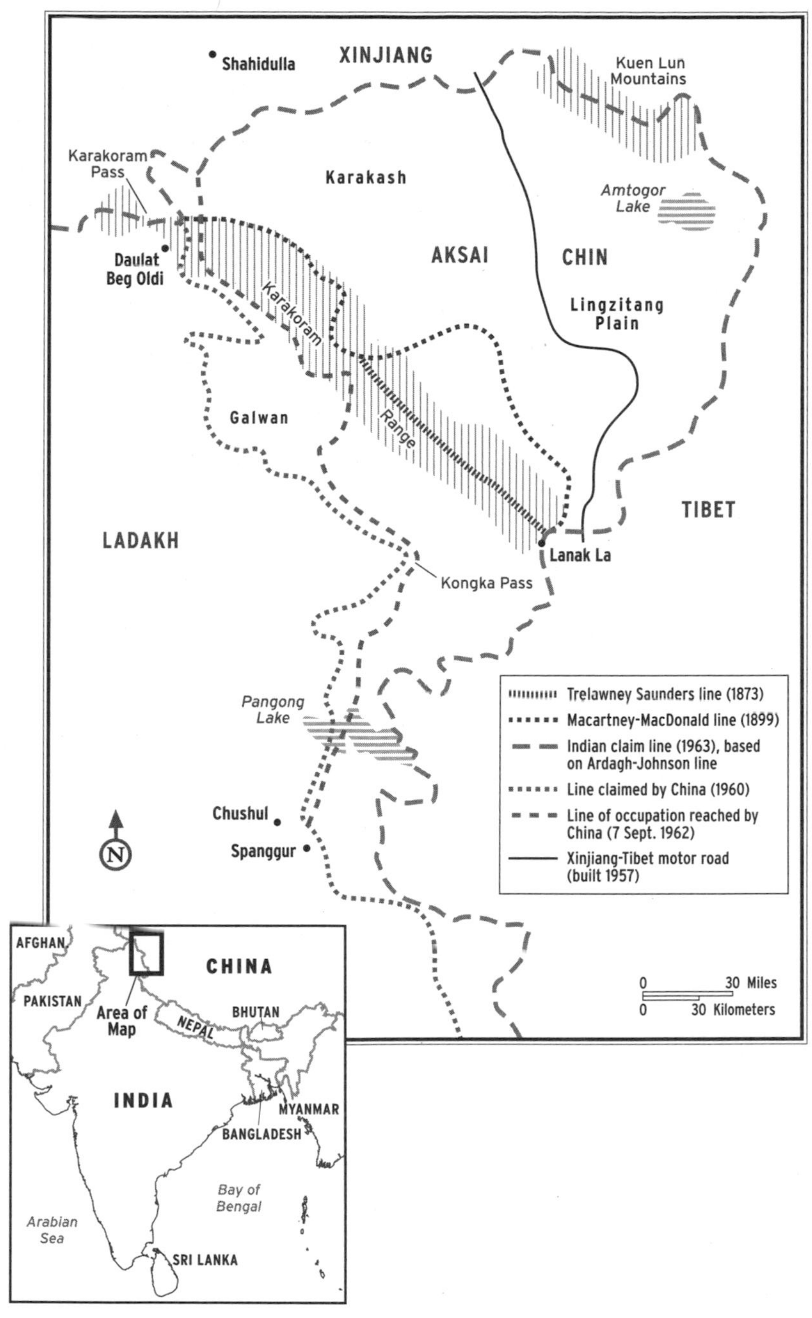

Figure 4.1 *British-formulated boundaries for Ladakh*

away from superpower entanglements.[19] Furthermore, his insistence on promoting economic development and eradicating mass poverty[20] required that India reduce the opportunity costs that would be posed by significant defense expenditures.

This approach to defense policy required a largely nonhostile neighborhood for India. Despite a war with Pakistan in 1947–48 and a succession of subsequent crises, Indian leaders did not perceive the military threat from Pakistan to be substantial.[21] A military challenge from the People's Republic of China (PRC), however, would require India to look for substantial foreign military assistance or to significantly boost its own military prowess. The pursuit of nonalignment foreclosed the former strategy, while the fear of Bonapartism and the perceived need to prioritize economic development undermined the latter.[22] Consequently, Nehru's strategy in dealing with the PRC was one of conciliation and appeasement.[23]

The Indian historian P. C. Chakravarti superbly summarizes Nehru's dilemma and the strategy he devised to deal with China:

> India's attitude toward China was determined, in large measure, by her unrealistic assessment of Chinese leadership. In Nehru's eyes, the supreme need of the moment was peace, particularly in Asia. The only power that might disturb Asian peace was China with her irredentist ambitions. Once those ambitions were satisfied, China, it was believed, would settle down to peaceful internal development. Unfriendly policies would merely antagonize the Chinese Communists and make them belligerent.[24]

Given this outlook, it is not surprising that Nehru quickly sought to conciliate China and boost its case in various international forums. To this end, India campaigned for China's inclusion in the negotiations in San Francisco for a post–World War II peace treaty with Japan, argued in support of China's bid for a seat on the United Nations Security Council, and refused to condemn China when its troops crossed the Yalu River during the Korean War.[25]

Yet Nehru was not entirely oblivious to a potential security threat from China. Although anxious to avoid a military confrontation, he did upbraid the Chinese following their occupation of Tibet in 1950.[26] He could do little in the military realm, however, to contest the PRC's annexation of a state that had once had a distinct international legal personality. Furthermore, he underestimated the geographic advantages that the occupation of Tibet would confer on China in its dealings with India along the Himalayan frontier.[27] Also, at a diplomatic level, Nehru did not deem it possible or worthwhile to raise the Tibetan question before the United Nations. According to one scholar, Nehru may have been inhibited from raising the Tibet issue before the United Nations because he had yet to tackle the vexing issues of French and Portuguese colonial enclaves still existing on Indian territory. Additionally, he wanted to maintain India's role as an interlocutor in the Korean crisis.[28]

The extraterritorial privileges in Tibet that India had inherited from the British included the right to station a small garrison of troops and a diplomatic mission there. The Chinese, preoccupied with the prosecution of the Korean War, did not immediately act to challenge and dismantle these privileges after their annexation of Tibet. Once the war waned, however, and Chinese control over Tibet was more firmly in place, Beijing instructed the Indians to cede what it deemed to be anachronistic colonial-era concessions. India, recognizing the superior military might of the Chinese and also sympathetic to the anti-imperial rhetoric, acquiesced to the Chinese demands. (In part, the Indians conceded because the Tibetans had already been forced to accept the Chinese incorporation of Tibet in the Seventeen-Point Agreement signed in Beijing in May 1951.[29])

The 1954 agreement in which India recognized China's sovereignty in Tibet also encoded the Five Principles of Peaceful Coexistence, or *Panch Shila.* Although in retrospect it seems quite naive, Nehru neglected at this stage to secure a Chinese endorsement of India's border claims and special rights in the other Himalayan states inherited from the British. In an act of supreme self-delusion and wishful thinking, Nehru assumed that his concessions to the Chinese and the ideational propositions embodied in the *Panch Shila* amounted to an agreement with the Chinese on the border question.[30] According to an important student of Sino-Indian relations, in Nehru's view the Chinese had tacitly conceded India's position on the border in what was a "gentleman's deal."[31] This failure on Nehru's part to secure a formal agreement would prove extraordinarily costly later on.

The Chinese occupation of Tibet and Beijing's harsh attempts to consolidate political power there contributed to a rebellion among the Tibetans as early as 1954.[32] Discontent with and resistance to the Chinese occupation pervaded Tibet, but, interestingly, the insurrection started in the eastern Tibetan regions of Kham and Amdo, which had nominally accepted

Chinese rule since the Qing period. Following the communist takeover, however, attempts to alter the traditional lives of the Tibetans were carried out with particular vigor in these regions.[33]

The issue that most upset the Tibetans in Amdo and Kham was the draconian Chinese program of land reform. Resistance to land reform became violent by the mid-1950s, and the Chinese People's Liberation Army (PLA) was used to repress the violent opposition. The full-blown revolt broke out after a harsh PLA assault in 1956 on the Changtreng Sampheling monastery, one of the largest and most revered Buddhist religious sites in Kham. The monastery was targeted because the three thousand resident monks had provided refuge to thousands of Tibetans who had resisted the land reform program.[34] Other monasteries were shut down, lamas and monks were forced to take part in manual labor, and all religious activity was ruthlessly suppressed. Simultaneously, all significant economic and social activities were brought under the control of the cadres of the Chinese Communist Party. Tibetan lands and herds were also collectivized.[35] Despite harsh PLA response, the revolt gathered strength and spread across Tibet.

Over the next two years, the Tibetans received limited support from the U.S. Central Intelligence Agency through its operatives in Kalimpong and Darjeeling in the Indian state of West Bengal. This assistance, however, was insufficient for the Khampas to put up significant armed resistance against the PLA. Worse still, it enabled the PLA and the Chinese leadership to portray the Khampas as stooges of what they characterized as American "imperialism."[36]

Amid the turmoil of the Khampa rebellion, the Chogyal (ruler) of Sikkim invited the Dalai Lama to attend celebrations of the twenty-five-hundredth anniversary of the birth of Buddha, to be held in Bodh Gaya in India during 1956–57. The government of India had attempted to invite him through diplomatic channels, via the Chinese regime in Beijing, but the Chinese had made no effort to pass on the invitation to the Dalai Lama. Despite attempts by Chinese Premier Zhou Enlai to dissuade him, the Dalai Lama chose to go to India. While there, he not only attended the ceremony but also visited with various Tibetan émigré groups, who sought to impress on him the horrors that the Chinese regime was visiting on them in remote parts of Tibet. The Dalai Lama also met with Indian officials, but they refused to involve themselves in the internal affairs of Tibet for fear of offending the Chinese.[37]

In 1957, the Dalai Lama returned to Tibet. The regime in Beijing had meanwhile stepped up its repressive policies in Tibet. As the Khampa rebellion continued and after a 10 March protest against a rumored PLA plot to kidnap the Dalai Lama escalated into a full-blown national uprising against Chinese rule, in 1959 the PLA attacked the Dalai Lama's palace in Lhasa. Fearing imminent incarceration at the hands of the Chinese authorities, he and the members of his immediate family fled for India. New Delhi was quick to grant political asylum, which infuriated the Chinese government in Beijing. China saw the government in New Delhi as not only complicit in fomenting the rebellion in Tibet in collusion with the United States, but also responsible for orchestrating the flight of the Dalai Lama to India.[38] There is little question that New Delhi had provided limited assistance to the Tibetan rebellion, largely in concert with the Central Intelligence Agency.[39] However, no evidence has been unearthed that would provide any semblance of support for the Chinese claim that India helped orchestrate the flight of the Dalai Lama. (This flawed Chinese belief in Indian malfeasance would dog Sino-Indian relations over the next several years.) On the contrary, the Dalai Lama's flight to India posed a serious diplomatic problem for Prime Minister Nehru. Nehru had for the past decade sought to appease China and had adopted a circumspect, and even timorous, policy on the Tibetan question because he was acutely cognizant of India's military weakness.[40] While he unhesitatingly granted the Dalai Lama asylum, he also sought to limit the political activities of his guest for fear of invoking the wrath of the Chinese.

Dealing with the Troubled Frontier

As early as 1950, Indian diplomats had encountered Chinese maps that depicted as Chinese territory that India deemed to be its own. Initially, Nehru had brushed off suggestions that this matter be forthrightly discussed with the Chinese. In his view, the inherited boundaries of the British Empire were legal and therefore sacrosanct. This legalistic worldview was in marked contrast to the Chinese position, which was largely shaped by considerations of power as well as notions of historical grievance.

Only at the urging of other Indian officials did Nehru eventually raise the matter of the maps with Zhou Enlai in the course of official discussions during a visit to Beijing in 1954. Zhou answered that the maps were old Nationalist documents and that the new regime in Beijing had not had an opportunity to examine and possibly rectify them.[41] Nehru chose not to press the matter any further. His unwillingness to seek a more unequivocal answer on the subject would later pose grave problems for the Sino-Indian relationship.

Even when Indian troops in 1955 encountered a Chinese encampment at Bara Hoti in the Garwhal district of the northern Indian state of Uttar Pradesh, the Indian Foreign Office issued a rather bland and equivocal statement that glossed over the issue of Chinese intrusions. Further intrusions took place throughout 1955, after which the Foreign Office did send notes to Beijing indicating its displeasure. However, Nehru made little effort to inform Parliament, for fear of provoking a wider anti-Chinese reaction and in the hope that he might be able to reach some amicable settlement with the Chinese.

In 1958, the government of India learned that during the preceding two years Chinese military engineers had constructed a road through the Aksai Chin region of Ladakh, in territory that India unequivocally claimed as its own (see map 4.1). Faced with this fait accompli, Nehru complained directly to Zhou in a letter stating that the Chinese had transgressed into Indian territory. Zhou replied that the portion of Ladakh through which the road, the Tibet-Xinjiang Highway, had been constructed was Chinese territory.[42]

Tensions between the two countries mounted in 1959 after Chinese troops surrounded and attacked an Indian patrol at Longju and another position in Ladakh (figure 4.2). Nehru again refused to significantly bolster Indian military capabilities along the Himalayan frontier for fear of starting a larger military confrontation with China. However, he did permit a modest increase in the overall defense budget.[43]

Simultaneously, he invited Zhou to New Delhi for talks in 1960, which turned out disastrously. At this meeting Zhou informally offered to swap the occupied Aksai Chin region for the territory China claimed within India's North East Frontier Agency (now the state of Arunachal Pradesh).[44] This proposal was fundamentally unacceptable to Indian decision makers; thanks in part to Nehru's dissembling on prior Chinese incursions, members of the opposition in Parliament were in no mood to negotiate with the Chinese. As a consequence, Nehru's room for maneuvering was significantly smaller, and he had to adopt a more unyielding position. Zhou, largely unfamiliar with the workings of a parliamentary democracy, perceived Nehru's stance to be one of extreme rigidity.

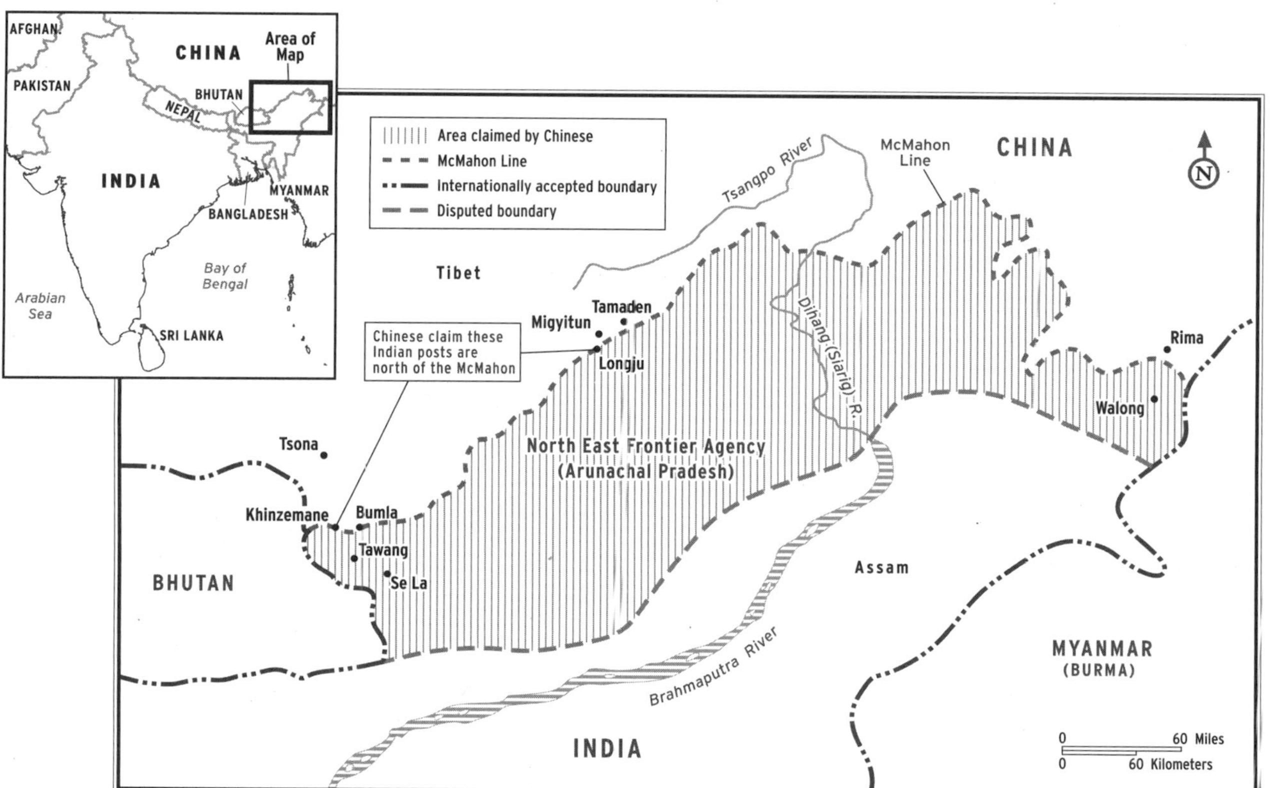

Figure 4.2 *Boundary dispute in the eastern sector, 1959. (From Alastair Lamb,* The China-India Border *[London: Oxford University Press for the Royal Institute of International Affairs, 1964]. Reprinted by permission of the Royal Institute of International Affairs.)*

Prelude to War

Following Zhou's infelicitous visit to New Delhi, all discussions on settling the border dispute ended. In an attempt to assert India's position on the Chinese-claimed areas, the Indian government formulated its "forward policy," which involved sending small numbers ("penny packets," in military jargon) of lightly armed Indian troops into the disputed areas in and around Ladakh where, in India's view, the Chinese had made cartographic claims. The forward policy amounted to a strategy of compellence—namely, an effort to force an adversary to undo the consequences of a hostile act.[45]

Unfortunately, the strategy as it was actually implemented made little or no military sense. In the words of one senior Indian general, it had "neither teeth nor tail"[46]—the troops lacked sufficient firepower to inflict significant costs on an adversary and also did not have adequate logistical support to carry out sustained operations.[47]

The Border War

The Sino-Indian border war started on 20 October 1962, when units of the PLA attacked a number of Indian positions in the eastern sector at Khinzemane, Dhola, and Tsangdhar.[48] Other units struck simultaneously at Indian positions in the western sector: in the Pangong Lake area and at Daulat Beg Oldi, Chusul, and Demchok.

Unprepared for this onslaught, the Indian troops initially were traumatized. However, they managed to overcome their initial shock and moved to strengthen their defensive positions in both the North East Frontier Agency and Ladakh. They also sought to block other routes through Sikkim and Bhutan that the Chinese might have used to make further ingress in the eastern sector.[49] The Indians put up a particularly spirited resistance in Ladakh but were forced to concede posts at Rezang La, Gurung Hill, and Spanggur Lake.[50] The resistance of the Indian forces was remarkable in one respect: they were equipped with World War I vintage bolt-action rifles, whereas their battle-ready Chinese adversaries were armed with modern automatic weapons.[51]

The major military debacle for India unfolded in the North East Frontier Agency. The Chinese managed to penetrate deep into the Assam foothills, threatening the town of Tezpur and India's oil fields at Digboi. The entire

Fourth Division of the Indian Army was all but decimated in the eastern sector by the Chinese. The disarray of the Indian forces led Prime Minister Nehru to remove the commandant of the eastern front, Lieutenant-General B. N. Kaul, and the chief of army staff, General P. N. Thapar.[52]

The war lasted about a month. On 21 November, the Chinese declared a unilateral cease-fire and started to withdraw their troops from the eastern sector. In the western sector, however, they came to occupy some 14,500 square miles of territory, including areas that they had previously claimed. They also issued a stern warning to the Indians that any attempts to dislodge Chinese troops from the areas that they had come to occupy would result in a Chinese attack.[53]

The Aftermath of 1962

The consequences of the war for India, apart from the loss of life and the demoralization of the armed forces, were far-reaching and sweeping. One commentator has aptly summarized the larger political and strategic consequences of the border war for the Indian polity:

> The conflict dispelled any lingering illusions in the official Indian circles regarding Chinese inhibitions about employing force against India. It brought into focus a grave threat in a quarter where geography had been regarded as an almost insurmountable barrier against serious attack by land. It confirmed India's dependence upon external help against attack by a major power and the availability of Western military aid involving Communist China.[54]

The impact of the war on Indian defense planning, strategy, and military organization cannot be overestimated. The Chinese attack on India left Nehru a broken man; he died shortly thereafter of a heart attack. Though his successors continued to invoke the language of nonalignment, fundamental shifts took place in Indian foreign and defense policies.[55] Among other matters, the Indian leadership sought to forge a new defense relationship with the United States. Limited military cooperation with the United States did emerge after the 1962 war, including on the unsettled question of the Chinese occupation of Tibet.[56] The ambit of military cooperation, however, failed to significantly expand because of profound Pakistani misgivings, the inability of the two sides to reach a settlement of the Kashmir dispute, and

India's own ambivalence about the relationship.[57] Nevertheless, India did embark on a massive "self-help" program of military modernization,[58] raising ten new mountain divisions trained in high-altitude warfare, acquiring a forty-five-squadron air force equipped with supersonic aircraft, creating a million-man army, and making a modest effort at naval expansion.[59]

The Pakistan Factor

The border war had effectively shattered any hopes of Sino-Indian amity. Any willingness on India's part to renew a more positive relationship with China would not emerge until the late 1980s as the Indo-Soviet relationship started to decline. In the aftermath of the border war, yet another factor started to exacerbate the already frayed Sino-Indian relationship: China's growing ties to Pakistan, India's principal adversary. India's long-troubled relationship with Pakistan would further complicate its relations with China.

Soon after their emergence from the detritus of the British Indian colonial empire in 1947 India and Pakistan had become embroiled in war over the status of the state of Jammu and Kashmir. The origins of the Kashmir dispute are complex and have been explored at length elsewhere.[60] Suffice to say that Pakistan's claim to Kashmir, the only Muslim-majority state in the former British Indian empire, was irredentist. Pakistani leaders believed that they had to incorporate Kashmir into their domain to ensure the completeness of Pakistan, the putative homeland for the Muslims of South Asia. India, which had been founded on the principles of secular and civic nationalism, argued with equal force that Kashmir had to remain within the Indian Union to demonstrate that a Muslim-majority population could thrive under the aegis of a secular polity. These two competing visions of nationalism placed the nascent states on a collision course shortly after they obtained their independence from the United Kingdom.

The first Kashmir war of 1947–48 resulted in a division of the state. India came to control some two-thirds of the state and Pakistan the remaining one-third. India, on the advice of Lord Mountbatten, the last viceroy, referred the Kashmir issue to the United Nations on 1 January 1948. Later in 1948, even as the war continued, the United Nations passed two critical resolutions. Pared to the bone, these resolutions called for Pakistan to vacate its aggression in Kashmir and for India to hold a plebiscite to determine the wishes of the Kashmiri population.[61] Not unexpectedly, India insisted that Pakistan first withdraw its forces from Kashmir before India would allow a plebiscite to be held. Pakistan, in a similar vein, insisted that only after the wishes of the Kashmiris had been ascertained in a plebiscite would they withdraw their troops. As a stalemate ensued on this process, the issue quickly became enmeshed in Cold War politics in the United Nations, and the positions of the two sides steadily hardened. By 1960 the United Nations had largely lost interest in the Kashmir dispute, given the intractable positions of both sides.

In the aftermath of Pakistan's independence, despite Pakistani overtures, Sino-Pakistani relations were not especially close. Pakistan's early ties to the United States and its membership in the U.S.-sponsored Central Treaty Organization (CENTO) and the Southeast Asia Treaty Organization (SEATO) had made China wary of Pakistan. The PRC was also irked by Pakistan's unwillingness to support its claim for membership in the United Nations. The evolution of the Indo-Pakistani deadlock over Kashmir was not lost on China. Despite the professed anticommunist sentiments of Pakistan's military dictator, the self-styled Field Marshal Mohammed Ayub Khan, who seized power in 1958, the Chinese made overtures toward Pakistan, especially after the 1962 border war. Pakistan quickly reciprocated the overtures, and a relationship based upon a common hostility toward India started to emerge.[62]

The warming trend in Sino-Pakistani relations was first evident in China's willingness to change its position on the crucial Kashmir issue. Initially, the Chinese had hewed to the position that the Kashmir problem was the result of British colonial perfidy and not the result of Indian machinations.[63] The most significant shift in Sino-Pakistani relations occurred after the 1962 border war. During the war, under pressure from the United States, Pakistan had refrained from opening a second front. In the aftermath of the war, the Pakistanis reacted with considerable dismay as the United States instituted a modest arms transfer and military relationship with India to bolster India's defenses against renewed Chinese aggression.[64] This unhappiness with the United States led the military regime of Mohammed Ayub Khan to make some overtures toward China.[65] China reciprocated these Pakistani moves. Most important, China proved willing to settle conflicting border claims in the area of Xinjiang abutting the disputed state of Jammu and Kashmir. An exchange of maps took place in mid-July 1962, and formal negotiations began in October of that year against a backdrop of steadily deteriorating Sino-Indian relations. By late December, the two sides had reached a common understanding of the alignment of the border. The settlement involved a two-hundred-mile stretch of territory extending from the Afghanistan, Pakistan, and Xinjiang trijunction to the Karakoram Pass. Under the terms of the settlement, Pakistan gained some 750 square miles of territory from the Chinese while ceding its claim to 1,050 square miles.

Interestingly enough, the settlement was announced on 2 March 1963, literally hours before Indo-Pakistani talks over Kashmir were about to begin. Obviously, the timing of this announcement was hardly accidental. The territories that Pakistan and China had traded as part of the border settlement involved portions of the original princely state of Jammu and Kashmir, the principal subject of Indo-Pakistani discord. India, predictably, denounced the agreement but nevertheless did not pull out of the planned negotiations.[66]

The border settlement with Pakistan marked the beginning of what one scholar has characterized as the development of an "entente cordiale" between China and Pakistan.[67] In subsequent years, the two countries coordinated policies on a number of crucial issues, often to India's distress. Some episodes, in particular, are important to highlight. In September 1965 when Pakistan attacked India, China sided with Pakistan and threatened India with adverse consequences during the course of the war.[68] However, China's support for Pakistan during this war was mostly symbolic; it did not open a second front along the Himalayan border.[69] Despite the limited Chinese support for Pakistan during the 1965 war, Sino-Pakistani relations continued to improve during the remainder of the decade. Indeed another military regime in Pakistan, under General Yahya Khan, played a critical role in enabling Henry Kissinger to make his secret trip to the PRC in 1970 to reopen diplomatic relations with China.[70]

During the 1971 war, China loudly denounced India's military intervention in East Pakistan but did not resort to any military intimidation of India. Three factors explain Chinese military nonintervention in East Pakistan crisis. First, the People's Liberation Army was deeply implicated in China's internal politics as the most tumultuous years of the Cultural Revolution drew to a close. Consequently, it was not in the best possible form to undertake significant military action. Second, in 1965 China had intervened on behalf of the Kashmiris, some of whom were disaffected from India. In 1971, a military intervention against India would have placed China squarely against the self-determination of the Bangladeshis.[71] Finally, from a logistical standpoint, India had carefully waited until November–December 1971 to start its intervention; by this time most of the Himalayan passes were closed.

In the aftermath of the 1971 war, Prime Minister Zulfikar Ali Bhutto made an important strategic calculation. He realized that in subsequent wars with India, Pakistan would no longer have the option of ceding any territory and could no longer open a second front elsewhere. Also, faced with India's emerging arms acquisition relationship with the Soviet Union, Pakistan could not hope to match India's inevitable conventional military superiority. Accordingly, Pakistan needed nuclear weapons to guarantee its future security. To this end Bhutto embarked upon the acquisition of a Pakistani nuclear deterrent.[72]

As the Pakistanis avidly pursued a nuclear weapon program throughout much of the next two decades, the Chinese provided assistance. China's calculations in favor of aiding the Pakistani program were clear, especially after India's initial nuclear test in 1974. Nuclear arms capability, coupled with India's substantial conventional superiority, would enable India to dominate the subcontinent and relegate Pakistan to the status of a vassal state. Such an outcome was intolerable to Beijing, which sought to keep India tied down in the subcontinent and mired in its continuing conflict with Pakistan.[73] In subsequent decades China played a critical role in aiding and abetting the Pakistani nuclear and ballistic missile programs. China has dissembled and denied any significant assistance to these programs, but the evidence of Chinese involvement is overwhelming.[74]

Continuing Tensions

Through the 1960s Sino-Indian relations remained acutely strained. The first Chinese nuclear test at Lop Nor in 1964 set off a renewed firestorm of controversy in India and led to demands for an Indian nuclear deterrent. Despite significant pressures to acquire an overt nuclear capability, Prime Minister Lal Bahadur Shastri deferred the decision.[75] Shortly thereafter, in October 1965, war broke out between India and Pakistan over the unresolved question of the status of Kashmir. Although it did not resort to any military malfeasance during this war, China assailed India with hortatory statements of support for the Pakistani position.[76] Tensions again flared along the Sino-Indian border in 1967 when the two sides exchanged artillery fire in the eastern sector.

Throughout the late 1960s and beyond, China was also deeply involved in supporting the Naga and Mizo separatists in India's troubled northeast. This support to the various tribal groups stemmed largely from China's broader strategy of supporting "national liberation movements" directed against regimes "unfriendly" to China. Like most separatist movements, these two tribal insurgencies had indigenous roots stemming from local grievances.[77] However, Chinese assistance to the insurgents expanded the scope and prolonged the duration of the conflicts. As long as China, in its revolutionary zeal, continued to support these insurgents the prospects of rapprochement with India remained nonexistent. It was only in the late 1970s, with the accession of Deng Xiaoping to power, that the Chinese chose to cut off assistance to the separatist guerillas, thereby making possible some movement on the improvement of relations.[78]

Attempts at Normalization: The "Mao Smile"

China initiated the first effort to improve relations. Quite unexpectedly, in May 1970, Chairman Mao Zedong approached the Indian chargé d'affairs, Brajesh Mishra, in Beijing at a reception and greeted him warmly, suggesting that Sino-Indian relations should be repaired.[79] It appears reasonable to argue that Mao's sudden desire to improve relations with India stemmed at least in part from his predicament with the Soviet Union; only a year earlier, Soviet and Chinese troops had fought a bitter border war along the Ussuri River.[80]

Despite this Chinese interest in improving relations with India, the opportunity was lost because of the onset of the East Pakistan crisis of December 1970, which culminated in the creation of Bangladesh in 1971. During this period of upheaval in the subcontinent, the Chinese felt compelled to show at least verbal solidarity with Pakistan, their long-standing ally in South Asia. China vituperatively criticized Indian actions on behalf of the Bengali insurgents and staunchly defended the territorial integrity of the Pakistani state.[81] Consequently, any prospect of improving relations with India was vitiated for the next several years.

Matters worsened in 1975 when India absorbed the Himalayan kingdom of Sikkim into its domain. Unsurprisingly, the Chinese bitterly attacked the Indian decision, but they confined their protests to the diplomatic realm. Despite this setback, in an attempt to mollify Chinese sensibilities Prime Minister Indira Gandhi offered to restore full-fledged diplomatic relations, which had been suspended after the 1962 border war. The Chinese responded favorably to this proposal, and in 1976 full diplomatic relations were restored. Before either side could make further diplomatic overtures on the vexed question of the border dispute, however, Indira Gandhi was ousted from the prime ministership.

The new Janata coalition regime in New Delhi came to office with the promise of returning India to a policy of "genuine nonalignment" and also sought to improve relations with all of India's neighbors.[82] To this end Foreign Minister Atal Behari Vajpayee visited Beijing in 1979 in an attempt to revive discussions on settling the border question. This visit proved to be singularly ill-timed: the Chinese attacked Vietnam during that week and, to the acute discomfiture of their Indian guest, declared that they were "teaching Vietnam a lesson" just as they had taught India a similar one in 1962. Understandably, Vajpayee cut short his visit in protest and returned home.

The rancor that this episode generated in India foreclosed any further talks on the border issue for the next several years. In fact, it was the Chinese who reinitiated the dialogue process in 1981 at the instance of Deng Xiaoping. The border talks started in 1981 and concluded in 1988. The particulars of what transpired in these eight rounds of negotiations have been discussed elsewhere.[83] The first four rounds were focused primarily on the development of basic negotiating principles, and the second four dealt with "the situation on the ground."[84] In the sixth round, in 1985, the Chinese returned to their package proposal of swapping China's claims in the western sector for concessions in the eastern sector. However, following the talks, in the wake of Indian defense ministry statements alleging that China was actively aiding the Pakistani nuclear program, the Chinese again hardened their position. In mid-June of 1986, the Chinese vice foreign minister and leader of the delegation to the border talks told a group of visiting Indian journalists that the eastern sector remained the biggest hurdle in the Sino-Indian border negotiations. More to the point, he added that India was in illegal occupation of some ninety thousand square kilometers of territory in the eastern sector. In fact, in the seventh round of talks, held in July 1986, the Chinese started to press their claims on an area south of the McMahon Line in the eastern sector.[85] The talks failed to produce any fundamental breakthroughs on the border question, but they did contribute to an overall relaxation of tensions and to various confidence-building measures (CBMs) designed to reduce the likelihood of accidental conflict along the Himalayan border.[86]

Hands across the Himalayas?

A congeries of factors explain Prime Minister Rajiv Gandhi's decision to visit China in 1988. One of the principal, if unstated, factors was the waning of the Cold War and the growing uncertainty of unstinting Soviet support for India's security needs.[87] With the Soviet Union under Mikhail Gorbachev showing some signs of unreliability, it behooved India to try and improve relations with its major long-term adversary, China. Second, in 1986 tensions along the Sino-Indian border, especially at Sumdurong Chu in Arunachal Pradesh, an area of east-west mountain ranges that forms the trijunction of India, Bhutan, and China, had brought the two states to the brink of another military confrontation.[88] Although subsequent meetings and agreements had dampened the immediate tensions, political relations had remained strained. Finally, eight rounds of border talks had accomplished all that they possibly could. More substantive questions regarding a settlement of the contentious border dispute would necessarily require higher-level political consultation and direction.[89]

During his visit Rajiv Gandhi made two significant concessions. First, he agreed that the settlement of the border dispute need no longer be a precondition for the improvement of bilateral relations. Second, he conceded that some members of the Tibetan émigré community were engaged in "anti-Chinese" activities within India.[90] These two concessions were significant because China had repeatedly sought Indian acquiescence on these two issues. Separately, at the insistence of his Chinese interlocutors, Gandhi had to reiterate that Tibet was "an internal affair of China." The outcomes of the negotiations at this visit were clearly asymmetric: the Indian delegation neither sought nor received any similar support on the Kashmir dispute from the Chinese.[91] These facts again underscored the stark debility of India's negotiating capabilities vis-à-vis the Chinese.

One of the more tangible achievements of the trip was the creation of a high-level Joint Working Group (JWG). This entity was charged with seeking a political settlement of the border and other extant problems in Sino-Indian relations.

Glacial Progress: Assessing the Border Negotiations

Despite the concessions that Rajiv Gandhi made during his historic visit to the PRC, attempts to resolve the border dispute since then have moved at a glacial pace. The Chinese, who occupy a fundamentally advantageous position in the negotiations, appear to be in no particular rush to reach a final resolution. In the words of one American strategist with substantial knowledge of the region and the border dispute, the Chinese claim to Arunachal Pradesh amounts to a "dagger held against the heart of India."[92] Such a characterization is hardly chimerical. In recent years, despite the seeming improvement in Sino-Indian relations, especially on the border question, deep differences remain between China and India in the northeast. It is also important to underscore that China formally refuses to accept India's incorporation of the Himalayan kingdom of Sikkim. In the Chinese view, India's incorporation of Sikkim and the ending of the monarchy in that country was tantamount to "annexation."[93] Finally, India fears increasing Chinese military influence in Burma/Myanmar, as well as in the Himalayan kingdoms of Bhutan and Nepal.[94] Chinese involvement in Burma/Myanmar, in particular, is of no trivial significance to India. For example, the radar monitoring facility that China has developed on the Cocos Island, just north of India's Andaman archipelago, enables the Chinese to track Indian naval movements in the region.

Two developments pertaining to the border dispute require some discussion. The first is the agreement that was reached during Prime Minister Narasimha Rao's visit to China in September 1993. It enjoined the two sides to respect the so-called Line of Actual Control along the Himalayan border and not to conduct military maneuvers in designated zones even though there is no agreement on the precise position of the LAC in many sectors. This agreement is widely referred to as the "peace and tranquility" agreement.

Two factors made it possible to forge this agreement in 1993. First, five prior meetings of the JWG had already contributed to an atmosphere more conducive to the formulation and implementation of this CBM. In fact, at the fourth meeting of the JWG, held in New Delhi in February 1992, the two sides had agreed on a system of telephone links between local commanders and had also set up a schedule of regular meetings. Second, by 1993 both sides, especially Rao in India, were keen on pursuing various domestic development agendas. Consequently, peace along the border was a necessity. Despite this agreement, Rao failed to obtain any satisfactory answers from his Chinese interlocutor, Premier Li Peng, on China's sales of military equipment to Pakistan and its growing military presence in Burma/Myanmar.[95]

The other significant development was the emergence during the next three years, from a variety of dispassionate sources, of further details about Chinese military involvement in Burma/Myanmar and continuing Chinese technological assistance to the Pakistani nuclear and missile programs.[96] These reports led to continuing contention during the meetings of the JWG, as Indian diplomats pressed their Chinese counterparts for explanations. The Chinese did not respond seriously to the Indian misgivings, simply stating that their dealings with Pakistan and Burma/Myanmar remained within the ambit of normal state-to-state relations.

India's failure to obtain some clarification of what it deemed to be inimical Chinese behavior did not inhibit the government of Prime Minister H. D. Deve Gowda from forging another important set of CBMs in 1996. These were put into effect when President Jiang Zemin visited India in November 1996. Among other matters, the CBMs addressed the reduction of troops in border areas, prior notification of troop deployments, and other communication measures. Perhaps most important, the two sides agreed not to attack each other's forces along the disputed Himalayan frontier.[97] A central question still eluded the Indian and Chinese negotiators, however, even as they agreed on these important CBMs: the precise location of the Line of Actual Control.[98]

These CBMs have survived the considerable rhetorical acrimony that characterized Sino-Indian relations in the aftermath of the Indian nuclear tests of May 1998. However, a settlement of the border question still appears illusory. During his visit to India in January 2001, Li Peng expressed some willingness to start a discussion about the least contentious segment of the border, the middle sector.[99]

Contemplating the Future

Sino-Indian relations, despite fitful improvements, will remain competitive.[100] The two states have divergent self-images and different political systems. They also each wish to emerge as major powers in Asia and beyond. Though the two sides will find occasions for cooperation, they will nevertheless be at odds on a number of issues. At an international and strategic level, the PRC political and military leadership will not easily accept India's status as a full-fledged nuclear power.[101] Simultaneously, India's political leadership, regardless of coloration, will not forswear the nuclear weapons or ballistic missile programs. These issues will keep the two sides at odds.[102] In a related vein, subject to fiscal constraints, India will continue to expand the strength, scope, and reach of its naval capabilities. The growth of such capabilities will provide the Chinese with further reason to be wary of Indian intentions.

The larger Sino-Indian relationship will also, in all likelihood, remain competitive in Southeast Asia. In January 2001, India signed defense pacts with Indonesia and Vietnam. Prime Minister Atal Behari Vajpayee visited Malaysia in February 2001. These attempts to woo the countries of Southeast Asia were actually begun under the Congress Party regime of Narasimha Rao in the early 1990s, as part of his "look East" policy. After Rao's demise, political uncertainties in New Delhi led to the lapse of a coherent policy toward Southeast Asia, a region long ignored by India's foreign policy makers. Under the Vajpayee regime, India is making a renewed attempt to court those states of Southeast Asia that have long-term concerns about Chinese interests and behavior in the region.[103] During its two years in office, Vajpayee's regime has signed a defense agreement with Indonesia, held joint naval exercises with Vietnam, and started exercises with the Japanese coast guard to combat piracy. More recently, it has also started to strengthen ties with the military junta in Myanmar/Burma to counter growing Chinese influence in that country.[104]

At a regional level, China's continuing ties with Pakistan and its unwillingness to endorse India's position on the Kashmir question will remain important irritants in the Sino-Indian border relationship. Though China no longer unequivocally supports Pakistan on Kashmir, it does not endorse India's position either—nor is it likely to do so in the foreseeable future. India can neither offer sufficient inducements nor sufficiently threaten the Chinese to alter their position. Furthermore, given their own difficulties with the recrudescence of radical Islam in Xinjiang, the Chinese now perhaps more than ever need Pakistan as a possible interlocutor to rein in Islamic zealots.[105]

Other territorial issues also dog the Sino-Indian relationship. Even today China does not accept Sikkim's incorporation into India.[106] To demonstrate its firmness on its claim to Arunachal Pradesh, China has even refused to grant visas to the speaker of the Arunachal Pradesh assembly to visit China. Nor will it grant visas to any member of Parliament from Arunachal Pradesh. Improvements in relations have not led to any Chinese concessions on these issues.[107]

Finally, any progress on the border dispute will be glacial. Only in November 2000 at the eighth meeting of the Expert's Group, a spinoff of the JWG, did the two sides exchange maps of the least controversial segment of the border, the middle sector.[108] After the ninth meeting, held on 28 July 2001, the Indian spokesperson stated that the talks had been held in a "friendly and constructive atmosphere" but revealed little else.[109] The subsequent meetings yielded little more.[110] In fourteenth meeting, held in Beijing in late March 2002, the two sides agreed to a time frame for clarifying the LAC.[111] An initial exchange of maps of the eastern sector in early 2003 would be followed shortly thereafter by an exchange of maps of the western sector.[112]

The PRC does not appear to attach any great urgency to the settlement of its border dispute with India. From a strategic standpoint, Beijing's lack of alacrity makes sense. The PLA can effectively tie down significant numbers of Indian troops along the Himalayan border without expending too many resources.[113]

On the other side of the border, India is unlikely to depart significantly from its present policy of limiting the political activities of the Tibetans. For example, India has refused to allow the American representative to the Tibetan government-in-exile to meet with the Dalai Lama for fear of provoking a harsh reaction from the Chinese. On the other hand, India is also unlikely to further hem in the activities of the Tibetans or limit the Dalai Lama's ability to freely travel to and from India. As long as the Dalai Lama is alive, the continued existence of the Tibetan community in India will remain irksome to the Chinese.

Yet India is unlikely to exploit the Tibetan question to exert pressure on China. A variety of factors explain India's reluctance to use the Tibetan issue to its political advantage. At one level, the current Bharatiya Janata Party (BJP)-led coalition's tougher political rhetoric notwithstanding, elements of a Nehruvian worldview still stalk the corridors of South Block, the home of India's Ministry of External Affairs. In practical terms, this means that India's foreign policy decision makers remain unwilling to dramatically alter a well-established policy of caution and circumspection with respect to China. Additionally, many Indian foreign and security policy officials fear that the Chinese can still sow considerable discord in India's unsettled northeast where Mizo and Naga tribals remain somewhat disaffected.[114]

Even though the likelihood of India's exploiting the Tibetan issue is all but negligible, China's decision makers remain extremely concerned about any hint or event prospect of international disapprobation of their control over Tibet. Despite their long occupation of Tibet, the Chinese still have not succeeded in completely suppressing Tibetan resistance and legitimizing Chinese rule; consequently, this issue will continue to roil Sino-Indian relations. All these factors will necessarily limit the scope, pace, and extent of improvements in Sino-Indian relations and impede the settlement of the border dispute.

Notes

1. On the matter of Chinese involvement in Burma (Myanmar), see J. Mohan Malik, "China-India Relations in the Post-Soviet Era: The Continuing Rivalry," *China Quarterly* no. 142 (June 1995): 317–55.

2. For a useful discussion of Chinese concerns about India, see Gary Klintworth, "Chinese Perspectives on India as a Great Power," in *India's Strategic Future: Regional State or Global Power?* ed. Ross Babbage and Sandy Gordon (Houndmills: Macmillan, 1992).

3. For a thoughtful assessment of Chinese reactions to the Indian nuclear test, see Mark W. Frazier, "China-India Relations since Pokhran II: Assessing Sources of Conflict," *AccessAsia Review* 3, no. 2 (July 2000); also see Ming Zhang, *China's Changing Nuclear Posture: Reactions to the South Asian Nuclear Tests* (Washington, D.C.: Carnegie Endowment for International Peace, 1999).

4. Denny Roy, *China's Foreign Relations* (Lanham, Md.: Rowman and Littlefield, 1998), 170.

5. Personal communication with Professor John Garver, Georgia Institute of Technology, Atlanta, Georgia, March 2001.

6. V. Sudarshan, "On the Li-war side," *Outlook,* 15 January 2001.

7. For one discussion of such questions, see Stratfor's Global Intelligence Update, "Asian Alliance on the Horizon," 14 October 1999, available at www.stratfors.com.

8. For an early and perceptive treatment of the 1962 border war, see S. S. Khera, *India's Defence Problem* (Bombay: Orient Longman, 1968).

9. The literature on this subject is far too vast to adequately catalog. For one assessment of British imperialism, see Sir Penderel Moon, *The British Conquest of India* (London: Duckworth, 1989). For the impact of European imperialism on China, see Jonathan Spence, *The Search for Modern China* (New York: Norton, 1990). Also see K. M. Pannikar, *Asia and Western Domination* (London: George Allen and Unwin, 1959).

10. On this point, see Gopal Krishna, "India and International Society," in *The Expansion of International Society,* ed. Hedley Bull and Adam Watson (Oxford: Clarendon, 1984).

11. For a discussion of the significance of colonially inherited borders in the context of the Sino-Indian border dispute, see Steven Hoffmann, *India and the China Crisis* (Berkeley: University of California Press, 1990).

12. For a discussion of Nehru's "discovery" of India, see Teresa Hubel, *Whose India? The Independence Struggle in British and Indian Fiction and History* (Durham, N.C.: Duke University Press, 1996).

13. This theme is discussed in Allen S. Whiting, *The Chinese Calculus of Deterrence: India and Indo-China* (Ann Arbor: University of Michigan Press, 1975).

14. For a comprehensive study of the legal dimensions of the Sino-Indian border question, see Alastair Lamb, *The McMahon Line: A Study in the Relations between India, China and Tibet,* vols. 1 and 2 (London: Routledge and Kegan Paul, 1966); also

see Alastair Lamb, *The Sino-Indian Border in Ladakh* (Canberra: Australian National University Press, 1973). For an alternative assessment, see Parshotam Mehra, *The McMahon Line and After* (Delhi: Macmillan, 1974); for a less legalistic and more geopolitical account, see John Rowland, *A History of Sino-Indian Relations: Hostile Co-Existence* (Princeton, N.J.: Van Nostrand, 1967), 25–40. Much of the evidence and argument presented here is derived from the excellent distillation of evidence presented in Hoffmann, *India and the China Crisis.*

15. For an excellent treatment of the evolution of India's border policies from the British colonial period to the postindependence era, see P. C. Chakravarti, *The Evolution of India's Northern Borders* (New Delhi: Asia Publishing House, 1971).

16. Pro-Chinese analysts, of course, question this contention. For statements of the Chinese position on the border alignments, see Liu Xuecheng, *The Sino-Indian Border Dispute and Sino-Indian Relations* (Lanham, Md.: University Press of America, 1994); and Neville Maxwell, *India's China War* (New York: Pantheon Books, 1970). For the evidentiary basis of the Indian claims, see the *Report of the Officials of the Governments of India and the People's Republic of China on the Boundary Question* (New Delhi: Ministry of External Affairs, 1962).

17. A substantial body of literature exists on this subject. See, for example, Girilal Jain, *Panchsheela and After: Sino-Indian Relations in the Context of the Tibetan Insurrection* (Bombay: Asia Publishing House, 1960); B. N. Mullik, *My Years with Nehru: The Chinese Betrayal* (Bombay: Allied Publishers, 1971). For a particularly pro-Chinese and vituperatively anti-Indian analysis of India's key decisions pertaining to the Sino-Indian border question, see Maxwell, *India's China War.*

18. On this point, see A. P. Rana, *The Imperatives of Nonalignment: A Conceptual Study of India's Foreign Policy in the Nehru Period* (Delhi: Macmillan, 1976).

19. Nehru's hostility toward the profession of arms is discussed carefully in Stephen P. Cohen, *The Indian Army: Its Contribution to the Development of a Nation* (Delhi: Oxford University Press, 1990).

20. For a detailed discussion of Nehru's commitment to economic development, see Francine R. Frankel, *India's Political Economy: The Gradual Revolution, 1947–1977* (Princeton, N.J.: Princeton University Press, 1978).

21. The Indo-Pakistani wars and crises are described and analyzed in Sumit Ganguly, *Conflict Unending: India-Pakistan Tensions since 1947* (New York: Columbia University Press; Washington, D.C.: Woodrow Wilson Center Press; and New Delhi: Oxford University Press, 2001).

22. The fear of a Bonapartist threat is discussed in Sumit Ganguly, "From the Defense of the Nation to Aid to the Civil: The Army in Contemporary India," in *Civil Military Interaction in Asia and Africa,* ed. Charles H. Kennedy and David J. Louscher (Leiden: E. J. Brill, 1991).

23. I use the term *appeasement* in its pristine, pre-Munich sense. In its original formulation "appeasement" did not have a negative connotation. It meant that states could accommodate the legitimate demands of rivals without compromising their own vital interests. For a particularly nuanced discussion of this subject, see Paul Kennedy, ed., *Strategy and Diplomacy, 1870–1945: Eight Studies* (London: Allen and Unwin, 1983).

24. P. C. Chakravarti, *India's China Policy* (Bloomington: Indiana University Press, 1962), 59.

25. An excellent account of Indian efforts to conciliate China can be found in Chakravarti, *India's China Policy.*

26. For a discussion of the Indian reaction to the Chinese conquest and occupation of Tibet, see Wayne A. Wilcox, *India, Pakistan and the Rise of China* (New York: Walker and Company, 1964), 48–49. For Nehru's utterly flawed assessment of the strategic impact of China's occupation of Tibet on Indian security, see the nuanced discussion in John W. Garver, *Protracted Contest: Sino-Indian Rivalry in the Twentieth Century* (Seattle: University of Washington Press, 2001), 50.

27. The question of Tibet's international legal personality is discussed in Michael C. van Walt van Praag, *The Status of Tibet: History, Rights, and Prospects in International Law* (Boulder, Colo.: Westview Press, 1987); for further historical evidence, see Hugh E. Richardson, *Tibet and Its History* (Boston: Shambala Press, 1984); for a more political account of Tibet's relationship with China, see Melvyn C. Goldstein, *The Snow Lion and the Dragon: China, Tibet and the Dalai Lama* (Berkeley: University of California Press, 1997).

28. This point is made in Wilcox, *India, Pakistan,* 53; on the latter issue, see Goldstein, *Snow Lion and the Dragon,* 46.

29. For an excellent discussion of the circumstances surrounding the formal incorporation of Tibet into China, see Tsering Shakya, *The Dragon in the Land of Snows* (New York: Penguin Compass, 1999), 523–71.

30. The politics surrounding the negotiation of the *Panch Shila* are dealt with in Rowland, *History of Sino-Indian Relations,* 84–87.

31. This issue is discussed with considerable care in Dawa Norbu, "Tibet in Sino-Indian Relations: The Centrality of Marginality," *Asian Survey* 37, no. 11 (November 1997): 1078–95.

32. For a first-person account of the Tibetan rebellion, see Gompo Tashi Andrugtsang, *Four Rivers, Six Ranges: A True Account of Khampa Resistance to Chinese in Tibet* (Dharamsala, India: Information and Publicity Office of the Dalai Lama, 1973).

33. For the Chinese attempts to change the social and political order of Tibet, see Dawa Norbu, *Red Star over Tibet* (London: Oxford University Press, 1987).

34. For a detailed account, see Shakya, *Dragon in the Land of Snows,* 140–41.

35. Garver, *Protracted Contest,* 22–56.

36. The details of American involvement with the Khampas can be found in Garver, *Protracted Contest,* 170–80; also see the account of a former Central Intelligence Agency case officer, John Kenneth Knaus, *Orphans of the Cold War: America and the Tibetan Struggle for Survival* (New York: Public Affairs Press, 1999).

37. For an insightful discussion of the intricacies of Indian decision making at this time, see Jain, *Panchsheela and After.*

38. For a discussion of Beijing's views, see Rowland, *History of Sino-Indian Relations,* 112–16. For an account that suggests that there was more active American involvement in the Tibetan revolt, see Whiting, *Chinese Calculus of Deterrence,* 12–19.

39. S. Mahmud Ali, *Cold War in the High Himalayas: The USA, China and South Asia in the 1950s* (London: Curzon Press, 1999), 78–79.

40. For a thoughtful discussion of Nehru's dilemma, see Knaus, *Orphans of the Cold War,* 169–70.

41. For the Chinese perspective on the disputed maps and Indian accusations of "cartographic aggression," see Liu, *Sino-Indian Border Dispute.*

42. Chakravarti, *India's China Policy,* 71.

43. Wilcox, *India, Pakistan,* 67.

44. Some uncertainty exists in India about the precise terms of Zhou's offer. A retired Indian foreign secretary who had dealt extensively with Sino-Indian relations, Jagat Mehta, categorically denied in a meeting in New Delhi in July 2000 that there was any such clear-cut offer from Zhou.

45. For a discussion of the concept of compellence, see Thomas Schelling, *Arms and Influence* (New Haven: Yale University Press, 1966).

46. Author interview with a senior retired Indian general, New Delhi, July 1988.

47. For an excellent discussion of the forward policy and its goals, see Lorne J. Kavic, *India's Quest for Security: Defence Policies, 1947–1965* (Berkeley: University of California Press, 1967).

48. For a remarkably candid and perceptive account of the Indian military debacle in the face of the Chinese attack, see Major-General D. K. Palit (ret.), *War in High Himalaya: The Indian Army in Crisis, 1962* (London: Hurst, 1991), 240–41.

49. For details of military operations see Palit, *War in High Himalaya.*

50. Kavic, *India's Quest,* 176.

51. Ibid., 184.

52. Ibid., 177.

53. Ibid., 182.

54. Ibid., 187.

55. For a thoughtful discussion of the shift in Indian foreign policy orientation, see Michael Brecher, "Non-Alignment under Stress: The West and the India-China Border War," *Pacific Affairs* 52, no. 4 (Winter 1979–80).

56. For a discussion of Indo-U.S. clandestine cooperation on the Tibetan question *after* the 1962 border war, see Shakya, *Dragon in the Land of Snows,* 286.

57. For a supple discussion of this period in U.S.-Indian relations, see Dennis Kux, *The United States and India: Estranged Democracies* (Washington, D.C.: National Defense University Press, 1996).

58. States, according to the canons of neorealist theory, have two basic strategies available to them to cope with extant security problems. They can either engage in "self-help," namely, mobilize internal resources to strengthen military capabilities, or they can forge an alliance with a stronger power or set of powers. For the standard statement on the subject, see Kenneth N. Waltz, *The Theory of International Politics* (New York: Addison Wesley, 1978).

59. For a detailed discussion of the evolution of this program after the 1962 border war, see Raju G. C. Thomas, *Indian Security Policy* (Princeton, N.J.: Princeton University Press, 1986). Also see Kavic, *India's Quest.*

60. Ganguly, *Conflict Unending.*

61. For a summary of the United Nations proceedings, see Jyoti Bhusan Das Gupta, *Jammu and Kashmir* (New Delhi: Martinus Nijhoff, 1968).

62. Shahid M. Amin, *Pakistan's Foreign Policy: A Reappraisal* (Karachi: Oxford University Press, 2000), 158.

63. Anwar Syed, *China and Pakistan: The Diplomacy of an Entente Cordiale* (Amherst: University of Massachusetts Press, 1974), 69–71.

64. On this point, see Dennis Kux, *The United States and Pakistan, 1947–2000: Disenchanted Allies* (Baltimore: Johns Hopkins University Press, 2001).

65. Syed, *China and Pakistan,* 84.

66. For details pertaining to the Indian reaction, see Russell Brines, *The Indo-Pakistani Conflict* (New York: Pall Mall, 1968).

67. Syed, *China and Pakistan.*

68. For a discussion of the forces that contributed to the Pakistani attack on India, see Ganguly, *Conflict Unending.*

69. The Chinese failure to more fully assist Pakistan during the 1965 war stemmed from a number of likely factors. First, the timing of the Pakistani attack made it exceedingly difficult for China to open a Himalayan front as most of the mountain passes were closed. Second, renewed Chinese hostilities along the border would, in all likelihood, have provoked an adverse American reaction. Third, China was also at odds with the Soviet Union, a state with which India had improved its ties.

70. For details, see Kux, *Disenchanted Allies.*

71. Garver, *Protracted Contest,* 213.

72. For a useful discussion of Pakistan's quest for nuclear weapons, see Ziba Moshaver, *Nuclear Weapons Proliferation on the Indian Subcontinent* (New York: St. Martin's Press, 1991).

73. Garver, *Protracted Contest,* 341.

74. One of the best sources is Ashley J. Tellis, *India's Emerging Nuclear Posture: Between Recessed Deterrence and Ready Arsenal* (Santa Monica, Calif.: RAND, 2001).

75. The politics surrounding this decision are discussed in Tellis, *Between Recessed Deterrence and Ready Arsenal.*

76. For a description and analysis of Chinese behavior during the 1965 border war see Sumit Ganguly, *The Crisis in Kashmir: Portents of War, Hopes of Peace* (Cambridge: Cambridge University Press; Washington, D.C.: Woodrow Wilson Center Press, 1999).

77. Mandavi Mahta, "India's Troubled Northeast," *South Asia Monitor,* 5 July 2001.

78. Dinesh Kotwal, "The Naga Insurgency: The Past and the Future," *Strategic Analysis* 24, no. 4 (July 2000): 751–72; for a discussion of China's involvement, see Sreeradha Datta, "Security of India's Northeast: External Linkages," *Strategic Analysis* 24, no. 8 (November 2000): 1495–1516; also see Onkar Marwah, "Northeastern India: New Delhi Confronts the Insurgents," *Orbis* 21, no. 1 (1977): 353–73; for evidence of China's decision to end support to the guerillas, see Garver, *Protracted Contest,* 94.

79. Author interview with Ambassador Brajesh Mishra, New Delhi, July 1988.

80. The war is described in some detail in Harrison Salisbury, *The Coming War between Russia and China* (London: Secker and Warburg, 1969).

81. For Chinese behavior during the 1971 crisis, see Ganguly, *Conflict Unending.*

82. For an assessment of foreign policy during the Janata years, see K. P. Mishra, ed., *Janata's Foreign Policy* (New Delhi: Vikas, 1979).

83. Sumit Ganguly, "The Sino-Indian Border Talks, 1981–1989: A View from New Delhi," *Asian Survey* 29, no. 12 (December 1989): 1123–35.

84. Author interview, Ministry of External Affairs, New Delhi, July 1989.

85. Garver, *Protracted Contest,* 103–5.

86. Rosemary Foot, "Sources of Conflict between China and India as Seen from Beijing," in *Mending Fences: Confidence and Security-Building Measures in South Asia,* ed. Sumit Ganguly and Ted Greenwood (Boulder, Colo.: Westview Press, 1997).

87. Interview with a senior Indian foreign service officer with long experience in Indo-Soviet relations, New York City, September 1986.

88. According to one prominent American scholar, the pressures that the Chinese exerted at Sumdurong Chu were directly linked to China's efforts to establish a claim on territory south of the McMahon Line. On this subject, see Garver, *Protracted Contest,* 105.

89. Much of this material has been drawn from Ganguly, "Sino-Indian Border Talks."

90. Swaran Singh, "Sino-Indian CBMs: Problems and Prospects," *Strategic Analysis* 20, no. 4 (1999): 543–59.

91. A decade after Rajiv Gandhi's visit, India has had no success in persuading China to change its position on the Kashmir dispute except in a mostly semantic fashion. Instead of unequivocally supporting the United Nations resolutions on Kashmir, China now alludes to the Shimla Agreement of 1972. However, Chinese officials categorically refuse to accept any suggestion that Tibet and Kashmir constitute similar problems. On this point, see "Chinese Ambassador to India Explains Chinese Foreign Policy, 'Kashmir Dispute and Tibet Are Totally Different Issues,'" *Mainstream,* 24 October 1998, 22–28. Some Indian commentators, however, deem the Chinese semantic shift on the Kashmir issue to be of symbolic value and therefore indicative of a shift in China's official attitude toward the Kashmir question.

92. Personal correspondence with an American strategic analyst, January 2001.

93. On this matter, see Garver, *Protracted Contest,* 172–73.

94. "Bhutan Today: India's Security Stakes Remain High," *The Statesman* (Calcutta), 25 August 2000.

95. For a discussion of Indian concerns about Chinese forays into Burma/Myanmar, see P. Stobdan, "China's Forays into Burma: Implications for India," *Strategic Analysis* 16, no. 1 (April 1993): 21–37; also see Garver, *Protracted Contest,* 242–74.

96. For an assessment of these reports, see Renato Cruz De Castro, "Probing the Bounds of the Post-1991 Sino-Indian Rapprochement: A Focus on the Border Talks," *Issue and Studies* 35, no. 3 (May–June 1999): 61–104.

97. The full range of measures are discussed in the "Agreement between the Government of the Republic of India and the Government of the People's Republic of China on Confidence-Building Measures in the Military Field along the Line of Actual Control in the India-China Border Areas," New Delhi, 29 November 1996, text available at www.stimson.org.

98. De Castro, "Probing the Bounds," 95.

99. Atul Aneja, "India, China Seek to Narrow Down Differences," *Hindu,* 14 February 2001.

100. For an earlier assessment that reached similar conclusions, see John W. Garver, "China and South Asia," *Annals* 519 (January 1992).

101. P. Jayaram, "Differences Persist over Nuclear Issue with China," *India Abroad,* 23 February 2001, 18.

102. For some discussion of this issue, see John W. Garver, "The China-India-U.S. Triangle: Strategic Relations in the Post–Cold War Era," *NBR Analysis* 13, no. 5 (October 2002).

103. M. G. G. Pillai, "Archipelago of Dreams," *Outlook,* 12 February 2001, available at www.outlookindia.com.

104. For a discussion of India's overtures toward Vietnam and Japan, see Nayan Chanda, "After the Bomb," *Far Eastern Economic Review,* 13 April 2000, 20. For a discussion of Jaswant Singh's visit to Burma/Myanmar, see Celia W. Dugger, "Indian

Aide's Visit Warms Ties with Burmese Junta," *New York Times,* 16 February 2001, A10; also see Syed Zarir Hussain and P. Jayaram, "'Look East' Policy Now Also Includes Myanmar," *India Abroad,* 23 February 2001, 18.

105. For a detailed discussion of the rise of radical Islamic fervor in China, see Dru C. Gladney, *Muslim Chinese: Ethnic Nationalism in the People's Republic* (Cambridge: Council on East Asian Studies, Harvard University, 1996); for China's concerns about Islamic radicalism in Xinjiang and its concomitant willingness to shift its position on the Kashmir dispute, see Roy, *China's Foreign Relations,* 173.

106. Surjit Mansingh and Steven I. Levine, "China and India: Moving beyond Confrontation," *Problems of Communism* 38, nos. 2–3 (March–June 1989): 49.

107. See Sujit Dutta, "Sino-Indian Diplomatic Negotiations: A Preliminary Assessment," *Strategic Analysis* 22, no. 12 (March 1999): 1821–34.

108. Reuters, "India, China to Exchange Maps on Himalayan Border," 28 June 2001, available at www.chinaonline.com.

109. "Border Talks with China 'Friendly': India," *Indian Express,* 29 June 2001, available at www.expressindia.com.

110. For a chronology and discussion of key statements, see B. Raman, "Sino-Indian Relations: A Chronology," South Asia Analysis Group Papers, 23 April 1999, available at www.saag.org/papers/paper49.html.

111. V. Mohan Narayan and Anil K. Joseph, "India, China Agree on Timeframe to Clarify LAC," 29 March 2002, available at www.rediff.com/news/2002/mar/29china2.htm.

112. Narayan and Joseph, "India, China Agree on Timeframe."

113. Some commentators have suggested an alternative explanation, namely, that China wants to defer the settlement until such time as it is militarily more powerful and has resolved the Taiwan question to its advantage. An anonymous reviewer of this manuscript made this suggestion.

114. Personal correspondence with senior Ministry of External Affairs and Ministry of Defense officials, August 2001.

5

China and India in Asia

Ashley J. Tellis

For most of the postwar period, Sino-Indian political interactions in Asia attracted little interest. Although both states had great potential power, they were still relatively weak entities in Asian geopolitics: emerging as new political entities after World War II, they confronted enormous problems of economic development, political restructuring, and social stability. Nonetheless, China and India appeared destined for competition almost from the moment of their creation as modern states. The history of this competition has been explored in great and revealing detail elsewhere.[1] This chapter explores future Chinese and Indian interactions in Asia. It is divided into four sections. The first briefly examines the structural context defining future Sino-Indian relations. The second section describes the key drivers underlying this bilateral relationship and explains how critical political dilemmas have led both Beijing and New Delhi toward strategic interactions beyond their immediate geographic locale, in the larger theater of the Asian continent. The third examines specific subregions within Asia where

Chinese and Indian interests are likely to intersect and with what effects. The conclusion briefly summarizes the characteristics of Sino-Indian competition in Asia and their implications for U.S. interests.

The Structural Context of Sino-Indian Relations in Asia

The potential for Sino-Indian interactions to play out in Asia writ large is driven by three factors. To begin with, the growing economic strength and rising geopolitical standing of the two countries will reinforce the view in Beijing and New Delhi that the Asian continent remains the most appropriate arena for their ambitions, even as they seek to accumulate the capabilities necessary to underwrite more extensive aspirations. The relatively high growth rates exhibited in China since 1978 and in India since 1991 suggest that the desire to play a greater political role may actually be sustained by the underlying material expansion.[2] When this economic performance is assessed relative to that of other Asian countries such as Japan, Korea, and Indonesia in the 2000–2015 time frame, a truly dramatic reordering of power-political patterns in Asia seems possible. One analysis has concluded, for example, that if current trends hold, the Chinese and the Indian economies will become the two largest economies in Asia by 2015 when measured in 1998 U.S. dollars based on purchasing power parity.[3]

If this projection is borne out, the Chinese and Indian economies could provide their state managers with the resources necessary to pursue wider strategic interests across the continent. This does not imply that Chinese and Indian power will suddenly become visible in every corner of Asia, or that their military capabilities will palpably appear in every one of its subregions, but rather that the traditional image of China and India remaining confined primarily to their limited and separate regional worlds will become less and less accurate. In fact, the growing ability of both states to dominate their immediate geographic locales economically (and perhaps even politically) while sustaining—if not enlarging—their power-political capabilities will inevitably compel China and India to interact in other subregions, either to secure access to resources or to forestall the other from acquiring the preponderant influence.

While growing economic and military capabilities will thus propel China and India to expand their interests beyond East and South Asia, respectively, the impetus for such interactions will also derive from their desire to co-opt the United States into helping them resolve their mutual security dilemmas and those that may arise in their relationships with other Asian states—even as this mutual and possibly competitive desire for American support is likely to be exploited by the United States itself to preserve its own primacy and stabilize the international order. The critical role of the United States in conditioning Sino-Indian interactions in Asia cannot be underestimated. The United States will certainly remain a hegemonic power in Asia at least until 2025, with strong economic links to the Asian trading and innovation system, a set of alliances that guarantee access, and unmatched forward-based and forward-deployed military capabilities.[4] Future Sino-Indian interactions in Asia will occur, therefore, under the shadow of superior American power. Given this fact, both China and India will seek to entice the United States into supporting their strategic preferences vis-à-vis one another, with India rather than China possibly leaning more heavily on the United States because of its own relative weakness. Both China and India also need at least American acquiescence, if not assistance, if they are to resolve security problems involving other states such as potential Taiwanese independence, contested territorial claims in the South China Sea, the possible rearmament of Japan, and the potential dangers of a Chinese-supported Pakistan.

Although American hegemony will condition Sino-Indian interactions in Asia in different ways, that hegemony will not always be engaged as a result of Sino-Indian competition. In some instances, China and India could cooperate to limit U.S. actions, for example, with respect to aspects of state sovereignty, human rights, global governance, environmental management, and humanitarian intervention. Such Sino-Indian cooperation is unlikely to be either durable or robust, but it could be significant in any given instance. What complicates matters, however, is that the United States will not always passively receive competitive Chinese and Indian attention, but often enough will actively play off China and India against each other to garner support for maintaining a stable Asian international order that has as a crucial component the preservation of American primacy.[5] Sino-Indian interactions in Asia are thus likely to become far more complex than they would otherwise be, because the United States is liable to be just as active in soliciting Chinese and Indian cooperation in support of its own objectives even as the two Asian states seek U.S. assistance in furthering their own.

Sino-Indian relations in Asia will thus be driven, first, by the growth of Chinese and Indian economic and military capabilities and, second, by the interaction of their interests with those of the United States. The third and final variable defining the complexity of these relations will be the critical role played by the other Asian states. Those states are likely to become active participants in any future Sino-Indian interaction: although mostly weaker than China or India, they would probably pursue their own national goals, either independently or as part of a coalition that includes other regional or extraregional powers (like the United States). Irrespective of the strategies chosen, all the Asian states actively participating in the Sino-Indian relationship will seek to play off the two major regional powers against one another so as to secure some benefit for themselves, even if in the process they turn out to be more valuable to the principals than the principals are to them.

The potentially crucial role of the other Asian states in the presumed Sino-Indian competition, therefore, implies that whatever Chinese or Indian preferences may initially be, they will never obtain in pure form. Instead, they will be mediated through both the processes of mutual competition and the preferences of those states that appear to be bystanders. Since many of the regional states will exploit Sino-Indian competition just as much as China and India seek to take advantage of them, the Sino-Indian interaction in Asia will thus be considerably more complex than is suggested by any crude model of dyadic rivalry. Thanks to the exigencies of both power and history, this interaction will be influenced, first, by the continental presence of the United States. Because this presence is likely to continue well into the future, it will have many derivative effects, among the most important of which will be its ability to empower the peripheral Asian states that seek American assistance in coping with the uncertainties of future Sino-Indian competition. Even states that forgo U.S. assistance could cope with the challenges imposed by such competition through other means such as participation in local coalitions, bandwagoning with other regional powers, continued nonalignment, or accepting protection from one protagonist in the rivalry. All told, therefore, mapping the patterns of Sino-Indian interactions in Asia requires sensitivity to many more factors than simply dyadic rivalry between China and India.

The Drivers of Sino-Indian Competition and Their Carryover into Asia

Ever since the Sino-Indian conflict of 1962, relations between China and India have remained unsettled. The overt tensions that dominated their interactions into the 1980s have dissipated, but latent suspicions remain.[6] The reasons for this precarious equilibrium are not hard to find. India views China as the most important constraint on its search for security and status in Asia. Although Pakistan has been India's most immediate and nettlesome security problem, Indian policy makers recognize that the subcontinental balance of power more than favors New Delhi over Islamabad. They appreciate, however, that Pakistan's ability to mitigate its unfavorable position is rooted in the assistance it has received from extraregional states, especially China. To that degree, Beijing's relationship with Islamabad functions as the critical impediment that prevents the fullest normalization of Sino-Indian ties that might otherwise be possible. Current Chinese activities in Myanmar (Burma) exacerbate this problem further. Perceived in the context of past Chinese initiatives vis-à-vis the other small South Asian states, these actions are seen as an effort on Beijing's part to undercut New Delhi's natural dominance in South Asia: they compel India to commit resources toward maintaining its preeminence within the subcontinent instead of allocating them toward expanding its sphere of influence in other areas that might be of greater significance to China.

This "indirect strategy" of confining India within South Asia through the use of multiple "proxies" is viewed by many Indian analysts as both deceptive and sinister insofar as it allows Beijing to garner all the benefits arising from improved bilateral relations at a diplomatic level even as China implements a larger grand strategy aimed at containing India as a future competitor. As one Indian analyst concluded, "While China professes a policy of peace and friendliness towards India, its deeds are clearly aimed at the *strategic encirclement of India* in order to marginalise India in Asia and tie it down to the Indian sub-continent."[7] Such perceptions gain greater credence in Indian assessments because of other outstanding issues such as the Chinese unwillingness to rapidly settle the disputed border; China's disinclination to recognize Sikkim's merger with India (even as it insists on India's recognition of Tibet as an inalienable part of China); the fear that China might resume support for the insurgency in the Indian northeast; and the persistent Chinese reluctance to admit that its nuclear capabilities threaten India. Taken together, these issues leave many Indian elites and policy makers distrustful of China.

Because, as states, India is weaker than China, New Delhi is more concerned about China's capabilities, intentions, and policies than Beijing is concerned about those of India. Such a pattern is not surprising because in any relationship between unequals, the weaker is usually more anxious about the policies of the stronger. This dynamic, for example, explains why Pakistan is far more obsessed with India than India is with Pakistan—and if New Delhi does not betray a comparable fixation with Beijing, it is only because the exigencies of history and the asymmetry of relative capabilities in the Sino-Indian case are far less acute than they are in the case of India and Pakistan. Given the peculiar relationships between unequal states, China's supposed indifference toward India cannot be used to justify the conclusion that New Delhi's concerns about its northern neighbor are misplaced because the evidentiary record corroborates a consistent Chinese anxiety only about Northeast and Southeast Asia to the relative neglect of its southwestern periphery, including South Asia.[8]

That China's southwestern periphery has less salience than that of maritime Asia is undeniable, but the lack of priority here does not equate to neglect. Rather, the disparity between Chinese and Indian capabilities, their relative international standing, and the character of their immediate threats (India's, emanating from an adjacent land power, demands far more attention than the more extended sea and air power challenges faced by China today) has enabled Beijing to do much with little. Aided by favorable geography, adequate conventional capabilities, robust nuclear forces, and effective, if only tacit, allies within South Asia, China could afford to treat India as a lesser priority because so long as the latter did not actively undercut Chinese interests—either by supporting insurgencies and separatist movements within Chinese territory, by developing nuclear capabilities aimed at Chinese targets, or by fostering counterencirclement strategies—Beijing could be satisfied that its current geopolitical strategy vis-à-vis India would suffice to ensure security along its southwestern frontier.

Broadly speaking, this strategy has five components: first, a feigned indifference toward India coupled with the consistent denial that New Delhi remains a potential rival;[9] second, an effort to minimize direct conventional military competition with India, even as Beijing continues subtly to treat New Delhi as a significant nuclear threat;[10] third, maintenance of an enduring strategic relationship with Pakistan while avoiding any encouragement of Islamabad's revisionist policies toward India;[11] fourth, bolstering of Chinese links with various Southeast Asian states while remaining engaged with the smaller countries within South Asia;[12] fifth—and as part of a larger grand strategy that transcends India—a continued focus on maintaining a high economic growth rate that attracts increased foreign investment, produces growing international political status, and generates a larger quantum of resources for power-political purposes.[13]

When these five elements of China's strategy toward India are viewed in their totality, the evidence suggests that Beijing has paid New Delhi more geostrategic attention than it has been willing to publicly admit and, further, has put in place an effective defensive policy that makes its relative disregard of India a justifiable entailment of its larger grand strategy. Accordingly, the purported Chinese *neglect* of India must be judged a myth. The facts suggest instead that China views India very much as a potential challenger, albeit a lower-order threat, but recognizes that only benefits accrue from its consistent refusal to own up to this perception. At the very least, such reticence holds the potential of mitigating active security competition with India at a time when New Delhi has formidable conventional superiority along the disputed Himalayan frontiers, but, more important, Beijing faces far more formidable challenges—among them, the possibility of Taiwanese independence, potential U.S. military intervention in a Sino-Taiwanese conflict, Japanese rearmament, the potential for new regionwide balancing in the face of growing Chinese power, and, finally, its own need to preserve a pacific geopolitical environment so that it may complete its ongoing economic reform and technological modernization. Further, the refusal to name India as a potential rival could help to dampen tensions along China's southwestern frontier and contribute greatly to denying New Delhi the status that would accrue if it were to be viewed by Beijing as a genuine, if only long-term, competitor. It is not surprising, therefore, that these two benefits—when combined with the fruits of the surreptitious investments already made in deepening Indian enmeshment within South Asia—are attractive to Beijing, given the many and complex domestic and international problems that China must surmount if it is to sustain its rise to power.

Even as it proceeds along this trajectory, however, China has to confront important, potentially unsettling realities with respect to India. First, unlike most of the states located along its periphery, India is large and represents a substantial concentration of economic, political, and military capabilities. India's sheer size and location make it difficult for Beijing to forget New Delhi altogether, in part because India's strong and continuing grievance about "status incongruity" in international politics—that is, the discrepancy between India's standing as a "great civilization" and its lack of status as a "great power"—could result in strategic surprises by India that redound to China's disadvantage. This issue holds special significance because India remains, together with Japan and Russia, one of three major contestants for influence in Asia and one with whom China also shares a disputed land border.

Second, India's large and competent conventional military forces, especially their advantages in logistics and air power, could pose a significant military threat to the Chinese southwest. Coupled with the continuing weaknesses in Chinese political control, especially in Tibet, and the possibility that future Indian strategies could justify actively assisting the Tibetan resistance, the character of both India's political objectives and its military presence vis-à-vis the Chinese borderlands remain issues that Beijing cannot ignore. The certain emergence of India's nuclear capabilities over time—capabilities that will transform India's current abject vulnerability with respect to China into something resembling a mutual vulnerability, attenuating many of Beijing's present strategic advantages—will only compound the challenges.

Finally, India's emerging economic strength and its geophysical location make it relevant to China's long-term security in multiple ways: India could become a major regional rival for influence in Central and Southeast Asia and in the Persian Gulf; its large and growing naval capabilities will dominate the sea lanes through which will pass most of the oil supplies vital for China's energy security; and India's capabilities, fears, and location make it a potential link in any containment strategy that might be developed either independently by the countries of maritime Asia or in concert with the United States. In the context of the last issue particularly, Beijing cannot afford to place much faith in the common Sino-Indian desire for "multipolarity" because American unipolarity offers India geopolitical advantages that are far more attractive to New Delhi than any prospective multipolarity that brings with it grave imbalances in future Sino-Indian power.

Given all these considerations, Beijing has no alternative but to treat India warily. Not surprisingly, India in turn has responded to China's prevailing strategy with a subtle, multidimensional approach of its own.

First, it has avoided picking rhetorical, political, and military fights with China to the maximum degree possible.[14] Consistent with this, New Delhi has negotiated a variety of confidence-building measures with Beijing; it has persisted in negotiations relating to the border dispute, even in the face of sluggish progress resulting from Chinese prevarication; it has accepted the Chinese principle that intractable issues ought to be put on the back burner so that they may not impede improving relations; and it has attempted to assuage core Chinese concerns on important sovereignty disputes over Taiwan and Tibet by essentially accepting Beijing's claims even as it has sustained a quiet dialogue with the Taiwanese and provided asylum to thousands of Tibetan refugees. Even on issues that directly threaten India's security—such as the transfer of nuclear and missile technology to Pakistan and Beijing's targeting of India with nuclear weapons—Indian policy makers have been reticent to challenge Chinese actions publicly. Instead, they have responded by either complaining politely to the United States or obliquely mumbling to various Chinese counterparts during bilateral meetings.

Second, India has sought to improve relations with China in those areas where rapid improvement is possible. The most critical area of convergence is economic relations, particularly bilateral trade.[15] India has endeavored to expand the volume and composition of trade with Beijing, and it has sought to enlarge the number of border outposts through which local, cross-Himalayan trade is conducted. Outside of trade issues, however, Chinese and Indian interests also converge with respect to the fight against terrorism, the threat of fundamentalist Islam, Western pressures with regard to human rights, fears of American intervention in sensitive domestic political questions, and a gamut of international problems such as the environment, intellectual property rights, and restrictive technology control regimes. Although India has *not* gone out of its way to seek or express solidarity with China on these issues, Indian policy makers clearly recognize a useful potential for convergent political action, and, hence, they have been careful not to foreclose possibilities for collaboration in the future.

Third, even as India has attempted to minimize discord with China, it has sought to protect itself against the worst should Sino-Indian relations sour. The decision to test its nuclear capabilities and develop a modest deterrent is the best example of such an insurance policy. Other examples include its determination to continue its long-postponed conventional force modernization and to pursue research and development efforts in traditional strategic technologies as well as in newer, leading-edge areas such as information technology, biotechnology, aviation, and advanced materials and manufacturing. The pursuit of these insurance policies suggests that while New Delhi seeks to improve relations with Beijing, it is not blind to the ways Chinese power could undercut its interests. Therefore, a continued commitment to maintaining India's defensive capabilities, primarily through domesticating the best military technologies available, remains at the heart of India's security policy.[16]

Fourth, the prospect of having to cope with a powerful China has stimulated India to revitalize its relations with the peripheral Asian states. Southeast Asia and East Asia, long neglected by Indian diplomacy, now form the core of India's extraregional economic and political outreach.[17] Reaching out to other states that may one day feel threatened by Chinese actions represents a clever effort at adding India's geopolitical weight to the evolving regional balance of power without compromising New Delhi's desire to maintain freedom of action. Even as it has reached out to the Asian rimlands, however, India has salvaged its previously disrupted military supply relationship with Russia, while forging significant new relations with second-tier suppliers like France and Israel and dramatically transforming its relations on various fronts with the United States.

The interaction of these multidimensional strategies pursued by both sides suggests that the judgment advanced almost a decade ago still holds: "The Sino-Indian relationship is . . . an uneasy one. India still regards nuclear China as a major threat to its security. It sees China's South Asian policies as anti-Indian, divisive, opportunistic and interfering. China perceives India to be an ambitious, overconfident yet militarily powerful neighbor with whom it may eventually have to have a day of reckoning."[18]

With sentiments such as these defining Sino-Indian relations, it is not surprising that policy makers in both capitals hold mutual suspicions; though it must be noted that Chinese security managers take India a tad more seriously than is commonly believed—if their strategic decisions have any geopolitical significance—while Indian policy makers are far less fearful about China than is commonly believed.[19] In any event, both sides have attempted to repair their relationship since 1988, endeavoring to manage mutual competition and encourage cooperation in at least those areas where joint gains might be achieved. In the areas of bilateral trade and maintaining tranquility along the Line of Actual Control, significant progress has occurred. Yet on the critical problems bedeviling the relationship—the border dispute, horizontal proliferation, and competitive efforts at encirclement and counterencirclement—little has been accomplished. To the degree that mutual suspicions have been the chief culprit, they have not been allayed by the fact that the two sides have moved asymmetrically to address them. If the public record is anything to go by, India appears to be far more anxious than China is to discuss the core problems afflicting the relationship. Where these issues are concerned, New Delhi appears to be convinced that resolving them speedily would offer the best opportunity to eliminate the thorniest mutual dilemmas and thereby shape the two states' larger interactions in Asia in more cooperative ways. Beijing, by contrast, has not displayed a comparable alacrity in engaging these questions, in part because of other, more pressing problems.

Other considerations intervene as well. So long as China's policies of strategic insurance vis-à-vis India remain fairly robust, policy makers in Beijing do not feel compelled to resolve disputes with New Delhi quickly. As far as the border dispute is concerned, for example, they reckon that the balance of power between China and India today is sufficiently stable that no disadvantage results from their unwillingness to resolve this disagreement. Further, they believe that the balance of power will only tilt further in their direction, and, consequently, they will have more options when the dispute must finally be engaged. With respect to horizontal proliferation, they recognize that no advantage inheres in any change in their current behavior: China has not suffered any penalties worth the name for its infraction of various nonproliferation regimes, and, if anything, it has been advantaged by the reality that India now has to cope with two effective nuclear adversaries rather than one. Because the Chinese recognize that India's evolving nuclear capabilities will not challenge the existing Sino-Indian nuclear balance, assistance to Pakistan can continue at whatever pace Beijing desires. With respect to the competitive encirclement-counter-encirclement dynamic, Chinese strategists view such developments as part of the rough-and-tumble of international politics. They are not convinced that any benefits will flow from discussing their third-country strategic relationships with India, except generally; and, even if they did enter into such discussions, they are unlikely to be persuaded to modify those relationships simply because of New Delhi's concerns about them. On balance, therefore, there appear to be good reasons why the speedy resolution of the bilateral irritants that India desires may not hold a candle from a Chinese perspective. It may be an error in judgment on Beijing's part, but so long as this conviction holds, Indian apprehensions about Chinese intentions and interests will only grow—as will, in turn, Chinese anxiety about Indian initiatives in Asia and beyond.

A significant by-product of the failure of both sides to resolve outstanding disputes is that these problems will cease to remain primarily localized matters but will appear instead as part of a larger struggle for power and security in Asia. In part, the "amplification" of particular Sino-Indian disputes onto the larger Asian canvas will occur because of concurrent Chinese and Indian economic growth, the unavoidable engagement with the United States, and the critical interactions with various Asian states. But it is also likely to receive a fillip from several other factors: first, the increasing emphasis by both sides on the "indirect approach" to competition, in addition to all the old instruments of direct rivalry; second, the emerging changes in military technology, which will compel both sides to operate across wider geostrategic spaces; third, the ongoing efforts by both sides to develop extra–South Asian strategic relationships that will inevitably expand this competition; and, fourth, the complexity of evolving Sino-Indian relations, which have expanded to include both economic instruments relating to prosperity and ideational and institutional instruments pertaining to the recognition of status. In the final analysis, therefore, even purely bilateral Sino-Indian interactions are certain to carry over to the Asian continent writ large simply because of their growing multidimensionality. Since every major regional actor in Asia, not to mention the United States, is likely to be involved in these interactions over the next two decades, it should not be surprising to find that what began as a local affair could potentially have wider geostrategic consequences.

Analyzing Specific Sino-Indian Interactions

When Sino-Indian security interdependence is analyzed more finely, most of the critical interactions materialize along three broad dimensions: the struggle for security; the accumulation of wealth; and the recognition of status. As figure 5.1 indicates, some problem issues appear at the interstices of these dimensions, while others remain unique to each. Of the three

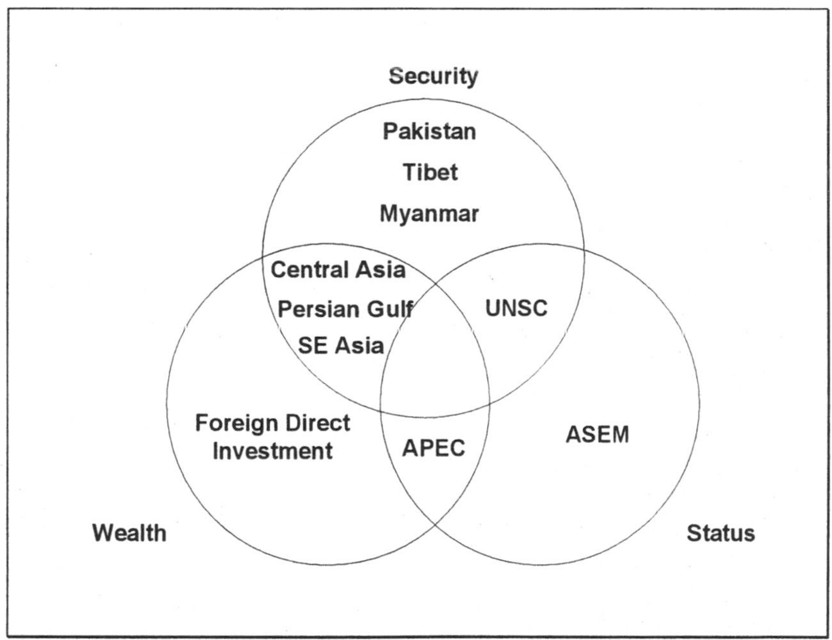

Figure 5.1 *Sino-Indian interactions along three dimensions. APEC = Asia-Pacific Cooperation; UNSC = UN Security Council; ASEM = Asia-Europe Meeting*

dimensions, the struggle for security is likely to be the most important because of its impact on the physical safety and political autonomy of both protagonists; it is followed in importance by the quest for wealth and the recognition of status. This section reviews each issue identified in the graphic and briefly assesses the outcomes for Sino-Indian interactions as a triangular product of (1) the convergence or conflict in key Sino-Indian objectives; (2) their intersection with the United States; and (3) the particular objectives of the local states.

The Struggle for Security

The following simple and direct issues of security impinge directly on Chinese and Indian safety.

Pakistan

Ordinarily, the issue of Pakistan would not pose a problem for Sino-Indian relations, since the most important elements of the dispute—territory, ideology, and power-political ordering—relate primarily to India and Pakistan. Pakistan, however, has become a critical issue in Sino-Indian relations because of, first, the Chinese decision to supply Pakistan with nuclear and missile technologies[20] and, second, the Pakistani attempt at exploiting these capabilities to prosecute a low-intensity war against India.[21] Both components directly affect Indian security because they reinforce India's perception of China as a strategic competitor and as a direct security threat. Many Western and Indian analysts believe that Beijing transferred nuclear technologies to Pakistan with the principal intention of constraining India.[22] Irrespective of whether this is actually the case, Chinese horizontal proliferation to Pakistan certainly increased the threat posed to India. With successive developments in New Delhi's nuclear weapon program, the Indocentric rationale for continued Chinese strategic transfers to Pakistan appears to have strengthened further, as was evident from the spurt in Chinese assistance to Pakistan following India's May 1998 nuclear tests. From Beijing's perspective, however, such assistance is intended solely for the defense of Pakistan against India and is intended neither to underwrite nor to endorse Islamabad's wars against New Delhi.

Pakistan, unfortunately, appears to have other ideas. Given its anti–status quo orientation in South Asia, Islamabad has sought to use its nuclear capabilities not simply for deterrence but to secure contested political goals.

First, Islamabad believes that its nuclear weapons create permissive conditions that enable it to pursue policies of "strategic diversion"[23]—that is, to enervate India through low-intensity conflict waged by proxy on the expectation that New Delhi cannot retaliate conventionally for fear of sparking a nuclear holocaust.[24] Second, Islamabad with views nuclear weapons as critical for both deterrence and defense insofar as they function as the means by which Pakistan can ward off—through an operational strategy resembling "flexible response"—the worst Indian conventional counterresponses that may be precipitated by Islamabad's efforts at strategic diversion.[25] Finally, Islamabad views nuclear weapons as catalytic instruments that ensure international intervention on Pakistan's behalf should a South Asian political-military crisis threaten to spin out of control.[26]

Recognizing the potential for serious crises, China has clearly signaled the limits of its support to Islamabad. Depending on the circumstances, China might extend Pakistan every form of diplomatic and moral support that it believes is justified; it might even be willing to provide Islamabad with the military instruments necessary to preserve its security, but it will neither provide Pakistan any formal guarantees of security nor extend deterrence. Nor will it prepare joint defenses that imply coordinated military action against India. These factors suggest that China has pursued a rather subtle partnership with Pakistan: it will do the minimum necessary to preserve Pakistani security from a distance, but it has sought to avoid overt entanglements.[27] Thus, for example, China has moved away from its previously unqualified support of the Pakistani position on Kashmir, and it had signaled its displeasure with Islamabad's support of the Taliban well before the events of September 11 precipitated a change in Pakistan's strategic policies vis-à-vis Kabul. Beijing's low-cost/high-payoff commitment to Pakistani security, therefore, does not translate into support for Pakistani revisionism.[28]

Whether Pakistan will remain a trigger for intense future Sino-Indian competition, then, depends on several variables. First, if the Indian nuclear program makes technological strides and acquires a manifestly anti-Chinese orientation, the incentives for Beijing to respond with changes in its own nuclear posture and to increase assistance to the Pakistani program will grow. Second, if Sino-U.S. relations deteriorate either because of political reasons or because of technical changes in the current offense-dominant global nuclear order, Beijing will have greater incentive to respond by increasing strategic assistance to Pakistan, if for no other reason than to "get back" at the United States. Third, if Pakistan grows weaker, is increasingly dominated by Islamists of various stripes, and pursues an ideological foreign policy aimed at exporting a *jehadi* ideology, China's incentives to support Pakistan will decrease. Other factors will also condition the relevance of Pakistan as a trigger in Sino-Indian relations: these include the state of U.S.-Indian relations, the possibility of anti-Chinese coalitions developing in maritime Asia, and the relative economic performance in China and India. When all these factors are considered, Pakistan is likely not only to remain a serious problem in Sino-Indian relations but also to compel India to pursue indirect approaches more resolutely to even the score with China.

Tibet

Tibet exemplifies a situation in which India could respond by indirect strategies to any future augmentation of the challenge that China poses to India via Pakistan. On the face of it again, Tibet ought not become an issue in Sino-Indian relations. After all, China's political and military presence on the Tibetan plateau has been established since 1950, and under the terms of the 1954 Sino-Indian agreement, India has recognized China's sovereignty over Tibet. As one scholar noted, "by the terms of this treaty, India gave up all the special privileges in Tibet it had inherited from the British," which in effect "signified India's acquiescence to China's conquest of Tibet."[29]

Therefore, at the legal level, the issue of Tibet as a potential trigger in Sino-Indian competition is nonexistent; however, it remains a source of tension. This concern is rooted in several mutually reinforcing realities. To begin with, the indigenous Tibetan population has been struggling to recover the autonomy that the Tibetan state enjoyed during the last decades of the Qing dynasty. The brutal Chinese occupation of Tibet in 1950 resulted in a significant emigration of Tibetans to India. Their spiritual head, the Dalai Lama, and a large Tibetan exile community live in northern India. While most Tibetans in the Tibet Autonomous Region (TAR) have reluctantly come to terms with Chinese rule, this "accommodation" has always been highly unstable, and the repeated Chinese attempts at repopulating Tibet with Han Chinese, repressing Tibetan Buddhism, and manipulating monastery politics in Tibet have resulted in the resident populace constantly seeking to redefine the meaning of Tibetan autonomy within the framework of the Chinese state. This process has only been helped by the fact that the Tibetan cause enjoys considerable visibility in the United

States; the Dalai Lama is an articulate spokesman for the cause of autonomy; and the Tibetan exiles abroad remain a significant political "force-in-being" which, assisted by the United States and India, has in the past undertaken costly resistance operations against the People's Liberation Army. So long as these ingredients persist, China's control over its Tibetan territories will remain relatively infirm, and, by implication, the possibilities of serious discord remain.[30]

It is in this context that Chinese concerns about Indian intentions become critical. Despite the fact that India has recognized Chinese "suzerainty" over Tibet, Beijing realizes that the material ingredients for change in India's diplomatic position already exist. The Dalai Lama, although living in controlled conditions in India, has a large following in the West and could become the nucleus of more active Tibetan resistance should altered geopolitical circumstances make such a change viable. Further, India houses a large body of second-generation Tibetan exiles who believe that the Dalai Lama's pacifist politics have been unsuccessful and who consequently appear willing to spearhead more radical challenges to Chinese rule. More important, Indian elites display an increased willingness to play a more hard-nosed game of political bargaining with China over Tibet. Arguing that China has continually undermined Indian security interests with impunity, whether through support of insurgency movements, or through nuclear transfers to Pakistan, or through a refusal to compromise on the border dispute, these constituencies have urged their government to give China only as much reassurance about long-standing Indian commitments on Tibet as India receives in terms of Chinese sensitivity to its own interests. Finally, the critical imponderable in this whole process remains the United States. The growing American perception of China as a strategic competitor coupled with long-standing U.S. concerns about Tibetan autonomy for all the motives unique to liberal societies increases the chances that the United States could intensify its support for Tibetan autonomy, which Beijing fears could only provide more opportunities for potential competitors like India to further undermine its objective of "national reunification." Not surprisingly, then, almost every bilateral Sino-Indian colloquy ends with the expectation that India will reaffirm its 1954 position on Tibet—an expectation that seems to be grounded in the Chinese belief that a repeated incantation of the Indian position serves to bind New Delhi publicly to policies that cohere with Chinese interests.

The Indian government, thus far, has shied away from adopting any positions that intimate a reconsideration of its 1954 agreement. This is in spite of the fact that New Delhi recognizes Tibetan autonomy, if not independence, as a desirable outcome: a genuine autonomy would attenuate the threat posed by Chinese military forces along India's northern frontier; it would almost eliminate the border dispute; and it would restore the geopolitical balances within the Indian subcontinent by eliminating the threat of a two-front war that would reduce India's freedom of action versus Pakistan. The costs of pursuing such an objective by repudiating the 1954 agreement, however, are correctly seen as high, and consequently New Delhi has refrained from pursuing Tibetan autonomy as an objective of state policy. The problem of Tibet, however, demonstrates that forces outside the direct strategies adopted by China and India could affect even issues appearing to be only bilateral. These forces include, for example, the success of China's efforts at distributing the fruits of its economic reforms more equitably among its constituent provinces; the future of Tibetan nationalism after the passing of the present Dalai Lama; the complex character of monastery politics; the psychology of the second generation of Tibetan exiles in India; and, last, the willingness of the United States, and the West more generally, to support Tibetan resistance against what is ordinarily quite oppressive Chinese rule. These factors taken together suggest that Tibet will remain "an enduring irritant"[31] in the relationship between China and India, because—the latter's formal accommodation notwithstanding—the material elements that stabilize the present equilibrium could change quite dramatically thanks to events beyond the control of Beijing and New Delhi and, in so doing, could transform the local problems of Tibet into larger geopolitical challenges in Asia.

Burma (Myanmar)

Sino-Indian interactions in Burma, now Myanmar, although often and correctly viewed as an example of a case where Beijing and New Delhi are waging an open and determined struggle for influence and domination, actually represent a good case of how third parties can affect the Sino-Indian relationship.[32] Although it lies at the intersection of Chinese and Indian interests at the western tip of Southeast Asia, the Burmese state was largely neglected by India and actively opposed by China for most of its independent existence. Both powers have had long-standing linkages with Burma: northern Burma remained the natural economic hinterland of the Chinese province of Yunnan, while the country as a whole had been a loosely controlled tributary of China historically; the erstwhile northeastern kingdoms of India too, historically, had economic and cultural relations with northern Burma, and Burma as a whole was eventually conquered by British India, an event that colored the perceptions of the Burmese toward India.

After India's independence and the formation of the modern Chinese state, Indian and Chinese relations with Burma did not enjoy any particular priority, given the strict nonalignment practiced first by the civilian regime of U Nu and later by the military regime of Ne Win. From 1962 to 1988, when Ne Win was in Rangoon, Sino-Burmese relations were actively hostile, as the People's Republic of China actively supported the Burmese Communist Party (BCP) and both India and China supported various ethnic rebel groups. Burma's consistent neutrality, however, was transformed when the violent suppression of popular opposition to military rule in 1988 brought a new military group, the State Law and Order Restoration Council (SLORC), to power. This brutal suppression precipitated a hostile international reaction and led to the isolation of the SLORC, with India in particular leading the criticism of Burma. The SLORC, exemplifying "the siege mentality that combines autocratic rule at home with extreme defensiveness abroad,"[33] responded by looking around for any friends it could find and fell into the arms of China. In a remarkable but nimble policy change, the communist regime in Beijing quickly mended relations with the Burmese junta by offering support.

This support has taken multiple forms: a substantial investment in infrastructure aimed primarily at developing Burma as an avenue for Yunnan's trade with the rest of the world; significant arms sales ranging from small arms to heavy weapons; public demonstrations of political support through high-level visits by Chinese officials and pressure on ethnic minority insurgents to make peace with the SLORC; and, most controversially, efforts to develop Burma's military infrastructure and some modest military facilities "that could pave the way for a significant Chinese presence in the Indian Ocean." Good information about this last feature of Sino-Burmese relations is hard to come by, and most accounts in the open literature are clouded by exaggeration, disinformation, and speculation about the extent and number of facilities. In any event, this increase in Chinese support appears oriented to achieving several goals: to develop Burma to integrate it more effectively with the regional economy in Yunnan; to use Burma as a possible entrepot for trading activities with the western portion of Southeast Asia; and eventually to acquire additional military access to the Indian Ocean.

India has viewed these developments with considerable consternation as a parallel attempt by China to replicate in Burma its achievements vis-à-vis Pakistan, namely, to develop a robust presence on India's eastern seaboard with the aim of encircling New Delhi. This outcome, although plausible, is not foreordained. China does have a significant presence in northern Burma, due in part to legal and illegal border trade, significant population movements, and early SLORC policies that permitted easy Chinese penetration. At the grand-strategic level, China may even desire to transform this presence over time into a robust military capability that "encircles" India, but Rangoon's incentives to support this policy diminish with time. Burma is not Pakistan: it does not share a parallel security dilemma with India and is unlikely to give up its identity and independence merely to assist China to encircle India. Rangoon's alignment with Beijing was a product of isolation, which forced it to rely on the Chinese far more than it might have done otherwise. In fact, Burma is likely to exploit China just as mercilessly as China is supposed to dominate Burma, because Chinese investments in infrastructure improvements, trade linkages, and military modernization serve the SLORC's state interests even before they do China's.

The recent Indian decision to change course and directly engage the SLORC gives both New Delhi and Rangoon new options. The new Indian efforts at engagement with Rangoon further reduce the regime's isolation and help attenuate the disadvantages accruing from its dependence on China. Not surprisingly, the SLORC appears to have accepted Indian overtures enthusiastically, and India has responded with a new strategy that includes a renewed commitment to developing Burmese infrastructure, increased cooperation in the development of technologies, and a willingness to extend both military and political cooperation. For India, the benefits of a revitalized Indo-Burmese relationship are obvious. The SLORC's principal goal of "restoring law and order" offers India opportunities to secure Burmese cooperation in minimizing the troubles caused by insurgents in the Indian northeast. The SLORC has in fact made some headway in establishing state control in Burma's peripheral regions and in attacking narco-terrorism and drug smuggling in cooperation with UN agencies. India also stands to gain from emerging as a secondary source of supply for Burma's military needs, particularly insofar as these result in direct military-to-military contacts, modest arms sales and the establishment of a small indigenous defense production infrastructure, coordination in counterinsurgency and counterterrorism, access to Indian technical and military training establishments, and naval cooperation. The SLORC's secondary goal of increasing "state development" also offers India the opportunity to become a primary supplier of imported goods because seaborne Indo-

Burmese trade is far easier than overland trade between Burma and Yunnan. Further, it allows India to compete in areas where great complementarities exist in Indo-Burmese economic relations: agrotechnical, forestry, and metallurgical industries; oil and gas exploration; automobile and two-wheeler industries; communications development; and tourism.

Burma will thus remain the cynosure of Sino-Indian competition for some time.[34] While China is likely to use economic and military instruments to secure outcomes such as strategic access, India is likely to emphasize similar instruments to block them. In this contest, Burma is likely to be an active participant, manipulating both sides into providing the state with the resources required to enhance both regime and national survival. Although China leads in this competition, India is not entirely disadvantaged: New Delhi has substantial resources of its own as well as locational advantages vis-à-vis both Burma and China as far as naval competition is concerned. More important, however, India's objectives in this competition are primarily negative rather than positive, being grounded in the desire to see Burma free of undue foreign influence. The goals of Indian grand strategy more closely cohere with those of the Burmese state, and this alignment of interests minimizes the disadvantages that may otherwise handicap India in its competition with China in Burma.

Even if India were to fail conclusively and China were to acquire bases along the Andaman Sea, this presence would be a strategic liability both to Burma and to China. Situated at the end of a long and precarious internal line of communications and far from the main concentrations of Chinese military power, such a forward presence could fall easy victim to Indian military power in case of war. Even in peacetime, Chinese bases would become strategic liabilities for Burma: an open Chinese presence would also alarm Indonesia, Malaysia, Singapore, and possibly even Thailand, not to mention the United States. At a time when the SLORC has succeeded in playing the "China card" to reduce its international isolation, it is unclear why the Burmese state would want to reverse these victories by increasing China's military presence in a way that would heighten regional pressures on itself, diminish its independence, and make it a target for foreign military planning.

Russia

Although the Russia-India-China "strategic triangle" enthusiastically advocated by Yevgeny Primakov remains a distant dream, the key bilateral relationships, between Russia and India and between Russia and China, remain good examples of the complicated realignments that have arisen with the end of the Cold War. The notion of a strategic triangle itself is born out of certain common interests. All three countries are challenged by the problems of Islamist terrorism; are more or less uncomfortable with a global unipolarity defined by American hegemony; and are acutely interested in the arms trade with Russia as the principal supplier of relatively advanced modern weaponry. Despite these common interests, however, a triangular coalition of the three states is unlikely to emerge for several reasons. First, the common challenge of Islamist terrorism manifests itself in different guises in each of the three countries and consequently engenders little joint action. Second, the common discomfort with the United States varies in intensity where each country is concerned: India is more threatened by the unresolved border disputes between India and China than it is by U.S. hegemony; China's interest in unfettered access to the American market is greater than its concern over the challenges posed by American primacy; and Russia, too, is more concerned about sustaining U.S. economic aid and political support than it is about American coercive power. On balance, then, the relations each of these countries enjoys with the United States are more important than most other issues, and this limits their propensity to gang up against Washington.

Where Sino-Indian interactions are concerned, the individual bilateral relations both countries enjoy with Russia are far more important to their strategic future than any chimerical strategic triangle. Astutely managing these bilateral relations has become all the more important now because India, a former Soviet ally, is at best another friend, while China, a former Soviet adversary, is increasingly Russia's largest customer of sophisticated arms. Russia's own search for an independent foreign policy, in which it seeks to maintain good relations with the West while still struggling to balance its European and Asiatic orientations, complicates the picture further, creating a situation where Moscow's foreign policy choices, too, are determined entirely by interest rather than ideology. In such circumstances, the grand-strategic choices of all three countries are far more fluid than they have ever been historically now that both Sino-Russian and Indo-Russian relationships are driven largely by the laws and logic of the market.

This reality is what makes Russia so interesting from the perspective of Sino-Indian relations. While Moscow has become increasingly sensitive to the problem of both nuclear proliferation and the growth of new powers in Asia, its own precarious economic condition has created a new willingness to sell advanced military and dual-use technologies to any country based simply on its ability to buy.[35] Arms sales have in fact become critical to the survival of Russia's defense industry because the state cannot afford to procure weapons for its own military forces. Exports remain practically this industry's sole source of income, and although many Russian defense firms receive subsidies of one sort or another, arms exports are still their principal means of survival. Given the privatization of the Russian defense industry, the continued jostling over the definition of national interest in Moscow, and the widespread corruption within the Russian state, it is not surprising to find all Russian arms manufacturers aggressively promoting foreign military sales in the guise of advancing Russian national interest.[36]

In this context, the Chinese and Indian desire for advanced arms matches Russian need. Both countries taken together currently account for more than 60 percent of Russia's arms exports. China, for example, has purchased from Russia Su-27 and Su-30 fighter jets, Kilo-class diesel-electric submarines, and Sovremenny-class destroyers, in addition to advanced surface-to-air missiles and other munitions. India similarly has purchased Su-30 fighter aircraft, long-range theater bombers, Kilo-class diesel-electric submarines, major surface combatants, advanced surface-to-air missiles, and the T-90, Russia's most advanced main battle tank. The consequence of such unconstrained Russian sales to both China and India could be significant from the viewpoint of Sino-Indian competition over the far term. First, it makes relative economic performance even more central to the maintenance of a stable bilateral balance of power: superior China's economic growth in this context could lay the basis for eroding India's current military superiority along the Himalayan border. Second, it paves the way for the creation of two rival military forces armed with similar weaponry: this by itself creates interesting operational challenges as war-fighting outcomes would increasingly depend on relative tactical proficiency, imaginative strategies, and concepts of employment, rather than on gross differences in technology. How China and India will cope with these two challenges is not entirely clear, but they combine to make Russia an increasingly important actor in long-range Sino-Indian competition in Asia.

The Intersection of the Struggle for Security and the Accumulation of Wealth

In contrast to the four previous cases of Sino-Indian interaction, the present and future Sino-Indian interactions in Central Asia, the Persian Gulf, and Southeast Asia represent instances where concerns about security intersect with economic interests.

Central Asia

China and India have security and economic interests in Central Asia. The security interests revolve primarily around the containment of Islamic fundamentalism in the newly independent Central Asian republics, and in this respect the interests of the two countries mostly converge. Militant fundamentalism could intensify ethnonationalism in the Xinjiang-Uighur Autonomous Region, populated by more than 8 million Muslim Uighurs, as well as threaten the stability of China's northwestern provinces. The stability of the Xinjiang region in particular is especially critical because it has vast natural resources, including significant unexploited petroleum reserves in the Tarim Basin (which some believe sufficient to free Beijing from future dependence on Middle East petroleum) and large deposits of natural gas, iron, and coal—resources that make the region's security critical both to China's economic modernization and to its overarching political objective of preserving national unity. Apart from ensuring local stability, China's security interests in Central Asia also derive from its desire to keep the region as free as possible from Russian influence. The breakup of the Soviet Union and the absence of Soviet military power in Central Asia for the first time in a century have increased the security of western China considerably, but Beijing's strategic conundrum now consists of how to prevent the destabilizing currents emerging in Central Asia as a result of state weakness in the newly independent republics from inciting a renewed Russian or other foreign presence that appears under the guise of suppressing Islamic fundamentalism. Finally, China seeks to exploit the emerging Central Asian markets as a catalyst, both to create a new prosperity zone in Xinjiang for foreign investment and to revive the old Silk Road to push Chinese economic interests beyond Central Asia to the Persian Gulf and perhaps even on to Europe. Beijing expects that the creation of such an integrated market would strengthen the secular governments of Central Asia against those groups favoring Islamic rule, prevent the republics from returning to dependence on Russia, and expand Chinese influence beyond its western peripheries.[37]

India views the Central Asian republics as important for similar reasons. Thanks to the problems in Kashmir and the links between those problems and the crisis in Afghanistan, Indian security is intertwined with the turbulence in Central Asia. Consequently, a critical Indian security objective has been to develop an integrated strategy aimed at combating Islamist insurgencies, small-arms proliferation, drug trafficking, and transnational terrorism so that the newly independent Central Asian republics may sustain themselves as secular societies. Attaining this objective bolsters other Indian strategic goals. It undercuts the Pakistani search for "strategic depth," which Islamabad has sought to consolidate by extending the Economic Cooperation Organization (ECO) to include Central Asian states (while excluding India) and by deliberately exploiting metaphors like the "Silk Road" that include Kashmir as a part of Central Asia. And, more important, it provides an opportunity to revitalize India's previous political and economic presence in the region.[38]

Although China and India thus have mostly parallel security goals in Central Asia, the potential for conflict could arise, mainly from any Chinese efforts to transform cooperation with the local states into a larger system of influence dominated by Beijing. In this regard, China has the advantage of geographical contiguity, but this could be counterbalanced by the willingness of the Central Asian states to accord India greater priority precisely because its distance from them makes New Delhi less threatening. In the final analysis, India's more limited resources and its insufficient investable capital reduce its importance to the Central Asian states. Sino-Indian political interactions in Central Asia in general, however, are likely to be muted because of the enormity of Russian influence (and now, U.S. presence), which renders the other two Asian rivals less significant.

The possibility of genuine Sino-Indian rivalry in Central Asia, curiously, is more likely to arise in the realm of economics than of security, and this rivalry will be conditioned primarily by the strategies adopted by China with respect to the region's natural resources. It is generally believed that the Central Asian region contains somewhere between 90 billion and 200 billion barrels of oil and about 46 percent of the world's gas reserves. The struggle to tap these resources has already begun with Western multinationals, China, and Russia pursuing competitive efforts at exploration, drilling, and export. So long as the oil and gas deposits in the region ultimately reach the international market and their consumption is regulated by ordinary market mechanisms, Sino-Indian rivalry over these resources is unlikely to become significant. But if China seeks to acquire exclusive access to these resources, then the Sino-Indian rivalry could take on new colors. As one analyst noted, the

> advent of the "China Century" depends on stable energy resources, domestic stability, and positive economic growth. It is estimated that China will have to import 100 million tons of crude by 2010 unless it

> finds new sources. China's new, weak Central Asian neighbors are the potential, new "Kuwaits" of the 21st century. If the Chinese build a pipeline (over Russian resistance), Central Asia's importance to China will shift immeasurably in the next century, as will Chinese military attitudes towards safeguarding their strategic oil reserves.[39]

Under such circumstances, Sino-Indian rivalry in Central Asia could take new forms, with both sides jockeying for preferential access in exchange for technology, economic assistance, military technologies, and possibly even security guarantees.

Persian Gulf

Despite all the potentialities resident in the energy reserves of Central Asia, most analysts conclude that the Persian Gulf will remain central to world energy supplies.[40] During the next twenty years, the demand for energy is projected to expand by more than 50 percent, and Asian demands will account for the bulk of the increase. In this context, China and India are likely to become the largest Asian consumers of oil and natural gas, requiring, respectively, around 100 quadrillion and 30 quadrillion Btu of energy annually to sustain economic growth. Although Central Asia and Southeast Asia will play an increasingly important role as new suppliers of oil and natural gas to both countries, they will not be able to supplant the Persian Gulf as the principal supplier of energy. Consequently, the Persian Gulf will remain the main arena where potential Sino-Indian rivalries over security and wealth will intersect, because cheap and abundant energy remains the motor for sustenance of high growth rates domestically—economic performance that both China and India define as essential.[41]

A functioning market should keep the Sino-Indian demand for energy from creating conflict. But this mitigating factor could be less effective in practice for several reasons. First, China and, to a lesser degree, India remain suspicious about the effectiveness and viability of market mechanisms for regulating access to raw materials. Because both countries are still not powerful enough, they have been compelled to accept the realities of the market even as they seek to foster a variety of nonmarket strategies to ensure energy independence. Should such strategies come to dominate their political attitudes, their behaviors and interactions would correspondingly change. Second, the logic of an effective energy market that attenuates political competition over access assumes stability in the Middle East. But such stability remains a precarious problem as domestic instability and infirm governing structures within the energy-producing states combine with external threats emerging both from regional predators and from the unresolved Israeli-Palestinian conflict. Should instability in the Gulf worsen, incentives for regional states to seek outside intervention will only parallel the interest that extraregional entities may have in pursuing strategies that minimize the effects of such instability on their own security and in developing exclusive access arrangements to ensure energy for their own requirements. Third, the stability offered by market mechanisms relies disproportionately on the strategic protection provided by the United States to the regulatory processes themselves, the trade routes over which the energy moves, and the moderate Arab regimes. So long as American protection remains unchanged, the worst consequences of any local perturbation arguably would be minimized, but continued U.S. protection may itself be at issue because it depends so much on contingent variables such as domestic opinion in the United States, changes in American relative power, and the diminishing American dependency on Gulf (though not on imported) oil.

These variables implicitly reinforce the issue highlighted earlier: that Sino-Indian rivalries in Asia will often be mediated by external realities and cannot be viewed as purely dyadic struggles. The potential for Sino-Indian conflict over Persian Gulf oil represents a case in point because the autarkic solutions to energy dependence that must be adopted by at least one side to trigger serious bilateral conflicts require a concatenation of several critical contingencies, such as increased instability in key Gulf states, the growth of radicalism within key energy-producing countries, an increase in external regional threats, a U.S. disengagement from Persian Gulf politics after the final resolution of the Israeli-Palestinian conflict or if U.S. energy demands are satisfied by other sources, and a possible dislocation or atrophy of key primary commodities markets due to either U.S. retrenchment or decline. Precisely because some of these contingencies could materialize, China and India have already embarked on a variety of strategic solutions anticipating the worst outcomes. Some solutions are relatively benign and are in fact desirable: they include expanding oil and gas exploration at home; increasing the technical efficiency of energy-consuming activities; developing regional energy management networks; investing in noncarbon energy alternatives; and, finally, liberalizing internal energy markets to rationalize production and consumption. Other strategies that both sides, but particularly China, could contemplate, could exacerbate competition. As one analysis concluded,

> As countries in Asia seek to secure growing levels of energy imports, two geopolitical risks emerge. First, historical enmities might boil over into armed conflict for control of specific energy reserves in the region. Second, the rising dependence of China on Persian Gulf oil could well alter political relationships within and outside the region. For example, China might seek to build military ties with energy exporters in the Persian Gulf in ways that would be of concern to the United States and its allies.[42]

If either or both states, therefore, come to believe that autarkic strategies promise the best solutions to their energy needs, they might launch determined efforts to forge exclusive energy access arrangements with producers located along their periphery. Efforts to secure exclusive access arrangements are likely to ensue even if only one of the competitors pursues an autarkic strategy. Such a strategy would consist of a competitive search for specific zones of influence where each of the "metropolitan" powers—China and India—would enjoy privileged access to the raw materials in exchange for political protection and economic payment. If such strategies were pursued, it is likely that China would seek such privileged access initially in Central Asia and obviously the Persian Gulf, while India would focus primarily on the Persian Gulf. In each zone, the metropolitan powers would be likely to seek and support key local influentials, like Kazakhstan in the case of China and Iran in the case of India. Given the importance of the Persian Gulf, the pursuit of such autarkic solutions would likely result in a Sino-Indian struggle for influence in key centers like Saudi Arabia, Iraq, and the smaller Gulf Cooperation Council states. The objective of both powers would be to secure some kind of energy-for-protection arrangements. And although it is possible that separate geopolitical strategies could manifest themselves at first—with China focusing on securing energy via land routes and India via the sea—a collision of these strategies would be inevitable because the extraordinarily high levels of Chinese and Indian energy demands would expand their interests beyond other peripheral suppliers into the Persian Gulf, which will remain the mother lode of energy supplies well into the future.[43]

The search for exclusive access arrangements is likely to be complemented by some military modernization to safeguard the new access arrangements. This will almost certainly require both states to create large naval forces to protect their sea-lanes of communication; new land force expeditionary capabilities to protect distant pipelines or assist their client states; and new long-range precision strike assets to defend their interests against other extraregional states. In general, the creation of such capabilities is likely to fuel regional tensions, exacerbate Sino-Indian competition, and impinge on larger American regional interests.

Although such exigencies could come to pass if the contingencies identified earlier were to materialize, it is unlikely that Sino-Indian rivalries in the Persian Gulf will develop in such stark form. This is because China and India are not core powers in the international system, and consequently any emerging bilateral competition with respect to the Persian Gulf would only become attenuated because of the overwhelming power and influence of the United States in the region. Further, even if U.S. energy dependence on the Gulf remains absolutely minimal, the fact that many of its allies depend on Gulf energy implies that the United States cannot become indifferent to the region's security. Moreover, the very fact that control of the area's resources would not only privilege the controller asymmetrically but could also help underwrite a larger strategic challenge to U.S. global hegemony implies that Washington could never become simply a bystander in the region's geopolitics—the necessary condition for any significant Sino-Indian rivalry over Gulf oil. Finally, the preferences of the regional states themselves almost ensure minimized Sino-Indian rivalry: faced with a choice of suitors, many of the principal energy producers are likely to prefer either U.S. protection or at least the protection offered by multiple entities.

For all these reasons, Sino-Indian rivalries in the Persian Gulf, while possible, are unlikely to materialize in the worst forms. Even if they do materialize, they will exist under the shadow of overwhelming U.S. power.[44] Clearly, both countries have the potential to become significant players in Gulf politics. China possesses a range of disruptive technologies that could become available to various regional states, and it will certainly have the economic resources and political incentives to seek access. India will also acquire a comparable set of disruptive technologies over time and, more important, will possess a large and capable fleet that will enable it to maintain a sustained presence in the region. India also considers the Gulf to lie within its zone of strategic interest. In the face of U.S. power, however, Sino-Indian competition over the Persian Gulf is likely to take political rather than military form: within the ambit of a functioning energy market, both sides will seek supplemental arrangements for oil and natural gas; both sides will seek privileged political relations with the key regional states; both sides may even become modest suppliers of some military technologies, with China in particular becoming a potential supplier of disruptive technologies depending on its larger relations with the United States; and India will more likely than not work with the United States to ensure freedom of navigation along the Gulf transit routes.

Southeast Asia

The Southeast Asian region historically formed the meeting point of the Sinic and Indic empires and in contemporary times has become the focus of parallel and often competitive Sino-Indian diplomacy. Just as in the Persian Gulf, Sino-Indian interactions with the various countries of the region are driven by considerations of security and prosperity. The Southeast Asian states themselves are key players in this interaction because they can often choose between China and India.

China has always had a strategic interest in Southeast Asia. The region traditionally subsisted as the southern periphery of the imperial Chinese security system, and most of the regional kingdoms had tributary relations with the Chinese imperial court. During the postwar period, the region was viewed as vital enough for China to aid what was otherwise a bitter rival, Vietnam, in its struggle against the United States. Today, the importance of the region derives from sources beyond historical legacies. The economic liberalization program under way in China has created vastly successful provinces along its southern coast. The poorer countries of Southeast Asia flank these provinces, and China is compelled to treat the region as part of its defensive perimeter. Apart from the direct consequences for defense, China is also involved in Southeast Asia because of significant territorial disputes with regional states. China is locked into direct competition with Vietnam, the Philippines, Malaysia, Brunei, and Indonesia over the Spratly Islands. Finally, the relevance of Southeast Asia to the Chinese grand strategy is simply a matter of geopolitics: the region lies athwart the principal sea-lanes of communication, carrying roughly $100 billion worth of annual Chinese trade. It also represents a potential means of access through which extraregional states could attack the southern Chinese periphery, and it hosts significant entities, such as the Philippines, Singapore, and Indonesia, that could become critical links in a future containment of China. Finally, it remains one of the two crucial bridges to Asia for maritime powers seeking to attack China with land power. The permanent nature of geopolitics thus ensures that Southeast Asia will remain fundamentally valuable to the Chinese grand strategy.[45]

Other factors only enhance the region's importance. Among the most important is the presence of a large Chinese diaspora in Southeast Asia, which happens to be one of the largest single blocs contributing to foreign investment in metropolitan China. Southeast Asia also remains a growing secondary area of importance for trade. Merchandise trade between the five members of the Association of Southeast Asian Nations (ASEAN) and China, for example, has grown at double-digit rates in the last couple of decades, and the trade volume of the ASEAN five countries with China has increased at a rate faster than the group's total trade volume. Sino–Southeast Asian trade will continue to grow, and, in a remarkable turn, is likely to be sustained despite the increasing similarity in comparative trade profiles.[46]

In contrast to China, Southeast Asia—at least historically—has remained only of indirect value to India. Not surprisingly, Indo–Southeast Asian relations went into the cold for the most part after the 1962 Sino-Indian war: the Indian defeat in that conflict ended New Delhi's infatuation with the pan-Asian anticolonial movements that had justified its diplomatic involvement with various Southeast Asian states; and its subsequent preoccupation with domestic crises, the rise of Pakistan as a regional challenger, and multiple foreign policy failures all combined to weaken India's involvement with Southeast Asia. This condition might have continued indefinitely were it not for the dramatic success of China and the Southeast Asian economies. Motivated by a desire both to connect to the East Asian miracle and to engage the Southeast Asian states, then Indian Prime Minister Narasimha Rao initiated a new "Look East" policy, which has since defined India's relationships with the region.

India has three broad strategic objectives in Southeast Asia, and all rest on the conviction that the rise of China as a dominant power could pose significant threats to Indian security and possibly to its prosperity. The first objective is to prevent China from acquiring forward basing and presence that could threaten the Indian homeland and its freedom of action in South Asia. The second objective is to prevent China from acquiring sufficient regional influence so as to be able to coerce the local states into supporting Chinese policies aimed at undercutting Indian security. The third objective is to develop strategic relationships with the key states that enable India to operate within the region as required, and to extend support that may be requested by its regional partners. The "Look East" policy thus exemplifies New Delhi's recognition that although Southeast Asia is not intrinsically valuable to India in the way that it is to China, it is nonetheless important enough and therefore cannot be neglected. To the contrary, India must remain comprehensively engaged in the region if it seeks to influence the shape of its future extraregional presence in Southeast Asia and if it is to secure strategic outcomes that are important to its security.[47]

The economic dimensions of this engagement parallel India's strategic concerns. Although the Southeast Asian region is growing in importance from the perspective of Indian trade, some states are more important than others. India's economic relationship is strongest with countries like Singapore, Malaysia, and Thailand, which have emerged as important trading and investment partners. What is even more significant about India's economic strategies vis-à-vis Southeast Asia, however, is its drive to incorporate the region into a formalized free-trade area. Frustrated by the slow progress of regional cooperation within South Asia, India has begun to look beyond its immediate locale for trade opportunities. Toward that end, it has supported the rise of such new regional economic groupings as the Indian Ocean Rim Association for Regional Cooperation (IORARC) and the Bangladesh, India, Myanmar, Sri Lanka, and Thailand Economic Cooperation (BIMSTEC), while ranging even farther afield with ideas like the Bay of Bengal Community (BOBCOM), which would include India, Bangladesh, Myanmar, Malaysia, Singapore, Sri Lanka, and Thailand. Ideas such as these suggest that India increasingly views closer economic integration with Southeast Asia as critical to its economic health, and although progress on all such initiatives has been dreadfully slow, the very fact that these arrangements have been mooted signals the growing value of Southeast Asia for India's economic growth and development.[48]

While China and India have recognized the benefits of renewed attention to Southeast Asia, the local states have also understood the utility of engaging both China and India. The strong relationships many of these countries enjoy with extraregional powers like Japan, Australia, and the United States empower them to engage both China and India from a far more confident position than they might be in otherwise. Their record of strong economic growth and their relatively open economies also make many of the states attractive economic partners and provide them with the resources necessary to cope with their larger Asian neighbors. In any event, the strategic objective of the regional states vis-à-vis China and India has been to enmesh both Asian giants in a web of cooperative relationships while simultaneously using the power of each giant to limit the influence of the other. Although it is recognized that China has greater power-political capabilities than does India, the latter is seen to have attractive attributes as evidenced by its dynamic information technology sector, its effective conventional military capabilities, the absence of territorial disputes with the local states, and its growing ties with key extraregional powers like the United States. Accordingly, an enmeshment strategy that engages both Asian powers to exploit and limit them simultaneously makes eminent sense from a Southeast Asian perspective. As one regional analyst phrased it, "China and India, despite bilateral problems, are now both ASEAN dialogue partners and participants of the ASEAN Regional Forum (ARF). Indeed, in terms of power politics, the engagement of the two largest nations in the world, along with the U.S., Japan and Russia, might help create a regional balance of power in East Asia and the Asia-Pacific region as part of the global balance that includes the European Union."[49]

The willingness of the Southeast Asian states to play the balancing game has already paid rich dividends. It has reinforced the Chinese decision to put off final resolution of the Spratlys dispute in favor of advocating joint development of the islands in the interim and the enunciation of a code of conduct that would limit the aggressive actions of all parties. This strategy reduces the pressures on Beijing to embark on any large-scale use of force that might vitiate the political environment and create even stronger anti-Chinese sentiments, which could have grave consequences for the dispute that really matters to Beijing: Taiwan. Further, it has forced China to think about restructuring its relations with Southeast Asia by means of multiple bilateral agreements. These agreements, incorporating the principles of the Bandung Conference and a promise by the regional partners to respect the "one China" policy, have prompted Beijing to guarantee that only peaceful means would be used in settling local disputes; to support the stability, integrity, and prosperity of the partners; to engage in high-level exchanges and consultations; and to promote political, diplomatic, economic, and military ties with the regional states. Finally, it has encouraged China to advocate consultative processes that help "to resist hegemonism and power politics [and] to promote East Asian economic cooperation."[50] These processes are envisaged as devices to promote local solidarity while simultaneously weakening the influence of extraregional powers like the United States.

While seeking to use its relations with the Southeast Asian states to its advantage, India has been careful to tread lightly. It has sought to develop the instruments required to safeguard its interests, even as it recognizes that its welcome in the region is a function of being a quiet, not an overbearing, partner. In this regard, it has often let its regional partners take the initiative, letting Singapore, for example, coordinate the ASEAN-India dialogue, leaving Indonesia, for example, to extol India's virtues as a secular multiethnic, multilingual, and multireligious model for Southeast Asia. In this delicate engagement, India has recognized that tact and sensitivity are required for its success. It cannot be seen as seeking to export South Asian problems to the region, nor can it be viewed as attempting to ensnare the Southeast Asian states in its own security dilemmas. Consequently, the ARF's decision not to invite Pakistan's membership has not only been cheered by New Delhi but advocated on the grounds that the organization's effectiveness would be compromised by Pakistan's incessant interest in "internationalizing" the Kashmir problem. Accordingly, the ASEAN determination that Indo-Pakistani rivalries fall outside the "geographical footprint" of its interest and hence ought not to be solicited via Pakistani membership accords with Indian interests. In its interactions with the Southeast Asian states, India has been guided by the desire to see ASEAN become a regional security system robust enough to ward off the worst potential Chinese blandishments and coercion. Toward that end, it has emphasized integrated strategies that include economic, diplomatic, and strategic components. In large part, this emphasis on diversification has been conditioned by the joint desire to minimize offense to China while still developing regional ties capable of limiting Chinese penetration. Since this objective is shared fully by most of the critical states in Southeast Asia, the success of Indian regional strategy is assured, provided India pays consistent attention to the region, pursues its diplomacy with tact and grace, and remains both a vibrant economy and a stable polity.

On balance, then, of all the geographic areas where Sino-Indian rivalry is likely to materialize, the Southeast Asian region will probably become one of the most important.[51] This rivalry, however, will continue to be characterized both by asymmetric goals and by a triangular pattern of interaction: at least in the security area, China is likely to seek influence to use the region and its assets to secure positive ends—access to resources, a proscenium for forward operations, and the re-creation of a sphere of privileged influence—while India will attempt to use its influence primarily for negative ones—ward off Chinese penetration, minimize Beijing's ability to use the area to engage in forward operations, and attenuate Chinese goals of developing veto rights over local political choices. In the context of such interactions, the regional states themselves are likely to play a critical role, reassured in great measure by the enduring superiority of U.S. power and perhaps even the growing U.S. regional military presence.

With such quadrangular components, the Sino-Indian rivalry in Southeast Asia is likely to transform primarily into an influence game in which both sides devote considerable attention to competitively influencing the region's capitals.

The Quest for Wealth (and the Intersection of Wealth and Status)

Unlike most of the arenas pertaining to security and to wealth and security jointly, wherein the actions undertaken by one side are oriented toward the other, the struggle for foreign direct investment (FDI) is unique: it is characterized solely by actions undertaken within one's own state but which nonetheless have serious consequences for the long-run balance of power. The competitive dimensions of the quest for increased FDI arise primarily because capital is scarce and must be competed for despite the fact that such competition does not have any immediate consequences for safety and security. In principle, the competition for FDI stems from the national economic strategies pursued by China and India, which require both sides to invite significant quantities of foreign investment. In this context, FDI is particularly favored because, unlike portfolio investments, which represent highly mobile forms of short-term capital, FDI not only embodies greater stability but also helps to increase national competitiveness because it brings along new capital, technology, managerial expertise, and access to foreign markets.

Both China and India have actively solicited new FDI since the beginning of their liberalization programs, and thus far the evidence suggests that China has "won the race" hands down. As one analysis put it,

> India's neighbors that are relying heavily on FDI, such as China, Indonesia, Malaysia, and Thailand, have been pulling far ahead of India in economic growth, income levels, and productivity, while also increasing their security and geopolitical influence in the world community. India's continuing ambivalence to FDI, as a result, exacts a heavy toll on the Indian economy. Undoubtedly, India is ceding billions of dollars of FDI to its neighbors each year. While China achieved actual FDI inflows of around $45.3 billion in 1997, India settled for a mere $3.2 billion![52]

The Sino-Indian FDI race, consequently, resembles a sprint in China and a crawl in India. The reasons for this asymmetry are many. In the areas of export-oriented FDI, domestic market-oriented FDI, and infrastructure

FDI, New Delhi has simply not moved as quickly as Beijing, with the result that China, which had virtually no foreign investment in the 1970s, is now a major host country for large quantities of FDI in all three areas. Three significant issues stand out. First, despite India's big-bang reforms in 1991, the Indian government has made no systematic effort to attract expatriate investment. China has promulgated laws and regulations specifically designed to attract investment from the Chinese diaspora in Hong Kong, Taiwan, Macau, and Southeast Asia. Second, India has offered no special benefits to foreign investors, unlike China, which has offered favorable treatment to foreign firms that is not offered to domestic enterprises. Third, India fares poorly with respect to China in the following areas: openness to foreign trade, investment, and financial flows; the role of the state in the economy; the effectiveness of financial intermediaries and the level of competition in financial markets; and the efficiency and competitiveness of the domestic labor market. It is marginally better than China with respect to the quality of institutionalization and the extent of corruption and vulnerability to organized crime; the use and spread of new technologies, including information technologies; the level and quality of research and development; and the overall quality of management, marketing, and staff training and motivation practices. And it is marginally worse than China as far as the quality of its physical infrastructure, telecommunications, transportation, and overall infrastructure investment are concerned.[53]

Given these facts, the Sino-Indian "competition" for FDI would be inconsequential were it not for the fact that the Indian government is now committed to increasing annual FDI flows from the current totals of approximately \$3 billion to \$10 billion annually. This commitment will obviously require a substantial transformation of the national business climate if it is to succeed. So long as the ratio of China's FDI to India's FDI remains on the order of fifteen to one, there will be no Sino-Indian competition in this issue area worth the name, but should the Indian government succeed in improving the ratio in its favor, the stage could be set for some modest rivalry. This rivalry will obviously be very different from that occurring in the geopolitical issue areas examined earlier, but its consequences will be far more significant for India's continuing search for security and status.

Apart from the issue of competitive FDI, Sino-Indian relations interact in another issue area: India's desire to join the Asia-Pacific Economic Cooperation (APEC) forum to consolidate its increasing commitment to open trade and practical economic cooperation and to signal its arrival as a consequential player on the Asia-Pacific geopolitical scene. APEC, which consists today of twenty-one members, has become both a forum for discussions on regional economic integration in areas such as trade and investment, energy, transportation, telecommunications, and science and technology and, more important, an avenue for annual meetings at the highest political level. The economic and political benefits of formal participation in an organization representing the most productive sections of the international economy are not lost on India, which has made a serious effort to join since APEC's founding in 1989. The APEC decision in 1997 not to admit India during its most recent wave of expansion, coupled with its imposition of a ten-year moratorium on new admittances, constitutes a setback for India's "Look East" policy. This decision, however, exposed the critical political nature of APEC and opens the door to possible Sino-Indian cooperation or competition—depending on the position Beijing takes on future Indian membership. Thus far, the United States has led the opposition to Indian membership formally on the basis of questions about New Delhi's sincerity about its economic reforms, especially with regard to tariff and nontariff barriers, quantitative restrictions, implementation of intellectual property rights, and high protectionism in the area of services. China has been content to ride behind U.S. opposition because Indian membership would bring no particular economic benefits to China and would elevate India's stature in the Asia-Pacific. It is likely that U.S. opposition to Indian membership will abate over time, and Beijing's position on the issue could become an important symbol that clarifies its own attitudes toward a rising India. To that degree it could function either as an irritant or as a lubricant in future Sino-Indian relations.

The Recognition of Status (and the Intersection of Status and Security)

The issue areas pertaining to status remain the third and perhaps least important arena of Sino-Indian interactions. The problems of status are affected by the critical asymmetry identified earlier: China already has standing as a great power, whereas India is a rising power that seeks recognition. Pure status issues, however, are hard to find in Sino-Indian interactions in Asia. The best example of what is arguably a status issue remains India's desire to join the Asia-Europe Meeting (ASEM) process. ASEM is an informal process of dialogue and cooperation that brings together the fifteen European Union member states and the European Commission and ten Asian countries.[54] The ASEM dialogue addresses political, economic, and cultural issues with the objective of strengthening the relationship between Asia and Europe. The ASEM process includes a summit-level meeting every second year, annual ministerial-level meetings, and more frequent working-level meetings. ASEM activities are concentrated in three areas: political discussions (for example, on human rights), economic discussions (for example, on reducing barriers to trade and investment), and cultural discussions (for example, about developing increased people-to-people contact).

Obviously, India's participation in such activities does not provide immediate material benefits but rather signals its emergence as a key player in the Asian arena. For that reason, India has lobbied heavily to be admitted into the ASEM process—but thus far, without success, in part because of Chinese opposition. As one analyst explained this position,

> The main objective of China's Asia policy has always been to prevent the rise of an Asian rival or peer competitor to challenge its status as the Asia-Pacific's sole "Middle Kingdom." As an old Chinese saying goes, "one mountain cannot accommodate two tigers." That China does not want India to emerge as an equal is evident from its staunch opposition to India's membership of the P-5 (UN Security Council), N-5 (Nuclear Club), ASEM (Asia-Europe Summit), and APEC (Asia-Pacific Economic Cooperation).[55]

If Beijing's attitudes on this question were to harden over time, they would only exacerbate the prevailing suspicions in Sino-Indian relations and make reaching a modus vivendi on issues of joint interest more difficult. Irrespective of how this specific question is resolved, status disputes in Sino-Indian relations will not disappear, in part because the problem of managing the status claims of two simultaneously rising powers will continue to elude easy solutions in many instances. Both countries have worldviews based on a hierarchical order wherein securing appropriately superior positions in the "warrant of precedence" are critical for stability. Other great powers could be tempted to play off the status claims of these two Asian emerging powers against one another to further their own political interests.

In contrast to relatively pure status claims represented by membership in processes like ASEM, India's desire for a permanent seat on the United Nations Security Council (something China already possesses) reflects both status and security considerations. The basic Indian argument for being considered as a permanent council member is rooted in India's vision of itself as one of the world's great civilizations; as an emerging economic power that will also soon be the most populous country in the world; as one of the founding members of the United Nations; as one of the few countries that has enthusiastically participated in all UN-mandated peace operations; and as a robust democracy that is a model for the management of linguistic, racial, ethnic, and religious differences amid great poverty. These arguments are often advanced to underscore the status justification for India's claim to permanent representation on the Security Council, but strong security imperatives underlie this claim as well. New Delhi clearly recognizes that permanent membership in the Security Council with full veto powers would enhance India's autonomy in a way that very few other political instruments could. The ability to wield the veto independently guarantees that New Delhi would never have to rely on the political cover offered by other great powers as it has in the past for safeguarding its interests; it would immunize India completely against any future Pakistani efforts at "internationalizing" the Kashmir issue and would render infructuous past UN resolutions on this issue; and it would enable India to pursue its own interests in the face of potential opposition by other great powers.

Because the acquisition of permanent UN Security Council membership would advantage India dramatically, many of the other great powers, including the United States and China, have been reluctant to support its claims. Although this opposition has been expressed thus far through a variety of procedural hurdles, the principal reason for it, ultimately, is the uncertainty about how India would use its newly acquired powers vis-à-vis larger American and Chinese interests. Although it is possible that Washington might relent in its opposition to Indian membership if U.S.-Indian ties continue to strengthen, Beijing's privately expressed opposition to India's candidacy for permanent membership is only likely to deepen if India is increasingly viewed as a significant rival. Although the ultimate consequences of such opposition are difficult to assess, the fact remains that concerted Chinese resistance to Indian membership in the Security Council will have the corrosive effect of deepening Sino-Indian suspicions in many other issue areas.

On balance, then, even in the area of status, delicate shadowboxing rather than tentative cooperation will probably define Sino-Indian relations over the next two decades.

Conclusion

The discussion in this chapter suggests that the Sino-Indian relationship in Asia will be complex and multidimensional and will include elements of cooperation and competition simultaneously. In contrast to Indo-Pakistani competition, which represents a localized rivalry in South Asia, Sino-Indian interactions will manifest themselves both in areas *outside* South Asia proper *and* over nontraditional issues. These interactions, which could dethrone the extant Indo-Pakistani rivalry as the primary security challenge in southern Asia, will arise because of the fact that two power transitions—not one—appear to be occurring concurrently in Asia today. Both China and India are emerging powers that, growing at historically rapid rates, having fought wars previously, and abutting one another along the Asian landmass, remain natural competitors. This potential for competition becomes additionally interesting because both states represent major concentrations of conventional capabilities, with significant types of technical modernization yet to come. Both countries also possess the capability to develop various kinds of nonconventional military technologies and would thus be increasingly able to mount asymmetric challenges against one another and against many others.

The many facets of Sino-Indian competition explored in this chapter suggest, however, that the term "competition" itself masks a variety of complex interactions and ought not to be translated as simple dyadic rivalry. The range of issues confronting Beijing and New Delhi are sufficiently varied so as to engender complex, possibly antinomous, national strategies. In most instances, China and India will be faced with the task of deterring, defending, and reassuring each other simultaneously in the presence of multiple actors, each with its own capabilities, preferences, and constraints. In this context, Sino-Indian relations—on balance—will be defined more by competition than by cooperation, but such competition is unlikely to become malignantly rivalrous, as U.S.-Soviet competition was during the Cold War. This outcome will obtain primarily because both China and India are still subordinate states in the global system that lack untrammeled freedom of action; have sufficiently different strategic orientations in Asia that, while intersecting, offer hope of avoiding unvarnished confrontation; and have assured defense capabilities wherein geography, nuclear weaponry, and conventional forces combine to produce fairly robust defense dominance vis-à-vis each other. If and when these three conditions change, however, the stage would be set for serious dyadic rivalry.

As the United States monitors changes in these conditions, it ought to remember three things about the Sino-Indian relationship from the perspective of its own grand strategy.

First, the Sino-Indian relationship will involve political interactions beyond South Asia proper *and* will encompass a gamut of issues subsuming both high and low politics: this includes precipitants that are physically located extraregionally, or that have their origins in "catalytic" sources (that is, in the actions of entities not entirely under the control of the two states), or that emerge from nonconventional sources of tension.

Second, the history of Sino-Indian relations, the current differences in the countries' rates of relative growth, and the prognostication that this relationship is likely on balance to be more competitive than cooperative, implies that New Delhi will increasingly look for U.S. support as both Sino-Indian and possibly Sino-U.S. competition deepens over time.

Third, both the idealist tradition, which emphasizes the natural harmony of democratic societies, and the realist tradition, which emphasizes the primacy of the differences in relative power, tend to make India the more desirable object of American geopolitical attention in comparison with China. Since Beijing, however, remains the more important American trading partner today, and is currently more critical for the success of U.S. strategic objectives in Northeast Asia, managing the tensions between a China-dominant short-term policy and a longer-term policy focused on maritime Asia (including India) ought to consume significant American attention as Washington adjusts its grand strategy for the new century.

Notes

1. John W. Garver, *Protracted Contest: Sino-Indian Rivalry in the Twentieth Century* (Seattle: University of Washington Press, 2001).

2. Wayne M. Morrison, "China's Economic Conditions," *CRS Issue Brief for Congress,* 21 September 2000; World Bank, *India at a Glance,* 25 August 2000; Ashley J. Tellis, "South Asia," in *Strategic Asia 2001–02: Power and Purpose,* ed. Richard J. Ellings and Aaron L. Friedberg (Seattle: National Bureau of Asian Research, 2001), 223–67.

3. Charles Wolf, Jr., Anil Bamezai, K. C. Yeh, and Benjamin Zycher, *Asian Economic Trends and Their Security Implications* (Santa Monica, Calif.: RAND, 2000), 25–61.

4. For more on this issue, see Zalmay Khalilzad et al., *The United States and Asia: Toward a New U.S. Strategy and Force Posture* (Santa Monica, Calif.: RAND, 2001).

5. A good review of the challenges involved in preserving U.S. primacy can be found in the *Quadrennial Defense Review Report* (Washington, D.C.: Department of Defense, 2001).

6. Damon Bristow, "Mutual Mistrust Still Hampering Sino-Indian Rapprochement," *Jane's Intelligence Review* 9, no. 8 (1997): 368–71.

7. Colonel Gurmeet Kanwal, "Countering China's Strategic Encirclement of India," *Bharat Rakshak Monitor* 3, no. 3 (November–December 2000), emphasis in original.

8. A very useful assessment of Chinese attitudes toward South Asia (and in particular India) relative to its other Asian interests can be found in Michael Pillsbury, *China Debates the Future Security Environment* (Washington, D.C.: National Defense University Press, 2000).

9. Jonathan Pollack, "China and Asia's Nuclear Future," in *Bridging the Nonproliferation Divide: The United States and India,* ed. Francine R. Frankel (Lanham, Md.: University Press of America, 1995).

10. Ashley J. Tellis, *India's Emerging Nuclear Posture* (Santa Monica, Calif.: RAND, 2001), 58–75.

11. A useful survey of the Sino-Pakistani relationship can be found in "Sino-Pakistani Strategic Cooperation" (omnibus issue), *Peace Initiatives* 5, nos. 3–6 (May–December 1999).

12. Shaw-Fawn Kao, "China and ASEAN: Strategic Interests and Policy Prospects," Ph.D. diss., University of Virginia, 1990; Yaacov Vertzberger, *China's Southwestern Strategy: Encirclement and Counterencirclement* (New York: Praeger, 1985).

13. Michael D. Swaine and Ashley J. Tellis, *Interpreting China's Grand Strategy: Past, Present, and Future* (Santa Monica, Calif.: RAND, 2000).

14. For a good survey, see Sujit Dutta, "Sino-Indian Diplomatic Negotiations: A Preliminary Assessment," *Strategic Analysis* 22, no. 12 (March 1999): 1821–34.

15. "Indo-China Border Trade: Trading on Top of the World," *India Today,* 30 September 1992, 64; Raman A. Thothathri, "Indo-Chinese Trade: A Change for the Better," *Business India,* 21 June 1993, 34; "Hindi-Chini Buy, Buy," *Business India,* 16 December 1996, 77.

16. See Kapil Kak, "India's Conventional Defence: Problems and Prospects," *Strategic Analysis* 22, no. 11 (February 1999): 1639–65, and Tellis, *India's Emerging Nuclear Posture,* 477–671, for a survey of these issues.

17. V. Jayanth, "India's 'Look East' Policy," *Hindu,* 2 April 1998; Sandy Gordon, *India's Rise to Power* (New York: St. Martin's Press, 1995), 290–317; and C. S. Kuppuswamy, "India's Policy: Looking Eastward—Update No. 2," available at www.saag.org/notes2/note151.html.

18. Gary Klintworth, "Chinese Perspectives on India as a Great Power," in *India's Strategic Future,* ed. Ross Babbage and Sandy Gordon (New York: St. Martin's Press, 1992), 96.

19. For more on this issue, see Ashley J. Tellis, *The Changing Political-Military Environment: South Asia,* document no. RP-947 (Santa Monica, Calif.: RAND, 2001).

20. For details, see Center for Nonproliferation Studies, "China's Nuclear Exports and Assistance to Pakistan," available at http://cns.miis.edu/research/india/china/npakpos.htm.

21. Ashley J. Tellis, *Stability in South Asia* (Santa Monica, Calif.: RAND, 1997).

22. See, for example, John W. Garver, "Nuclear Weapons and the China-India Relationship," paper presented at the conference on South Asia's Nuclear Dilemma, Weatherhead Center for International Affairs, Harvard University, 18–19 February 1999.

23. Tellis, *Stability in South Asia,* 42–43.

24. For a good survey of how Pakistani nuclear coercion fits into its larger grand strategy, see Eric Arnett, "The Future Strategic Balance in South Asia," in *The Balance of Power in South Asia,* ed. Herro Mustafa (Abu Dhabi: Emirates Center for Strategic Studies and Research, 2000), 95–108.

25. For details, see Rodney W. Jones, "Pakistan's Nuclear Posture: Quest for Assured Nuclear Deterrence—A Conjecture," *Spotlight on Regional Affairs* 19, no. 1 (January 2000): 3–39.

26. Tellis, *Stability in South Asia,* 44–46; Ashley J. Tellis, "India's Emerging Nuclear Doctrine: Exemplifying the Lessons of the Nuclear Revolution," *NBR Analysis* 12, no. 2 (May 2001): 107–10.

27. This critical point is correctly emphasized in Leo E. Rose, "India and China: Forging a New Relationship," in *The Asia-Pacific in the New Millennium: Geopolitics, Security, and Foreign Policy,* ed. Shalendra Sharma (Berkeley, Calif.: Institute of East Asian Studies, 2000), 224–38.

28. Swaran Singh, "Sino-South Asian Ties: Problems and Prospects," *Strategic Analysis* 24, no. 1 (April 2000): 31–49. This judgment, however, raises interesting questions about China's long-term attitude toward Indian hegemony in South Asia. Leo Rose, for example, has argued that China's behavior since 1971 suggests a permanent acquiescence to Indian regional hegemony, while Garver, by contrast, has maintained that the evidence suggests that Beijing's accommodation is at best transient and perhaps only temporary. Unfortunately, it is difficult to resolve this dispute conclusively right now. Beijing's current behavior certainly suggests acquiescence to Indian primacy in South Asia, but whether this condition will change depends greatly on China's own future power capabilities, the successful resolution of its current disputes in East Asia, the larger global balance of power, and the state of Sino-Indian relations.

29. Warren W. Smith, Jr., *Tibetan Nation: A History of Tibetan Nationalism and Sino-Tibetan Relations* (Boulder, Colo.: Westview Press, 1996), 376.

30. For further information, see S. K. Bahl, "China's Failure in Tibet: Pulls and Pressures of Domestic Politics," *China Report* 25, no. 3 (1989); June Teufel Dreyer, "Unrest in Tibet," *Current History* 88, no. 539 (1989); and Donald S. Lopez, Jr., "'Lamaism'" and the Disappearance of Tibet," *Comparative Studies in Society and History* 38, no. 1 (1996).

31. Ramesh Thakur, "Normalizing Sino-Indian Relations," *Pacific Review* 4, no. 1 (1991): 5.

32. Andrew Selth, "Burma and the Strategic Competition between China and India," *Journal of Strategic Studies* 19 (June 1996): 213–30.

33. Donald M. Seekins, "Burma-China Relations: Playing with Fire," *Asian Survey* 37 (June 1977): 532.

34. J. Mohan Malik, "Myanmar's Role in Regional Security: Pawn or Pivot?" *Contemporary Southeast Asia* 19, no. 1 (June 1997).

35. Stephen Blank, "Playing with Fire: Russian Sales in Asia," *Jane's Intelligence Review* 9, no. 4 (April 1997): 174–77.

36. Stephen J. Blank, *The Dynamics of Russian Weapons Sales to China* (Carlisle, Pa.: Strategic Studies Institute, 1997).

37. For more on these issues, see Mark Burles, *Chinese Policy toward Russia and the Central Asian Republics* (Santa Monica, Calif.: RAND, 1999).

38. P. Stobdan, "Regional Security Issues in Central/South Asia and Potential for Cooperation," *Strategic Analysis* 22, no. 10 (January 1999): 1561–76.

39. Dianne L. Smith, *Central Asia: A New Great Game?* (Carlisle, Pa.: Strategic Studies Institute, 1996), 22.

40. Rosemarie Forsythe, *The Politics of Oil in the Caucasus and Central Asia: Prospects for Oil Exploitation and Export in the Caspian Basin,* Adelphi Papers no. 300 (1996).

41. A good survey of these issues can be found in Fereidun Fesharaki, "Energy and the Asian Security Nexus," *Journal of International Affairs* 53, no. 1 (Fall 1999); and Energy Information Administration, U.S. Department of Energy, *International Energy Outlook 1995,* available at www.tonto.eia.doe.gov/FTPROOT/forecasting/048495.pdf.

42. Center for Strategic and International Studies, *The Geopolitics of Energy into the 21st Century: The Report of the CSIS Strategic Initiative* (Executive Summary, November 2000), 4.

43. The centrality of the Gulf to India and China is described in Satyanarayan Pattanayak, "Oil as a Factor in Indo-Gulf Relations," *Strategic Analysis* 25, no. 3 (June 2001): 465–80, and in Erica Strecker Downs, *China's Quest for Energy Security* (Santa Monica, Calif.: RAND, 2000).

44. For an analysis of U.S. power in relationship to the Persian Gulf, see Geoffrey Kemp and Robert E. Harkavy, *Strategic Geography and the Changing Middle East* (Washington, D.C.: Brookings Institution Press, 1997).

45. For a good review of this issue in a contemporary perspective, see Robert Sutter, "China's Policy Priorities and Recent Relations with Southeast Asia," *SAIS Policy Forum Series,* report no. 7 (October 1999).

46. Ellen Palanca, "China's Changing Trade Patterns: Implications for ASEAN-China Trade," *PIDS Policy Notes,* no. 2000-15 (November 2000).

47. "India Looks East," *CSIS South Asia Monitor,* 6 July 2000.

48. V. V. Bhanoji Rao, "Indian Economic Reforms and ASEAN-India Economic Relations," *Journal of Asian Economics* 7, no. 4 (1996): 759–68; Charan Wadhwa, "Revitalising India-ASEAN Economic Partnership: Recent Trends and Future Prospects," in *India and ASEAN: The Growing Partnership for the 21st Century,* ed. K. S. Nathan (Kuala Lumpur: Institute of Diplomacy and Foreign Relations, 2000), 51–74.

49. S. Djiwandono, "India's Relations with East Asia: New Partners?" paper presented at the IISS conference on Rethinking India's Role in the World, Neemrana Fort, India, September 1997 (mimeo), 13.

50. Carlyle Thayer, "China Consolidates Long-Term Regional Relations," *Comparative Connections* 1, no. 3 (January 2000).

51. J. Mohan Malik, "Sino-Indian Relations and India's Eastern Strategy," in *India Looks East: An Emerging Power and Its Asia-Pacific Neighbors,* ed. Sandy Gordon and Stephen Henningham (Canberra: Strategic and Defence Studies Centre, Australian National University, 1995), 119–63.

52. Nirupam Bajpai and Jeffrey D. Sachs, "Foreign Direct Investment in India: Issues and Problems," discussion paper no. 759, Harvard Institute for International Development, March 2000, 7.

53. Jeffrey D. Sachs, Nirupam Bajpai, Mark F. Blaxill, and Arun Maira, *Foreign Direct Investment in India: How Can $10 Billion of Annual Inflows Be Realized?* (policy

report for the Government of India) (Cambridge, Mass.: Center for International Development, Harvard University, 11 January 2000).

54. The Asian countries are Brunei, China, Indonesia, Japan, South Korea, Malaysia, the Philippines, Singapore, Thailand, and Vietnam.

55. J. Mohan Malik, "The India-China Divide," available at www.arts.monash.edu.au/mai/savirtualforum/PaperMalik2.htm.

6

The Nuclear and Security Balance

George Perkovich

This chapter begins by summarizing the historical drivers of China's and India's nuclear and ballistic missile programs and policies. It then describes the current status of these programs and policies and their likely future trajectories. A separate section analyzes Chinese motivations in assisting Pakistan's nuclear and missile programs. The chapter concludes with a comparative discussion of China's and India's approaches toward major arms control and nonproliferation initiatives.

The past and current dynamics affecting China's and India's nuclear policies and the two states' interactions are too various and complicated to allow neat definitions or future projections. India has not been factored heavily into China's nuclear policy making, and China has been only one of several important factors influencing India's nuclear policies. Since the early 1990s China's profile in India's threat assessment has grown, primarily because of Beijing's assistance to Pakistan's nuclear and missile programs. Thus, a complex web of domestic and international relationships within and among India, Pakistan, China, the United States, and others complicates each state's approach to nuclear weapons. This complexity and interconnectedness explains why the three principal antagonists—India, Pakistan, and China—and important extraregional actors such as the United States have failed to establish reliable rules and procedures for managing their nuclear affairs. Without a structured dialogue, let alone the transparency and predictability that come with arms control agreements, future trajectories remain unpredictable.

Historical Drivers of China's and India's Nuclear and Missile Programs

China

Mao Zedong, with counsel from Zhou Enlai, set China on its quest for nuclear weapons in January 1955.[1] The United States was the precipitating cause. The United States had threatened China with nuclear weapons in the Korean War (1950–53) and was now mobilizing to exert military pressure in the Taiwan Strait crisis. Chinese leaders feared that the United States would threaten or actually use nuclear weapons in this crisis.[2] Given the unknowable lead time required to build nuclear weapons, the decision in 1955 represented a longer-term calculus that Washington would feel free to coerce China with nuclear weapons unless and until China had nuclear weapons of its own.

Chinese leaders also believed that nuclear weapons would bring respect and geopolitical power. "As for the atomic bomb," Mao said in 1958, "this big thing, without it people say you don't count for much. Fine, then we should build some."[3] China's aspirations for strategic autonomy, defense, and global standing required the awesome power of nuclear weapons. Chinese leaders also felt that the genius of the Chinese nation and the communist system would be impressed upon their citizens and the broader world by the scientific prowess displayed in the acquisition of nuclear weapons.[4]

China turned to the Soviet Union for assistance in beginning its nuclear program. The Soviets obliged, but by 1960 the Sino-Soviet rift caused Moscow to end this cooperation.[5] Soviet help no doubt contributed significantly to the Chinese effort. Still, when China tested its first nuclear weapon in October 1964, the success was owed largely to the massive and enormously costly exertions of Chinese scientists, engineers, and laborers numbering in the tens of thousands.

In the 1960s and 1970s, the Soviet Union replaced the United States as the principal external threat that Chinese nuclear weapons were to deter.[6]

Alastair Iain Johnston and other leading experts on this topic argue that for nearly three decades after acquiring its first nuclear weapon China lacked a coherent nuclear doctrine.[7] However, this assessment may somewhat misleadingly apply the doctrinal standards set by U.S. and Soviet theorists and practitioners. The Cold War model of nuclear doctrine called for massive, variegated arsenals of tactical, intermediate, and long-range systems and elaborate nuclear war–fighting operations predicated on first use and/or extremely rapid response. Each side targeted the other's nuclear forces, command and control systems, as well as conventional forces and economic targets, in the ultimately futile quest to find a way to win nuclear war. By this standard, China's approach was inadequate. Yet it was not necessarily incoherent. China developed and deployed a relatively small nuclear arsenal for purely defensive purposes to deter nuclear blackmail and possible military aggression against Chinese territory. Accordingly, China committed itself to not to being the first to use nuclear weapons in a conflict. China then organized and operated its nuclear forces consistent with this defensive strategy and no-first-use commitment. For technical and political-doctrinal reasons, Chinese nuclear forces were not deployed in launch-ready configurations. Warheads were not routinely mated to delivery systems. Forces were concealed to help ensure survivability against a possible enemy first strike. Technological limitations explained much of this conservative approach. Still, Chinese political leaders could have pushed harder and spent more to expand and modernize their arsenal earlier.

China's self-restraint reflected the political leadership's political-strategic devaluation of nuclear war fighting. At least through the mid-1990s, Chinese political leaders appeared to perceive nuclear weapons not as war-fighting instruments, but rather as political deterrents against major military aggression or blackmail. To deter sane adversaries from committing such aggression against China, it was sufficient to be able to threaten a *few* of their major cities or *major* military bases on their allies' territory. This can be called a doctrine of minimal deterrence. It seemed to guide or at least reflect China's nuclear and ballistic missile capabilities until the late 1980s. China's leaders seemed to believe that adversary political leaders—as opposed to military theorists—would find the basic, existential threat posed by nuclear weapons sufficient to deter them from risking military aggression against China. The Cuban Missile Crisis, the Sino-Soviet clash along the Ussuri River in 1969, and the refusal of American leaders to risk nuclear escalation in Vietnam all suggested that the specter of nuclear weapons inspired political caution.

A number of factors stimulated new trends in China's approach to nuclear weapons in the late 1980s and early 1990s. China's political leadership and ideology evolved. The Cold War ended. China developed new missile and warhead technologies. The prospect of U.S. ballistic missile defenses emerged on the horizon. Chinese military intellectuals were more exposed to U.S. theories of nuclear doctrine. Chinese defense decision making became more professionalized. Taiwan's political evolution looked more ominous to Beijing. Seeing these trends, Chinese strategists took more seriously the possibility that the minimalist approach to deterrence was insufficient. The advances made by the United States in conventional military operations, and its overwhelming nuclear arsenal, raised doubts about the survivability of China's nuclear deterrent in the face of U.S. attack.[8] In essence, Chinese strategists worried that the United States (or Russia) could call the bluff of a deterrent based on rudimentary capabilities.

China's technological gains made it possible to consider new approaches to deterrence.[9] The central concept was the need to be able to conduct nuclear strikes against a growing array of military targets at relatively early stages of a conflict, instead of ceding a range of military options to the adversary while holding back until the threshold had been crossed for nuclear attacks on major cities. Relying on the last rung of the escalation ladder allowed for too much damage while the adversary climbed the lower rungs. This was militarily unacceptable because it rested deterrence on the perhaps implausible threat that China would jump from the first stage of conventional conflict right to counter-city nuclear attacks.

An evolving concept of "limited deterrence" has appeared to gain favor in China, as distinct from "minimal deterrence."[10] To deny an adversary the initiative in dominating the military escalation process, China needs the capacity to strike enemy missile bases, naval and air bases, regional and national command and control centers and communication hubs, and strategic warning and defense systems, as well as military, economic, and political infrastructure centers. This array of targets in turn requires at least hundreds of accurate missiles that can be rapidly launched. Sophisticated reconnaissance and target acquisition capabilities and command and control systems will also be needed to conduct the envisioned nuclear operations.

The doctrine of limited deterrence proffered by Chinese analysts focuses more on war fighting at the theater level in Northeast Asia than on the capacity to wage strategic nuclear war involving homeland attacks against the United States or Russia. The latter would require a still more ambitious array of weapons, delivery systems, and command and control infrastructure. Lower on the escalation ladder, Chinese strategists call for building up their conventional missile forces to engage Taiwan and U.S. and allied conventional forces in Northeast Asia.[11]

China's actual capacity to achieve these deterrent desiderata remains highly problematic, as will be discussed in later sections of this chapter. The point here is that the factors guiding China's nuclear strategy and policy evolved in the 1990s. Perceived threats from the United States, primarily to Chinese interests in Northeast Asia, remain central. The greatest change is the possible shift from an intuitive, political understanding of deterrence to a militarized process for defining forces and operational plans sufficient to engage adversaries along the spectrum of possible military conflict.

It must be emphasized here, in summary, that India has not figured significantly in motivating or guiding the evolution of China's nuclear doctrine and its acquisition of nuclear weapons and ballistic missiles.[12] China has not regarded India as a strategic peer; nor has China wished to provoke India with threats. China quietly has targeted medium- and intermediate-range nuclear-tipped missiles at India since the mid-1970s. This unadvertised targeting of India represented a low-marginal-cost form of strategic insurance. Beijing did not see India as a threat that should drive China's acquisition and doctrinal adaptation of nuclear forces. Beijing has not relinquished its claims in the border dispute with India or its interest in keeping India from achieving global-power status, but China has not used nuclear or other threats to push these claims either. Chinese leaders no doubt appreciate that India has been forced to take China's nuclear capabilities into account, but Beijing has preferred to let these capabilities speak for themselves rather than make overt nuclear threats against India. Paradoxically, Chinese insouciance and condescension toward India increased New Delhi's interest in acquiring nuclear weapons as a way to compel Beijing to give greater heed to India's interests vis-à-vis China.

India

India's decision to make nuclear weapons was not nearly as assertive as China's. India acquired the bomb ambivalently and haltingly. Whereas

China's highest political leaders launched a crash nuclear weapon building program in 1955, culminating in the first weapon test nine years later, India's program evolved incrementally and ambiguously from 1947 to the first *peaceful* nuclear explosion in 1974, and then to the first avowed *weapon* tests in 1998.

This slow-motion process reflected several factors. The impetus for India's nuclear program came originally from a charismatic scientist, Homi Bhabha, who believed that mastery of atomic energy would demonstrate Indian intellectual prowess, national greatness, and modernity. Bhabha recognized the general military power that could derive from nuclear weapons, but he and his successors did not approach the endeavor in military-strategic terms. India's prime ministers, beginning with Jawaharlal Nehru, retained ultimate authority over the nuclear realm. They, too, thought of nuclear weapon capability in political terms more than in military-security terms. Almost without exception, India's prime ministers have been reluctant to militarize—intellectually and institutionally—India's nuclear capabilities. In this attitude they were joined by the scientific leaders of the nuclear establishment, who consciously excluded military leaders from significant roles in setting nuclear policy and evaluating the direction and performance of the nuclear scientific establishment. For personal and bureaucratic reasons, the scientists and prime ministers did not wish to lose their autonomy over nuclear policy. They also felt that militarization of the program would generate pressures to build a larger and more costly arsenal than they thought the nation could afford. Instead of focusing on military formulae for evaluating "winners" in nuclear war–fighting scenarios, they saw nuclear deterrence as an existential, political condition. In their view the mere prospect that India could visit nuclear destruction on a Pakistani or Chinese city posed sufficient costs to outweigh the political-strategic gains that adversary leaders might seek through nuclear blackmail or aggression against India. They believed that doctrines of nuclear war fighting, which military logic almost inevitably favors, would undermine security and violate India's moral traditions and identity.

China played an important, but not decisive, role in shaping the course of India's nuclear history through the 1998 tests. Bhabha and Nehru privately and in veiled public statements evinced interest in acquiring the capacity to make nuclear explosives in the mid-1950s, before China loomed as a military-security threat. Bhabha's plans to build India's first plutonium reprocessing plant were approved in 1958. India's defeat at the hands of China in 1962 forced the nation to take military security more seriously.

Immediately after the war, India dramatically increased defense spending. Yet the nation did not alter its cautious approach to acquiring nuclear weapons.

China's first nuclear weapon test, in 1964, shortly after Nehru's death, occasioned a major parliamentary debate on India's nuclear options.[13] This remarkable debate revealed competing strategic, political-economic, and moral views regarding the course India should take. Prime Minister Lal Bahadur Shastri ultimately accommodated the urging of Bhabha and his supporters to intensify India's nuclear preparations, but he did so, characteristically, by authorizing work to begin toward developing *peaceful* nuclear explosives. At the same time—from late 1964 through 1967—Indian officials vaguely and ambivalently sought security guarantees, first from the West and then through the United Nations, to protect against possible Chinese nuclear threats. Washington, London, and Moscow were unreceptive. The nascent peaceful nuclear explosive project was halted in 1966 by Bhabha's successor, Vikram Sarabhai, who evinced moral and practical doubts about the wisdom of directing the nuclear establishment toward work on explosives.

A handful of leading scientists then resumed the effort on their own, though Sarabhai did not object when he learned about it. Yet, as the scientists labored on in the late 1960s and early 1970s, China did not figure in their expressed motivations. Rather, they were driven by a more basic desire to prove that they, and India, could master the awesome power of the atom and thus ensure that no state could boss India around. The bomb represented the final repudiation of colonialism and the ultimate guarantee of autonomy. To the extent that the 1974 test had international motivations, they had more to do with showing the United States that it could not treat India contemptuously, as it had in the 1971 Indo-Pakistani war, than with countering Chinese threats. More broadly, Indira Gandhi wanted to signal the United States, China, and the Soviet Union that they could not impinge on India's autonomy.[14] This general valuation of nuclear capability helps explain why the 1974 blast was not followed by others, as would have been the case if Indian leaders had felt a military-strategic imperative to counter China with an operational nuclear deterrent.

In the 1980s, Pakistan emerged as the primary external threat affecting India's nuclear policy. Western press reports and occasional statements by Pakistanis, particularly the director of the Kahuta research laboratories, A. Q. Khan, indicated that by 1987 Pakistan possessed at least one nuclear weapon.[15] China contributed significantly to this threat by providing vital assistance to Pakistan's maturing nuclear weapon program. China reportedly supplied Pakistan with blueprints for a fission weapon around or before 1983.[16] In 1986, China and Pakistan concluded a comprehensive nuclear cooperation agreement. Chinese scientists began assisting Pakistani counterparts to enrich uranium to weapon grade.[17] China also reportedly transferred enough tritium gas to supply neutron initiators for ten nuclear weapons. China also made possible the construction of the Khushab plutonium-production reactor that began operating in 1998.[18]

China grew as a perceived threat to India in the 1990s, notwithstanding improvement in Sino-Indian relations following Prime Minister Rajiv Gandhi's visit to Beijing in 1988. China's assistance to Pakistan's missile program was the most acute cause of concern, along with greater awareness of earlier Sino-Pakistani nuclear cooperation. According to the Center for Nonproliferation Studies at the Monterey Institute of International Studies, China had begun discussing sales of M-11 missiles to Pakistan in the late 1980s. The first contract reportedly was signed in 1988.[19] The United States announced that it had detected a shipment of an M-11 missile to Pakistan in 1991, and imposed sanctions. After negotiations between Washington and Beijing, China assured the United States that it would abide by Missile Technology Control Regime guidelines barring sales of missiles with ranges greater than 300 kilometers. Washington lifted sanctions in March 1992. However, during the U.S. presidential election in September 1992, President Bush agreed to sell 150 F-16 fighters to Taiwan, perhaps to win votes in Texas and California where the plane was produced. This angered China deeply, and may have provided Chinese officials a tactically useful rationale for continuing to assist Pakistan's missile program in the face of U.S. objections. In December 1992, intelligence emerged that China had transferred thirty-four complete M-11 missile systems to Pakistan. In the mid-1990s, China reportedly provided major assistance in the design, construction, and equipment of a missile production plant in Rawalpindi, Pakistan. Thus, the most direct Chinese nuclear threat to India actually came through China's assistance to Pakistan.

More broadly, China's economy continued a second decade of robust growth. In 1947, India started ahead of China in terms of economic development and scientific capabilities, including atomic energy, and therefore thought it should win the contest to be the leading power in Asia. Yet by the 1990s, China had surpassed India by most indices of economic modernization and wherewithal.[20] The rest of the world spoke of China as the rising great power on the world scene. India was seen as a still-struggling poor country with good potential. China's economic expansion facilitated military modernization. While India's conventional force improvements from the mid-1960s onward led to superiority over China in the relevant theaters of potential conflict, China's strategic capabilities outclassed India's. Beijing's condescending, sometimes contemptuous attitude toward India exacerbated resentment and concern. Looking ahead, some in India worried that China could be tempted to bully India in the future. China's unabated claim on Arunachal Pradesh could be pursued more forcefully in the future, as Chinese economic and military power grew. China could also seek to challenge India's influence in the territory and waters abutting the subcontinent.

By 1996, the nationalistic, security-minded Bharatiya Janata Party (BJP) had concluded that India should buttress and display its nuclear weapon prowess as the quickest available means to show the Indian people, China, and the world that India, too, was a power to be reckoned with. Pressure to conduct nuclear tests had been mounting acutely in India since the international community's May 1995 decision to extend indefinitely the Nuclear Nonproliferation Treaty. Many Indian strategists and the key figures in the nuclear establishment feared that India must test now or forfeit its nuclear weapon ambitions. Prime Minister Atal Behari Vajpayee first ordered a nuclear weapon test in his brief tenure in 1996, but reversed the decision pending a parliamentary vote of confidence, which his government ultimately lost.[21] In 1998, Vajpayee ordered tests as one of his first acts in power. The government cited the shadow of China as the major justification for these tests. The demonstration of nuclear capability was intended to give the Indian people confidence, China reason to take India more seriously, and the Indian state the capacity to develop a sufficient nuclear deterrent against China in the long term.

In sum, although a desire to hedge against an uncertain future with China has imparted momentum and intensity to India's quest for nuclear weapons, India's nuclear program through the 1990s was not driven by military requirements or by an acute sense that without "the bomb" India would fall victim to predation. Rather, key scientists and political leaders have seen nuclear weapon capabilities as accoutrements of modernity and world-class power. Nuclear weapons could guarantee India's strategic autonomy and capacity to resist outside political, diplomatic, or military pressure—whether from China, Pakistan, the United States, or any other power. Moral tradition stemming from Gandhi has made the Indian polity and its leading institutions reluctant to treat "the bomb" as a militarily usable weapon, as will be elaborated in later sections. But if great powers have nuclear weapons, and having nuclear weapons compels others to treat one more deferentially, then India will have nuclear weapons. In the coming decades, as distinct from the prior half-century, the realities of being an overt nuclear weapon possessor will force India to address more directly the technical and operational challenges of deterring China.

Current Status and Future Trajectories of Chinese and Indian Nuclear Forces and Doctrines

Nuclear Forces: China

China does not yet possess remotely sufficient nuclear forces and command and control capabilities to fulfill the ambitious missions envisioned under the concept of limited deterrence. This is true both at the theater level in Northeast Asia, primarily the Taiwan Strait, and at the strategic level where nuclear exchanges against core homeland targets would be envisioned. However, if Chinese nuclear capabilities were geared toward India, then China would possess significant advantages in theoretical moves up the nuclear escalation ladder.

China possesses only a rudimentary, largely notional nuclear triad.[22] It has one ballistic missile submarine with twelve missiles capable of carrying a single nuclear warhead 1,700 kilometers. However, this submarine has been beset by technical problems since entering into service in the early 1980s and is not considered operational.[23] The air leg of the Chinese triad consists of aged bombers, mostly of the 1960s-vintage H-6 variety. These pose practically no threat to Russian or U.S. and allied defenses.

Land-based missiles are the only muscular leg of the Chinese arsenal. According to public sources, China possesses 120-plus land-based missiles with ranges exceeding 1,800 kilometers.[24] Each can carry one nuclear warhead. The longest-range missile, the DF-5A (or CSS-4), is dedicated to the United States and can carry a three- to five-megaton warhead 13,000 kilometers. Between seventeen and twenty-four of these silo-based systems are believed to exist. Twenty DF-4 (or CSS-3) missiles are deployed with a range of 4,750 kilometers, and may be targeted at India (as discussed in the next paragraph). Roughly fifty DF-21 (CSS-5) missiles with a range of 1,800 kilometers are also deployed. These have warheads with two- to three-hundred-kiloton yields. Roughly thirty-eight DF-3A (or CSS-2) missiles with a range of 2,850 kilometers are deployed with warheads estimated to have one- to three-megaton yields. However, the DF-3A is a thirty-year-old, liquid-fueled system that is being replaced by the DF-21. China also deploys several hundred shorter-range missile systems capable of carrying nuclear warheads. These are known as the DF-11 and DF-15, or M-9, M-11 classes of missiles.

China's land-based missiles are slated to cover a broad array of targets. The longest-range missiles are dedicated to the United States. DF-3A and DF-21 missiles based in Jilin are likely targeted at Japan, Korea, Okinawa, and the Russian Far East.[25] Missiles at other bases target countries to the south and southwest of China, including the Philippines, Vietnam, and India. Others target the former Soviet Union. Many of the shorter-range DF-11 and DF-15 (M-9, M-11) missiles are dedicated to Taiwan-related scenarios.

China is modernizing its missile force. It is developing the mobile, solid-fueled DF-31 missile with a range of 8,000 kilometers, which is expected to be deployed in the next several years. Another program, the DF-41, reportedly has been canceled, but is being succeeded by an as-yet-unnamed system that the CIA estimates will be targeted at the United States and may be tested within several years.[26] An improved submarine-launched missile, the JL-2, also is reportedly under development, though the fundamental problems experienced by China's ballistic missile submarine program raise questions about that system's viability. Each of these longer-range systems is geared primarily toward the United States. Missile modernization is intended to improve force survivability. China's older, liquid-fueled missiles are typically deployed without fuel and warheads, meaning they are vulnerable to preemption and cannot be launched on warning of attack. All of this is consistent with minimal deterrence, but not with the war-fighting doctrine favored by some Chinese analysts. By increasing launch readiness and mobility, the newer missile systems should enhance survivability. Chinese strategists and technologists also seek to develop the space-based or land-based early warning systems needed to execute more militarily robust deterrence strategies. Execution of war-fighting strategies also requires greater missile accuracy. Much of the modernization effort is dedicated to enhancing these capabilities and, more broadly, to reaping the benefits of the revolution in communication and computing technology.

The intensity and scale of China's future strategic modernization efforts will be affected significantly by the threats China perceives of Taiwanese independence and of U.S. initiatives to contain China's power and influence directly and through relations with Taiwan, Japan, and perhaps India. U.S. missile defense policies bear on these relationships insofar as Washington may buttress Japanese and Taiwanese positions against China, as perceived by Beijing, through cooperative deployments of theater missile defenses. U.S. national missile defenses would pose a direct threat to China's strategic deterrent. China likely would seek to counter such defenses through a more extensive quantitative and qualitative buildup of long-range offensive nuclear forces with innovations to penetrate defenses. Beijing also may choose to supply countermeasure technology to U.S. adversaries.

China's nuclear arsenal is more than sufficient to prevail in theoretical nuclear exchanges with India. This is true even discounting the Chinese bomber fleet, which cannot penetrate alerted Indian air defenses, and the Chinese naval nuclear force, which is highly unlikely to be deployed to the Bay of Bengal or the Indian Ocean.[27]

Three categories of Chinese ballistic missiles, totaling at least sixty-six missiles, are believed to include India among their targets. They are deployed at two missile bases. Base 53, headquartered at Kumming, in Yunnan province in south-central China, hosts DF-3A (or CSS-2) missiles with ranges of 2,800 kilometers, and mobile DF-21 (or CSS-5) missiles with ranges of about 1,800 kilometers. Base 56, headquartered at Xining, Qinghai province, in north-central China, hosts a subset of the thirty to forty total CSS-2 missiles, and ten or more DF-4 (or CSS-3) missiles with a range of 4,750 kilometers, great enough to cover all of India. The DF-3A missiles are each believed to carry one three-megaton thermonuclear warhead, enough to destroy a major city in a single blast. The DF-21 missiles reportedly carry warheads with yields in the two- to three-hundred-kiloton range, while the 10 DF-4s carry one- to three-megaton warheads. The liquid-fueled DF-3As are being replaced by more modern, solid-fueled DF-21s in at least two modernized versions with extended range.[28] This array of missiles and warheads ensures that China can destroy with high confidence any city or other major target in India.

The fact that China's thermonuclear weapons and long-range ballistic missiles constitute nuclear superiority over India provides relatively little useful advantage to Beijing. No realistic scenario exists under which these forces would be required to deter Indian aggression or to facilitate Chinese aggression against India. Indeed, the Sino-Indian military balance along the Himalayan frontier makes such aggression highly unpromising for Beijing. As Ashley Tellis concludes, the quality of Indian personnel, training, and infrastructure, especially its relative logistical advantages, make Indian defenses very robust in the Himalayan region. India's tactical air power unambiguously surpasses that of China along the frontier.[29] In Tellis's words, "there are in fact few circumstances under which Chinese use of nuclear weapons as warfighting instruments would be either plausible or advantageous to it in the context of a conventional conflict with India."[30] Moreover, it is very difficult to imagine what interests would motivate China to launch the sort of aggression against India that would be threatening enough to prompt New Delhi to run the grave risks of countering by using nuclear weapons.[31] A conventional aggression large enough to cause strategic peril against defensively robust India would make no sense and would require long mobilization that would provide strategic warning to India and to outside powers such as the United States and Russia. Even if China calculated that it could resort early to nuclear use to overcome India's defensive advantage, the realities of moving follow-on forces through Himalayan terrain in the aftermath of nuclear detonations would be practically overwhelming. It further defies credibility to think that China would risk the incalculable consequences of escalating to strategic nuclear attacks against India to overcome the problems of conventional and tactical nuclear conflict along the disputed frontier.

For the foreseeable future China will lack the combination of geopolitical interests and military capabilities that would make limited aggression against India plausibly tempting. Although China could leap beyond limited conflict and "win" an all-out nuclear exchange against India in the coming decade, such a scenario stretches all geostrategic credulity. Rather, China's nuclear capabilities provide a strong and low-cost reinsurance policy that India will be deterred from seeking militarily to revise the results of the 1962 war or settle the border dispute on India's terms.[32]

Nuclear Forces: India

India does not yet deploy assembled nuclear weapons that could be launched for attack immediately or even in a few hours as China's strategic nuclear weapons could be. Thus, references to India's "nuclear forces" pertain more to capabilities that could be mobilized over time than to ready-to-fire assets. This is not necessarily a weakness or vulnerability, insofar as India faces no immediate nuclear threat from China and has committed itself not to be the first to initiate use of nuclear weapons in any case.

The most plausible nuclear threat to India would come from Pakistan. According to David Albright, writing in 2000, Pakistan probably possesses roughly 690 kilograms of highly enriched uranium, enough for perhaps thirty-nine fission weapons.[33] The quantities likely have increased slightly in the intervening months. Pakistan also has begun to operate an unsafeguarded Chinese-supplied plutonium production reactor at Khushab and reportedly has an operating reprocessing plant at "New Labs," near the Pakistan Institute of Nuclear Science and Technology in Rawalpindi. China's assistance in constructing the Khushab reactor violated the nuclear Nonproliferation Treaty. Pakistan has a suite of ballistic missiles under development and production. The most threatening of these are the 700-kilometer-range Shaheen, with Chinese parentage, and the 1,500–2,000-kilometer-range Ghauri-1 and -2, with North Korean parentage.[34] Additional variants of these missiles are reportedly under development. Pakistan also fields roughly two dozen rather aged F-16 aircraft that could deliver nuclear weapons against Indian targets. Pakistan from the beginning, unlike India, has treated nuclear weapons as military instruments. The Pakistani armed services have been involved in nuclear policy and doctrine formation for decades now and should be expected to have developed coherent doctrines and operational procedures to employ nuclear weapons in a conflict with India. Pakistan's program reflects a determination to ensure the invulnerability of its strategic missiles (and warheads) to preemption and their capacity to penetrate Indian defenses to reach a growing range of targets in India.

With strategic warning, and in response to a nuclear attack, India probably could conduct the final assembly operations necessary to enable aircraft to deliver a nuclear riposte against Pakistan within twenty-four hours. (India's short-range Prithvi ballistic missile could carry a nuclear warhead to Pakistani targets, but would have to be deployed and fueled within range of Pakistani interdiction, making it an undesirable nuclear delivery vehicle.) India's strategic modernization programs and evolving operational and command and control systems will increase New Delhi's confidence that it can withstand a Pakistani first strike and deliver a devastating counterblow. It is difficult to argue that this does not constitute a serious nuclear deterrent against Pakistan.

Still, as Ashley Tellis has pointed out, Pakistan's growing nuclear wherewithal poses the most fundamental threat to India's security. Rawalpindi's strategic capabilities severely undermine India's conventional military advantages. Indian security managers will have to attend to this reality as the first-order security problem, even if pundits and others prefer to focus on the more ennobling challenge of competing with China.[35] This may seem paradoxical insofar as India today does possess a viable capacity to retaliate to a Pakistani nuclear attack and is much less capable of holding major Chinese targets hostage. The difference lies in the relative likelihood of conflict that could escalate to the strategic level between India and Pakistan, on one hand, and India and China, on the other. The former is a more realistic threat than the latter.

Fission warheads with explosive yields somewhat greater than the bombs the United States dropped on Hiroshima and Nagasaki probably make up the core of India's nuclear weapons capabilities. This sort of weapon was tested in a nondeliverable configuration in 1974, and in an improved, deliverable form in 1998. There is reason to think that India can deploy fission weapons that use weapon-grade and non-weapon-grade plutonium, the latter having lower yields. India also has tested designs of more efficient and powerful nuclear explosives. The 1998 tests included a thermonuclear device whose primary, or first stage, was a boosted-fission explosive. Boosted-fission devices use a small amount of mixed deuterium and tritium to provide large numbers of neutrons that greatly increase the rate of fission of plutonium before the chain reaction ends. Successful boosting vastly increases the explosive power of a given amount of plutonium, enabling the production of devices with yields typically in the one- to two-hundred-kiloton range. Thermonuclear weapons can have still greater explosive yields. However, international and Indian sources have continued to debate whether the two-stage boosted-fission/thermonuclear device tested by India worked effectively.[36]

At the end of 2002, the best open estimates suggested that India possesses between three and four hundred kilograms of separated weapon-grade plutonium, derived from the weapons-dedicated CIRUS and Dhruva plutonium production reactors at the Bhabha Atomic Research Centre at Trombay.[37] This is enough for perhaps fifty to sixty-five fission weapons. The potential number of weapons is larger if India is able and chooses to fashion weapons from non-weapon-grade plutonium. These likely would have small yields equivalent to one hundred tons of TNT. Continuing production of fissile materials means that India's potential arsenal size will grow. The desired end point will depend on many variables that cannot be specified today; informed Indians suggest that an arsenal of 100 to 175 weapons would be a reasonable goal.[38]

Tactical fighter-bomber aircraft, most likely the French Mirage-2000, make up India's current nuclear weapon delivery capability. India has thirty-five of these planes, which have to be modified to deliver nuclear weapons.[39] Jaguar fighter-bombers also could perform this role, as could Russian Sukhoi-30s. Whichever aircraft Indian military planners prefer for nuclear missions, they all have adequate range to cover desired targets in Pakistan.[40] None possesses the range to hit strategically significant targets in China. India could in the future seek to procure advanced aircraft with ranges sufficient to reach such targets.

Missiles are the key to reaching Chinese targets. India began its Integrated Guided Missile Program in 1983. By the late 1980s, the short-range Prithvi missile system had been fully flight-tested and had entered production. It has a 150-kilometer and a 250-kilometer variant. Yet the Prithvi was not designed to perform nuclear missions, and Indian leaders appear unlikely to assign it this role.[41]

The Agni missile is clearly the nuclear-delivery vehicle of choice. The original configuration of the Agni was tested three times, with mixed results, between 1989 and 1994. It achieved a range of 1,000 kilometers. An improved version, the Agni II, has been flight-tested twice, in 1999 and 2001. With an all-solid-fuel propulsion system, this missile reportedly has achieved a range of 2,000 kilometers. According to the Defense Research and Development Organization, the missile is now ready for production. Reports in August 2001 declared that the Indian army would field these weapons in a nuclear deterrent role.[42] Yet, even if two tests are sufficient to prove the reliability and effectiveness of this missile, its range still falls more than 1,000 kilometers short of China's major cities, the most logical targets if the India deterrent is to be robust. As the Indian Air Force recently concluded in a classified report quoted in *India Today,* the range of "Prithvi is too short to qualify as a nuclear platform . . . Agni is some distance away from being operational . . . the only vector is the aircraft and will be so for about a decade."[43] India would need a test-proven ballistic missile with a range of at least 3,500 kilometers to hold targets such as Chengdu, Chongqing, and Yichang at risk, and a missile with a 5,000-kilometer range to target Beijing and Shanghai. A new variant of the Agni could someday achieve the former, but an entirely new missile system would be necessary to go beyond 3,000–3,500 kilometers.[44] Thus, India remains probably more than a decade away from an extensive missile-based deterrent against China.

India also is developing a suite of cruise missiles. Russia is helping significantly in this area and in the overall missile program.[45] Cruise missiles based on surface ships and attack submarines could augment India's nuclear deterrent by providing mobile and, especially in the case of submarines, hard-to-detect nuclear platforms. To this end, Indian and Russian sources indicated in 2002 that Russia would lease to India two new nuclear-powered Shchuka B-class submarines (Akula II, in NATO parlance).[46] These (nonballistic missile) submarines are capable of carrying land-attack cruise missiles with four-hundred-kilogram warheads and a 300-kilometer range. It remains unclear how long it would take India to develop, test, and integrate nuclear-tipped cruise missiles for launch by submarines, if India sought to achieve this objective while pursuing the more distant goal of a submarine-based ballistic missile nuclear deterrent. Unlike land-based and air-based nuclear systems, sea-based systems would require the military to take possession of nuclear warheads in peacetime and to maintain warheads mated with delivery systems. This raises difficult political and doctrinal questions for India.

Ultimately, India's most ambitious strategists and defense technologists hope that nuclear-powered ballistic missile submarines will become the centerpiece of the nation's nuclear deterrent. Such submarines would be difficult to track and target, thereby greatly enhancing the survivability of the deterrent. But the submarine program has been plagued with technical problems from its inception in the 1970s. Doubts remain as to whether India can produce a safe and effective nuclear propulsion system, master the extreme challenge of building an advanced submarine, and develop the capacity to launch long-range ballistic missiles underwater. India secretly approached Russia for help in this program in the 1980s, and it is possible that recently reintensified Indo-Russian defense cooperation could boost the effort. Still, an effective submarine-based ballistic missile capability remains a rather distant prospect.

India's nuclear doctrine rests on one grand concept and three fundamental operational principles. The grand concept is that nuclear weapons are not war-fighting instruments, but rather means to deter other nuclear-armed states from using or threatening to use nuclear weapons against India. Put another way, the challenge of deterrence is to persuade adversary decision makers not to undertake the risks of aggression that could likely escalate to nuclear weapon use. Authors of Indian doctrine see this as a political more than a military process. They believe that real-life political leaders are unlikely to run such risks, and that nuclear weapons strongly reinforce the rather simple intuition that none of India's potential adversaries has so much to gain by massive military aggression against India that they would risk being hit with nuclear weapons in return. Thus, Indian decision makers—all civilians—have resisted the abstract, nuclear war–fighting logic that American and Russian nuclear strategists built into their nuclear doctrines.[47]

The most important of the three major operational principles that flow from this basic approach to deterrence is that India will not be the first to use nuclear weapons in a conflict. No-first-use removes much of the temptation to develop nuclear war–fighting plans and tactical weapons to go with them. A state following no-first-use would assume that some of the militarily significant targets that might be desirable to hit on a first-strike basis will have already "left the barn" and therefore do not merit targeting. This leads to the second operational principle: Indian nuclear weapons would be unleashed to punish an aggressor rather than to limit potential damage by destroying adversaries' nuclear weapon installations, conventional forces, and other war-fighting assets. Punishment means that India's nuclear forces would be targeted primarily at adversary cities or other high-value targets in sociopolitical and economic terms. India does not have a real alternative vis-à-vis China, insofar as India could not locate and target China's concealed and mobile nuclear weapons. This so-called countervalue targeting is the third operational principle of India's nuclear doctrine.[48]

If India were to possess nuclear weapons and delivery systems capable of hitting Chinese targets, New Delhi's doctrinal precepts would reserve use of these weapons until after China had initiated nuclear conflict. But this is a highly unlikely contingency for the foreseeable future. The public record suggests that the distant nature of the Chinese military nuclear threat and the state of India's still evolving technical capabilities combine to dampen the urgency for India of elaborating detailed plans for nuclear operations against China.

Technological developments and political-strategic adjustments to the exigencies of managing overt nuclear arsenals could cause erosion in each of the three cardinal premises of Indian doctrine. For example, deployment of nuclear weapons at sea would require transfer of peacetime control of nuclear weapons from civilians to the military. The military then would gain a more integral role in the nuclear policy process than civilian leaders have traditionally accepted. Strategists also may worry that Pakistan or China will doubt the credibility of India's threats to rely only on second-strike retaliation against countervalue targets. Such concerns could engender pressure to deploy tactical nuclear weapons and adopt counterforce plans to convince adversaries that India would in fact use nuclear weapons, thereby strengthening deterrence in a manner similar to U.S. and Soviet policies.

Public sources do not detail India's current command, control, and operational plans and capabilities. There is reason to think that the political and scientific leadership, at least, are comfortable with the procedures and resources that have been established to muster an effective nuclear retaliatory blow against Pakistan if needed. At the same time, greater attention is now being given to the integration of military professionalism into nuclear planning. In 2000, the government tasked Arun Singh to head a commission to devise recommendations for reforming India's defense management. This commission recommended that a new post, chief of defense staff, be created to provide an apex military adviser to the government.[49] Analogous to the U.S. chairman of the Joint Chiefs of Staff, the chief of defense staff (CDS) would organize greater coordination between the three separate military services, reconciling competing claims for resources and integrating strategic planning. One of the CDS's top functions would be to coordinate nuclear weapon and delivery system development, acquisition, and operational planning, presenting the political leadership with integrated recommendations. The CDS would be the principal liaison between the political leadership and the armed forces in nuclear weapon matters. Civilians would retain possession and control of nuclear weapons themselves; the military's role would focus on delivery systems and operational planning.

Unsurprisingly, however, implementation of the recommendation to create and staff the CDS post has been slow. For diverse reasons, the three services have been reluctant to embrace the idea, feeling that their service interests would be better served without an intermediary figure at the apex of the military establishment. The Indian Air Force reportedly is particularly reluctant to cede what has been its primacy in nuclear missions.[50] Opposition political parties have protested that they were not consulted adequately on such a momentous change in defense management and, potentially, in civil-military relations.[51] Through 2002, the reform had been put on hold. The Indian democracy's long-standing ambivalence about treating nuclear weapons as military instruments has expressed itself again.

India's nuclear doctrine and command system to date represent the political-moral judgments of India's leaders more than the considered analysis of military professionals. If India were to follow a military logic and produce nuclear doctrine inductively—beginning with threat assessments and working back to operational requirements—rather than deductively, it would confront a great challenge.

India faces two qualitatively and quantitatively different potential nuclear adversaries in Pakistan and China. An arsenal numerous and powerful enough to threaten China on a second-strike basis would alarm Pakistan and cause it to ratchet up its own capabilities in an unwanted action-reaction cycle. Doctrine and forces suited to deter just Pakistan might be insufficient to guarantee credible nuclear retaliation against China. The Indian strategist Rear Admiral (ret.) Raja Menon has recognized this well: "An Indian attempt to structure an arsenal beyond Pakistan's would first lead to a South Asian arms race (unless Pakistan accepts India's perceived threat from China), followed by a needless Sino-Indian arms race. In both cases India will be pushed economically—the result of having to defend against two nuclear states. An understanding with China on nuclear arsenals is mandatory at the very beginning."[52] Menon acknowledges further that India and Pakistan need to agree on rules of the road to guide and limit their nuclear competition. To date, neither India and Pakistan nor India and China have approached agreements that would regulate their current and potential competition in strategic weaponry.

India cited the threat from China in justifying the 1998 nuclear tests. Since then, leading military and security strategists have added nuance to this portrayal. In January 2001, Army Chief of Staff General Sundarjan Padmanabhan said that "the level of confrontation, the level of tempers and the tendency to jump off the edge is much less with China" than with Pakistan.[53] Foreign Minister Jaswant Singh declared in Beijing that "the threat chapter is over."[54] The Ministry of Defense's 1998–99 annual report stated that India did not regard China as "an adversary."[55] However, the ministry's report for 2000–2001, released in May 2001, returned to a less sanguine appraisal of China. It noted that "our largest neighbour China is working towards achieving super-power status in the new millennium."[56] The report continued that China was extending its political and military influence in India's "neighbourhood," and that every Indian city is within reach of Chinese missiles." Yet, as Rear Admiral (ret.) Raja Menon averred in his thoughtful, hawkish monograph on Indian nuclear strategy: "The Indian arsenal is not required because of an immediate military threat from China"; India does not need nuclear weapons to defend its territory.[57]

Nuclear forces and doctrine will not attain what India wants from China. A highly respected Indian government adviser recently offered that India seeks Chinese acknowledgment that

> we have legitimate rights and interests and there cannot be a meaningful relationship unless such an acknowledgement is unequivocal and public. China must show signs of abandoning its specific policy to use Pakistan as its 'counter-irritant' in its relationship with India. China will have to show signs that it intends to build a bilateral relationship not governed by its own third party requirements. China will have to show signs that it considers an improvement in Sino-Indian relations as important or at least meaningful to China.[58]

The nonnuclear nature of Sino-Indian tensions fortuitously corresponds with India's low capability to deliver nuclear weapons against China. India cannot do what it does not presently need to do. Practically, Indian doctrine and capabilities must address Pakistan as the first-order challenge. Once this is recognized, India's doctrine and capabilities as adduced above appear sufficient. Over the longer term, India may require long-range nuclear weapons to give New Delhi confidence that it could rebuff future instances of Chinese "blackmail" or "coercive diplomacy"—that is, mobilization of Chinese forces against India paired with threats to move the escalatory ladder of conflict if India did not accede to Chinese demands. This need could arise if China reversed the current conventional force balance along the Sino-Indian frontier, and/or if Sino-Indian relations became so intensely competitive in Asia that either side appeared inclined to prefer the high risks of war to the chronic frustration of diplomacy and political-economic jostling. (Both halves of this scenario presuppose that China's more fundamental interests vis-à-vis Taiwan, Japan, and the United States would be resolved positively or negatively to the point that Beijing would have little to lose by diverting its military and political capital to a conflict with India.) To prepare for this unwelcome eventuality without causing it, India would have to develop the technical capability to hold vital Chinese targets hostage without alarming China about India's intentions and thereby reversing the positive trend in Sino-Indian relations. In the meantime, the challenge of dissuading China from continuing its troublesome assistance to Pakistan's missile program will require greater progress in Indo-Pakistani relations to remove the incentives that both Beijing and Islamabad perceive in balancing India's strategic advantages over Pakistan.

China will affect India's future actions in at least three ways. First, if China continues major assistance to Pakistan's nuclear and missile programs, India will more energetically advance its own capabilities in response. Second, China's nuclear and missile modernization program affects the environment to which India adapts. India's sense of global equity leads it increasingly to speak and act as the other major powers do. If China, Russia, and the United States reintensify competition in the nuclear and missile spheres, India will more energetically seek to extend the range and diversity of its nuclear weapon delivery capabilities. Third, China's specific attitude and policies toward India will affect how New Delhi defines its nuclear and missile requirements. If China takes a forthcoming path toward India, Indian political leaders will prefer not to divert their nation's resources and attention to strategic military rivalry with China. If Beijing exhibits bullying and condescending attitudes toward India, New Delhi will see displays of growing nuclear and missile capabilities as a means of reassuring the Indian people and warning China that India will not be coerced or slighted.

In any case, India will continue to expand and refine the quantity and quality of its nuclear weapons and missile delivery systems. It will develop operational procedures and command and control systems to provide greater confidence that it has an assured retaliatory capability, especially against Pakistan. Indeed, the Pakistan threat alone is sufficient to drive India's nuclearization process forward. This would be true even if China fulsomely adhered to its pledges to "prevent the export of equipment, materials or technology that could in any way assist programs in India or Pakistan for nuclear weapons or for ballistic missiles capable of delivering such weapons."[59] Pakistan now has the expertise and facilities to "grow" its arsenal indigenously. However, if China continues to dodge its non-proliferation obligations, the pressure for an Indo-Pakistani arms race will increase. India could resist this pressure by remaining "satisfied" with the capacity to destroy Pakistani cities and society on a second-strike basis, regardless of the future quantitative and qualitative levels of each side's forces. Yet maintaining such self-restraint poses political challenges. Arms control could serve both India and Pakistan by circumscribing their potential competition and the opportunity of political forces to exacerbate it.

Chinese Missile and Nuclear Proliferation to Pakistan

Public sources reveal little about the motives behind China's nuclear and missile proliferation to Pakistan. Neither China nor Pakistan has acknowledged, let alone explained, the nuclear assistance. China has been compelled by U.S. diplomacy to acknowledge implicitly its missile proliferation, but the actual motivations behind it remain cloudy.

As early as the mid-1960s, Zulfikar Ali Bhutto requested Chinese assistance to help Pakistan develop nuclear weapon capabilities to match the Indian program. Pakistan, following the 1964 claims of Homi Bhabha, believed that India would produce a nuclear weapon in the near future. China did not oblige then, but in 1976, according to a subsequent intimation by Bhutto, the Beijing government agreed to be more forthcoming. If true, this suggests that Beijing sought to help Pakistan respond to India's detonation of a nuclear explosive in 1974. Still, the public record indicates that provision of key inputs did not occur until the early and mid-1980s. This coincided with the Soviet aggression in Afghanistan, which alarmed Beijing (and Washington and Islamabad) with the prospect that Moscow could extend its reach into Central Asia and the Persian Gulf. China and the United States cooperated in extending assistance to Pakistan and to the Afghan resistance. Beijing was already disposed to assist Pakistan in balancing India's nuclear capability; the interest in strengthening Pakistan's capacity to shield itself (and China) against Soviet incursions into the region could help explain the timing of the supply of a weapon blueprint, neutron initiator(s), and other materiel. Beijing also correctly calculated that Washington would not vigorously punish China and Pakistan for this proliferation, given the Sino-American-Pakistani cooperation in repulsing Soviet aggression.

Chinese assistance to Pakistan's missile program appears to have been directed first and foremost at helping Pakistan to balance India and at creating local nuisances that would keep India from becoming more than a hamstrung regional power. China's ongoing assistance to Pakistan's missile program also has paralleled India's development of a suite of ballistic missile systems. A strategically armed Pakistan would limit India's regional hegemony and provide an indirect lever to influence India. China constantly worries that Indian-based Tibetan leaders could intensify their quest for autonomy or even independence from China; the threat to increase Pakistan's capacity to challenge India can be seen as a tool to ensure that India limits the political activities of the Tibetan community in India. Chinese officials argue that assisting friends in maintaining a balance of power is "normal" behavior.[60]

American officials and analysts have suggested that the commercial interests of missile technology enterprises and "brokers" in China also played a role. Beijing also has used missile-related exports to protest American actions that China disliked—for example, in the aftermath of the U.S. sale of F-16s to Taiwan. To the extent that nonproliferation is a U.S.

priority, China appears to view compliance or noncompliance with American "demands" as tactical tool. This sometimes befuddles American officials insofar as missiles in Pakistan do not pose direct threats to the United States, but rather to the general nonproliferation regime in which the United States believes China should share an interest. To date, China apparently has placed greater value on helping Pakistan balance India regionally than on strengthening the global nonproliferation regime.

In any case, by late 1996 Beijing appeared to be recalculating its interests in South Asia. The Soviet collapse greatly reduced the need to contain Moscow's regional influence. The increasing global hegemony of the United States and its prominence in South Asia elevated China's interest in balancing the United States in the region. At the same time, India appeared to be a rising global player. By all indices of power, India was beginning to dwarf Pakistan. Worse still, from Beijing's perspective, Pakistan was becoming an increasingly problematic partner. Extremist Islamist organizations born of the Afghan struggle were distorting the character of Pakistani politics. Networks of terrorist and drug-trading organizations threatened to foment Islamist resistance groups in China's Xinjiang. And China was becoming more uncomfortable with the drift of conflict in Kashmir. Thus, as a Chinese commentator recently noted, Beijing began to recognize that in South Asia "China and India have more common interests than differences."[61]

The most dramatic signal of China's reassessment came with President Jiang Zemin's late-1996 visit to India and Pakistan. China and India signed four agreements during the visit. The most important was a measure to further the withdrawal of forces and enhance confidence-building along the Line of Actual Control. In a press conference, a Chinese foreign ministry spokesman denied that China had provided nuclear weapon technology or M-11 missiles to Pakistan and also declared that China would not sell advanced weapons to its neighbors.[62] The denial of past activities was false. The statement about future activities, made on Indian soil, was potentially significant, though past performance indicated that China would find ways to continue helping Pakistan within the letter but not the spirit of the nonproliferation pledges sought by India and the United States.

The most important development of Jiang's trip occurred in Pakistan. Jiang delivered a diplomatically veiled blow by calling for Pakistan and India to negotiate a settlement on Kashmir. As a Pakistani daily noted, this seemingly banal statement signified that Beijing "no longer recognises [Kashmir] as an international issue."[63] China was shifting the balance of its interests relative to Pakistan and India.

However, following the Indian nuclear tests of May 1998, U.S. intelligence noted a resumption of Chinese assistance to Pakistan's missile program (which China in 1996 had said would stop). The Shaheen-1 missile tested by Pakistan in April 1999 bore the traits of China's M-9 missile. Pakistan's Ghauri missile derived from North Korea. The U.S. Central Intelligency Agency (CIA) concluded in 1999 that Chinese and North Korean entities "continued to provide assistance to Pakistan's ballistic missile program" in 1998. A knowledgeable U.S. official told the author that following the Indian nuclear tests, "the Pakistanis called on their old friends to show loyalty and we saw problems in the missile proliferation area again in late 1998 and 1999."[64] This prompted the United States to warn China that sanctions might once again be applied. That warning led in early 2000 to a stronger Chinese commitment to Washington not to supply Pakistan's missile program.[65]

From 1999 to early 2001, Sino-Indian relations recovered from the damage caused by the 1998 nuclear tests and the Indian rhetoric surrounding them, as discussed by Susan Shirk in chapter 3 of this volume.[66] China rebuffed Pakistani bids for diplomatic buttressing during the 1999 Kargil war. In the midst of the conflict, China received the Indian foreign minister, Jaswant Singh, and announced the formation of a "strategic dialogue" between the two countries. In May 2000, Indian President K. R. Narayanan traveled to China where he was received warmly. China refrained from hectoring on nuclear issues, and the two states generally boosted the momentum in their relations. The effort to put a positive face on the Sino-Indian relationship continued in January 2001 when Li Peng, the second most powerful figure in China, made a nine-day visit to India.[67]

Still, China's assistance to Pakistan's strategic programs remains arguably the greatest impediment to Sino-Indian relations. Notwithstanding repeated (and varying) commitments to the United States to cease missile-related exports to Pakistan, China has continued some such exports, according to U.S. officials in July 2001. "After November 2000, there have been instances that make the [agreement with the United States] meaningless and show China has no intention of implementing it," a U.S. diplomat told the *Washington Post*.[68] China and Pakistan have denied any "violations of the Missile Technology Control Regime."[69] The dispute was taken up by Chinese and American diplomats in late August 2001 with no public outcome. Indian officials privately remain frustrated that Chinese officials have not admitted past assistance to Pakistan's nuclear weapon program, let alone ongoing proliferation.[70] China may see its assistance to Pakistan's missile program as a means of balancing India's capabilities. To the extent that Russia is now providing major assistance to India's missile program, it may be more difficult for Indians and others to insist on complete Chinese forbearance vis-à-vis Pakistan. In any case, Beijing's unwillingness to acknowledge its assistance to Pakistan's strategic programs and to address directly India's concerns about China's role in the Indo-Pakistani security equation raises Indian (and U.S.) concerns about China's intentions.

It appears that China has not reconciled its ongoing policies toward Pakistan's missile program with its overall diplomatic strategy to warm ties with India. As the twenty-first century begins, China places great strategic emphasis on balancing U.S. power and fostering global multipolarity in lieu of unipolarity. China worries most about the future of Taiwan and about U.S.-Japanese influence in Northeast Asia. Beijing detects American interest, especially among Republicans, in enlisting India in an effort to contain China. China seeks to improve ties with India to forestall such collusional containment. India's traditional resistance to Western domination gives China hope that New Delhi, with Russia, shares an interest in campaigning for multipolarity. This strategic interest drives Beijing to offer New Delhi greater hope that the pace and degree of improvement in their bilateral relationship will intensify.[71] If India does not align itself too closely with the United States, China will be more likely to accommodate India's bilateral concerns. However, if India does appear to align with the United States against China, then China would be more tempted to punish India through reintensified assistance to Pakistan and by taking more hostile positions in Sino-Indian diplomacy.

Chinese and Indian Approaches to Arms Control and Nonproliferation

Not surprisingly, China and India display differences and similarities in their approaches to arms control and nonproliferation. The differences stem from the character of the two polities and governmental regimes, and from the divergence between China's status as a juridically accepted nuclear weapon state and India's status as an outlier in the nuclear Nonproliferation Treaty "system." The similarities stem from both states' feeling that they still need to catch up to the strategic capabilities of their rivals, and that arms control and nonproliferation proposals seem intended to lock them into positions of inferiority. At bottom, both countries tend to see more costs than benefits in formal arms control agreements. These dynamics can be seen in the ways that Beijing and New Delhi have responded to the nuclear Nonproliferation Treaty (NPT), the Comprehensive Test Ban Treaty (CTBT), a prospective ban on fissile material production for explosive purposes, and various controls on missile development and exports.

China signed the NPT in 1992, twenty-two years after the treaty entered into force. India has refused to sign the treaty. For the analytical purposes of this chapter, the NPT can be seen to have three elements. First, it legitimated the possession of nuclear weapons by the five states that had tested nuclear devices prior to 1967—the United States, the United Kingdom, Russia, France, and China—while erecting barriers to the spread of these weapons to other countries. Second, the treaty has a moral-political dimension in that the states that gave up the right to acquire nuclear weapons insisted that the nuclear powers make a reciprocal commitment eventually to eliminate their own nuclear arsenals. This weak and reluctant commitment was embodied in Article 6 of the treaty. Third, the treaty established the basis for export controls and nuclear safeguards that would give teeth to the mission of stopping the spread of nuclear weapons.

China's and India's perceptions of these three elements of the NPT illuminate their overall approach to nonproliferation and arms control. China obviously welcomed the legitimation of its nuclear arsenal, which it was not prepared to abandon. Yet Beijing criticized the NPT's failure to commit the United States and Russia to not expanding their nuclear arsenals. Indeed, China saw the treaty as an exertion of U.S.-Soviet superpower hegemony and likely viewed assistance to Pakistan's nuclear weapon program as a means to further erode superpower nuclear dominance.[72] China abandoned its objections to the NPT only in 1992 when the United States and Russia appeared to cease their nuclear arms race and embarked on arms reduction agreements befitting the end of the Cold War. India always has objected to the NPT because, among other reasons, New Delhi was not prepared to foreclose the option of acquiring nuclear weapons. New Delhi also noted that China did not sign the treaty and therefore did not commit itself to eventual nuclear disarmament or promise to eschew assisting other countries to acquire nuclear weapons. By 1992, when China finally signed the treaty, Beijing already had provided major assistance to Pakistan's acquisition of nuclear weapons. From India's perspective, the damage had been done. China's signature of the treaty did nothing to improve the treaty's attractiveness to India. Thus, both India and China found the treaty to be of little benefit to their basic needs and aspirations regarding nuclear weapons and national security. India today would accept entry into the treaty, but only as a recognized nuclear weapon state with the attendant removal of all technology embargoes. However, the treaty would have to be amended to admit India under these terms, and there is no sign that a majority of the parties would support this.

On the political-moral level, India and China agreed, at least until 1992, that the treaty perpetuated unacceptable inequities. It granted the United States, Russia, Britain, and France advantages in nuclear technology and arsenals while giving lip service to the demands of the developing world for nuclear disarmament. Both Beijing and New Delhi tended to be champions of these demands. Beyond their political interests in representing the world's "have-nots" against the "haves," India and China also saw the process of nuclear disarmament as a means to reduce strategic imbalances. China demanded that the United States and Russia reduce their nuclear arsenals down to the level of China's arsenal before Beijing would enter discussions about reducing its own nuclear forces. India demanded that all of the recognized nuclear powers, including especially China, come down to India's level. Once again, these respective positions reflected both political-moral perspectives as well as hardheaded national security calculations.

By 1992, however, Beijing's international political calculus had shifted somewhat. U.S.-Russian force reductions facilitated this shift, as mentioned above, but other considerations affected the change too. In the early 1990s, after the Tiananmen Square protests and related carnage in Beijing, the Chinese government recognized that its international image required it to take a more forthcoming position in nonproliferation and international trade regimes.[73] The benefits of being seen as a constructive player in international regimes on nonproliferation outweighed the political value of dissenting against the NPT. (This calculation also appeared to inform China's signature in the same year to the Chemical Weapons Convention [CWC]. India made a similar calculation in signing the CWC in 1993. To the surprise of many, India secretly had built chemical weapons, and therefore the government of India committed itself to destroying its stocks.)

Significantly, the Chinese government decided to sign the NPT and the CWC without public debate. These were executive decisions free from the partisan and media pressures that attend such decisions in democracies. India's government decided to sign the CWC in a similar manner. Political organizations and the media did not know that India possessed chemical weapons; whatever discussions surrounded the convention tended to be abstract and not of widespread interest. The government's decision was in effect a fait accompli. Conversely, an Indian decision to sign the NPT would entail giving up publicly celebrated assets and would have to be debated democratically.

The third element of the NPT relates to abstinence from exporting sensitive nuclear technology, materiel, and know-how to states that do not possess nuclear weapons. As noted, China in the 1980s perceived an interest in providing such exports to Pakistan, a clear violation of the spirit and letter of the NPT (which China had not signed). After 1992, China flirted with providing sensitive nuclear equipment and know-how to Iran, but evidently was persuaded by Washington to desist. In 1996, the United States threatened to impose sanctions because China had supplied ring magnets to Pakistan. Beijing then pledged not to provide nuclear assistance to unsafeguarded facilities in any country. This qualified limitation on nuclear assistance left open numerous possibilities for China to train personnel at safeguarded facilities who could then work on weapons-related projects, and to provide equipment that could be reverse engineered or otherwise used for "proliferant" purposes. Insofar as China still has not agreed to abide by 1992 Nuclear Suppliers Group guidelines that prohibit exports to states that have not put *all* of their nuclear facilities under fullscope international safeguards, Beijing has kept options open to export to countries such as Pakistan that have safeguards only on certain facilities. Thus, the United States has continued to press China to accept and act upon the notion that all nuclear exports to proliferation-sensitive countries such as Pakistan, Iran, and Iraq should be rejected.

Notwithstanding China's lingering ambivalence, some Beijing officials have gradually recognized that China's security interests, as well as its international political interests, are served by supporting international efforts to prevent the spread of nuclear weapons.[74] In October 2002, on the eve of President Jiang Zemin's visit to President George W. Bush's ranch in Texas, China issued long-awaited comprehensive new export control regulations covering missile technology, chemical weapons precursors and technology, and biological agent–related items. (China in 1997 had joined the Zangger Committee, the multilateral consortium that regulates nuclear exports.) The new regulations did much to bring China into conformity with key nonproliferation regimes and closed a number of loopholes, although their ultimate effect will depend on the rigor with which they are implemented and enforced.[75] The Chinese government retains the right to issue export licenses on a discretionary basis pending the state's assessment of particular risks that exported items would be misused.

Unlike China, India is not known to have exported any sensitive nuclear technology, materiel, or know-how to countries of proliferation concern. In this sense, India has complied with the broader international nonproliferation regime's mandate not to facilitate the spread of nuclear weapons, even if India remains outside the NPT and in possession of nuclear weapons itself. However, India has been willing to buy and receive materials, equipment, and know-how from states that violate their own nonproliferation commitments in providing these assets to India.[76] Nor has India been immune to temptation to export sensitive equipment. In the 1980s, the Indian Atomic Energy Commission considered exporting a nuclear research reactor to Iran, but the government of India was dissuaded from this course by the United States.[77] Ultimately India's restraint as a proliferator stems from the normative insistence that the world would be better off without nuclear weapons and that India's acquisition of these weapons has been reluctant and compelled by the failure of others to achieve nuclear disarmament. The moral dimension of India's national perspective on nuclear weapons has been internalized by the public and by many political leaders. This consensus would make prospective exports to proliferation-sensitive countries a highly controversial issue in Indian politics. This democratic check on Indian policy is yet another manifestation of the differences between the nature of the Indian and Chinese systems of government.

Beyond moral-political considerations, India's interests in exporting sensitive nuclear technology are circumscribed by geostrategic factors. The number of potential nuclear weapon "proliferators" is very small. Iran, Iraq, and Libya tend to be the primary states of concern. India would undermine seriously its more important relationships with the United States, Israel, and other states if it were to abet proliferation to these states of concern. The proposed sale to Iran in the mid-1980s exemplifies this circumstance. In recent years India and Israel quietly have intensified their cooperation in defense technology development and production, giving New Delhi still greater reason not to export nuclear technology or know-how to states of proliferation concern.[78]

In sum, China is a less than fully reliable participant in the international nonproliferation regime, whereas India behaves (thus far) as a responsible possessor of nuclear weapons even if India remains outside of the nonproliferation treaty upon which the broader regime is based. The challenge remains for the parties to the NPT and India, Israel, and Pakistan to find mutually acceptable means to bring these three states into the international system of rules to prevent further proliferation without appearing to "reward" their acquisition of nuclear weapons. Meeting this challenge will require more sustained and creative high-level diplomacy than any of the parties involved has yet applied to the problem.

The Comprehensive Test Ban Treaty is another seminal arms control and nonproliferation treaty that reveals similarities and differences in Beijing's and New Delhi's perspectives.

The CTBT was China's first experience with a nuclear arms control treaty that would actually constrain a Chinese nuclear activity. China had signed other treaties and protocols to nuclear-weapon-free zone agreements, but these did not limit current or prospective Chinese activities or deployments.[79] Ending nuclear testing was different. When the CTBT negotiations began in January 1994, China had conducted fewer than forty nuclear tests, compared with nearly fourteen hundred by the United States. China's small nuclear arsenal was unsophisticated compared with that of its principal rivals, the United States and Russia. Thus, a test ban would greatly limit China's capacity to fill the gaps between its nuclear weapon capabilities and those of the its nuclear rivals.

Unsurprisingly, the Chinese military and nuclear establishment expressed grave reservations about signing the treaty. As in the United States and other nuclear weapon states, Chinese nuclear weapon laboratories were particularly reluctant to abandon testing.[80] The arguments for signing the treaty came principally from the Ministry of Foreign Affairs. It argued that China's international standing would suffer enormously if it were the lone nuclear weapon state refusing to sign the treaty.[81] Not only the United States, but also Japan, Central Asian states bordering on China, and leading developing countries all pressured China to accede to the test ban. China's political leaders ultimately concluded that the national interests articulated by the diplomats outweighed the arguments of the military and the nuclear establishment. This decision was no doubt difficult and contested, but it would have been even more so had it been made in the context of a multiparty system of government with a free media.

To educate leaders on the costs, benefits, and practical issues involved in arms control and nonproliferation, China had to develop expertise on these matters and integrate it into relevant institutions. In 1997, following signature of the CTBT, the Chinese foreign ministry created a department dedicated to arms control and disarmament issues. The People's Liberation Army (PLA) and its related think-tanks and departments also developed cadres with expertise on arms control and disarmament issues, as did nuclear and defense-industrial entities.[82] It remains difficult to ascertain the mechanisms by which PLA views on these issues are developed and conveyed to decision makers, but it seems that the military and defense-industrial establishments are acquiring substantial expertise to match that of the foreign ministry.

India continues to refuse to sign the CTBT. Notwithstanding Indian sponsorship of UN resolutions in the early 1990s calling for completion of negotiations on the treaty, the Indian polity shifted its regard for the CTBT between 1995 and the current day. Like India's general approach to nuclear weapons, attitudes toward the CTBT reflect institutional, political, moral, and security considerations.

Unlike China's, India's foreign ministry has long possessed expertise on nuclear arms control and disarmament issues. India signed the Partial Test Ban Treaty in 1963, and Indian diplomats have participated fully in debates on the CTBT ever since. Prior to 1995 they championed the treaty as a fundamental measure of progress toward nuclear disarmament. Yet, whereas the Chinese PLA has had a central role in shaping Chinese nuclear policy, including arms control policy, the Indian military has been excluded from this realm until very recently. Perspectives and participation in the Indian debate began to shift in late 1995 when the international community opted to extend the NPT indefinitely. This decision, taken without requiring a time-bound commitment by the nuclear weapon states to achieve nuclear disarmament, surprised Indians and presented them with a thorny problem. It now appeared that a Comprehensive Test Ban Treaty would be completed soon, and that India's opportunities to prove and improve its nuclear weapon capabilities could be severely impaired. The stark reality that nuclear disarmament was not to be taken seriously by the recognized nuclear powers made Indian officials and pundits conclude that India must energetically build a credible deterrent. This could not be done without nuclear weapon tests. Thus, India withheld signature of the treaty in 1996 and conducted nuclear tests in 1998.

By making its nuclear capabilities overt and declaring itself a nuclear weapon power, the Indian government significantly increased the military-security salience of what heretofore had been a largely political-diplomatic capability. National security thinking and the perspectives of military professionals now entered the nuclear policy making domain as never before. This shift continues to have implications for the Indian state, for example, with regard to the role of the military in decision making, as discussed earlier. One of the most acute problems now concerns the technical adequacy of India's nuclear weapons. Since the tests of 1998, Indian nuclear scientists and the government have insisted that those tests yielded enough data to guarantee that the nation possesses proficient weapon designs. The government, at the highest levels, has declared repeatedly that India does not need to and will not conduct further nuclear explosive tests. However, doubts remain internationally and among the Indian military whether enough tests have been conducted to establish confidence in the reliability and robustness of India's nuclear weapons and, therefore, whether India can "afford" to sign the CTBT. Indian military leaders and scientists have less certainty about their nuclear weapons than their Chinese counterparts who argued against signing the CTBT have about theirs.

The greatest difference between India's and China's approaches to arms control lies in the political character of the CTBT debate. In India, the CTBT has assumed tremendous political symbolic importance. The treaty was roundly lambasted in 1996 as a hollow disarmament measure. Indian critics portrayed the CTBT as a cynical ploy led by the U.S. imperialists to impose nonproliferation on India. Signing the treaty would be tantamount to submitting to latter-day nuclear colonialism or nuclear "apartheid." Foreign Minister Jaswant Singh and Prime Minister Atal Behari Vajpayee pledged to their American counterparts from 1998 onward that they would seek a national consensus in favor of signing the treaty, but these men shied away from the severe political challenge of creating such a consensus.[83] The issue receded when the U.S. Senate refused to ratify the treaty in October 1999. It has fallen further off the stage since the ascension of the Bush administration, which opposes the treaty. The point here is that even if Indian leaders concluded that signing the treaty was in India's overall interest, India's raucous democracy would stay their hand.

Another major item on the international arms control and nonproliferation agenda is a ban on the production of fissile material for explosive purposes. Here, too, India and China take relatively similar positions. In the 1990s, China was wary of but somewhat receptive to such a treaty. However, as relations with the United States and Taiwan have become more strained, and the prospect of ambitious American missile defenses has grown, China has become more reluctant to limit its options. This attitude parallels India's reluctance to agree to end fissile material production without redressing the disparity in global nuclear arsenals and fissile material stockpiles, particularly the disparity between China and India. Pakistan echoes this concern, wanting any treaty to remove India's presumed advantages in fissile material stocks vis-à-vis Pakistan.

Similar considerations make India reluctant to agree formally to limit its options to refine and expand its nuclear and missile arsenals. India continues to favor nuclear disarmament, but does not wish to accept intermediate arms control measures unless and until the de jure nuclear weapon states make, and probably begin to implement, binding disarmament agreements that India considers equitable. So, too, China will not agree to forgo modernization of its nuclear arsenal without reciprocal measures by the United States and Russia to reduce drastically their larger arsenals and, in the case of the United States, to forswear or at least significantly limit plans for ballistic missile defenses.

Overall, to the extent that China perceives the United States and its allies to be pursuing a strategy to contain China, the security rationale for arms control, if not nonproliferation, becomes weaker. The norms and rules of related international regimes appear more like cynical traps. China, like other states, frets over American global hegemony. To the extent that cooperation with the United States in international regimes and institutions—such as the UN Security Council—will temper U.S. unilateralism and encourage U.S. decision makers not to treat China as an enemy, Beijing is motivated to comply with international norms. Conversely, if and when China sees itself the object of containment or diktat from the United States, and concludes that Washington will run roughshod over key Chinese interests, Beijing likely will take countermeasures.

One way that China could "fight back" against perceived bullying by the United States would be to expand missile and/or nuclear cooperation with Iran and, more likely, Pakistan. Such proliferation in turn would affect Indian security interests significantly. The point here is that China's security policies, including its proliferation behavior, can be affected by U.S. security policies toward China and India's reactions to them.

Finally, it is worth discussing China's and India's pledges not to be the first to use nuclear weapons in a conflict. Such a pledge is not properly an arms control policy, insofar as it is not backed up by binding, verifiable agreement. Moreover, if and when China develops and deploys the range of nuclear forces and command and control capabilities envisioned by proponents of limited deterrence, the sincerity of its no-first-use pledge will be more difficult to ascertain. India is further from developing, let alone deploying, the mixture of tactical and longer-range nuclear weapon systems and command and control capabilities that would make first use feasible, but such capability in future decades cannot be ruled out. In a further complication, China's pledge not to use nuclear weapons first does not apply to possible use on Chinese territory. This caveat seems to emphasize that China does not intend to launch aggression on other states' territories, but reserves the right to use any weapon any time in defense of Chinese territory. The complication is that to the extent that China actually regards Arunachal Pradesh as Chinese territory, the no-first-use pledge would not apply to a conflict in what is de facto Indian territory.

That said, China and India have invested political and diplomatic credibility in their no-first-use pledges. This doctrine has helped rationalize China's rather modest nuclear force posture and India's current rejection of tactical nuclear weapons. No-first-use commitments do not comport well with nuclear war–fighting doctrine, in which the advantages of "going first" are often noted. Eschewal of nuclear war fighting also "allows" states not to pursue counterforce targeting and large, variegated nuclear arsenals, and as such has implications for arms control and for potential confidence-building agreements. As Banning Garrett and Bonnie Glaser reported, Chinese officials have held that no-first-use pledges hold strategic significance and augment mutual reassurance by conveying benign intentions that, in the Chinese view, are as vital as capabilities in effecting strategic assessments.[84] Indian leaders and strategists make similar points. They tend to see no-first-use as a bulwark that will keep India from sliding over the costly and destabilizing precipice of nuclear war fighting.[85]

The former U.S. principal deputy undersecretary of defense, Jan Lodal, recently buttressed these points in ways that should be of interest to all. Lodal argues that if the United States were to abandon its nuclear first-use doctrines related to Europe, and the related strategy of damage-limiting counterforce targeting, it could readily reduce its strategic nuclear arsenal to fewer than a thousand warheads.[86] If Russia were to reciprocate, Moscow and Washington would significantly reduce risks of inadvertent or accidental nuclear use. Insofar as China and India currently favor no-first-use, they may wish to consider how to encourage the United States and Russia to move in this direction as a potentially important innovation in international arms control. For this to be feasible, however, China would first have to specify that its no-first-use doctrine applies to India, including scenarios concerning the disputed border regions.

Conclusion

The Sino-Indian nuclear relationship cannot be separated usefully from the larger, more complicated web of concerns and actors that joins these two states. Since 1962, Beijing and New Delhi have managed their direct engagements soberly if not satisfyingly. Pakistan has become the primary locus of Sino-Indian friction. Given the already grave tensions between India and Pakistan, the proxy Sino-Indian rivalry conducted through Pakistan exacerbates the danger. This danger will not be resolved without more forthcoming and constructive initiatives from Pakistani, Indian, and Chinese leaders. Pakistan must be willing to abandon strategies of violence against India in Kashmir and to acknowledge that the only viable solution there will entail compromise. India must implement meaningful steps to bring all Kashmiris into a fair political process predicated on greater autonomy, while reassuring Pakistan that India recognizes its stakes in Kashmir and its need for lasting security. China must cease assisting Pakistan as a means to keep India off balance, and adopt policies to calm Indo-Pakistani competition while strengthening bilateral relations with India. If these conditions do not occur, neither India nor Pakistan is likely to restrain its development of nuclear weapons and ballistic missiles. Pakistan will seek more and "better" weapons to rival India, perhaps with Chinese help. India will do the same to match or surpass Pakistan and to show China that India cannot be disregarded or intimidated. However, under foreseeable local and global conditions, war and even nuclear arms racing will not improve India's, China's, or Pakistan's circumstances. No leader in any of these states can make a plausible case to the contrary. The challenge is to translate this reality into bilateral and trilateral policies.

Notes

1. John Wilson Lewis and Xue Litai, *China Builds the Bomb* (Stanford: Stanford University Press, 1988), 38–39.

2. Ibid., 37.

3. Quoted in Alastair Iain Johnston, "China's New 'Old Thinking': The Concept of Limited Deterrence," *International Security* 20, no. 3 (Winter 1995–96): 8. Full citation appears in Johnston's footnote 9.

4. Lewis and Xue, *China Builds the Bomb,* 231.

5. Ibid., 72.

6. Paul H. B. Godwin, "China's Nuclear Forces: An Assessment," *Current History* 98 (September 1999): 261.

7. Alastair Iain Johnston, "Prospects for Chinese Nuclear Force Modernization: Limited Deterrence versus Multilateral Arms Control," in *China's Military in Transition,* ed. David Shambaugh and Richard H. Yang (Oxford: Oxford University Press, 1997), 288.

8. Soviet military leaders in the early 1980s, most famously General Nikolai

Ogarkov, came to similar conclusions regarding the implications of American breakthroughs in computing and electronic communication technology. The Gulf War deepened Chinese, Russian, and other states' sense of vulnerability.

9. See Mark A. Stokes, *China's Strategic Modernization: Implications for the United States* (Carlisle, Pa.: Strategic Studies Institute, 1999).

10. For descriptions and analyses of the evolving concept of limited deterrence, see Johnston, "China's New 'Old Thinking'" and "Prospects for Chinese Nuclear Force Modernization"; and Bates Gill, James Mulvenon, and Mark Stokes, "The Chinese Second Artillery Corps: Transition to Credible Deterrence," in *The People's Liberation Army as Organization,* ed. James Mulvenon and Richard H. Yang (Washington, D.C.: RAND, 2002).

11. See Gill, Mulvenon, and Stokes, "Chinese Second Artillery Corps."

12. For a discussion of the low salience of India within Chinese threat assessments, see Michael Pillsbury, "PLA Capabilities in the 21st Century: How Does China Assess Its Future Security Needs?" in *The Chinese Armed Forces in the 21st Century,* ed. Larry M. Wortzel (Carlisle, Pa.: Strategic Studies Institute, 1999), 138–39.

13. See George Perkovich, *India's Nuclear Bomb* (Berkeley: University of California Press, 2001), chapter 2.

14. India and the Soviet Union had signed the Treaty of Peace, Friendship, and Cooperation in 1971. While they welcomed the strategic protection the treaty afforded, Indian leaders preferred the autonomy of nonalignment and resisted falling into too tight an embrace with the Soviet Union.

15. Perkovich, *India's Nuclear Bomb,* 252–54, 279–81; and Shahid-Ur-Rehman, *Long Road to Chagai* (Islamabad: Shahid-Ur-Rehman, 1999).

16. "The Pakistani Nuclear Program," State Department Briefing Paper, 23 June 1983, in NSA Electronic Briefing Book No. 6, *India and Pakistan: On the Nuclear Threshold,* ed. Joyce Battle, National Security Archive, Washington, D.C., 2000, available at www.gwu.edu/nsarchiv/NSAEBB/NSAEBB6/.

17. Center for Nonproliferation Studies, "China's Nuclear Exports and Assistance to Pakistan," available at www.cns.miis.edu/research/india/china/npakpos.htm, p. 1.

18. Ashley Tellis, *India's Emerging Nuclear Posture* (Santa Monica, Calif.: RAND, 2001), 47.

19. Center for Nonproliferation Studies, "China's Missile Exports and Assistance to Pakistan," available at www.cns.miis.edu/research/india/china/mpakpos.htm, p. 2.

20. For a trenchant comparison, see Jairam Ramesh, "Mao to Murthy," *India Today,* 29 January 2001, 25.

21. Perkovich, *India's Nuclear Bomb,* 374–76.

22. Gill, Mulvenon, and Stokes, "Chinese Second Artillery Corps," 42.

23. Godwin, "China's Nuclear Forces," 261.

24. International Institute for Strategic Studies (IISS), *The Military Balance 2000–2001* (London: Oxford University Press, 2000), 194; National Resources Defense Council (NRDC), Nuclear Notebook, "Chinese Nuclear Forces, 2001," in *Bulletin of the Atomic Scientists,* September–October 2001, 71.

25. Gill, Mulvenon, and Stokes, "Chinese Second Artillery Corps," 34–35.

26. NRDC, "Chinese Nuclear Forces, 2001," 72.

27. Tellis, *India's Emerging Nuclear Posture,* 136–40.

28. Bill Gertz, "New Chinese Missiles Target All of East Asia," *Washington Times,* 10 June 1997; Dunbar Lockwood, "The Status of U.S., Russian, and Chinese Nuclear

Forces in Northeast Asia," *Arms Control Today,* November 1994, 24; Gill, Mulvenon, and Stokes, "Chinese Second Artillery Corps"; and Tellis, *India's Emerging Nuclear Posture,* 56–57.

29. Tellis, *India's Emerging Nuclear Posture,* 136–140.

30. Ibid., 136.

31. History suggests that nuclear-armed adversaries may engage in major proxy wars against each other—e.g., Soviet support of Vietnam against the United States, U.S. support of Afghanistan against the Soviet Union—and also "low-intensity conflicts"—China-Russia along the Ussuri River in 1969, India-Pakistan in 1999. Thus, in some ways, nuclear weapons provide shields under which certain forms of conflict may become more likely insofar as combatants assume they can initiate a limited military campaign with some confidence that their adversaries will be unlikely to escalate, fearing the risk of nuclear use. The notion that nuclear weapons provide the possessor with an effective deterrent against border skirmishes and other limited military challenges does not withstand practical scrutiny. However, nuclear-armed adversaries have been extremely reluctant to undertake direct aggression of such a scale and strategic significance that it would be likely to trigger nuclear counterstrikes.

32. China, like other states, does not reveal its operational plans for possible use of nuclear weapons against India, and given the unlikelihood of Sino-Indian war the secret operational plans developed by nuclear strategists would not necessarily predict the crisis behavior of Chinese decision makers.

33. David Albright, "India's and Pakistan's Fissile Material and Nuclear Weapons Inventories, End of 1999," Institute for Science and International Security, 11 October 2000, available at www.isis-online.org/publications/southasia/stocks1000.html. The 690 kilograms is a median estimate for a range of 585 to 800 kilograms. Similarly, the 39 weapon figure is a median between 30 and 52.

34. Carnegie Endowment for International Peace, "World Missile Chart," available at www.ceip.org/files/projects/npp/resources/ballisticmissilechart.htm.

35. Tellis, *India's Emerging Nuclear Posture,* 53.

36. See, for example, Terry C. Wallace, "The May 1998 India and Pakistan Nuclear Tests," Seismological Research Letters, September 1998, available at www.geo.arizona.edu/geophysics/faculty/wallace/ind.pak/; Brian Barker et al., "Monitoring Nuclear Tests," *Science,* 25 September 1998, 1967–68; S. K. Sikka, Falguni Roy, and G. J. Nair, "Indian Explosions of 11 May 1998: An Analysis of Global Seismic Body Wave Magnitude Estimates," *Current Science,* 10 September 1998, 491; D. Ramana, Matt Thundyil, and V. Sunder, "The Indian Nuclear Tests: Summary Paper," *Bharat Rakshak Monitor* 3 (May–June 2001), available at www.bharat-rakshak.com/Monitor/issue3-6/ramana.html.

37. See Albright, "Fissile Material and Nuclear Weapons Inventories"; and Tellis, *India's Emerging Nuclear Posture,* 481–85. India's stockpile of weapon-usable fissile material could be greater if India has used or in the future plans to use the civilian Madras nuclear reactors and nearby reprocessing plant to produce and separate plutonium for weapons purposes.

38. Tellis, *India's Emerging Nuclear Posture,* 490.

39. IISS, *Military Balance 2000–2001,* 163.

40. For the best discussion of the relevant attributes of India's aircraft, see Tellis, *India's Emerging Nuclear Posture.*

41. "According to highly placed Government sources, it has been decided not to arm

the 150-km range Prithvi missile or any of its variants with a nuclear warhead." Atul Aneja, "India Has 'Problems' Managing Nuclear Arms," *Hindu,* 14 August 2001.

42. "*Brahmos* May Be Inducted in Two Years," *Times of India,* 26 August 2001; Aneja, "India Has 'Problems.'"

43. Shishir Gupta, "Down to Brasstacks," *India Today* (international), 28 May 2001, 30.

44. Tellis, *India's Emerging Nuclear Posture,* 561–67.

45. See for example, Rahul Bedi, "Agni II Now in Production," *Jane's Missiles and Rockets,* 1 August 2001, regarding Russian assistance to the submarine-launched cruise missile Sagarika; Atul Aneja, "Indo-Russian Missile Tested," *Hindu,* 13 June 2001, for Indo-Russian cooperation on the Brahmos cruise missile; *Defense News,* 26 March 2001, 1, for Indo-Russian cooperation in missile guidance technology.

46. Center for Nonproliferation Studies, "Russia to Lease Two Nuclear Submarines to India," 19 February 2002, available at http://cns.miis.edu/pubs/week/020218.htm.

47. The Indian approach may be closer to American and Russian *political* leaders' understanding of deterrence sufficiency. However, American and Russian political leaders generally have not comprehended, let alone shaped, their states' operational nuclear doctrines. See Janne E. Nolan, *Guardians of the Arsenal: The Politics of Nuclear Strategy* (New York: Basic Books, 1989) and *An Elusive Consensus* (Washington, D.C.: Brookings Institution Press, 2000); and McGeorge Bundy, *Danger and Survival* (New York: Random House, 1988).

48. Space here does not allow engagement of the frequently oversimplified American debate on the morality of countervalue versus counterforce targeting. India's moral qualms are salved by the determination to use nuclear weapons only after sustaining an adversary's nuclear attack on India, after which point the moral burden is off India. This retaliation-only posture, unlike war-fighting doctrine, reduces the chances of inadvertent nuclear use or crisis escalation, further buttressing the moral quality of Indian doctrine, if the underlying moral principle is to prevent mass casualties whether through accident or purposeful exchanges.

49. Atul Aneja, "Chief of Defence Staff Must Head Strategic Force," *Hindu,* 1 November 2000, available at www.indiaserver.com/thehindu/2000/11/01/stories/0201000a.htm; "State Set for N-Force Command Structure," *Hindustan Times,* 18 January 2001, available at www.hindustantimes.com/nonfram/180101/detFRO02.asp; Gupta, "Down to Brasstacks"; author interviews with knowledgeable Indian officials, New Delhi, April 2001.

50. Aneja, "India Has 'Problems.'"

51. Gupta, "Down to Brasstacks."

52. Raja Menon, *A Nuclear Strategy for India* (New Delhi: Sage, 2000), 191.

53. Interview with Rahul Bedi, *Jane's Defence Weekly,* 17 January 2001, 32.

54. Jyoti Malhotra, "China's No Threat, Says Jaswant," *Indian Express,* 16 June 1999.

55. "India for Friendly Ties with China: Defence Ministry," *Hindu,* 17 April 1999.

56. Quoted in Ashwani Talwar, "Defence Ministry Beats Less around the Bush," *Times of India,* 31 May 2001, available at www.timesofindia.com/today/31indu4.htm.

57. Menon, *Nuclear Strategy for India,* 182, 179.

58. Private communication, 19 April 2000.

59. U.S.-China Joint Statement, 27 June 1998, Beijing, available at www.cns.miis.edu/research/india/china/mpakchr.htm.

60. Interview with knowledgeable Indian official, New Delhi, 23 April 2001.

61. Du Youkang, "Security Patterns in Post–Cold War South Asia—and Effects on China," *International Affairs* (Shanghai), no. 2 (2000): 12–15, translated for the author by Sun Liang.

62. Delhi Doordarshan Television, 29 November 1996, in FBIS-NESA, 96-322, drnes232-r-96003.

63. *Frontier Post,* 3 December 1996, 6, in FBIS-NESA, 96-233, drnes233-v-96001.

64. Interview with U.S. official, 26 January 2001.

65. U.S. Department of State, statement by Acting Assistant Secretary Richard Boucher, 21 November 2000. According to the United States, China made a "clear policy commitment not to assist, in any way, other countries to develop ballistic missiles that can be used to deliver nuclear weapons and to further improve and reinforce its export control system, including by publishing at an early date a comprehensive export control list of missile-related items, including dual use items."

66. For a more detailed chronicle of these developments, see the afterword in the paperback edition of George Perkovich, *India's Nuclear Bomb* (Berkeley: University of California Press, 2001).

67. Indian observers noted four important trends: China displayed genuine warmth toward India; Chinese leaders acknowledged India's growing economic and political importance; Beijing appeared more willing than before to engage openly on matters of tension, including the border dispute; and Chinese leaders eschewed polemical discourse on the nuclear issue.

68. John Pomfret, "U.S. Protests Exports of Missiles by China," *Washington Post,* 27 July 2001, A21.

69. Ambassador Maleeha Lohdi, letter to the *Wall Street Journal,* 24 August 2001.

70. Interview with knowledgeable Indian official, New Delhi, 23 April 2001.

71. "Over almost 2 decades, China has steered a long-term course for good relations with India. Despite the inevitable difficulties that will arise, Beijing appears intent on maintaining that course. Regional stability is something in which China now has a very big stake." Eric A. McVadon, "The Chinese Military and the Peripheral States in the 21st Century: A Security Tour D'Horizon," in *The Chinese Armed Forces in the 21st Century,* ed. Larry M. Wortzel (Carlisle, Pa.: Strategic Studies Institute, 1999), 70.

72. The author thanks an anonymous reviewer of this chapter for adding this point.

73. Bates Gill and Evan S. Medeiros, "Foreign and Domestic Influences on China's Arms Control and Nonproliferation Policies," *China Quarterly* 161 (March 2000): 68.

74. See Banning N. Garrett and Bonnie S. Glaser, "Chinese Perspectives on Nuclear Arms Control," *International Security* 20, no. 3 (Winter 1995–96): 50–53.

75. Research notes available at www.cns.miis.edu/research/china/chiexp/index.htm.

76. For India's clandestine acquisition of heavy water, see Perkovich, *India's Nuclear Bomb,* 249–51, 285–86. India's current and prospective procurement from Russia of low-enriched uranium fuel, new reactors, and missile technology and know-how are highly suspect from the standpoint of Russia's nonproliferation obligations.

77. See Perkovich, *India's Nuclear Bomb,* 324.

78. "India and Israel Sign Big Arms Deal," *Information Times,* 20 July 2001, www.InformationTimes.com.

79. Ibid., 68.

80. Garrett and Glaser, "Chinese Perspectives," 59.

81. Ibid., 90.

82. Ibid., 86–88.

83. Singh said, "If this treaty is unilaterally abrogated, abridged or adjusted, this will lead to greater uncertainty instead of promoting a new more cooperative security framework. . . . That is why we are recommending to the United States that any step in that direction must be made with Russia and in consultation with Russia." "Russia 'Sways' India on ABM Treaty," *Hindu,* 7 June 2001, available at www.the-hindu.com/stories/0107000a.htm.

84. Garrett and Glaser, "Chinese Perspectives," 65.

85. Tellis, *India's Emerging Nuclear Posture,* 302–12, esp. 306.

86. Jan Lodal, *The Price of Dominance* (New York: Council on Foreign Relations Press, 2001), 33–37.

7

Economic Reforms and Global Integration

T. N. Srinivasan

In the last two decades of the twentieth century, China and India enjoyed historically unprecedented average annual rates of real income growth—around 10 percent and 6 percent, respectively.[1] Although still very poor, with their large populations (still mostly rural) and rapid growth of gross domestic product (GDP), both countries constitute large domestic markets for a variety of agricultural and industrial products and services (table 7.1).

The first three main sections draw on T. N. Srinivasan, *Agriculture and Trade in China and India* (San Francisco International Center for Economic Growth, 1994), chapter 1. This is a revised version of a paper presented at seminars in Beijing, New Delhi, and Shanghai. I thank my discussants, Zhan Minqiu and Wen Fude at Beijing, V. S. Seshadri at New Delhi, and Huang Renwei at Shanghai, and participants of these three seminars for their valuable comments. Thanks are also due to the editors, Harry Harding and Francine Frankel, for their valuable substantive and editorial suggestions. I thank the Center for Research on Economic Development and Policy Reform at Stanford University for research support, and Jessica Seddon Wallack for research assistance.

Table 7.1 *Population, Urbanization, Real Income, and Growth, China and India, ca. 2000*

	China	India
Population (millions)	1,278[a]	1,027[b]
Urban proportion of population (2000)	32%	28%
Gross national income (GNI) per capita (2001)	$840	$450
GNI at purchasing-power parity exchange rate (2001)	$3,920	$2,340
Rate of growth of GDP (% per year)		
1965–1979	8.1	4.6
1980–1990	10.1	5.8
1990–2000	10.3	6.0

Sources: J. K. Banthia, *Provisional Population Totals, Census of India, 2001,* Series 1, Paper 1 of 2001 (New Delhi: Registrar General and Census Commissioner, India); World Bank, *World Development Indicators 2002* (Washington, D.C.: World Bank, 2002), tables 1.10, 3.10, 4.1; World Bank, *World Development Indicators 2001* (Washington, D.C.: World Bank, 2001), table 1.4.
a. On 1 February 2000.
b. On 1 March 2001.

The prospects of selling profitably in these huge markets have attracted exporters and investors of the industrialized countries. Since both countries are engaged in integrating their economies with the world economy, they now compete in markets in the rest of the world for exports and for external capital. Given the emerging economic strength of China and India, as well as their possible competition for dominance as the leading Asian power, it is important to analyze their recent economic performance in a comparative framework.[2]

Indeed, this chapter is devoted to such an analysis and not to a theme more in keeping with the other chapters of the volume, namely, bilateral economic relations between the two countries. The reason is that, historically, economic interactions between China and India have been much less important than their cultural interactions. This is in part due to the high cost of transport across the Himalayan border. The border war of 1962, and the subsequent chill in bilateral political relations, effectively eliminated much trade and other economic relations between the two countries. Although in the nineties bilateral trade grew rapidly, and the prospects for a substantial penetration of each in the other's market are good, these phenomena are very recent. On the one hand, with China's entry into the World Trade Organization (WTO) and the launch of a new round of multilateral trade negotiations under the auspices of the WTO in 2002, competition between China and India in third markets is likely to intensify. On the other, as large poor and labor-abundant developing countries the two should find much common ground in their negotiating positions. James Clad covers these issues in chapter 8 of this volume.

Because there is not much to describe or analyze about India-China economic relations of the last half of the twentieth century, this chapter is devoted to a comparison of their economic development strategies and performance since the early fifties. Although it might seem natural in a comparative analysis of two economies to devote equal space to each economy and to discuss each within a common structure, it is not so in this case. The reason is that the dominance of the state in the Chinese economy, which was total and direct prior to the reforms, is still very significant, and the control of the Communist Party of the government is complete. By contrast, in India's multiparty democracy, with a large private sector, state control over the economy has been incomplete, indirect, and subject to political pulls. Because of these differences, not only is more space devoted to India, but a rigid common structure is not adopted for the discussion.

After all, China and India, the two most populous countries of the world and among the poorest, have attempted to develop economically and alleviate poverty through similar development strategies, but under vastly different political frameworks, namely, a single-party (communist) authoritarian rule in China and a multiparty democracy in India. China began its economic reforms and opening to the world economy in 1978. India began relaxing its rigidly controlled economy in a piecemeal fashion in the 1980s, but its significant opening to the world economy and deeper domestic reforms did not begin until after the severe macroeconomic crisis of 1991. With the experience of reforms and globalization for more than twenty-five years in China, and a decade in India, much more information and critical analysis (particularly of the Chinese economy) have become available.

The primary focus of this chapter, divided into several sections, is an analysis of the economic reforms, post-reform performance, and future prospects of both economies. The section "Economic, Political, and Social Frameworks and Economic Performance" describes the state of the two economies as they initiated their development efforts, their politico-economic social frameworks, and their achievements in terms of important socioeconomic indicators. The section "Development Strategies prior to Reforms" is devoted to their pre-reform development strategies. In the subsequent three sections, I describe the background to, the rationale for, and the contents of reforms in China since 1978 and in India since 1991. I concentrate primarily on reforms of the foreign trade, industry, and the financial sectors. I discuss agricultural reforms only briefly, primarily because the reforms of the two countries in this area are not comparable; India has yet to initiate significant reforms. The section "Results of Reform" details the achievements of reforms in both countries. The sections "Looking Ahead" and "Conclusion" discuss reforms that are needed but are yet to be initiated, and the likely future prospects of the two economies.

Economic, Political, and Social Frameworks and Economic Performance

The governments of both China and India turned to planning for national development in the early 1950s. Until the reforms initiated in 1978, China's was a command economy wherein the private sector played an insignificant role in resource allocation. Although India's was, and still is, a mixed economy with a large private sector, state regulation of economic activity was very extensive until the reforms of 1991.

In its first detailed report on the Chinese economy, the World Bank concluded that India and China had roughly similar per capita incomes, in the range of $50 to $60 (in 1952) in the early fifties,[3] though Maddison's recent estimates suggest otherwise (see table 7.2). China's population was a little more than 1.5 times that of India's 360 million in 1951. India had a more diversified industrial structure and a more extensive network of transport and communications (three times the route kilometers of railways and more than three and a half times the extent of highways per square kilometer of land area) as compared with China even in 1979. On the other hand, in China the average yields per hectare of rice and wheat were twice and more than one and a half times, respectively, those of India. Crude birth rates were about the same (around 37–38 per thousand), while the crude death rate of China, at about 17 per thousand, was significantly lower than India's 24 per thousand (again in the early fifties), perhaps reflecting the better nutritional status enjoyed by the Chinese population because of higher food-grain output per head.

Maddison provides estimates of per capita real GDP for China and India going back to the beginning of the eighteenth century (table 7.2). There is likely to be a wide margin of error surrounding each of Maddison's estimates. Still, they are consistent with the widely held belief that real gross national product (GNP) per capita grew much faster in China than in India after China's reforms of 1978. Even more interesting, they show that while India's per capita income grew under direct British rule from 1858 until

Table 7.2 *Growth of Gross Domestic Product, China and India, 1700–1998*

	1700	1820	1870	1913	1950	1973	1998
China	600	600	530	552	439	839	3117
India	550	533	533	673	619	853	1746

Source: A. Maddison, "Growth and Interaction in the World Economy: The West and the Rest, 1000–2000 A.D.," paper presented at Harvard University, 24 May 2002.
Note: Table shows real GDP per capita (1990 international dollars).

1947 (albeit with some reduction between the two world wars), China's declined by more than 25 percent between 1820 and 1950. Indeed, China's per capita income did not catch up with India's until the late 1970s. In terms of absolute size of gross national income (GNI) or product, China was the seventh and India the twelfth largest economy in the world in 2000.[4]

In the 1980s, the rates of economic growth and export growth were much faster in China than in India (table 7.3). Between 1950 and 1980, real growth in China's foreign trade was about the same as that in GNP, so that the share of trade in GNP hardly changed.[5] Since 1980, however, China's trade has expanded phenomenally and faster than GDP, raising its share in GDP. In India, the share of trade (exports plus imports) in GDP, around 10 percent until the eighties, rose slowly until 1990, and then more rapidly

Table 7.3 *Foreign Trade, China and India*

	Period	China	India
Rate of growth (% per year)			
Value of exports	1980–1990	12.8	7.4
	1990–2000	14.6	9.6
Value of imports	1980–1990	13.5	4.2
	1990–2000	12.6	9.9
Share in GDP (%)			
Exports of goods and services	1990	18	7
	2000	26	14
Imports of goods and services	1990	14	10
	2000	23	17
Share of world merchandise exports (%)	1948	0.9	2.2
	1983	1.2	0.5
	1993	2.5	0.6
	2000	4.0	0.7

Sources: World Bank, *World Development Indicators 2002* (Washington, D.C.: World Bank, 2002), table 4.4; WTO, *International Trade Statistics 2001* (Geneva: World Trade Organization, 2001), table II.2.

thereafter until 2000.[6] China was the fourth largest exporter in the world in 2001 while India was a distant thirty-first.[7]

China was far ahead of India in 2000 in social indicators, such as life expectancy at birth (70 years in China versus 63 in India), rate of infant mortality (10 per thousand live births versus 63), and adult illiteracy (8 percent versus 32 percent among males, and 24 percent versus 55 percent among females).[8]

Development Strategies prior to Reforms

Not only were India and China at a similar stage of development in the early fifties, but both also adopted similar development strategies at that time. Leaders of both countries were heavily influenced by the then-perceived success of the Soviet Union in rapidly industrializing a largely rural economy in a relatively short span of four decades without significant external assistance. The influence of the Soviet experience, of course, is no surprise in the case of the communist leadership of China. The future Indian prime minister Jawaharlal Nehru had visited the Soviet Union in the late 1920s and came away very impressed with their planning. Nehru later acted as chairman of the National Planning Committee established in 1938 by the Indian National Congress, the then-dominant political party that led India's independence struggle. The committee, which managed to complete most of its work before Nehru's arrest by the colonial government in 1940, articulated a development strategy whose main elements were incorporated into postindependence planning.[9]

The development strategy of the Soviet Union, emulated by China and India, emphasized investment in heavy industry. It had its analytical foundation in an economic model formulated in the Soviet Union by Gregorii Alexandrovic Fel'dman in the 1920s. In the model the share of investment devoted to augmenting the stock of capital in the equipment-producing (heavy industry) sector determined the long-run rate of growth of the economy: the larger this share, the greater was the growth rate. The very same model was independently arrived at by Professor P. C. Mahalanobis, who authored India's second five-year plan (1956–61).

Both China and India emphasized industrialization as the sine qua non of economic development. Even prior to independence Indian political leaders, technocrats, trade union leaders, and businessmen had advocated a planned economy and rapid industrialization as the only means to eradicate India's poverty.[10] After independence, the government's industrial policy resolutions of 1948 and 1956 had set the broad outlines of industrial strategy by assigning exclusive responsibility for development of major industries, particularly in infrastructure (transport and communication), to the state. A few (most prominently agriculture) were left for the private sector to develop, and for the development of a few others both state and private sector were jointly responsible. In China, the communist government followed the Soviet communists in emphasizing industrial development. Of course, all private enterprises were nationalized fairly early on.

The actual extent of industrialization, measured by share of industry in value added or in employment, differed substantially between the two countries. In India, the share of agriculture in GDP fell by half between 1950–51 and 1999–2000.[11] The share of the manufacturing industry in GDP rose by less than a third in the same period. In China, the manufacturing industry's share tripled between 1949 and 2000.[12] In both countries, the capital-intensive nature of investment in industry meant that the share of agriculture in total employment remained high, at least in their pre-reform periods, though comparable data are not available for agricultural employment. It is very likely that after more than two decades of reforms, the share of agricultural employment in China has fallen significantly, but in India it is still high, nearly two-thirds in 2000 (table 7.4).

Both China and India implemented their industrialization programs through state controls on investment and on foreign trade. Indeed, both economies followed virtually autarkic policies, which imposed a heavy cost on both in terms of efficiency of resource allocation and forgone growth. Further, in the early 1950s both China and India had virtually no capital goods–producing industry. This meant that most of the equipment needed for investment had to be imported, at least until enough capacity for producing equipment had been built. Heavy industry was capital-intensive as well. Thus, the emphasis on heavy industry made substantial demands on foreign exchange and investment resources. In order to generate these resources, both countries relied on administrative controls on investment and import quotas, rather than on the markets and the price and fiscal mechanisms. In China, prior to the reforms of 1978, state control over economic activity was direct and total: agriculture was collectivized, almost all of industry was state-owned, and most services were supplied by the state. In India's mixed economy, the control mechanism had to ensure

Table 7.4 *Structure of Value Added (GDP) and Employment, China and India*

	China		India	
Share of GDP (%)	1949	2000	1950–51	1999–2000
Agriculture	68	16	55	25
Industry	12	35	11	17
Services	30	49	34	58
Share of employment (%)	1980	2000	1972–73	1999–2000
Agriculture	69	50	73.9	61.7
Industry	18	23	12.3	15.8
Services	13	47	14.8	22.5

Sources: Justin Lin, "Chinese Agriculture: Institutional Changes and Performance," in T. N. Srinivasan, *Agriculture and Trade in China and India* (San Francisco: International Center for Economic Growth, 1994); World Bank, *World Development Indicators 2002* (Washington, D.C.: World Bank, 2002); Central Statistical Organisation, *National Accounts Statistics, 1950-51–1979-80* (New Delhi: Department of Statistics, Government of India, 1989); Press Information Bureau, "Quick Estimates of National Income, Consumption Expenditure, Saving and Capital Formation, 1999–2000," press note, New Delhi, 30 January 2001; Press Information Bureau, "Advance Estimates of National Income 2000–01," press note, New Delhi, 5 February 2001; Ministry of Labour, *The Second National Commission on Labour Report* (New Delhi: Government of India, 2002), table 2.11.

that industrial development in the private sector conformed to the national plans by preventing the diversion of investable resources and foreign exchange to privately profitable but socially undesirable activities.

China's Economic Reforms

Background

I will be brief in describing the well-known and oft-told story of China's economic development prior to the watershed events of Mao Zedong's death in 1976, the fall of the Gang of Four, the rehabilitation of and assumption of power by Deng Xiaoping, and finally, the reforms initiated in December 1978 at the Third Plenary Session of the Eleventh National Congress of the Communist Party of China.[13] In keeping with communist ideology, the Chinese state had nationalized industry by 1958 and monopolized foreign trade even earlier. By 1956, when agricultural collectivization started, almost all rural households were members of a cooperative. Agricultural communes were initiated in 1958. Development strategy was Stalinist in its unbalanced emphasis on industrial growth (especially heavy industry). Autarkic policies ensured that the country's share of exports in world trade remained stagnant. Growth was achieved through higher rates of investment and labor force participation, but with a negligible increase in total factor productivity. The disasters of the Great Leap Forward (1958–62), entailing an estimated decline of two-thirds in grain output and excess mortality of more than 30 million, are well known. The decade (1966–76) of the Cultural Revolution resulted in a slowdown in the growth of output to about 4.5 percent per year, compared with 12.2 percent per year during 1949–57 and 15.3 percent per year during 1962–66. The worst economic performances were during 1958–62—the years of the Great Leap Forward (which was followed by the withdrawal Soviet aid) when growth in total output declined at the rate of 3 percent per year—and during the first two years of the Cultural Revolution (1966–67), when the decline was even faster, at 7 percent per year.[14]

Rationale

The turmoil of the Cultural Revolution severely dislocated the economy, and it would have been natural for those who came to power after the death of Mao to focus on economic recovery. But there were no obvious popular pressures for the institution of radical reforms. Of course, in the absence of any freedom for political expression or a free press in China, there is no reliable way of assessing popular support. Presumably, challenges *within* the party to its leadership can be viewed as reflecting the lack of popular support for the policies of the leadership. In any case, Deng Xiaoping, unlike Mao Zedong, had always been pragmatic, and in fact Mao himself had found Deng's pragmatism useful earlier. As such, with Deng's rehabilitation after the death of Mao in 1976 and with the fall of the Gang of Four, a shift toward pragmatism in Chinese policy was inevitable. On the other hand, rehabilitation itself would not have occurred had other leaders of the party not drawn the right lesson from the Cultural Revolution about the importance of economic development for staying in power. Indeed, Tony Saich suggests that by the late 1970s senior leaders of the party, including Deng, had concluded that the solution of the country's economic, political, and social problems required a major overhaul of the system.[15] Whether inevitable or not, radical economic reforms were initiated in 1978 at the Third Plenum of the Eleventh Central Committee of the Communist Party.

Contents

In important ways, integrating the centrally planned Chinese economy into a world economy that is driven largely by market forces differs from integrating the mixed economy of India. A reasonably well-functioning legal system for enforcement of contracts, and a financial system sufficiently well developed to include a range of financial intermediaries such as commercial banks, term lending institutions, and insurance firms, are the foundations of a market economy. Whereas India had functioning legal and financial institutions, in China they had to be built up from scratch. Much of China's foreign trade on the eve of reforms was carried out by state trading agencies. In India, except in food, fertilizers, petroleum, and minerals, foreign trade was in private hands.

Paraphrasing Gao Shangquan,[16] Chinese reforms during 1978–98 were undertaken in three successive stages. Reforms in the first stage (1978–84) consisted of the introduction of the household responsibility system in place of agricultural communes; free sale of output at market-determined prices except for a relatively small proportion delivered to the state at fixed prices; formation of township and village enterprises; replacement by taxes of surrender of profits by urban enterprises; and opening to the outside world through the creation of four special economic zones and fourteen coastal open cities.

The second-stage reforms (1984–85) were focused on urban areas and on state-owned enterprises. The reforms consisted of the introduction of a variety of contracts on enterprise leasing and management responsibility systems; creation of a shareholding system to facilitate mergers, leases, and auctions as well as bankruptcy of enterprises; development of markets for production materials and capital, labor, information, and technology; drastic reduction in the role of mandatory plans so that enterprises were free to make their own investment decisions; contracting of fiscal budgets, strengthening the regulatory role of the central bank; and further opening of the economy through the creation of the Hainan and Pudong special economic zones.

In the third stage, from 1992 on, reforms concentrated on the establishment of a socialist market economy. They consisted of replacing the fiscal contract system with a tax-sharing system, with turnover and value-added taxes at its core; entrusting to the central bank regulation of the money supply and supervision of financial systems; transformation of state-owned banks into commercial banks; extension and deepening of the price and foreign trade reforms of earlier stages; legal and regulatory reforms; and reform of government institutions concerned with education, science, and technology.

The first-stage reforms, by providing incentives for increasing the productivity of land and rationalizing the use of labor, were highly successful in raising the incomes and welfare of the overwhelming majority of the Chinese population, namely, the peasants. This success encouraged the leadership to proceed with subsequent stages of reform.[17] After two decades of reform, the Chinese economy had been radically transformed. Peasants and enterprises are essentially free to decide what and how much to produce in response to market signals; prices for most products are determined by the market; and market forces determine resource allocation, albeit under a regulatory system adapted to a market economy.

India's Economic Reforms

Background

The Indian economic reforms of 1991 represent a radical shift from the dysfunctional development strategy of the previous four decades. The prereform strategy pursued import-substituting industrialization, and the state played the dominant role in the economy. The foundations of the strategy were laid prior to independence and attracted wide support across the political spectrum. As such there was no significant political support for reforms until 1991, when a serious macroeconomic and balance-of-payments crisis forced a rethinking of the development strategy.

Until the early eighties, India's macroeconomic policies were conservative. Current revenues of the central government exceeded current expenditures so that there was a surplus available to finance in part the deficit in the capital account. In the early eighties, because of lax fiscal policies, current revenue surpluses turned into deficits, so that the government had to borrow at home and abroad to finance not only its investment but also its current consumption.

External borrowing was largely undertaken on concessional terms from multilateral lending institutions and via bilateral, government-to-government external aid until the eighties. As the eighties wore on, the government also resorted to borrowing from abroad on commercial terms, both from the capital market and from nonresident Indians. In 1983–84, out of

$22.8 billion of public and publicly guaranteed external debt, roughly 17 percent was owed to private creditors. On the eve of the macroeconomic crisis in 1990–91, external debt had tripled to $69.3 billion, of which around 30 percent was owed to private creditors.[18] Thus, debt to private creditors grew fivefold in seven years. Since the gross fiscal deficit was too large to be financed entirely by drawing on domestic and external savings, part of it was monetized.

Although fiscal expansionism was unsustainable, with some liberalization—in the form of delicensing of some industries and permitting flexible use of capacity in others through changes in product mix within the licensed capacity under so-called "broad banding," and of relaxing some import restrictions—it did generate growth. The average annual rate of growth of real GDP in the sixth and seventh plans, which covered the eighties, was 5.5 percent and 5.8 percent, respectively, much higher than the so-called Hindu rate of growth of 3.5 percent of the earlier three decades.[19]

Since the sixties, there have always been attempts at moderating the rigors and the unintended side effects as well as distributional consequences of the control system. The earliest of these occurred after a severe macroeconomic crisis in 1966 that forced the government to approach the International Monetary Fund (IMF) and the World Bank for assistance. As part of the agreement with the two institutions, the rupee was devalued in June 1966 and for a brief period of two years controls on foreign trade were relaxed. Prime Minister Indira Gandhi, who had come to power less than six months earlier, was politically vulnerable. Many senior leaders in her own party as well as opposition parties were adamantly against devaluation and liberalization. Their opposition, and the failure of the World Bank to deliver the substantial nonproject assistance that was promised in support of liberalization, led Mrs. Gandhi to abort ongoing liberalization. She did not attempt any liberalization thereafter until shortly before her assassination in 1984. The second liberalization, in the mid-eighties, was initiated by Rajiv Gandhi (who succeeded his assassinated mother) and the young economists appointed by him at senior levels in his office and economic ministries. They had served on the staff of the World Bank and were keen on releasing rigid controls. It so happened that reserves of food-grains and foreign exchange were comfortable at the time. This enabled Rajiv Gandhi's government to experiment with relaxing a few of the restrictive trade and investment policies without fear of triggering a balance-of-payments crisis. This liberalization did increase the potential output from existing capacity. But for the increased potential to be realized, demand had to be expanded. However, with no improvement in the international competitiveness of domestic producers, the demand increase would have to be domestic and not from exports. The domestic demand was stimulated by fiscal expansion, financed by borrowing at home and abroad and by some monetization of fiscal deficits. This expansion, although it turned out to be unsustainable, enabled the economy to absorb the increased output and to grow.

By 1990–91, the gross fiscal deficit had grown to about 10 percent of GDP. If one includes the losses of nonfinancial public-sector enterprises, the consolidated public-sector deficit stood at around 10.9 percent of GDP in 1990–91, of which nearly 4.3 percent of GDP was for interest payments on domestic and external debt.[20] An analysis by Willem Buiter and Urjit Patel showed that unless corrective steps were taken, India faced fiscal insolvency.[21]

The rising fiscal deficits, together with the steep rise in oil prices during the Gulf crisis of 1990, put pressure on prices and the exchange rate, fueling expectations of imminent devaluation of the currency. Political instability in 1990, as reflected in two changes of prime minister within a year, led to a lack of confidence among nonresident Indians in the government's ability to manage the economy. The expectation of a devaluation of the rupee and the decline in confidence led to the withdrawal of deposits in Indian banks by nonresident Indians and to the withdrawal of capital by other external investors. Foreign exchange reserves dwindled to a level that was less than the cost of two weeks' worth of imports. The specter of default on short-term external loans loomed and led to a downgrading of India's credit rating.

Rationale

The severe macroeconomic and balance-of-payments crisis called for immediate policy action. In earlier crises such as the one in 1966, the government had approached the IMF and the World Bank for assistance and been obliged to make such changes in policies as were mandated by the conditions attached to the assistance. But once the crisis eased, the government had reverted to its pre-crisis policies. By contrast, even though the government sought assistance from the IMF and the World Bank in the 1991 crisis, this time policy makers realized that a return to status quo ante with respect to policies was no longer tenable. There were two main reasons for this realization. The first was the collapse of the Soviet and East European economies, which undermined central planning as a means for achieving rapid growth and economic development. The second was the phenomenal growth performance of China since its opening and reforms in 1978. Although the rapid growth of other outward-oriented East Asian economies such as Korea and Taiwan had been evident much earlier, Indian policy makers had dismissed their experience as irrelevant with the argument that India was a much larger economy, even though Korea's industrial sector was rapidly approaching the size of India's. However, Chinese success was a different matter altogether: Not only was China a large economy that succeeded with economic reforms and opening to world markets, but its success exacerbated India's feeling of insecurity vis-à-vis China, acute since India's defeat by China in the border clash of the early sixties. Indian policy makers realized that systematic and deep reforms were needed, and in particular that India had to abandon its insulation from the world economy if its own economy was ever to grow rapidly enough to catch up with China's. Thus, the reforms of 1991 were born.

Contents

The major thrusts of the reforms of 1991 addressed the macroeconomic and balance-of-payments crisis through fiscal consolidation and limited tax reforms, removal of controls on industrial investment and on imports (other than consumer goods), reduction of import tariffs, and creation of a more favorable environment for attracting foreign capital. The reforms also included an initial devaluation and subsequent prudent management of movements in the exchange rate while allowing market forces to play a major role in its determination, making the rupee convertible for current account transactions, and finally, opening the energy and telecommunications sectors for private investment (both domestic and foreign).

Results of Reform

Macroeconomic Stabilization

India

Macroeconomic stabilization was the immediate objective of the Indian reforms. The central government's fiscal deficit was sharply reduced, from

6.6 percent of GDP in the crisis year of 1990–91 to 4.7 percent in 1992–93 and 4.8 percent the year after.[22] However, the deficit rose to 5.8 percent in 2000–2001 and was estimated at 6.1 percent for 2001–02.[23] Further, the fiscal deficit of states has risen substantially, from about 3 percent of GDP in 1990–91 to 4.6 percent in 1999–2000 and 4.2 percent in 2001–02.[24] In all, the deficit of the center, states, and nonfinancial public-sector enterprises in 2001–02, estimated at 11.7 percent of GDP, exceeded its level of 10.9 percent in the crisis year of 1990–91.[25] India's general government deficit is among the highest in the world, and government debt (domestic and foreign) is more than 80 percent of GDP. Thus, the task of fiscal consolidation is yet to be completed.

Tax reforms thus far have involved reductions in income and corporate tax rates, rationalization of customs and excise duties, and elimination of several tax exemptions. The current maximum marginal rate of income tax, at 30 percent, is moderate by international standards. Still, India's tax-to-GDP ratio is low by international standards.

China

Unlike India, China faced no macroeconomic crisis in the conventional sense when it began its reforms in 1978. Under central planning, the central government received all revenues and all expenditures were made through the central budget. Local discretionary spending through extrabudgetary means was minor. The tax system was simple, without personal or corporate income taxes other than on collective enterprises.

Planners' prices and taxes were interchangeable as revenue-enhancing tools, since revenues included the profits of state-owned enterprises (SOEs); those profits accounted for nearly half of total government revenues. With prices fixed by planners, the accounts of SOEs were easy to monitor. Although expenditure assignments were decentralized, intergovernmental transfers covered the gap between local revenues and planned local expenditure.

With reforms and the dismantling of central planning, the profits of SOEs declined as prices (no longer fixed) adjusted to market forces. Competition from private and other non-state-owned enterprises (such as township and village enterprises, TVEs) contributed to the decline in profits of SOEs. Monitoring the performance and tax obligations of SOEs became difficult. Also instead of collecting taxes from around fifty thousand communes, the state had to collect revenues from more than 200 million households and millions of township and village enterprises. Clearly, the fiscal system called for major reform. Four reforms were introduced: division of revenue and expenditure responsibilities among levels of government in 1980, a proportional sharing system in 1982, fiscal contracting in 1988, and a tax sharing system in 1994. A recent report by the World Bank points out that these changes have resulted in high and unsustainable expenditures relative to revenue assignments at subprovincial levels.[26] As a result, large (by international standards) regional disparities in fiscal spending and provision of services have emerged.

China's overall fiscal imbalance as conventionally measured is modest at around 3 percent of GDP over the last several years.[27] But this measure is misleading. Quasi-fixed liabilities arising from the growth of nonperforming loans in the financial system, costs of pension reforms, and the financial burden of supporting insolvent enterprises (bankruptcies are rare, given the absence of usable bankruptcy law) are all increasing. If these problems are not addressed, the fiscal situation will become unsustainable.

Industrial Reforms

India

The reforms of 1991 in India abolished industrial licensing except in a few industries and reduced the number of industries reserved exclusively for the public sector. Restrictions under the Monopolies and Restrictive Trade Practices Act were eased. Entry requirements (including limits on equity participation) also were eased, and private investment was allowed into sectors, such as power, which had been reserved for public-sector investment only. Disinvestment of equity in the public sector was also initiated. The reforms, by focusing primarily on the private sector and not addressing the problems of state-owned enterprises, have exacerbated the latter: SOEs can no longer expect their deficits to be financed through the budget, and at the same time the competition from the entry of private units has worsened the deficits of erstwhile public-sector monopolies. Paradoxically, SOEs still need ministerial and other bureaucratic clearances for their commercial decisions.

In the belief that the policy would generate employment, certain products had been reserved for production by "small-scale and cottage" industries. The fact that the reservation was an anomaly in the era of reforms and liberalization was recognized in 1997 by a government committee, which concluded that "the case for reservation is fundamentally flawed and self-contradictory. . . . The policy crippled growth of several industrial sectors, restricted exports and has done little for the promotion of small-scale industries."[28] Many of the reserved products were major export items, including garments accounting for a third or more of India's exports. Clearly, without a change in the reservation policy India stood to lose its market share in world exports of garments after the phase-out of quotas under the Multi-Fiber Arrangement in 2005, unless garment producers were enabled to compete effectively in world markets. After nearly a decade of reforms, the removal of the reservation of production of garments for the small-scale producers was announced, early in 2000. But orders for implementing the removal were issued only in August 2001. Removal of a similar reservation of leather products has been announced; the hope is that larger and more efficient firms will enter and compete efficiently in world markets.

China

In China, there was and is no analogue of India's small-scale reservation policy. However, the reform process opened significant room for the creation of new enterprises outside of the large SOE system. Most of these enterprises are collectively owned by townships and villages (they are thus known as TVEs). Perkins points out that the governments of townships and villages behave like miniature business conglomerates and have been active promoters of their local enterprises.[29] These governments receive benefits according to the enterprises they control and do not have to share these benefits with higher-level governments except to pay taxes on them. By 1998, the dynamic TVEs were producing 60 percent as much as the large SOEs. After growing rapidly from the mid-1980s to the early 1990s, the enterprises in the interior provinces apparently lost their competitive edge to enterprises from coastal cities.[30] When TVEs fail, it is often the local population that is forced to pay the debts. The total debt of rural administration was as high as $75 billion in 2001. No doubt part of rural administration debt, like SOE debt, is not being serviced and becomes part of the stock of nonperforming loans of the banking system.

Trade Barriers

India

The reforms of 1991 in India abolished licensing for most imports. External trade in agricultural commodities was largely left out of trade liberalization.

By 1996–97, import-weighted average tariffs on all imports had come down to 25 percent, from 85 percent in 1990–91. Since then, they have slowly risen, to 35.7 percent and 35.1 percent, respectively, in 2000–2001 and 2001–02. Quantitative restrictions on some imports were removed beginning in 1996–97. However, those remaining, mainly on consumer goods and agricultural products, were removed only recently, on 31 March 2000 and 1 April 2001.

China

China's average tariffs on the eve of its accession to the WTO in December 2001 were 18.9 percent, on agricultural products and 14.8 percent on industrial products. These averages are to go down to 15 percent and 8.9 percent, respectively, by 1 January 2005. Although Indian tariffs are expected to fall further from their levels in 2001, it would be a surprise if they were to fall as far as Chinese levels by 1 January 2005.

Growth in Aggregate Output

Although there was some limited economic liberalization in India in the 1980s, systemic reforms began only in 1991, more than a decade after China initiated its reforms in 1978. It is appropriate therefore to compare the performance of the two economies in the eighties and the nineties. China's average growth rate during 1990–2000 was the second highest among 140 countries; India's was tenth highest for the same period. During 1980–90, among 122 countries, China's average growth rate was again the second highest, whereas India's was eleventh. Even if one adjusts for possible overstatement of Chinese growth rates, by about 1.0 percent to 1.5 percent per year,[31] there is little doubt that both countries were star growth performers during 1980–2000.

Sectoral Composition of Growth

In both countries, economic reforms had differential impacts on different sectors of the economy (table 7.5). These differences are important from the perspective of the distribution of the costs and benefits of reform. For example, in both countries the bulk of the population, especially the poor, live in rural areas and depend on agriculture. The attention paid to, and the performance of, agriculture in the reform era is thus a key indicator of the impact of reforms.

Table 7.5 *Average Annual Percentage Rates of Growth, by Economic Sector*

	China		India	
	1980–1990	1990–2000	1980–1990	1990–2000
Agriculture	5.9	4.1	3.1	3.0
Industry	11.1	13.7	6.9	6.4
Manufacturing	11.1	13.4	7.3	5.2
Services	13.5	9.0	7.0	8.0
GDP	10.1	10.3	5.8	6.0

Source: World Bank, *World Development Indicators 2002* (Washington, D.C.: World Bank, 2002), table 4.1.

In China, the initial thrust of reforms was in the agricultural sector. This was no surprise given the poor performance of collectivized agriculture and the emphasis on industry prior to reforms. The introduction of the household responsibility system, the reduction in compulsory deliveries to the state, and increases in the proportion of output that could be sold in the market provided effective incentives for farm households to increase output. Their response was rapid, and agricultural output grew substantially. As might be expected, the initial rapid growth later slowed as the focus of the reform process shifted to improving the efficiency of the industrial sector. The industry- and export-oriented development of coastal cities and special economic zones and the growth of TVEs reflected this shift. In India, on the other hand, distortion prior to reforms was more pronounced in manufacturing and foreign trade, and the reforms were aimed at removing those distortions. Thus, the sectoral composition of output growth in the two countries reflects not only the differing targets of reform but also the lingering effects of pre-reform policies.

Because significant reforms in India were undertaken in the 1990s, the relatively modest change in the sectoral pattern and overall GDP growth during that decade might seem surprising. Part of the explanation lies in the fact that the reform process slowed remarkably in the second half of the 1990s. In China, the growth of agricultural and service output slowed markedly and that of manufacturing output accelerated in the nineties compared with the eighties. In India, on the other hand, the growth of manufacturing output slowed significantly and that of services rose.

Growth in Inputs and Productivity

The prime objective of economic liberalization in both countries was to increase the efficiency of resource use (as measured by gains in total factor productivity, or TFP) by promoting a greater role for markets in resource allocation and greater integration with the world economy. In the absence of such efficiency gains, any growth in output has to come only from increases in the quantum of resources used. On the other hand, if gains (or growth) in TFP are significant, then for any given aggregate growth rate achieved, growth in the quantum of resources used would be that much less.

Among the resources used, capital is an important component. Apart from attracting a considerably larger volume of foreign capital, China saved a much larger proportion of its income: gross domestic savings accounted for 40 percent of GDP in 2000 versus 21 percent in India. Gross capital formation in China was 37 percent of GDP in 2000 as compared with 24 percent in India.[32] In addition, there has apparently been no capital deepening in China—that is, no increase over time in the amount of capital used for producing a unit of output. A commonly used measure of capital use is the incremental capital-output ratio (ICOR). It is the ratio of the change in capital stock used to the resulting increases in output (as measured by real GDP). Sometimes an increase (decrease) in ICOR is interpreted as a decrease (increase) in productivity (or efficiency in use) of capital, although such an interpretation could be misleading. In any case, ICOR in China remained virtually constant during the period of rapid growth.[33] Srinivasan and Tendulkar estimate that the implicit ICOR for India's economy as a whole was 5.7 during 1950–80, and it fell to 4.0 during the 1980s, when there was limited liberalization, and to 4.1 during 1992–93 to 1999–2000.[34] Clearly, in both economies the period of liberalization and rapid growth was also one with no capital deepening, suggesting that both countries used resources efficiently by spreading capital over their abundant labor to enhance productivity.

However, there was a significant difference between the two economies in the relative contributions of factor inputs and productivity gains to growth. The growth accounting exercise of Hu and Khan for China suggests that "while capital formation alone accounted for 65 percent of pre-1978 growth, with labour adding another 17 percent, together they accounted for only 58 percent of the post-1978 boom, a slide of almost 25 percentage points. Productivity increases made up the rest."[35] The reason for this was that while average rate of GDP growth went up by 50 percent between the two periods, TFP growth more than tripled. Estimates of TFP growth in India by Ahluwalia, the IMF, and the World Bank are shown in table 7.6.[36] More disaggregated analysis by the National Council of Applied Economic Research (NCAER), using different methods (growth accounting and production function estimation), suggests that "where the

Table 7.6 *Growth in Total Factor Productivity (Percent per Year)*

China (Hu and Khan)		India (IMF)		India (World Bank)		India (Ahluwalia)	
1953–78	1.1	1960s	−1.0 to 1.1			1960–80	−0.5[a]
1979–94	3.9	1970s	−2.1 to 0.3	1979–80 to 1997–98	1.3 to 1.5		
		1980s	0.7 to 2.9			1980s	2.8[a]
		mid-1990s	1.5 to 3.4	1994–95 to 1996–97	2.4 to 2.8		
		late 1990s	0.3 to 2.9				

Sources: Z. Hu and M. Khan, "Why Is China Growing So Fast?" *Economic Issues,* no. 8 (Washington, D.C.: International Monetary Fund, June 1997); IMF, *India: Recent Economic Developments,* Country Report No. 02/155 (Washington, D.C.: International Monetary Fund, 2002), 11; World Bank, *India: Policies to Reduce Poverty and Accelerate Sustainable Development,* Report No. 19471-IN (Washington, D.C.: World Bank, 2000), 130; Isher Judge Ahluwalia, "Structural Adjustment and Productivity Growth in India," *Productivity* 33, no. 2 (New Delhi, 1992).

a. Figures for manufacturing sector only.

estimates indicate an increase in average productivity growth in the nineties, the change is insignificant."[37] Goldar summarizes the available TFP studies on India.[38] Taken together, these differing estimates indicate that the contribution of TFP growth to aggregate growth in the post-reform era was much less in India than in China.

There are serious and well-understood methodological and measurement error problems in TFP calculations, and depending on the method used, what one researcher attributes to TFP growth another might attribute to economies of scale and/or to positive externalities. Nonetheless, the foregoing estimates for China and India have been derived using similar methods. Moreover, they are consistent with other known features of the growth process in the two economies. In China, the move to the household responsibility system in agriculture after 1978 provided relatively more secure property rights. This move, together with the drastic reduction in forced deliveries to the state at below-market prices, greatly raised the incentives for more efficient use of resources, particularly labor, on family farms. Rapid growth in farm output enabled workers to move out of agriculture to work in township and village nonfarm enterprises. In the manufacturing sector, the post-1978 reforms granted greater autonomy to enterprise managers and allowed a larger proportion of output to be sold at remunerative market prices. Above all, foreign investment, particularly in the special economic zones, linked China to international markets and transferred productive technology. It is not at all surprising that these factors led to faster growth in, and greater contribution to total growth from, TFP.

In India, prior to the reforms of 1991, given the straitjacket in which producers were placed through controls on investment, location, choice of technology and inputs, imports of inputs, and foreign investment, and the absence of competitive pressures, it should surprise no one that there was no growth in TFP (except in the eighties when the rigor of some of the controls was relaxed). There is strong support for this conclusion in the TFP growth estimates of Ahluwalia, the IMF, and the World Bank, although other estimates by NCAER are ambiguous.[39]

Exports, Capital Flows, and External Debt

Integrating their domestic economies with the world economy was an important objective of reforms in both countries. Such integration would involve not only greater trade in goods and services with the rest of the world, but also greater inflows of external capital. Several indicators of integration are available, such as share of trade in GDP, growth of exports, trends in capital inflows, and external debt. Also, given the fact that the so-called information technology revolution of the 1990s opened up hitherto unavailable opportunities for exports of services, it is worth comparing Chinese and Indian achievements in this regard. It turns out that China outperformed India in most of the indications of global integration.

Both China and India experienced a significant increase in the average annual growth rate of the value of their merchandise exports in the eighties and nineties. A major contributor to India's exports of goods and services is the software sector. Receipts from software exports grew at an annual rate exceeding 50 percent in the five years ending in 1999–2000. Valued at $4.02 billion in 1999–2000, they accounted for nearly 8 percent of the total value of exports of goods and nonfactor services. If availability, cost, and efficiency of the telecommunications and power sectors do not constrain them, software exports are projected to grow even faster in the future. However, India's advantage relative to China, in terms of having a large pool of software technicians who operate in the English language, is eroding. China could surpass India as a software power in a decade. In fact, in 2000 China had 15.9 personal computers per thousand people as compared with India's 4.5, and had 22.5 million Internet users as compared with India's 5 million.[40]

Between 1990 and 1999, total long-term net resource flows to China quadrupled, from $10.1 billion to $42.7 billion. Flows to India fluctuated between $3.4 billion and $7.6 billion during the same period. Foreign direct investment (FDI) in China increased more than twelvefold, from $3.5 billion in 1990 to $44 billion in 2001. In India, FDI increased by about twenty times, but from a much smaller $162 million in 1990 to $3.9 billion in 2001.[41]

China's and India's total external debts in 2000 were, respectively, $149.8 billion and $100.4 billion. The World Bank classifies both as low, on the grounds that the present value of China's (India's) debt was only 3 percent (16 percent) of its GNI, and total debt service accounted for 9 percent (13 percent) of its exports. However, the share of volatile short-term debt in China's total debt, at 11.5 percent, was larger than India's 3.5 percent.[42]

Turning to FDI, the Indian reforms of 1991 affected FDI only to a limited extent. A Foreign Investment Promotion Board was established to approve FDI in some industries on a discretionary basis. In addition, the Reserve Bank of India granted automatic approval of FDI that met stipulated requirements. Indian firms with good standing have been allowed (since February 1992) with government approval to issue equity and convertible bonds abroad in European and American capital markets. Since September 1992, registered foreign institutional investors have also been permitted to purchase both equity and debt securities directly in the Indian capital market, subject to certain upper limits. As a consequence of the limited liberalization, FDI increased from $77 million in 1992 to $3.6 billion in 1997. It was estimated at $3.9 billion in 2001–02. India's share of total FDI in all developing countries rose from 0.6 percent in 1992 to a peak of 2.0 percent in 1997, and then fell to 1.0 percent in 2000 and rose to 1.7 percent in 2001.[43] India's share in the total portfolio investment for all developing countries increased from 1.7 percent in 1992 to 13.4 percent in 1994 and declined to 3.8 percent during 1999. Portfolio investment is volatile: it fell from $4.7 billion in 1994 to $1.5 billion in 1995, only to rise to $4.6 billion in 1996. It hit a low of $343 million in 1998.[44]

China has attracted and continues to attract massive inflow of FDI. It accounted for 21 percent of FDI flows to all developing countries in 2001.[45] In 1992–97, inflows to China amounted to $194.4 billion compared with India's $9.4 billion.[46] An inflow of $55 billion of FDI was expected for China in 2002, while an outflow of $48 billion was estimated by unofficial sources as capital flight for the same year. Part of the outflow is attributed to local bureaucracies sending their ill-gotten gains to their bank accounts abroad.[47]

A substantial part of China's foreign capital inflow came from overseas Chinese in the form of FDI. Although nonresident Indians contributed to India's external borrowing, their debt accounting for nearly a seventh of India's total debt of $97.8 billion at the end of March 2000, their participation in FDI was minor. Overseas Chinese have played a significant role in the spectacular growth of China's economy since 1978. Gopalan estimates that 54 percent of FDI inflows into China originated from Hong Kong, Singapore, and Taiwan, and 6 percent from the Virgin Islands, which is said to be a haven for illegal capital stashed abroad by Chinese.[48] Also, Gopalan suggests that "round-tripping" of capital that was deliberately sent abroad and brought back to take advantage of concessions offered for FDI might have accounted for 25 percent to 40 percent of the total.

Poverty and Other Social Indicators

Although serious conceptual and measurement problems encumber the assessment of poverty levels and their time trends in both countries, the available data suggest that rapid growth was associated with a significant reduction of poverty (see table 7.7). In India, poverty estimates based on large household surveys (annual until 1973–74, and quinquennial since then) are available. These data suggest that the poverty ratio (i.e., the proportion of population with consumption below a national poverty line) fluctuated around an average of about 50 percent with no downward trend from 1950–51 to 1973–74. The Indian household surveys after 1993–94 have been beset with problems of noncomparability. Angus Deaton has made adjustments for these problems, and these are reflected in the estimates for India in table 7.7. Chinese poverty data based on household surveys are relatively recent; official poverty lines and poverty head counts going back to 1978 were first announced in 1994, superseding some earlier ad hoc estimates.

India's education system is largely funded by governments at all levels, and private health care is costly and out of reach for the bulk of the population. In China, on the other hand, Saich points out that prior to the reforms, "the organization of the collective in the countryside and the inconsequentiality of cost meant that, for [the country's] developmental level, rural Chinese enjoyed a good preventive health care and basic education system."[49] In urban areas the social welfare system was linked to the enterprises that employed the workers. Because of this system, even though

Table 7.7 *Percentage of Population Living in Poverty, India and China, 1951–2000*

India			China		
				Rural	
	Rural	Urban		Official	World Bank
Aug. 1951–Nov. 1952	47.4	35.5	1978	30.7	
Sept. 1961–July 1962	47.2	43.6			
July 1970–June 1971	54.8	45.0	1990	9.5	42.8
July 1977–June 1978	50.5	40.5			
July 1987–June 1988	39.0	22.8	1997	5.4	
July 1993–June 1994	32.9	18.1	1998	4.6	24.2
July 1999–June 2000	25.3	9.5			

Sources: G. Datt, "Poverty in India: An Update," International Food Policy Research Institute, 1997; World Bank, "Has Poverty in India Declined since the Economic Reforms?" Washington, D.C.: 1999; A. Deaton, "Computing Prices and Poverty Rates in India, 1999–2000," Princeton University Research Program in Developmental Studies, 2001; A. Park and S. Wang, "China's Poverty Statistics," *China Economic Review* 12 (2001): 384–95.

direct public expenditures on education and health as a share of GDP were not high (in fact, in 1980 China was among the twenty countries in the world that spent the least on education as a share of GDP, according to Saich), China's achievements in social sectors were far superior to India's.[50] However, with the abolition of rural collectives and the poor financial condition of SOEs, alternative means for financing health and education have to be found if the pre-reform achievements are to be sustained in the future.

By and large, China had accomplished these successes by the early 1960s. For example, by the mid-1970s, life expectancy at birth had increased from around thirty-six years during 1948–49 to sixty-two years, and in the subsequent three decades the increase was only ten more years. Life expectancy of the Indian population reached sixty years only in the early 1990s. India has been catching up faster since 1980 in some indicators, but not in others. For example, the under-five mortality rate, at 177 per thousand, was nearly 2.7 times China's rate of 65 per thousand in 1980. By 2000, India's rate had dropped by half to 88 per thousand, which was about 2.5 times China's 39. On the other hand, adult illiteracy in India, at 45 percent among males over fifteen years of age, was only twice China's rate of 22 percent in 1980; by 2000 it had fallen by roughly a third to 32 percent in India, whereas in China it had fallen by more than a half to 8 percent, so that India's rate was nearly 3.7 times that of China.[51]

Looking Ahead

Slowdown in Aggregate Growth and the Importance of Further Reforms

The aggregate rate of growth in both China and India seems to have slackened. In China, the annual rate of growth of GDP steadily declined for seven years, from 14.2 percent in 1992 to 7 percent in 1999, and has since recovered to 7.3 percent in 2001.[52] India's growth rate recovered from a low of 0.8 percent in the crisis year of 1991–92, reached a peak of 7.3 percent in 1996–97, and then fell to 4.8 percent in 1997–98. In 1999–2000 and 2000–2001, the growth rate was, respectively, 6.0 percent and 4.0 percent; it is estimated to have been 5.4 percent in 2001–02.[53] Although growth rates of 14 percent or more could not possibly be sustained for long, the fall to around 7 percent in China and the stagnation at around 6 percent in India strongly suggest that the progress of reforms has slowed. Of course, without rapid growth sustained over a long enough period of time, it will be impossible for India and China to eliminate poverty and provide a reasonable standard of living for their large populations.

The broad thrust of reforms in both economies, despite differences in emphasis, was similar. It included a progressive reduction in the involvement of the state in the economy and a concomitant increase in that of the market. Another major goal of both countries was to integrate their economies with the world economy to a much greater extent than was the case before reforms. Finally, both engaged in reforms of economic (e.g., financial), political, and administrative (e.g., division of power and responsibilities between levels of government, legal system) institutions to enable those institutions to serve their market economies efficiently. The difference in nomenclatures in the description of the respective roles of the state and market, "socialist market economy" in the Chinese parlance and a "mixed economy" in the Indian parlance, are of little significance in differentiating the broad thrust of their reforms. However, the difference in nomenclatures does denote significant differences in political constraints on the future sustainability of reforms and of rapid economic growth.

The relative modesty of the success of Indian reforms cannot be attributed to their rapidity, that is, an attempt to reform too many areas and too fast. Indeed, India's reforms have been as gradual as China's if not more so. The more relevant distinction is in the political context of economic reforms in the two countries. India attempted to pursue a major restructuring of its economy in the context of a vibrant participatory democracy. The process of reform amid the competitive politics of India, where different parties rule in different states and a coalition of some of them rules at the center, was understandably a complex one of building, if not a political consensus, at least enough support to enact the needed legislation. In China, the reform process was centrally controlled by the authoritarian leadership of the Communist Party. This is not to say, of course, that the leadership of the party was unanimous in choosing among alternative courses of action; nor is it to say that the government in Beijing was fully aware of, and had a firm grip over, what went on in the provinces. It is only to say that the firm control held by the party made it much easier than in India to undertake and implement reforms. As Saich argues, a move toward democracy was never intended, and Deng Xiaoping and his successors

> have preferred to combine the introduction of market forces in the economy with tight political control. . . . Even here there has been adaptation in the party's role and some have begun to question whether it is viable for the long term future. . . . This strategy has appeared to be a success in economic terms. . . . However, the reforms have been deeply contested by those opposed on ideological grounds or by those who have felt that reforms have not progressed swiftly enough.[54]

The Sixteenth Party Congress that convened in Beijing in November 2002 chose a new general secretary, Hu Jintao, for the party and a new prime minister, Wen Jiabao. The challenge facing the party, and the new leaders, is to reinvent itself to maintain its continued acceptance by an increasingly diverse and assertive population. Many observers feel the party has lost its ideological soul and is groping for new ways to justify its monopoly of power. However, it seems unlikely that there will be any radical change. In his address to the Sixteenth Party Congress, President Jiang Zemin did not announce any proposals for political change but rather emphasized stability. His successor, Hu Jintao, is unlikely to deviate from Jiang's policies of opening China's economy to market forces and remaking the Communist Party while crushing all political movements and social unrest.[55]

The Politics of Reform of State-Owned Enterprises

The size of the state sector has obvious implications for the process of reform and globalization. In both countries, SOEs have provided a lion's share of infrastructural services such as electric power as well as other sources of energy. The efficiency of their functioning has implications for the cast of essential inputs, such as power and energy, and hence for the international competitiveness of the manufacturing sectors. Reforming SOEs, let alone privatizing them, runs into the strident opposition of their workers and their supporters among political parties. Yet the reform of SOEs is essential for the success of reforms and global integration.

Both China and India had heavily invested in SOEs, although, as would be expected in a communist state, in China the size of the state sector was much larger. In India, the share of total investment made by the public sector was 25.6 percent in 1950–51, the first year of planning; it grew to 49.8 percent in 1964–65 and declined to 38.8 percent by 1974–75, only to climb back to a peak of 53.6 percent in 1986–87. In the crisis and reform year of 1991–92 it had fallen to 43.0 percent. It stood at 29.9 percent in 1999–2000.[56] Lardy reports that on the eve of reforms in China in 1978, investment in state and collective enterprises accounted for 87 percent of total investment in China's fixed assets.[57] This share had come down to 69 percent by 1996. The Organization for Economic Cooperation and Development (OECD) reports the same 69 percent share for 1998.[58]

Both China and India tried to reform their large state-owned enterprises with limited and differing degrees of success. Their approach and strategies were also very different. There is no Indian counterpart to the dynamic township and village enterprises (TVEs) of China; the reform of SOEs, particularly where it involves privatization and possible retrenchment of workers, has been, and remains, a major political issue in both countries (as discussed further in the following section). Major differences between the two countries also exist in both the structure and reforms of their financial sectors. Although corruption is a significant issue in both countries, the fact that in India a legal system does not have to be constructed from scratch as in China (where the legal system, such as it was, was destroyed during the Cultural Revolution), and the absence of democracy in China, make the approach to elimination of corruption very different in the two countries.

The authorities in China, unlike their counterparts in India, did not have to deal with trade unions in SOEs in considering their options for reforms. Nevertheless, like their Indian counterparts, they were concerned about the possibility that reforms, particularly privatization, might result in large-scale unemployment of workers in SOEs. Besides, as Lardy points out, China

> initially lacked the legal, institutional, and governance structures that are required to support an economic system based predominantly on private ownership. Thus, early and rapid privatization of state-owned firms could not have been expected to improve economic efficiency. Instead China undertook other liberalizing measures that facilitated the extraordinary growth of nonstate industry, particularly township and village enterprises. As a result, the share of output produced by state-owned sector of the economy has fallen dramatically since the reform began.[59]

Although the share of China's output produced by SOEs declined, Lardy reports that employment in SOEs increased by 40 million between 1978 and 1984 and stabilized thereafter.[60] And SOEs continued to absorb a disproportionately large share of investment resources. What is more, despite a continuous increase in the number of loss-making SOEs, few were allowed to close down. Lardy suggests that, "unwilling to tolerate the level of urban unemployment that would accompany the widespread bankruptcy of loss-making firms, the state assumed the burden of subsidizing growing losses through fiscal subsidies and, increasingly, through so-called policy loans from the state-owned banking system. Since the late eighties these direct and indirect subsidies absorbed 10 percent or more of gross domestic product every year."[61] The fact that SOEs were responsible for pension, medical, and housing benefits for their workers compounded the problem. As subsidies from the government declined and competitive pressure from non-state-owned enterprises and imports increased, many SOEs could not meet their full range of social obligations or even their salary payments.[62] Without reform of the pension and health care systems, SOE reform is difficult. Mergers with and acquisition of failing SOEs by healthier ones have merely hidden the problem.

According to Lardy, China's gradualist reforms have created three economic trends that are unsustainable in the long run.[63] First, the growing debt of many SOEs, including their contingent liabilities on pensions and tax obligations, exceed the value of their assets so that they are insolvent, and other SOEs are headed that way. Second, unsustainable lending by state-owned banks and other financial institutions has led to a rapid rise in loans relative to output and to an unusually rapid expansion of the money supply, as well as to a large and rising share of nonperforming loans. Third, the decline in government revenues by two-thirds relative to output between 1978 and 1995 has eroded the capacity of the government to finance normal expenditures from the budget. The government has taken steps to address some of these problems. Four companies have been established to manage nonperforming loans (NPLs) and sales of distressed state-owned assets, at discounts exceeding 70 percent. One of the companies, Huarong, was to offer $2 billion of nonperforming assets for sale in London and has hired an international accountancy firm to promote the sale in New York after the London presentation.[64] Whether these efforts will revive the SOEs is open to doubt. By selling their debt to asset management companies and not paying interest on large nonperforming loans, "many bankrupt SOEs have turned around from basket cases to seemingly profitable enterprises overnight. Whether the problem of SOE inefficiency is really solved is an entirely different matter, and many of the SOEs have avoided the necessary structural reforms to enable them to compete in the future post WTO-entry market."[65]

Interestingly, the very same problems of restructuring or privatizing SOEs, NPLs in state-owned banks, and fiscal imbalance threaten the sustainability of India's growth. However, the origins and the seriousness of the problems, the political economy of the constraints faced by the government in addressing them, and their impact on the growth process are very different. For example, the budgetary implications of dealing with the NPLs of state-owned banks and recapitalizing them are far more serious in India than in China, given India's much higher ratio of public debt to GDP. In India, it is illegal to close down bankrupt enterprises (private as well as publicly owned) without government permission, which is rarely given. A Board for Industrial and Financial Reconstruction (BIFR) was set up in May 1987 to make recommendations to the government on appropriate actions to deal with enterprises that have to be restructured or wound up. The Indian government reported that up to the end of December 2000, 4,575 enterprises, including 251 SOEs, had been referred to BIFR.[66] The board registered 3,296 of them, recommending rehabilitation of 557 (45 SOEs) and the closing down of 824 (35 SOEs). Two hundred and forty-nine companies (8 SOEs) were declared no longer in need of restructuring, and for 35 (3 SOEs), net worth became positive. However, not a single enterprise has been wound up, although winding-up notices were issued in 102 cases (14 SOEs).

In India, for political reasons, privatization is described as "disinvestment," by which is meant the sale to private buyers of a part (but not enough to give the buyers management control) of the government's equity in an SOE. In 2000, the government committed itself to reducing its equity to 26 percent or less in nonstrategic SOEs and to 33 percent in state-owned banks. A Disinvestment Commission was set up in 1996 to advise the government on the modalities of disinvestment. Its term ended in 1999, and the commission was not renewed. Instead, a new Department of Disinvestment was created. During its existence, the Disinvestment Commission recommended action on fifty-eight of the sixty-four cases of SOEs referred to it. Yet as of mid-2000, the recommendations were being implemented in only thirteen cases. This shift, from disinvestments to strategic sales involving the transfer of management and control to private hands, has not resulted in any change. For example, Singapore Airlines, which was one of the bidders for the purchase of state-owned Air India, pulled out of the sale process, citing a hostile environment for privatization in India.

The political economy of privatization in India's competitive politics can be illustrated by two examples. In the state of Maharashtra, the government, then controlled by the Congress Party, had negotiated a contract in 1995 with Enron, a foreign energy firm, to invest in a large power plant. The power generated was to be sold to the state electricity board (SEB), a state-owned monopoly.[67] The Congress Party was voted out of office in 1996, and the newly elected government of the opposition Shiva Sena initially cancelled the contract. Later it renegotiated the power purchase agreement and the terms of investment in two phases. Enron completed the project and has been producing power. The Shiva Sena government was subsequently voted out of office, and the successor coalition government, in which the Congress Party is the senior partner, wants to renegotiate the power purchase agreement. Whatever the merits of the case, external investors in such a situation are very likely to conclude that investment in India is subject to significant political risk. The second example is that of a state-owned aluminum-producing plant in the newly created state of Chhattisgarh. The central government announced the sale of 55 percent of its equity in the plant to a private entrepreneur. However, the chief minister of the state, who belongs to the opposition Congress Party, demanded that the sale be rescinded and offered to buy the equity from the central government. After some legal wrangling, the sale finally went through.

Apart from privatization and foreign investment becoming issues of political competition, another concern is the opposition of labor unions, regardless of their political affiliation. In fact, the Bharat Mazdoor Sabha, a trade union affiliated with the ruling Bharatiya Janata Party (BJP), the dominant party in the coalition government at the center, has opposed privatization of SOEs. In his budget for 2001–02, Finance Minister Yashwant Sinha announced a proposal to introduce legislation that would require government permission to retrench workers or to wind up an enterprise only if the enterprise employed more than a thousand persons. He also proposed to increase the severance payment to retrenched workers. If introduced and passed, this legislation would be a major step forward because it would exempt an overwhelming majority of enterprises from having to seek government permission to restructure. Predictably, the labor unions are adamantly against the legislation. As of June 2003, the legislation had not been enacted.

The drag on growth from poorly performing SOEs arises from the fact that they are dominant in the infrastructural sector (e.g., power, railways, and ports). The state electricity boards, which generate, transmit, and distribute power, have been running losses, in part because of the heavily subsidized sale of power to politically important groups such as farmers, and even outright theft of power. Although they are required by law to earn a rate of return of not less than 3 percent of their fixed assets, the realized rate of return in 1999–2000 was minus 41.2 percent![68] Investment in future capacity is constrained by the poor resource position of the state electricity boards and the reluctance of private investors to enter the sector. In fact, three foreign investors decided in 2000 to cancel their announced investment. However, several states have enacted electricity reform acts. The central government has signed memoranda of agreement with some states, offering financial and technical support in return for their unbundling of transmission and distribution and privatization of distribution in a time-bound manner. It remains to be seen whether the center will be able to enforce reforms if the financial assistance is provided ahead of reforms. In the meantime, as disinvestment stagnates, the drag of loss-making SOEs on the public budget continues.

Fiscal and Financial Sector Reforms

Both China and India face challenges in reforming their fiscal and financial systems. Although both countries are large and have several levels of government, the modalities for assignment of tax and expenditure responsibilities and the sharing of revenues among levels of government are very different. In India, a constitutionally mandated Finance Commission (the twelfth Finance Commission was appointed in October 2002) reviews the fiscal situation of the central and state governments and makes recommendations every five years to the central government about revenue sharing and transfers from the center to the states. In China, as noted earlier, prior to reforms the system was heavily centralized. Since the tax reform of 1994, China has undertaken reforms in budget classification and preparation, procurement, and expenditure management and auditing. However, the state of intergovernmental fiscal relations and the problems with the existing system of decentralized finance have been described in a report by the World Bank as posing a significant bottleneck to development. The report makes several recommendations for putting in place incentives for intergovernmental cooperation.

The IMF has drawn attention to the likely future cost of pension reforms and meeting infrastructure and other needs, as well as the quasi-fiscal liabilities arising from the large nonperforming loans in the banking sector.[69] While acknowledging the difficulties in precisely estimating the impact of these potential liabilities, the IMF urged the authorities to reduce the budget deficit further over the next few years.

The OECD in its report in 2000 on China draws attention to the steady fall in the ratio of tax revenue to GDP between 1980 and 1996 and a slow recovery to less than 15 percent of GDP. It also points out that government spending on education, research and development, and other social endeavors has been low by international standards. Echoing the World Bank, it emphasizes the need for reforms of fiscal federalism arrangements so as to discourage the widespread imposition of ad hoc charges and other forms of resource extraction on enterprises and rural residents.

The OECD report states that the fundamental capabilities of the Chinese financial system, and its incentives to allocate credit efficiently, remain impaired. The reform of the banking system is closely linked with the reform of the SOEs. The report identifies three key objectives for reform: (1) restoring capital adequacy to financial institutions in the near term; (2) creating a more diverse and balanced system wherein financial outlets other than state-owned commercial banks have a much greater role; and (3) fostering the development of China's capital markets. Clearly, these are difficult tasks.

After a decade of reforms in India, the consolidated deficit of the public sector (including the center, the states, and nonfinancial SOEs) in 2000–2001, as noted earlier, is likely to exceed its pre-reform level of 10.9 percent of GDP in 1990–91. Thus, fiscal consolidation remains elusive. Tax and nontax revenue of the entire public sector as a proportion of GDP has remained virtually stagnant at around 19–20 percent over the last five years.[70] Major contributors to fiscal imbalance at the center and state levels are subsidies on food, fertilizer, irrigation water, and electricity, and the low charges assessed for public services such as education and health. Nonmerit subsidies (i.e., those that cannot be rationalized on social justice and externality grounds, such as on electricity used by farmers) accounted for more than three-fourths of the implicit and explicit subsidies, whose total was on the order of 14.5 percent of GDP in 1994–95.[71] Political considerations have precluded any serious attempt to reduce subsidies. Interest payments on the public debt and the expenditure on employee wages, salaries, and pensions eat up most of the revenue of government. In his budget for 2000–2001, the finance minister announced plans to reduce government employment, following the recommendations of the recently established Expenditure Reforms Commission.[72] This and introduction of a Fiscal Responsibility Act in Parliament are hopeful signs.

Reform of the financial sector in general, and of the banking system in particular, has been on the government's agenda for more than a decade. Several committees appointed by the government, including one appointed in February 1999 on reforming weak public-sector banks, had made recommendations. Although a few private domestic and foreign banks operate, the state-owned banks dominate the commercial banking sector. According to the IMF,[73] the risk-weighted capital ratio of twenty-seven large public-sector banks gradually increased to 11.2 percent in 1998–99. However, net NPLs accounted for 8.1 percent of the outstanding loans of public-sector banks, while the same ratio for their domestic private and foreign counterparts was, respectively, 6.9 percent and 2.0 percent in the same year. Even more disturbing is that the number of public-sector banks with net NPLs above 8 percent of all outstanding loans was as high as fourteen out of twenty-seven in 1998–99. Had norms for classification of a loan as nonperforming such as those in advanced countries been applied, instead of less stringent Indian ones, the quantity of NPLs would have been much higher. The banking system has a long way to go to become sound, and until it is, making the rupee convertible on the capital account would be premature.

Widening Regional Disparities and Income Inequalities

India's pre-reform state controls on economic activity spawned rampant economic and political corruption. The expectation that reforms, which did away with many of the controls, would reduce corruption has not yet been borne out. In China, at least until the reforms of 1978, the rents (as well as resources directed to rent seeking) were modest. The scope for consuming rents was limited because the goods available for consumption were few in number and poor in quality. Accumulating rents was not attractive either, because private wealth was difficult to hide and conspicuous consumption was politically risky. This is not to deny the existence of luxurious Party "guest houses," but only to suggest that the diversion of resources to such activities was limited. In post-reform China, wealth accumulation was no longer frowned upon, and with the phenomenal increase in the supply of consumer goods (particularly imported durables), the diversion of resources for rent seeking has increased substantially. Chinese policy makers, however, are said to have attempted to eliminate any potential rents quickly. Yet given the still rudimentary and segmented markets in China and the fact that *guanxi* (i.e., personal connection) is still important in getting ahead, it is unlikely that rents have been eliminated.

In the post-reform era a widening of regional disparities has been observed in both countries. To a certain extent this is natural: those regions (and individuals) that are better placed initially to take advantage of the opportunities opened up by the reforms are likely to grow faster. The real issue then is whether the socioeconomic system enables regions that are initially disadvantaged to catch up with the initially advantaged within a reasonable period of time.

At the aggregate level, one approach to this issue is to ask: do regions with initially different levels of income nonetheless converge over time to the same level and rate of growth of per capita income in the long run? This is the so-called absolute convergence hypothesis. It is to be contrasted with the conditional convergence hypothesis, which suggests that each region converges to its own long-run level and growth of per capita income. There is a growing literature on testing the hypotheses of absolute and conditional convergence in both countries.[74] In India, P. Cashin and R. Sahay found evidence of absolute convergence.[75] M. G. Rao and K. Sen, suggest that in fact the findings of Cashin and Sahay should be interpreted as supporting conditional convergence.[76] Clearly, a finding of conditional convergence, because it is consistent with regions growing at different rates in the long run, could mean growing disparities across regions. In India, there is evidence of growing disparities between southern and western coastal states, on the one hand, and the interior and northern states, on the other, in growth rates; the former are growing faster than the latter in the post-reform era. Coupled with the fact that the incidence of poverty is higher, and the share of the country's population larger, in the latter states, there has been legitimate concern that if sustained in the future, these growth disparities will threaten the stability of India's federal democracy.

In China, the report of the Central Committee of the Communist Party cites "growing social and economic inequality and official corruption as over-arching sources of discontent. The income gap is approaching the 'alarm level,' it says, with disparities widening between city and countryside, between the fast-growing East Coast and the stagnant interior, and also within urban populations."[77] In India, too, regional disparities are significant, and some states that were better placed in terms of human capital and infrastructure have grown faster than others after external opening and reforms. Clearly, in both countries growing regional disparities constitute a serious political issue.

China and India in the World Economy: Bilateral Trade and Competition in World Markets

After the border war of 1962 bilateral trade was suspended and did not reopen until 1977.[78] Although superficially it might appear that the two countries have similar factor endowment ratios and that there is not much complementarity between their commodity production structures to induce trade, there is still the potential for a much greater volume of trade than is taking place at present, particularly in intra-industry trade. There is evidence that after languishing in the eighties, trade grew significantly in the nineties. In the year 2000 total trade was on the order of $3 billion as compared with a paltry $2.45 million when trade reopened in 1977. India imported $1.56 billion worth of goods from China and exported $1.35 billion. The rate of growth of trade between 1999 and 2000 was a phenomenal 47 percent. There are a number of products, such as coking coal, iron ore, raw silk, and silk fabric, that present the potential for a substantial expansion of trade. Also, possibilities exist for two-way trade of items within broad product categories such as steel, textiles, and apparel.

Bilateral trade in services and bilateral flows of FDI are increasing as well. India's lead in software and China's capability in hardware have opened up possibilities of increasing trade in products and services of the information technology sector. Indian software companies and training institutes have a significant presence in the Pudong Software Park in Shanghai. A dominant Chinese software company has an office in India's software capital of Bangalore, and many Chinese software engineers are also being trained there. China has established a base for production of washing machines and color television sets in India to cater to the Indian market. India has just begun cultivating a Chinese-developed hybrid rice variety that can yield twice as much rice per unit of land as some of India's own dwarf varieties of high-yield rice.

Gopalan's estimates of labor productivity in manufacturing suggest that except in petroleum products and nonelectrical machinery, the productivity of a Chinese worker is higher than that of an Indian worker by anywhere from 30 percent to 180 percent, depending on the product.[79] Of course, these estimates must be treated with caution, given a number of factors including the heterogeneity of labor and of products within broad manufacturing sectors; possible biases in the exchange rates used to convert each country's output (or the value added in domestic prices) to U.S. dollars;[80] and the fact that the comparison is confined to the productivity of a single factor, namely, labor. Gopalan also provides price comparisons for Chinese and Indian manufactured goods, some of which both countries sell in third markets and some of which the Chinese export to India.[81] These comparisons indicate that China has lower costs in many products than India, though once again, one has to keep in mind that the exchange rates used might be distorted. It is no surprise that China has gained, and India has lost, market shares in third markets. Unless India catches up and becomes internationally competitive, this trend is likely to continue in the future.[82] The entry of cheaper Chinese products created an almost panicky reaction by some Indian producers, who demanded the imposition of antidumping duties on Chinese imports. The government unfortunately conceded this demand in May 2001 by imposing antidumping duties on some Chinese imports.

The contrast between China's and India's ability to attract massive inflows of foreign capital was noted earlier. Perkins argues that because much of the capital and direct investment came from overseas and Hong Kong Chinese who had expertise and experience in producing and selling in world markets, China was able to expand its exports and impart a dynamism to its economy without having to wait for the creation of domestic market institutions and culture.[83] However, whether flows of the magnitude that China has been receiving are sustainable into the future is an open question. Lardy suggests that the decline in foreign direct investment in 1996 and 1997 portends future reductions as well.[84] Whether or not there will be a future slowdown in FDI in China, it is clear that without creating a more welcoming climate and a less politically determined process of approval, India is unlikely to attract a substantial volume of FDI.

Even without being a member of the WTO (as India has been since the organization's founding) China already enjoyed one of the most significant benefits of membership, namely, most-favored-nation treatment, from every major country in the world (except the United States, which granted it on an annual basis until 2001). China and Taiwan became members of the WTO in December 2001. A World Bank study has estimated that with its accession to the WTO, China's share in world exports will rise to 6.3 percent in five years from its pre-accession level of 4.6 percent, with large gains in exports of apparel, textiles, electronics, and metals, in part because of the phase-out of the Multi-Fiber Arrangement on 1 January 2005 and also because some of Taiwan's electronics firms are relocating on the mainland.[85] India competes with China in world markets for many labor-intensive manufactures, including textiles and apparel. But China seems to be winning this competition (see table 7.8). Be that as it may, according to the Asian Development Bank, implementation of its commitments, undertaken as part of its agreement with existing members as preconditions of its entry into the WTO, to cut tariffs, remove nontariff barriers, and allow foreign participation across a wide range of sectors poses significant challenges to China. The possibility of a slackening in the growth of Chinese exports as China meets these challenges cannot be ruled out.

India and China have found it in their interests to cooperate in the negotiations that set the agenda for the next round of multilateral trade talks, launched at the ministerial meeting of the WTO at Doha, Qatar, in November 2001. They share a common interest in further liberalization of agricultural trade, tightening the rules on antidumping measures, and above all ensuring that non-trade-related issues, such as labor and environmental standards, are not brought into the WTO.

Conclusion

By 2000, after five decades of development, China had far outstripped India in economic performance in terms of levels of growth, of the education, health, and living standard of its population, and of integrating its economy with the world economy. In 1950, China's per capita real income was lower than India's by about a third, and both countries were very poor.[86] An overwhelming majority of both populations lived in rural areas and were dependent on agriculture for their livelihood. India had an initial advantage with more arable land per head, a more diversified industrial base,

Table 7.8 *Participation in World and Major Export Markets, China and India*

World Markets		1978–1981	1982–1984	1985–1987	1988–1991	1992–1994	1995–1997	1998–2000
China	Garments	3.93	6.93	8.74	14.95	18.78	19.70	20.45
	Fabrics	5.15	7.48	8.28	8.25	7.87	8.87	9.36
	Leather and leather manufactures	0.41	0.61	0.75	2.55	2.94	4.07	4.82
	Jewelry	1.13	1.05	1.36	2.69	5.97	7.14	9.48
	Others	1.07	1.93	3.27	7.73	14.6	16.9	18.1
India	Garments	3.95	3.43	3.46	3.82	4.40	4.97	5.27
	Fabrics	2.04	1.38	1.45	1.43	1.99	2.10	2.42
	Leather and leather manufactures	8.85	7.45	7.13	5.52	4.03	3.42	3.44
	Jewelry	0.61	1.02	1.40	2.18	2.21	2.97	4.61
	Others	0.31	0.24	0.20	0.25	0.29	0.30	0.31
North American Markets								
China	Garments	3.73	8.00	8.81	13.19	21.30	21.42	20.59
	Fabrics	3.73	5.31	5.61	5.66	6.25	5.84	6.52
	Leather and leather manufactures	0.14	0.45	0.49	2.57	6.67	7.65	8.44
	Jewelry	0.50	0.42	0.25	1.77	3.99	5.51	8.13
	Others	0.72	1.51	2.98	9.92	20.89	25.62	26.57
India	Garments	4.89	4.14	4.12	4.60	5.80	5.56	5.34
	Fabrics	6.02	2.64	2.69	2.98	4.62	5.93	5.73
	Leather and leather manufactures	9.38	8.89	6.51	4.09	3.05	2.33	2.05
	Jewelry	0.39	0.83	1.34	2.46	4.57	7.01	9.60
	Others	0.19	0.11	0.14	0.22	1.28	1.09	1.01
European Markets								
China	Garments	1.84	2.40	3.15	6.25	10.04	10.34	11.80
	Fabrics	1.54	2.15	2.08	1.78	1.70	2.05	2.92
	Leather and leather manufactures	0.33	0.37	0.31	0.86	1.14	1.27	1.89
	Jewelry	0.47	0.26	0.51	1.41	3.07	4.08	5.97
	Others	0.40	0.71	1.22	2.94	6.41	6.76	7.99
India	Garments	3.90	3.47	3.61	4.26	5.39	6.00	4.65
	Fabrics	1.54	1.18	1.30	1.60	1.99	2.28	2.26
	Leather and leather manufactures	9.90	8.51	8.26	7.65	7.45	7.09	6.12
	Jewelry	0.88	1.23	1.59	1.91	2.60	3.39	4.28
	Others	0.33	0.27	0.22	0.29	0.86	0.87	0.71

Sources: United Nations, *Comtrade Data Base* (New York: United Nations Statistical Office, 2001). I thank Francis Ng of the World Bank for providing the data.
Note: "Garments" refers to the three-digit SITC categories 843, 844, 848; "fabrics" to 652, 653, 654, 657; "leather" to 611 and 612; jewelry to 897; and "others" to categories 764, 778, 842, 847, 851, 893, 894.

and a better-developed transport and communications infrastructure. China had a more productive agriculture with higher crop yields per hectare of land. Both adopted state-directed, autarkic industrialization as their development strategy and virtually insulated their economies from the world economy.

Under Mao Zedong's dictatorship of nearly three decades there was little to commend China's performance relative to India's. It is true that China's faster average rate of growth of 6 percent per year during 1950–80, compared with India's 3.5 percent, enabled it to catch up with India's real per capita income.[87] But the faster growth was primarily due to the authoritarian Chinese regime extracting greater savings (around 10 percent of GDP higher) and labor from the Chinese population, and not due to any superiority in productivity growth. However, China had achieved higher rates of literacy and life expectancy compared with India's by the mid-seventies. Also, China devoted a greater share of investment to industry and infrastructure, so that by 1980 China was far more industrialized than India was. China abolished private property rights in land and forced the peasants into communes. India did not undertake any serious redistribution of land. However, Indians were not the subjects of cruel experimentation as the Chinese were during the Great Leap Forward and the Cultural Revolution. Nor did they experience famines and excess mortality of 30 million or more, as the Chinese suffered as subjects of those experiments. Above all, Indians, as citizens of a vibrant democracy, enjoyed personal and political freedoms that the Chinese are yet to enjoy.

The two decades after 1980 saw the emergence of both countries as star growth achievers in the world. However, China's growth rate during 1980–2000 was about 4 percent higher than India's, and its overall performance outstripped India's. The fact that China initiated reforms more than a decade earlier than India explains only a small part of this difference, since India also liberalized its economy to a limited extent in the 1980s. Also, China's investment rate continued to exceed India's by 10–15 percent of GDP on average in the eighties and nineties. A third contributing factor was China's greater success in export performance and in attracting FDI, though a large part of it came from overseas Chinese. However, these factor was in themselves are not adequate to dismiss the argument that Chinese reforms, in particular their contents and modes of implementation, are very different from their Indian counterparts and that this difference is a key to the Chinese success.

This argument, though plausible, can be stretched too far, as was done by the World Bank in its adulatory and insufficiently critical evaluation of Chinese reform.[88] The Bank found four consistent themes in the Chinese approach to reforms: gradualism, partial reform, decentralization, and mutually reinforcing reforms in several areas. It claims that "in almost all areas of reform, implementation has been spread over time, often several years, and usually after experimentation. Typically, such experiments take place in designated 'reform areas' and after the results of trials are observed, they are then spread to other parts of the country."[89] Given the vastness of China and the inadequacy of its transport and communication networks as of the early eighties, it is not credible that the leadership designed ex ante a large enough number of independent trials of alternative reform strategies, implemented them, then received and evaluated their results in time to implement the most successful alternative.

A more plausible story is that the success of Chinese reforms has been in part due to China's being an authoritarian society. Chinese leaders did not have to respond to pressure groups that stood to gain or lose from reforms, or to a critical press. The top leaders were thus able to resolve their different views about the direction and pace of reforms by putting into practice each view and letting the performance of the economy determine which was most appropriate. The reforms therefore appeared to proceed in a two-steps-forward, one-step-back manner. Further, the dominance of the Communist Party helped keep the bureaucratic apparatus intact and reasonably efficient while the pro-market policies of its paramount leader, Deng Xiaoping, took hold. The authoritarian roots of Chinese success were noted by the former Russian Prime Minister Yegov Gaidar, who is reported to have said that he too would have found China's method of change easier but that it was possible only with a "powerful structure of authoritarian rule."[90] This said, it is important to note that the Chinese success is also in part due to the gradual and experimental nature of the reforms, which allowed the possibility of correcting policies that failed and reinforcing those that proved fruitful.

Of course, the heavy investment in physical and social infrastructure prior to reforms paid off handsomely, once the reforms provided the incentives for peasants and producers to use resources efficiently. Clearly, the changes in incentives brought about by the move from a commune-based agriculture to the household responsibility system were phenomenal, and so was the response. In India, agriculture had always been in private hands, and there had been no major reforms of land ownership and tenancy. The reforms of 1991 also largely left agriculture out. As such, unlike in China, there could be no spectacular change in Indian agricultural performance after the reforms. Surprisingly, Indian agriculture did relatively well. The crop production index (in which each country's 1989–91 production is represented as 100) stood at 67.1 and 70.9, respectively, for China and India during 1979–81. It more than doubled to 141.6 by 1998–2000 in China, and in India it rose by 70 percent to 123.3.[91]

According to Lau et al., the "dual track" system of Chinese reforms—i.e., continuing to enforce the existing plan while simultaneously liberalizing the market—had the potential to avoid creating losers from reform.[92] While claiming that that potential was largely realized, the authors also recognize that by protecting workers in SOEs, the reforms compromised the interests of workers outside the state sector, particularly the migrant workers from rural areas, who have been hurt already. The World Bank, on the other hand, claimed that "by using the gradual approach, and by not subjecting the state sector to major shocks, China has succeeded in avoiding severe social costs during its transition. The Chinese effort has focused much less on changing old enterprises and more on generating new opportunities."[93] In fact, by keeping the SOEs dominant without attempting to make them competitive, China simply absorbed the cost of their inefficiencies. This option was not available to other developing countries such as India, which undertook reforms while in the midst of a macroeconomic and fiscal crisis. It would seem that China has not really avoided potential social problems but merely has postponed them, at a resource cost.

The agreements that China has signed as part of the process of its entry into the WTO would force China to deal with the SOEs and the problems of NPLs in its banks, to which the SOEs were the major contributors. Although India's SOEs need to be reformed, they are not as large a part of the industrial sector and the economy as a whole as are China's. The growing income disparity across regions and social groups is a potential problem for both countries. As a democracy, India has political safety valves to address the concerns of the losers and to ensure that the stability of the system is not threatened by social discontent. Whether the Chinese Communist Party, whose leadership is showing flexibility by admitting "capitalists" into the party, will be flexible enough to accommodate the problems of rural migrants and other losers from reforms is not clear. In any case, the substantial slowdown in growth that has been seen in both economies, if it persists, will make it considerably more difficult to tackle incipient social unrest and to eradicate poverty once and for all.

Notes

1. World Bank, *World Development Indicators 2002* (Washington, D.C.: World Bank, 2002), table 1.1.

2. Interestingly, such an analysis was already deemed important in the fifties; see W. Malenbaum, "India and China: Development Contrasts," *Journal of Political Economy* 64, no. 1 (1956): 1–24; and "India and China: Contrasts in Development," *American Economic Review* 49, no. 3 (1959): 284–309. At its annual meeting in December 1974, the American Economic Association (AEA) held a session on China and India with papers by B. Richman, "Chinese and Indian Development: An Interdisciplinary Environmental Analysis," *American Economic Review* 65, no. 2 (1975): 345–55; and T. Weisskopf, "China and India: Contrasting Experiences in Economic Development," ibid., 356–64; and comments by P. Desai, "Discussion," ibid., 365–68; and J. Gurley, "Discussion," ibid., 368–71. Malenbaum wrote fairly early in the development of the two countries, and the AEA discussion in 1974 preceded the death of Mao Zedong, a full revelation of the horrors of the Cultural Revolution, and Deng Xiaoping's initiation of reforms in 1978. Besides, as Desai pointed out, the information (particularly with respect to China) on which comparisons were then based left much to be desired. Nonetheless, Malenbaum was right about the importance of a comparative analysis of the development strategy, policies, and performance of China and India.

3. Figures from World Bank, *China: Socialist Economic Development,* vol. 1 (Washington, D.C.: World Bank, 1983). Compared with data on India, data on the Chinese economy, certainly for the period prior to 1978 and to a lesser extent thereafter, have been relatively sparse and of uncertain reliability, and their internal consistency has not been subject to rigorous examination. See "Round Table on Chinese Economic Statistics," in *China Economic Review* 12 (2001): 261–406. In China's command economy the relative prices of goods and services were distorted and did not represent the marginal rates of substitution in their use or of transformation in their supply. This meant that GDP and GNP at domestic Chinese prices were not good indicators of China's production capacity or of the welfare of Chinese citizens. Correcting for these distorted values and converting them to U.S. dollars using appropriate exchange rates are virtually impossible. For example, the World Bank (Jipin Zhang and Timothy King, *Case Studies of Chinese Economic Reform* [Washington, D.C.: World Bank, 1992]) reported China's per capita GNP in 1990 as $370 and India's as $350 and stated that the average annual rates of growth of GNP per capita during 1965–90 in China and India were, respectively, 5.8 percent and 1.9 percent. If these data are correct, then projecting backward, China's GNP per capita in 1965 would have been only 41 percent of India's! No knowledgeable analyst of the two countries would subscribe to this relative value of China's GNP per capita in 1965. A plausible explanation for these paradoxical figures is that the figure of $370 as China's 1990 per capita GNP reflects the consideration that a more realistic figure would have soon made China ineligible for loans from the Interna-

tional Development Association, the soft loan affiliate of the World Bank. In fact, G. Ma and R. Gaurnaut ("How Rich Is China: Evidence from the Food Economy," working paper, Department of Economics, Research School of Pacific Studies, Australian National University, Canberra, 1992) suggest that only if China's per capita income were three to four times the income reported by the World Bank would the consumption pattern of China be comparable, as one would expect, to that Taiwan and Hong Kong. Rawski reworked the estimates of output in China for the period 1914 to 1949 and concluded, "With the exception of the war period 1937–49, China's economy has now experienced seven decades of rising aggregate and per capita output stretching back to 1914 if not earlier" (T. G. Rawski, *Economic Growth in Prewar China* [Berkeley: University of California Press, 1989], 347–48]). However, Kumar's careful examination of Rawski's reworking of Chinese data and Indian data for the period 1914–49 led her to conclude that "the safest view is still that the overall growth story was not very different in the two countries—a slow growth of population, and slow or no growth in per capita income, in marked contrast to the post-1950 experience in both countries. The per capita income of both India and China was very low in 1949 and given the margin of error, it is not worth arguing about which country was the poorer. The demographic data suggest that the physical quality of life was higher in China, but this is based on unreliable data" (D. Kumar, "The Chinese and Indian Economies from ca. 1914–1949," CP no. 22, Research Programme on the Chinese Economy, STICERD, London School of Economics, 1992, 30).

4. World Bank, *World Development Indicators 2002,* table 1.1.

5. World Bank, *China: Socialist Economic Development,* vol. 1 (Washington, D.C.: World Bank, 1983).

6. World Bank, *World Development Indicators 2002,* table 4.9.

7. WTO, *International Trade Statistics 2001* (Geneva: World Trade Organization, 2001.)

8. World Bank, *World Development Indicators 2002,* tables 2.14 and 2.20.

9. A summary description of the committee's report can be found in Jawaharlal Nehru, *Discovery of India* (New York: John Day Company, 1946).

10. The first development plan of India was published by the engineer and statesman Sir M. Viswesvaraya, *Planned Economy for India* (Bangalore: Bangalore Press, 1934). A summary description of the committee's report can be found in Nehru's *Discovery of India.* At the close of the Second World War, a group of businessmen from Bombay formulated their own plan for India's development. Their plan, the so-called Bombay Plan, was published in 1944 (P. Thakurdas et al., *A Plan of Economic Development of India* [London: Penguin Books]). Trade union leaders published their own plan entitled the *People's Plan* (B. Bannerjee, G. Parikh, and V. Tarkunde, *People's Plan for Economic Development of India* [Bombay: Indian Federation of Labour, 1944]). All these plans emphasized the development of modern large-scale industries. However, followers of Mahatma Gandhi emphasized village self-sufficiency and the development of handcrafts as well as cottage and small-scale industries (see S. N. Agarwal, *Principles of Gandhian Planning* [Bombay: Kitab Mahal, 1960]).

11. Central Statistical Organisation, *National Accounts Statistics, 1950-51–1979-80* (New Delhi: Department of Statistics, Government of India, 1989); Press Information Bureau, "Quick Estimates of National Income, Consumption Expenditure, Saving and Capital Formation, 1999–2000," press note, New Delhi, 30 January 2001; and "Advance Estimates of National Income 2000–01," 5 February 2001.

12. Justin Lin, "Chinese Agriculture: Institutional Changes and Performance," in *Agriculture and Trade in China and India,* ed. T. N. Srinivasan (San Francisco: International Center for Economic Growth, 1994), table 2.2.

13. For a detailed and thorough discussion see Tony Saich, *Governance and Politics of China* (New York: Palgrave, 2001).

14. These data are drawn from a presentation of Peter Bottleier on the occasion of the fiftieth anniversary of the People's Republic of China, Stanford University, 16 November 1991.

15. Saich, *Governance and Politics of China,* 51.

16. Gao Shangquan, *Two Decades of Reform in China* (Singapore: World Scientific Publishing Co., 1999), 19–21.

17. I am glossing over the opposition to reforms and political problems that came to the fore in 1986 and culminated in the Tiananmen Square massacre in June 1989. However, the orthodox elements in the Communist Party lacked the strength to roll back reform. See Saich, *Governance and Politics of China,* chapter 3, for a detailed discussion.

18. World Bank, *India: Country Economic Memorandum,* Report No. 15882-IN (Washington, D.C.: World Bank, 1996), table 3.1a.

19. Government of India, *Economic Survey 1998–99* (New Delhi: Ministry of Finance, 1999), appendix table 1.2.

20. World Bank, *India: Policies to Reduce Poverty and Accelerate Sustainable Development,* Report No. 19471-IN (Washington, D.C.: World Bank, 2000), annex table 8.6.

21. W. Buiter and U. Patel, "Debt, Deficits and Inflation: An Application to the Public Finances of India," *Journal of Public Economics* 47 (1992): 171–205.

22. Government of India, *Economic Survey 2000–01* (New Delhi: Ministry of Finance, 2001), table 2.1.

23. IMF, *IMF Concludes Article IV Consultation with India,* Country Report No. 02/95 (Washington, D.C.: International Monetary Fund, 2002).

24. Reserve Bank of India, *Handbook of Statistics on the Indian Economy* (Mumbai: Reserve Bank of India, 2000).

25. IMF, *Article IV Consultation with India.*

26. World Bank, *China National Development and Sub-National Finance: A Review of Provincial Expenditures,* Report No. 22951-CHA (Washington, D.C.: World Bank, 2002).

27. IMF, *IMF Concludes Article IV Consultation with the People's Republic of China,* Country Report No. 02/97 (Washington, D.C.: International Monetary Fund, 2002).

28. World Bank, *India: Macroeconomic Update* (Washington, D.C.: World Bank, 1998), 27.

29. D. Perkins, "Industrial and Financial Sector Policies in China and Vietnam: A New Model or Replay of East Asian Experience Revisited?" mimeo, Department of Economics, Harvard University, 2000.

30. James Kynge, *Financial Times,* 31 October 2002, 5; see also Perkins, "Industrial and Financial Sector Policies."

31. Nicholas Lardy, *China's Unfinished Economic Revolution* (Washington, D.C.: Brookings Institution Press, 1998), 9.

32. World Bank, *World Development Indicators 2002,* table 4.1.

33. World Bank data suggest that India's ICOR was marginally higher than China's in the sixties and seventies. World Bank, *China: Socialist Economic Development* (Washington, D.C.: World Bank, 1983).

34. T. N. Srinivasan and S. D. Tendulkar, *Reintegrating India with the World Economy* (Washington, D.C.: Institute for International Economics, 2003), chapter 2.

35. Z. Hu and M. Khan, "Why Is China Growing So Fast?" *Economic Issues,* no. 8 (Washington, D.C.: International Monetary Fund, June 1997).

36. IMF, *India: Recent Economic Developments,* Country Report No. 02/155 (Washington, D.C.: International Monetary Fund, 2002), 11; World Bank, *India: Policies to Reduce Poverty and Accelerate Sustainable Development,* Report No. 19471-IN (Washington, D.C.: World Bank, 2000), 130; Isher Judge Ahluwalia, "Structural Adjustment and Productivity Growth in India," *Productivity* 33, no. 2 (New Delhi, 1992).

37. NCAER, "The Impact of India's Economic Reforms on Industrial Productivity and Competitiveness," National Council of Applied Economic Research, New Delhi, 2001.

38. B. Goldar, "Productivity Growth in Indian Manufacturing in the 1980s and 1990s," Institute of Economic Growth, New Delhi, 2000.

39. IMF, *India: Recent Economic Developments;* World Bank, *India: Policies to Reduce Poverty;* Ahluwalia, "Productivity Growth in India"; NCAER, "Impact of India's Economic Reforms."

40. World Bank, *World Development Indicators 2002,* table 5.1.

41. Planning Commission, *Foreign Investment* (New Delhi: Government of India, 2002), 13.

42. World Bank, *World Development Indicators 2002,* tables 4.16 and 4.17.

43. Planning Commission, "Foreign Investment," 13.

44. Srinivasan and Tendulkar, *Reintegrating India with the World Economy.*

45. Planning Commission, *Foreign Investment,* 13.

46. *Financial Times,* 28 October 2002.

47. James Kynge, *Financial Times,* 1 November 2002.

48. R. Gopalan, "A Discussion Paper on China's Competitiveness," Department of Commerce, Government of India, New Delhi, 2001, 611.

49. Saich, *Governance and Politics of China,* 243.

50. Ibid..

51. World Bank, *World Development Indicators 2002,* table 2.20.

52. IMF, *Article IV Consultation with the People's Republic of China.*

53. IMF, *India: Recent Economic Developments,* statistical appendix, table 1.

54. Saich, *Governance and Politics of China,* 52.

55. Erik Eckholm, *New York Times,* 5 November 2002 and 8 November 2002.

56. Central Statistical Organisation, *National Accounts Statistics, 1950-51–1979-80;* see also note 11.

57. Lardy, *China's Unfinished Economic Revolution,* table 2-2.

58. OECD, *Reforming China's Enterprises* (Paris: Organization for Economic Cooperation and Development, 2000), table II.1.

59. Lardy, *China's Unfinished Economic Revolution,* 3.

60. Ibid., table 2-1.

61. Ibid., 4.

62. Saich, *Governance and Politics of China,* 233.

63. Lardy, *China's Unfinished Economic Revolution,* 4, 5.

64. *Financial Times,* 6 June 2001, 8.

65. Saich, *Governance and Politics of China,* 236.

66. Government of India, *Economic Survey 2000–01,* 146.

67. Because the SEB was bankrupt, Enron insisted on a guarantee of payment from the state government, the owner of the SEB, if the latter failed to pay. Further, the state government itself was in financial difficulties so that Enron received a counterguarantee from the central government that it would pay if the state government failed to do so. The present situation is that the state government, led by the Congress Party, which is the opposition party at the center, does not want to pay, and the center refuses to honor its guarantee!

68. Government of India, *Economic Survey 2000–01,* table 9.4.

69. IMF, *Article IV Consultation with the People's Republic of China.*

70. IMF, *India: Recent Economic Developments,* table 1.7.

71. Government of India, *Economic Survey 1998–99.*

72. The previous government had raised emoluments of government servants over and above the levels recommended in 1997 by the Fifth Pay Commission while rejecting its recommendation to reduce government payroll by 30 percent over ten years. However, the savings from downsizing government are likely to be very modest.

73. IMF, *India: Recent Economic Developments,* table V.2.

74. S. Demurger et al., "Economic Geography and Regional Growth in China," paper presented at Asian Economic Panel, Cambridge, Mass., 26–27 April 2001; and A. Dayal-Gulati and A. Husain, "Centripetal Forces in China's Economic Take-off," working paper WP/00/86 (revised), International Monetary Fund, Washington, D.C., 2000.

75. P. Cashin and R. Sahay, "Internal Migration, Centre-State Grants, and Economic Growth in States of India," *IMF Staff Papers* 43 (1996): 123–71, and "A Reply to Rao and Sen," *IMF Staff Papers* 44 (1997): 289–91.

76. M. G. Rao and K. Sen, "Internal Migration, Centre-State Grants, and Economic Growth in States of India," *IMF Staff Papers* 44 (1997): 283–89.

77. *New York Times,* 3 June 2001, 8.

78. This section draws heavily, with thanks, on the comments of Zhang Minqiu at the Beijing Seminar. I have also relied on the handout "India's Trade with the East China Region" from the consulate general of India in Shanghai.

79. Gopalan, "China's Competitiveness," 35.

80. To the best of my knowledge, B. Lee and D. S. P. Rao ("Comparisons of Purchasing Power, Real Output and Productivity of Chinese and Indian Manufacturing") School of Economics and Finance, Queensland University of Technology, 2001), are the first to undertake a direct comparison for the period 1952–95 of the productivity of manufacturing industries of the two countries using sector-specific purchasing-power parity exchange rates. They found that labor productivity of India has declined from 71 percent of Chinese labor productivity in 1952 to 37 percent in 1995.

81. Gopalan, "China's Competitiveness," table 11, p. 48.

82. A. Wood and M. Calandrino, "When the Other Giant Awakens: Trade and Human Resources in India," *Economic and Political Weekly* 35, nos. 52–53 (2000): 4677–94, undertakes a detailed comparison of China's and India's manufacturing sectors in terms of employment and foreign trade. The authors decompose India-China differences according to the contributions of level of exports and imports and trade balance; composition of exports and imports; investment; household and government consumption; input-output coefficients; and relative sectoral and labor productivities.

Their bottom-line assessment, based on actual Chinese performance, is that if India were to reduce its existing barriers to trade, particularly to exporting, it could double its per capita income and increase its exports fivefold within a couple of decades.

83. D. Perkins, "Institutional Challenges for the Economic Transition in Asia," dicsussion paper, Harvard University, 2000.

84. Lardy, *China's Unfinished Economic Revolution,* 201.

85. E. Ianchovina, W. Martin, and E. Fukase, "Modeling the Impact of China's Accession to the WTO," World Bank, Washington, D.C., 2000.

86. A. Maddison, "Growth and Interaction in the World Economy: The West and the Rest, 1000–2000 A.D.," paper presented at Harvard University, 24 May 2002, table C.

87. Ibid.

88. Jipin Zhang and Timothy King, *Case Studies of Chinese Economic Reform* (Washington, D.C.: World Bank, 1992).

89. Ibid., 37.

90. *New York Times,* 7 October 1992.

91. World Bank, *World Development Indicators 2002,* table 3.3.

92. L. Lau, Y. Qian, and G. Roland, "Reforms without Losers: An Interpretation of China's Dual-Track Approach to Transition," *Journal of Political Economy* 108, no. 1 (2001): 120–43.

93. Zhang and King, *Case Studies of Chinese Economic Reform,* 67.

8

Convergent Chinese and Indian Perspectives on the Global Order

James Clad

Most analyses of Sino-Indian relations, no matter how cursory or from which country of origin, invariably assume an underlying element of competitiveness if not downright rivalry.[1] Within the specialist literature, the degree of Sino-Indian competition usually depends on how broadly the studies are cast. If the focus falls narrowly—as, for example, on the two countries' border dispute—then the competitive element becomes almost entirely dominant, lodged firmly within a bilateral security matrix.

Similarly, other studies comparing India and China—whether in ballistic missile or nuclear weapon development, in blue-water naval aspirations, in comparative diplomacy in Asia, in commercialization of technological competence, research and development spending, or even social welfare indicia—invariably carry a heavy assumption of rivalry as well. At the very least, their content conjures invidious comparisons between the two countries, with China generally faring better except, not surprisingly, in standards of democratic participation and (although India's counterinsurgencies in Kashmir and the Punjab have put a dent in the country's reputation) in respect for human rights. Habitual treatment of India and China as inherent rivals or even fated contestants, a tone some may find elsewhere in this book, also influences such seemingly straightforward exercises as comparative measurement of export performance and economic development policies—as in an elegant 1994 monograph comparing agricultural trade into and out of China and India.[2]

Given these ingrained habits, can an objective study of the impact of "globalization" on India and China—the term itself surely suggesting a uniformly nonnational phenomenon with undifferentiated world impact—avoid these competitive thought processes?

The remaining pages suggest that the answer may be yes. Some room exists for a more optimistic view of future India-China relations based on converging fortunes and steadily widening common interests as both countries engage ever more deeply in the international trading economy and as each becomes progressively more intertwined in global financial networks and increasingly mobile capital and business interests. Indeed, a review of recent literature on Sino-Indian relations reveals steadily increasing interest in the convergent impact of globalized trends on both countries and, indirectly, on the potential dynamics of the longer-term Sino-Indian relationship. Even the very nature of national identity in both countries may be shaped by the ongoing impact of globalized trends. For example, recent studies of India's or China's "state nationalism"[3] describe recurrent exogenous pressures on both civilizations as a type of "globalization" spawned in earlier eras. (In one view, "global" pressures from the European-dominated Age of Exploration had impacts just as acute in the New World or Africa as in China and India.) These earlier "globalizing" trends also achieved, in their time and context, radical redefinitions of cultural and "national" purpose in both China and India.

Nonetheless, and as one might expect, national security specialists in both countries remain skeptical of (what they see as) glib expectations that "globalization," a set of ideas seen as having a strong American pedigree, will usher in a more cooperative era of Sino-Indian ties. Yet both countries are succumbing to the forces of globalization—forces they both cannot evade *and* wish to harness in order to augment their national power. This creates an interesting tension in which new dependencies constrain the exercise of sovereignty. Indian analysts of the Sino-Indian connection share with their Chinese counterparts an old-fashioned attachment to traditional notions of absolute sovereignty. In their attitudes regarding territory, security, noninterference in domestic affairs, rejection of the obtrusion of social issues into international trade negotiations, and a raft of other issues, both the Chinese and Indian governments are very far from a "borderless world." Indeed, they espouse a view of sovereignty reminiscent of eighteenth- and nineteenth-century Europe.

Still, recent signs do point to willingness by national security elites in both countries to factor into their overall power equations a range of potentially common Sino-Indian issues and overlapping interests spawned by globalized production networks. Whether these can exert pressure toward an eventual formulation by Beijing and Delhi of common or joint policy responses is another question.

For example, India and China have broadly similar expectations from, and reservations about, the World Trade Organization (WTO) and other international trading regimes. Both countries' accommodation to the Uruguay Round (and to the resultant creation of the WTO) has focused on broadly similar issues—technical verification problems and phase-in arrangements of considerable complexity. India was a founding member of the WTO's antecedent grouping, the General Agreement on Tariffs and Trade (GATT), whereas China faced formal accession as a new WTO member. China has sought to use WTO adjustment to force the pace of domestic reform and economic restructuring, while India's tight entwining of electoral democracy, family corporate interests, and labor protections make a pro-reform embrace of the WTO much more problematic. Still, the successful adjustment by these two enormous Asian states—each undertaking large public-sector reductions and opening domestic markets to world commerce—will have profound consequences for the world trading system over time.

Most Western analysis focuses on Asian manufactured products penetrating existing markets and further accelerating the industrial competition first felt during Japan's competitive rise after the 1960s. But acceptance by India and China of free trade in agricultural products will present large domestic political challenges to the governments of both countries. Meanwhile, Western political reaction to burgeoning textile exports from both countries has prompted India and China to take similar trade advocacy positions in the WTO.[4]

The impact of international trade competition is being felt in both countries in similar ways. Both are experiencing geographical relocation of industries as firms choose best-cost solutions in defiance of earlier strictures promoting regional development and decentralization of industry. The

Uruguay Round also liberalized energy trade, and petroleum firms in both countries—notably Sinopec and China National Petroleum Corporation (CNPC) in China, and Indian Oil Corporation (IOC) in India—have already invested large sums in attempts to lock up retail gasoline networks before the entry of foreign multinationals mandated by the WTO accords. These are but some specific examples of the transformational nature of the new global trade regime for China and India.

Although this chapter focuses primarily on convergent global economic trends—notably in the areas of information technology and energy sourcing—another side of globalization also affects the Sino-Indian relationship. Religiously defined fanaticism of the type leading to the September 11, 2001 terrorist attacks also has a global dimension. So does the social and political impact on each country of information flows enabled by new technologies. In response to Islamic extremism, some modest level of intelligence sharing had already occurred between India and China with regard to the "spillover" of radical Islamist, anti-infidel politics into areas—Kashmir and Xinjiang—sensitive to each country's national security concerns.[5]

Chinese and Indian strategies for dealing with these global trends may be found in their respective diplomacy and positions in, first, *universal regimes* of an economic and security nature. These include the United Nations system (in particular the Security Council and such heavily politicized agencies as the Geneva-based UN Commission on Human Rights) as well as various special-issue agreements such as the Law of the Sea (LOS) and such international environmental agreements as the Kyoto and Montreal protocols.

Beyond that, one may also delve into various *regional regimes.* The approach of both countries vis-à-vis specific multilateral agendas such as river navigation, pollution, or regional infrastructure development says a lot about globalization in the regional context. These regional regimes include the ASEAN Regional Forum (ARF—which includes both China and India), the South Asia Association for Regional Cooperation (SAARC—India only), or the various multilateral Mekong river commissions (China only). Both global and regional regimes receive treatment later in this chapter.

The remainder of the chapter deals with some issues that show how a common experience of globalization by both India and China, together with a common interest in preserving traditionally defined sovereign prerogative, may work to create steadily more important parallel interests between the world's two most populous countries. These interests probably will not lead to joint action, but (I argue) they will increasingly augment, and dilute, the traditional security and border dispute agenda. Globalization therefore is not so much likely to strengthen Sino-Indian ties as to round them out. For example, China's competitive trading advantage is now leading to trade disputes with India. Although these disputes initially have arisen in the mundane matter of bicycles and wristwatches, deeper frictions and competitive impact seem inevitable, both for India and perhaps even (in areas such as Indian agricultural products) for China as well. But global trends also ensure that India and China will run increasingly on parallel tracks, particularly in energy and information technology, as the following pages suggest.

Global Energy Flows, Common Sino-Indian Policies, and Convergent Sino-Indian Interests

In recent years, both India and China have modified energy security doctrines that once emphasized security of supply over all other factors. This change reflects India's and China's reaction to global market trends as well as to changes in the technology of energy exploration, extraction, and utilization. With both India and China now standing as net energy importers (China became a net importer of oil in 1994), some degree of de facto common cause emerged in both countries' energy policy during the 1990s and is continuing into the new century. A good way to approach the impact of this most global of industries on both countries is to stress China's and India's *common predicament* in the face of global trends and pressures and often *common responses* to these trends and pressures. For example—and in the common predicaments category—both countries must adjust to dependence on foreign, especially Middle Eastern, oil. Both are net energy importers; both suffer appalling air pollution from coal-generated electricity plants, and both have maritime and coastal centers of energy demand that lie far from indigenous energy sources. Finally, the criticism both countries now apply to the performance of their once much-vaunted self-reliance strategies and state-owned enterprises applies with special force to the energy sector, which each country has sought to privatize and deregulate. China's major petroleum firms, once an exclusive state preserve, have shed hundreds of thousands of workers in a drive for profit-line results and efficiency.

In the common responses category, both countries now seek to spread supply risk via reliance on the market mechanism, especially procurement from external sources. Both seek fuel substitution strategies, moving away from coal to liquid natural gas (LNG). Both also flirt with long-distance sources of supply, which entail capital-intensive supply projects; in China's case, pipelines from the Tarim Basin, Kazakhstan, or Sakhalin in Russia's far east. For India, the supply options lie in its northeastern states, very far from demand centers, as well as from Bangladesh or from Turkmenistan via Afghanistan and Pakistan. In addition, both countries seek to head off disruption to sea-lanes of communication that might imperil delivery, or raise delivery costs, of oil and gas from the Middle East or Southeast Asia. This gives both countries a common stake in the stability of these regions of supply.

Finally, both countries share common experience in efforts to restructure their various state-owned enterprises (SOEs) involved in the energy business—though China's public listing of Sinopec and CNPC far outpace India's more tepid SOE reform efforts. The market approach favored by both countries applies to securing supply and organizing its distribution; neither objective contradicts their strategic concern about continuing dependence on foreign and especially (given the percentages) on Middle Eastern supplies. Although "resource diplomacy" concerns dating back to the 1970s exerted a long grip on the national security preoccupations in each country, neither concentrates any longer on long-term supply contracts. Each seeks instead to optimize short-term market opportunities for overall lower-cost deliveries over the long term.

For both India and China, a growing discrepancy between demand and domestic supply will pose tough choices, all the more so in the unsettled international environment after September 11, 2001. Solutions to this increasing energy insecurity include:

- pushing to develop oil and natural gas fields in out-of-the-way places despite large capital investment requirements, high production costs, and long distances from demand centers (these places include western China, offshore eastern China, India's northeast, and offshore western India);
- building pipelines to bring resources to demand centers from supply areas in adjacent countries, including Kazakhstan, Sakhalin, and east Siberia for China, and Iran, Bangladesh, and Turkmenistan (via Afghanistan and Pakistan) for India; and
- relying more on Persian Gulf and other area suppliers, such as Indonesia, despite the element of political risk involved. As 1970s-era

> long-term liquid natural gas supply contracts reach the end of their terms, renegotiation of supply may reorient Southeast Asian and Australian supply away from Korean and Japanese purchasers to import terminals in India and China.

In an energy world where adroit use of the marketplace seems to offer better security of supply than mercantilist strategies to lock in resources or guarantee long-term supply, are any of India's and China's energy security measures worth the cost? Evidence from both countries regarding corporate restructuring and the provision of exploration and production incentives suggest the common solution is a mixture of strategies: reliance on the market without abandoning efforts to maximize indigenous supply.

The strategic implications arising for both countries from a market-focused supply strategy should be fairly obvious. "China's rising oil import requirements and the physical constraints of its refining sector suggest that China will become increasingly dependent on the same energy sources as the U.S., Japan, and other industrialized countries. This could tie its strategic interests more closely to Western and Indian interests in the Middle East."[6] Occasionally Beijing hears hostile statements from politicians in Delhi suggesting efforts to interdict or obstruct Gulf oil contracted for delivery to China in truly extreme circumstances,[7] but such attempts by India would damage its own interests more than China's, even in the extremity of open hostilities. As global traders, both countries share an overriding, common interest in ensuring trouble-free sea-lanes.

Although structural reform in both countries' economies reflects the interface between various pressures from a globalizing economy, the largest single constraint on economic development in either country arises from egregious domestic energy supply deficits, most notably in India but also a recurrent provincial problem in China. But a rapid closing of that gap requires important choice-of-fuel decisions, and the competing options have important environmental consequences that are truly global in their impact—in particular, the production of greenhouse gases. Both India and China still rely heavily on coal; between them they account for nearly 50 percent of the greenhouse gases rising into the atmosphere. Heavy coal use by each national economy results in acid rain that affects neighboring states, notably Bangladesh and Nepal (for India) and Japan (for China), though the cumulative effect is, of course, global. Beyond that, coal reliance in both countries crimps energy efficiencies. More pervasively than in China, India suffers peak-load power shortages that badly affect enterprise productivity. Both countries must revisit the basic efficiency of their power grids, both fashioned in an era of top-down planning controls and investment dictates.

Beyond that, both India and China have unsustainable power tariff structures, but, in India especially, democratic norms also entrench cheap power in a web of political patronage and local voter support, subsidizing agricultural uses while penalizing industry. In China and India, businesses frustrated by local public energy bottlenecks build their own "captive power plants" to produce all the power needed by the enterprise without having to rely on the public power grid. Yet the resulting proliferation of small private generators exacerbates energy inefficiency problems in both countries.

Both India and China have sought a solution that is also global in effect. Each has invited independent power producers (IPPs) from a range of foreign countries to bid for projects to install new capacity. China receives a better response than do India's chronically insolvent state electricity boards; yet IPPs, even in China, generate less than twenty-five hundred megawatts in total. In India, the showpiece Dabhol IPP project, built by a consortium formed by the Enron Corporation, had by the onset of 2001 failed to receive reliable payment on contractually agreed tariff terms—a result that badly crimped IPP investor interest in India afterward. India's burdensome regulations require years to navigate; Enron needed seven years to win approvals to build the Dabhol plant in Maharashtra, by which time contractual provisions had become politically untenable for successive Maharashtra state governments. The American firms CMS Energy and AES also experienced long delays in financial closure of their India projects after the mid-1990s. In China, on the other hand, most IPP projects had a happier fate—although the amount of installed IPP capacity in the decade up to 2000 fell far short of Chinese (and foreign firms') ambitions.

Despite these formidable shortcomings, the outlines of a multipronged energy strategy for both countries are emerging. They include:

- relying on international markets for increasing supply segments;
- developing strategic energy reserves without committing enormous, up-front capital investments;
- establishing strategic and interdependent relationships with primary suppliers; and
- promoting natural gas as the fuel of choice.

While far less significant than coal, oil, and even nuclear energy in India's and China's energy mix, natural gas has become central to both countries' future maritime coastal dynamism. Impatient at chronic power deficits and their impact on export-oriented industries, coastal city and provincial authorities have entered into negotiations for terminals to receive LNG exports from the Middle East, Southeast Asia, Australia's northwest shelf, or even Sakhalin.

Both China and India see natural gas reducing their dependence on the Organization of Petroleum-Exporting Countries (OPEC) suppliers and allowing them to mitigate severe air pollution. But a comprehensive natural gas policy lies years ahead for both countries. In China and India, both the central authorities and provincial/state governments have planned LNG terminals to service maritime areas' industrial and residential power demand, which far outpaces demand in the interior.

China's and India's oil and gas companies also share common approaches toward seeking external supply arrangements, each reaching out in different geographical directions:

- Apart from ongoing discussions about piped gas from Iran or Turkmenistan—either of which must traverse Pakistan—India also began initial supply discussions with Indonesia during Indonesian President Abdurrahman Wahid's Delhi visit in mid-2000. Since the U.S.-led overthrow of the Taliban regime in Kabul, new interest in these cross-border pipeline projects has occurred.
- India also seeks to import gas from Bangladesh, where major gas reserves exist. One large American firm already has invested more than $370 million in prospecting and discovering this gas—for which the Indian market remains the only feasible destination. But gas exports to India remain controversial in Bangladeshi politics.
- As noted, China looks to import gas from Kazakhstan or Sakhalin, piped down via Japan and the bottom of the Korean peninsula. New LNG terminals, as in Shanghai, will rely on product from fields such as British Petroleum's concession off the western end of West Papua, Indonesia. (China—and to a lesser degree India—now have new and direct reasons to fret about Indonesian instability as each computes its energy security calculations; the Arun gas field's shutdown in Sumatra during 2001 raised Indonesia supply risk to hitherto unprecedented levels.)

Energy security issues thus offer policy makers in India and China a range of similar challenges and opportunities. Increased competition for energy within truly globalized energy markets became more pronounced as Asian demand rebounded after the 1997–98 financial crises and world prices rose. The new slump after 2001, exacerbated by the sharp fall-off in U.S. import demand after September 11, ignited new concerns over sea-lane protection and Indian Ocean naval and air activity. Chinese and Indian reliance on Persian Gulf energy offers the only constant trend line.

International instability after September 11, 2001, brought unsettled shipping schedules and higher marine insurance premiums right across the Indian Ocean while India and Japan conducted joint antipiracy exercises and planned new joint sea-lane security measures. India and the United States also share these same maritime and sea-lane security interests. Beijing's apparent acceptance of modest Japanese support for U.S.-led intervention in Iraq and Afghanistan belied intense misgivings about American goals—an anxiety not shared by India.

Globalized delivery, procurement, and supply of energy have important implications for the pace of urbanization in both China and India. How quickly will air pollution and toxicity become even more politicized in both countries? In Eastern Europe during the 1980s, environmental activism—initially thought "safe" politically—fed into broader and more destabilizing political movements.

Competition and Collaboration: Global Information Technology Trends

Information technology ("info-tech" or IT) provides a strong example of global trends characterized by high mobility of personnel, products, and research. This segment of the chapter identifies collaborative commercial and product development possibilities between Chinese and Indian firms. True, Chinese and Indian info-tech firms have formed only a very tiny number of joint ventures with each other. Yet out of both countries have emerged some of the world's most globalized marketing and product development networks.

Each country has a thriving IT sector. Both countries have given IT high strategic priority. In both countries the IT sector displays elements of commercial competitiveness and global integration. Behind the scenes, IT development in China and India has been driving adherence to WTO service trading norms even though the benefits have yet to win universal acceptance in each country's domestic arena. Just ten to fifteen years ago,

"North-South" rhetoric dominated debate on global integration. At that time, both India and China resisted bringing services into a GATT (and later a WTO) framework. From arguments and policies rejecting intellectual property protection, Beijing and Delhi have moved to endorsement of remarkably similar attitudes.

While much strategic thinking in both India and China focuses on IT's status- and power-enhancing potential, each country's info-tech experience also offers a study in contrasts. India's success comes in software development and export, whereas China's IT focuses on mobile phones and the Internet. Yet even these distinctions may prove transitory. China and Hong Kong already have issued thousands of work visas to Indian info-tech engineers since early 2000; collaboration by Indian IT firms with counterparts in Singapore and Taiwan have increased as well. India's IT trade with Taiwan and Singapore exceeded $8 billion in calendar year 2000, far surpassing that with mainland China alone.

Why this upsurge? The answer lies in the ways in which the earlier distinctions between software, mobile phone, and Internet technologies have become increasingly blurred. At present, each country's particular IT strengths matter less as technologies blend and mix, resulting in third-generation products diffusing wireless technology and data services via mobile phones.

Moreover, the global IT industry's competitive dynamics now involve networked production. Shifts in bargaining power have occurred, from integrated producers to major users. The end of integrated producers' dominance means that the old strategies based on "picking national champions" and then protecting them with high tariffs has become obsolete.[8] This, in turn, means that both India and China can maintain a competitive domestic IT industry only by shifting to tariff-free, open-market trade. The phenomenon, and their predicament, is global: For example, the major EU countries also face the same challenge.

Information technology and Internet diffusion have such profound social and commercial ramifications for India and China that treatment of each country's IT development is set out below. To take just one example, both countries have high savings rates and poor mobilization of savings and inefficient credit allocation. Computer-assisted savings mobilization and credit provision will provide enormous new economies of scale to each country. Programs enabling Chinese-language use of the Internet will both favor domestic businesses and exclude China from the dominant international commercial language, English. Proficiency in that language, plus low labor costs, have enabled India's lead in "backroom operations" servicing U.S. and other Western corporations' bookwork. Now consider the implications for continuing Indian skill migration, dual residencies in the West (and in India and China), and formation of civil society in India and China. These are but a few of the impacts that a global info-tech sector has in store for Asia's two giants.

The foregoing only sketches out the potential in an area of vibrant commerce in which, to date, only a tiny number of Sino-Indian joint info-tech ventures have been formed. More common are efforts by entrepreneurs from both countries to find a comparative engineering or manufacturing advantage by locating some production or research elements of their business in the other country. Albeit in a very limited way, some migration by Indian software engineers to China has already occurred. Several Chinese software firms—most notably the Chinese military-backed company Huawei—have set up operations in India's leading info-tech city, Bangalore. At a formal intergovernmental level, a 17 July 2000 Sino-Indian "Memorandum of Understanding on Information Technology" now sets out a broad framework for potential collaboration.[9] One thing is clear: during a 2001 Asia Society research tour, traveling in China and India, this volume's authors found their Chinese interlocutors grudgingly voicing admiration for India's software engineering skills and for its perceived edge over China in the fashioning of computer systems operating architecture.

One conclusion seems inescapable when current Asian outsourcing trends, steeply rising Chinese domestic info-tech demand, and India's software writing skills are examined. In this high-end area of value-added business at least, globalization's promise of a "borderless world" has some relevance for Sino-Indian relations.

Many impediments still constrain India's info-tech progress, despite overblown claims of that country's having become an "information superpower." By the end of 2000, cellular phone usage had reached only 2.3 million subscribers. By mid-2001, only 6 million personal computers (PCs) were in regular use in the entirety of India—an extraordinary mismatch between the sophisticated range of software exports and the degree of PC penetration in a country that frequently claims a middle class numbering more than 100 million.

Moreover, little or no chip fabrication exists in India—primarily because of the lack of reliable power supply—and little new hardware product development occurs. India's hardware manufacturers exist only within a high-tariff environment, dependent on import barriers for survival, prompting consumers to buy "gray market" (illegal) PC imports. By contrast, China by 2001 had become the world's third-largest hardware manufacturer, with $46 billion turnover for that year—more than 37 percent growth over just the previous year. By mid-2002, China appeared poised to become the world's largest hardware manufacturer, overtaking Taiwan whose factories have been relocating to the mainland since the late 1990s. Facing WTO-required tariff easing, India's hardware makers are in danger of extinction, although some manufacturers have displayed competitive skill by offering cut-rate machines capable of basic functions, including e-mail, without the memory and other functions that retail PCs have acquired in recent years. Known as "I-stations," these low-cost e-mail devices cost just a fraction of the price of a full PC, a machine that is grossly underutilized even in mature markets. Even the cheapest imported PC in India costs about five times the approximately $200 price of I-stations such as those produced under the Simputer brand. And I-station design rests completely on open-source information.

With these differences in mind, the phrase "digital divide"—most often applied to differential access by social classes to information technology—acquires a meaning based on longer-term Sino-Indian competitiveness in information technology. Yet for both countries, the digital divide *within* each society augurs an exacerbation of already skewed access to improved livelihood (table 8.1). If in coming decades the dispersion of information technology really assumes the transformational character its exponents now claim for it, the disparities engendered by differential info-tech access could exacerbate existing social divisions. India's high-tech boom has created a nouveau riche social class that displays scant interest in the country's social problems and is happy to benefit from its niche in a globalized world. In India's robust democracy, populist reaction could alter the political landscape in ways detrimental to long-term IT development. And studies of info-tech access in China show only minuscule penetration in the country's interior provinces.

As a new factor in the global migration of technical personnel, the IT revolution has put India on the map. China is not alone in seeking to facilitate the working entry of Indian info-tech professionals; an increasing number of states—including Germany, the United Kingdom, Japan, Hong Kong, and Finland—are also hiring Indians to support their IT industries. Does this enormous out-migration of engineers amount to an asset enabling India to project more power and influence in the world? As a "force multi-

Table 8.1 *Comparative Personal Computer and Telephone Penetration Rates, India and China, 2000*

	India	China	World
GDP[a]	480	1,030	—
1992–2000 average annual FDI inflows[a]	2.5	40	—
PC sales per million units	1.7	7.2	140
PC penetration per 1,000 people	6.2	13.2	26
Info-tech spending as GDP percentage	0.8	1.1	3.6
Internet user base (millions)	2.5	22.5	407.1
Telephone lines per 100 people	2.7	8.6	15.2
Cellular phones per 100 people	0.2	3.4	8.2

Source: Tyco Electronics Ltd., Bangalore, India, 19 July 2001.
a. In billions of U.S. dollars.

plier" for India in world leverage, this development does not seem promising. By comparison, China's decision to create an advanced information infrastructure across the country targets improved economic efficiencies across the board. For this reason, China experiences a much higher domestic IT investment than does India.

China's Internet expansion parallels the country's rapid mobile and wire line growth since 1995. The digital divide between the two countries is evident in their contrasting experience in domestic info-tech infrastructure expansion. China began to attract telecom infrastructure investment in the early 1980s, long before India became receptive to outside investment. China's IT sector had begun growing at three times the rate of the overall economy by 1990, and it has grown faster than any other sector since 1997; government telecom revenue increased *twentyfold* in the decade after 1991.

China's computer market grew 16.2 percent in 1999 (to $20.9 billion). The industry's total output reached $24.8 billion. Domestic brand computers had a market share of 51.7 percent, and foreign 25.3 percent, but foreign brands are still the major players for business computing. The manufacturing sector has been open for over ten years, and more than seventy foreign companies are involved. The software industry remains constrained by piracy rates that, at the retail level, approach 90 percent of all sales.

Meanwhile, Internet use in China has been doubling every year since 1996. The Internet "population" stood at 12.3 million in April 2000; estimates in mid-2001 from the International Data Corporation predicted that by the end of 2005 China's on-line population would reach 33.1 million, and e-commerce transactions would reach the equivalent of $11.7 billion. These are conservative estimates; the China Internet Network Information Center thinks there will be 120 million Internet users by 2004, and that another 70 million cellular phone subscribers will become Internet users through Wireless Application Protocol (WAP). Internet subscribers numbered 22.5 million at mid-2001 and are growing by more than 100 percent per annum.

China's mobile telecom network will have become the world's largest by the end of 2003, according to present growth projections. Its telephone subscriber base already exceeds 125 million. This rate of increase reflects liberalized investment policies, including permission for foreign manufacturers to sell in the domestic market and unique investment packages offered in the "special economic zones" in Shenzhen, Shantou, Zhuhai, Liamen, and Haimen. Shanghai, Guangzhou, and Beijing also compete for IT investments. In contrast to their specialized software research focus in India, firms such as IBM, Hewlett Packard, Cisco, Sun, Intel, Microsoft, Compaq, Dell, and Oracle have created major integrated facilities in China. These lie especially in the corridor between Zhangjiang's High-Tech Park and the Waigaoqiao free-trade zone and also in the new "science parks" created by Shenzhen–Hong Kong industry institutes.

The great multiplier effect for info-tech development comes through the expansion of telecommunication services. Here, again, the digital divide between India and China is striking. While both countries balk at the negative telecom revenue implications flowing from price reductions in domestic and international call rates, both seek lower Internet access charges. Yet telecom firms such as China Telecom have been reducing overhead while India's public-sector dinosaurs resist changes that would enable lower costs.

The Impact of Info-Tech on Sino-Indian Ties

The primary thrust of both trade strategy and business interests in the United States has aimed at India's and China's ever-deepening integration into a network of market-based rules and institutions. The WTO and its dispute resolution procedures encapsulate this system. Within both India and China, pro-WTO arguments have identified this integrative process with an acceleration of domestic reform.

In particular, the intrusion of WTO-backed rules and trading norms is viewed as accelerating "democratization" in China through deepening a "rules-based" culture. This is juxtaposed to the present way of doing business—one dominated by state arbitrariness, preferences for party elites, and *guanxi* ("personal relationships"). In India, the more open trading environment exemplified by the WTO is seen as widening a marketplace hitherto dominated by cozy alliances between bureaucrats, politicians, and a few business families. Thus, while often described exclusively as a globalizing force, WTO membership for China and India both reflects and augments societal transformations in each country.

American pressure caused China, as a price of WTO accession, to agree to an opening up of the info-tech sector to a 49 percent foreign direct investment ceiling, albeit only in "basic" telecom industries. For "value added" info-tech industries, the Chinese have accepted a foreign equity component of up to 50 percent. No one knows what these commitments will mean in specific terms in the coming years, although the experience of would-be competitors dealing with Legend, a Chinese firm cozy with the Chinese leadership, does not promise an easy road. Poor Chinese compliance with past bilateral U.S.-China import accords also provides scant reason for optimism.

Still—and in sharp contrast to India—foreign firms moved very visibly to pre-invest in China in preparation for its WTO entry. To give just one example, Motorola doubled its China investment during 2000 to $3.4 billion, including $700 million just for handset production. It also earmarked $1.2 billion for a semiconductor plant.

Given the info-tech emphasis in each country and an appreciation in each country of the other's comparative advantage in this field, what may be said about joint Sino-Indian efforts to commercialize IT applications? What efforts might firms from either country be making to invest personnel and resources to learn from, emulate, or absorb technologies and special strengths of the other country?

Information acquired during an Asia Society study tour of India and China in 2001 provides some insight into this question. In the technology zones in the Pudong district of Shanghai, senior personnel at a government-supported research center noted that the Indian firm NTT Data and three others had lodged applications to establish production and research facilities. In particular, the major Indian software-training firm, NIIT, has been operating in Shanghai since 1996; it is also providing advanced IT training in Beijing.

"Indian talent can help us get into particular markets," one Chinese researcher said. Another noted India's strengths in advanced software engineering training, stressing that China's IT strength lay in the application of software for use in China's domestic markets. Chinese-language content providers, and content, have grown enormously in the last two years, aiming at nothing short of maximal penetration of a 1.2 billion person market. China has also developed very cheap Internet access, in which some applications—such as gaming—are language-less. Yet India's strength, he and others conceded, still lies in fashioning software for basic systems.

Until retrenchment and scaling down of capital expansion occurred after early 2001, Indian firms also showed increasing interest in using Chinese engineers and basic technical personnel. As one Chinese analyst put it, "Indian firms are thinking of using China as an outsourcing base for Indian firms displeased by erratic reliability of supply from their own country." One senior Indian IT executive in Bangalore described China's engineers as "30 percent cheaper" than India's.

He anticipates that China will be graduating as many as 23,000 engineers in various IT fields by 2004–05, overtaking India's output. India's info-tech consulting firms, such as the NASDAQ-listed WIPRO and Infosys, achieve consistently higher software quality ratings than Chinese firms, but India is feeling the approach of Chinese competition as Chinese firms master and move up the value-added IT applications scale.

Until a few years ago, the only evidence of Chinese info-tech work in India could be found in such firms as Wanwei, which set up telephone production facilities in India. Now, analysts look at such firms as Huawei, which has close links to the Chinese military and is working in Bangalore, India's principal IT city. Huawei sends more than three hundred engineers per year to Bangalore.

Closing Observations on Info-Tech and Globalization

While occupying high prominence in both countries, India's and China's information technology strategies have created two very different postures. India aims to become the world's back office and center for software outsourcing. China, on the other hand, promotes information technology as a catalyst for overall economic growth. More clearly than India, China sees Internet use as a *domestic* engine for growth, and telecom service expansion as a way to help to bring in new foreign infrastructure investment. And not only does each country's info-tech focus vary considerably, but so do their respective connectivity achievements.

Surveying this comparative picture in a discussion with the author, Indian science and technology minister M. M. Joshi, among the four most senior and influential leaders of the Bharatiya Janata Party (BJP), focused on two levels. First there is what he calls the "micro-strategic" level, i.e., the social impact of wired households on Indian society. And then there is the "broad strategic" impact of the IT revolution. Joshi has publicly described information technology as a central component of China's "comprehensive challenge to India."[10] Another comparative comment comes from one of India's most respected IT entrepreneurs. "China's leadership is committed to lending its support to high-tech projects such as high-speed, wide band information networks," says Vijay Deshpande, CEO of India's Encore Software group. "With a sound hardware base in place, China is now focusing aggressively on the 'softer' side of the industry; with an economy 2.5 times that of India's and exports six times greater than India's, China has enough muscle to go full steam ahead in software," he adds.[11]

Broader consequences lie beyond these sectoral competitiveness issues. The rapidity with which international contact and communication now occurs has upset settled notions about how civic activity (business, politics, personal communication, scholarly endeavor) can be contained and controlled within national borders. Looking beyond the domestic arena—in which roughly equivalent populations dwell within the territorial shapes occupied by "China" and "India"—international trade growth, certainly the most important globalizing trend of all, has dramatically altered China's and India's impact *on the rest of the world* although not very much on one another.

This is surely an important point. The globalization of production and outsourcing that enriches info-tech entrepreneurs in Bangalore or Guangdong has not generated interaction of any depth between the two countries. Cheaper air travel has brought new commercial contacts (but no regular Delhi–Beijing air service existed until 2002). The info-tech revolution points to new synergies between Indian software skills and Chinese Internet expansion (but almost no joint ventures have been established to exploit these potential synergies).

Sovereignty, Intervention, and Sino-Indian Convergence

This chapter's final segment contrasts and compares Indian and Chinese approaches to state sovereignty. It also examines Beijing's and Delhi's attitudes to interventionist doctrines and touches indicatively on a few Sino-Indian approaches to international regimes.

A focus on sovereignty dominates attitudes in Delhi or Beijing toward proposed WTO rules on labor and environmental standards and toward key elements of the global diplomatic agenda. Here we see many parallel policy interests instead of the latent convergences in interest suggested by the review of energy and information technology trends above. By now reciprocal visits by the Chinese and Indian foreign ministers have become routine, and the communiqués resulting from those visits, especially since the BJP-led coalition won power in India in 1998, provide a useful checklist of areas where both countries take a common view. These areas of mutuality almost always concern their defense of national sovereignty, broadly defined.

For example, India and China share an interest in resisting notions such as the "humanitarian intervention" doctrine, the articulation of which reached an apogee during the Clinton presidency. Sino-Indian communiqués since 1998 have also displayed shared irritation at the presumptive agendas (human rights, minority policy, environmental concerns) of foreign nongovernmental organizations (NGOs) as they apply to India and China. The NATO-led intervention in Kosovo prompted expressions of unease; both countries asserted that only the United Nations can legitimate international armed intervention. Both countries display very conservative attitudes on the prerogatives of sovereignty. After initially welcoming international norms that, in the early post–World War II years, accorded priority to self-determination, India and China soon took a more skeptical view of self-determination doctrine—at least insofar as outside advocates applied it to the condition of restive minorities living within China and India. This hostility to the empowerment of minorities and dissidents results from a perception in each country that it remains well short of completing its own state-building enterprise. Each country contains, and confines, a multiethnic society within its frontiers—even though India prefers a nonethnic definition of nationality while China has moved in the direction of racial nationalism.

In a recent essay on Sino-Indian approaches to sovereignty, Surjit Mansingh and C. V. Ranganathan survey the impact of "this mid-20th century term [sovereignty] that assumes the existence of an independent territorial state with linear boundaries, legal equality with other states, freedom and autonomy of action externally to pursue its own interests . . . and a population under the legitimate authority of a government admitting no moral superior."[12] Mansingh and Ranganathan traverse such sovereignty-linked issues as defense of territorial integrity, nonintervention in internal matters of other states, UN peacekeeping, international human rights and/or environmental protection, and other special-issue international regimes. Their conclusions bear extended quotation:

> [Sino-Indian] differences are evident in historical experience, state formation and function, ideological preferences, type of society and policy, cultural values, military power and international status. . . . [The People's Republic of] China quickly established an international reputation for being able to look after itself . . . and became a "great power," whereas India's potential remains unrealized.
>
> [Still], there are commonalities of approach between China and India. . . . Their attachment to traditional concepts of absolute sovereignty is strong, especially on matters pertaining to territory and security. Neither is amenable to external interference on military and arms-related matters; both oppose external inspections and interventions elsewhere, especially if undertaken without benefit of UN validation. Their resentment of Western intrusiveness and hypocrisy, as on the subject of linking trade issues to social causes, is loud and insistent. . . . Both are highly defensive against the West on the issue of human rights but India's constitution and domestic institutions including pressure groups are more closely aligned with international norms . . . than are China's.

While the authors see in modern technological advances and evolving legal norms the eventual nemesis of the traditional concept of sovereignty, they judge that "the grip by national security elites on policymaking in each country makes any weakening of governmental attachment to sovereignty a long term proposition, at best."[13]

When contemplating minority issues, especially in dealing with separatist sentiment that garners sympathy and support from abroad, both countries oscillate between policies of assimilation, accommodation, and outright repression. Minority issues take center stage in the national security considerations of both Asian giants. Trouble in India's northeast, in the Punjab, in Kashmir, as well as earlier linguistic agitation that required extensive redrawing of the boundaries of India's states—all these have challenged Indian unity. For China, the coextensive reach of distinct (though numerically much smaller) Uighur and Tibetan minorities with the underpopulated western half of the country drives many security anxieties.

A detailed examination of comparative minority policy in India and China lies outside the reach of this chapter,[14] but it bears noting that rising concern in Beijing over radical Islamic influence in Xinjiang (including unreported assassinations of Chinese officials) had become apparent in the months before September 11, 2001. Large-scale army exercises occurred outside Kashgar, in the Artush area, in August of that year. Since then, a closer alliance of convenience has arisen between U.S., Indian, and Chinese interests in monitoring the impact of radical Islam in Central Asia. China is closely watching how the post-Taliban dispensation takes shape in Afghanistan. Beijing fears that Pakistan continues to enable the movement of militant Islam into the region.

Responses from Delhi and Beijing to minority agitation follow common paths. Both will not shrink from suppressing rebellions with force. Yet some approaches also provide a study in contrasts: India has a more variegated policy while Chinese policy often seems inseparable from the country's Han peoples, who comprise over 96 percent of the country's total population. India's federal system permits creation of new states within the Indian union—three emerged during 2000. Permitting new states often enables India to diffuse ethnic based or separatist tensions. Similarly, India co-opts disaffected minority leaders more successfully than China.

In China, by contrast, official attitudes vacillate between tolerance and, as during the 1960s and 1970s, some rather crude forced assimilation: the Great Leap Forward, the Cultural Revolution, and Deng's opening of China's economy have each had direct effects on Beijing's attitude to minorities. At present, the 1982 constitution (still in force) has enabled the creation of eighteen new autonomous counties. A "law on regional autonomy for minority nationalities," adopted in May 1984, created various set-aside provisions.

Given this record of applying, as deemed necessary, both palliatives and forceful means to end minority rebellions, neither Beijing nor Delhi have shown much sympathy for trends favoring internationally sanctioned intervention where central government violence falls on minorities. The NATO intervention on behalf of rebellious Muslim Kosovars in Yugoslavia worried China's leaders and discomfited India's. Both countries saw the NATO exercise as preparing the ground for further internationalization of conflicts that each country prefers to keep to itself, whether Kashmir or Tibet or Xinjiang. And a 1999 UN Security Council resolution legitimating Australian military intervention in East Timor caused misgiving in both Beijing and Delhi. Each says humanitarian doctrines being employed justify intervention in a multiethnic large Asian country—Indonesia.

Intelligence officials in both capitals monitor interaction between each country's minorities and ethnic brethren in adjacent states. Three hundred thousand Uighurs dwell in Kazakhstan and remain in contact with their cousins in Xinjiang. Islamist militants support Kashmiri insurgents from central Asia. Both countries see danger in linkages between restive Islamic minorities and radical wahabi-influenced movements. Sino-Indian intelligence cooperation has begun to share information on the influence of such groups. And although India still shelters the Dalai Lama (and thus helps keep émigré Tibetan hopes alive), both countries since the late 1980s have sought a lessening of provocation and covert support for separatist insurgency in the other's territory. These modest Sino-Indian convergences still fall well short of active collaboration, but they do point to an interesting countertrend. Ad hoc intelligence cooperation on counterterrorism and Islamist radicalism complements information sharing on global drug-smuggling cartels,[15] even though Indian suspicion about Burmese and Chinese connivance in cross-border drug smuggling into India's northeast remains high.

Careful examination of Beijing's and Delhi's approaches to various multilateral regimes also reveals commonalities. For example, both Chinese and Indian delegations at the UN Human Rights Commission in Geneva avoid encouraging agenda items that could embarrass the other—as when India votes against soliciting testimony about China's behavior in Tibet or when China discourages efforts to discuss Indian troop behavior in Kashmir. As one Indian specialist put it, "Human rights for the Tibetan people has been internationalized due mainly to U.S. pressure; it has long ceased to be a bilateral issue between India and China. . . . China's difficulties in Tibet facilitated a Chinese shift on Kashmir. . . . [Beijing] successfully has intervened with Pakistan after 1998 to withdraw Kashmir-directed human rights resolutions in Geneva."[16]

At a 2001 conference sponsored by the Indian external affairs ministry, successive speakers from both countries rose to condemn U.S.-backed doctrines justifying armed international intervention. Neither side welcomed an extension of this doctrinal interest to the questions of Tibet, Xinjiang, or Kashmir.

While falling short of joint policy, each country accepts that a coincident tactical approach applies in other issues where a mutual preference for a multipolar world joins them in trying to keep U.S. ascendancy in check. This does not mean total Indian acceptance of Beijing's articulation of "multipolarity"; that would amount, after all, to ceding to Beijing a special place—as a formal "legitimate" nuclear weapon state and as a UN Security Council Permanent Five member.

Just a few other examples will suffice. As noted, both countries articulate a mostly common skeptical response to environmental multilateralism. Several months before the global summit on the environment convened in Rio de Janeiro in 1992, Beijing assembled a pan-Asia meeting. China, India, and another two dozen signatories of a "Beijing Declaration" on the environment echoed Malaysian objections to "green imperialism," a phrase implying Western NGO arrogance and suggesting the signers' rejection of measures that would restrict states' sovereignty—in this case the sovereign right to use natural resources without international impediment.

A similar rhetorical stance characterizes Beijing's and Delhi's approaches to multilateral efforts to abate the emission of greenhouse gases. Both China and India remain highly dependent for electricity generation on domestic sources of often highly sulphurous coal. But both stand firm for a formula to attract aid from wealthier countries to achieve cleaner fuel substitution.

Concluding Observations

This chapter has examined convergent Chinese and Indian commercial and strategic goals in the context of global trends and challenges. It has reviewed China's and India's multilateral approach—to security, resource management, and cross-border issues. It has sought to identify areas of Sino-Indian convergence and competition in the post–WTO and post–September 11 world.

On trade matters, bilateral irritations between the two seem set to grow. From allegations of Chinese "dumping" of bicycles to national criticism in Delhi of Indian manufacturers opting to relocate in China (as did the Titana and Ajanta firms during 2001), Sino-Indian trade friction has appeared as a new bilateral irritant. Their trading relationship had remained miniscule until the late 1990s; it exceeded $6 billion by the end of 2002.

The overall picture that emerges reinforces a view that globalization in the current era simply represents a continuation of exogenous forces prompting China and India to generate nationalist responses during the nineteenth century. In far earlier years, India and China contributed mightily to previous phases of globalization. Earlier cultural florescence in each country produced mathematical and astronomical concepts and technologies such as the magnetic compass, flawless cast-iron foundry techniques, paper money, and even rocketry.[17]

"It is not a question of trusting China or not trusting it, but it is question, nevertheless, of realizing that China and India, two great countries, are going through enormous changes which are strengthening them, making them powerful modern states, and that they lie next to each other."[18] When India's first prime minister, Jawaharlal Nehru, said those words he intended something rather different from the connotation carried by the word *globalization* today. Yet his sense of two Asian civilizations, garbed in state structures of recent origin but undergoing transforming change, retains even more pertinence today.

In the writer's view, a return to a world in which a "concert of Asia" works to balance-of-power dynamics seems the most enduring post–Cold War reality.[19] But U.S. eagerness to treat India as a major Asian power in its overall foreign policy runs the risk of blinding American observers to areas where convergent thinking between India and China could make a tacit anti-China alliance between Delhi and Washington very hard to achieve. Asia's two largest countries share deep skepticism over the alleged perfection of global institutions nurtured by the United States after the Second World War. This is not just a rhetorical flourish in the Sino-Indian communiqués. While the competitive national security basis of Sino-Indian relations may very well continue to set the dominant tone, areas of commercial and even strategic cooperation do exist between the two most populous countries in the world. And "parallel track" interests spawned by globalization are already rounding out the too-severe rendering of Sino-Indian ties in simple terms of national security or border dispute.

Globalization is even spawning a set of parallel experiences at the subnational level. Both India and China are producing a different breed of chief ministers (India) and provincial Communist Party bosses (China) in response to changing economic circumstances. Entrepreneurial and executive skills win more respect these days, especially in the southern Indian states of Andhra Pradesh and Karnataka and in China's Guangdong and Fujian provinces. But the technocratic temperament reaches higher into the political hierarchy in China than in India—as reflected by the Shanghai-linked party politicians in China's central government. By contrast, India's most impressive technocrats reside only in the senior civil service, rarely crossing the line into active electoral politics.

Yet nearly all these examples fall into the parallel tracks category. Direct connections between two huge states remain fitful, whether at governmental, commercial, social, or migratory levels. The two countries remain only fleetingly in touch with one another. Xinhua, the Chinese official news agency, maintains just six correspondents in India, the Press Trust of India (PTI) just one journalist in all of China. Although ethnic Indian and Chinese diasporas reach deeply into the West, Southeast Asia, and elsewhere, Indian or Chinese migrants have next to no impact in China or India respectively. Even that most vibrant of Chinese cities, Shanghai, counts an Indian business community of fewer than two hundred people, including dependents. Despite the creation through globalized trends of new commercial, entrepreneurial, and technical constituencies, it is prudent to expect that national security elites in both countries will continue to preside over Sino-Indian relations.

For the United States, the globalized security challenges after September 2001 involve an ever more direct intrusion by U.S.-endorsed action into the sanctum sanctorum of national sovereignty. The United States has attacked and toppled two governments, in Iraq and Afghanistan, and both China and India are watching closely. Partly in response, they have edged more closely to one another while still conscious of deep divides—principally over nuclear rivalry and China's support for Pakistan, but more generally over questions of national status and the quest for primacy in Asia. Beginning with a mere mutuality of position, these convergences have proceeded over time to congruent views. Prime Minister Atal Bihari Vajpayee's Beijing visit in 2003 reflected this slow but unmistakable trend.

Yet all of these congruences for the foreseeable future continue to fall short of genuinely joint approaches or deliberately coordinated responses to international events. Even more distant is any bilateral crafting of international events. At a conceptual and strategic level, China and India are far from having a joint viewpoint on how to oppose the bogey of "unipolarity," by which China means American hegemony. Even the most obvious of global trends—the complex accession of both states to the WTO—has not prompted coordinated bilateral diplomacy despite declaratory intentions to the contrary. India stands alone among large powers in its opposition, right up to the WTO's Cancun meeting in 2003, to a new global trade round. The best outlook—if one seeks a collaborative agenda arising from the global trends affecting both countries—lies in the hope that a bilateral agenda narrowly concentrated for forty years on border and strategic security issues (and complicated by Beijing's quasi alliances with Pakistan and Myanmar) will continue to broaden in the coming years.

Notes

1. See, for example, "Sino-Indian Relations: Old Legacies and New Vistas," *China Report* 30, no. 2 (April–June 1994): "It needs to be borne in mind that relations between the two largest Asian nations are bound to be marked by an undercurrent of competition and contest, given the inherent logic of the unalterable realities of geographical proximity and national rivalry."

2. T. N. Srinivasan, ed., *Agriculture and Trade in China and India: Policies and Performance since 1950* (San Francisco: ICS Press, 1994).

3. See, for example, Torbjorn Loden's chapter "Nationalism Transcending the State: Changing Conceptions of Chinese Identity," in *Asian Forms of the Nation,* ed. Torbjorn Loden, Stein Tønnesson, and Hans Antlöv (Richmond, Surrey: Curzon, 1999).

4. The communique issued at the conclusion of Indian prime minister A. B. Vajpayee's June 2003 visit to China singled out the desirability of crafting joint Sino-Indian positions in the WTO as well as encouraging commercial cooperation in information technology. The communique identified these as among the most promising areas of future Sino-Indian collaboration.

5. The Indian home affairs minister L. K. Advani, in comments to the author in May 2000, described an invitation to Chinese intelligence officials to visit Srinagar, in Indian-occupied Kashmir, to meet Chinese nationals (ethnic Uighurs) found assisting the Islamist-influenced anti-India insurgency in Kashmir.

6. R. Soligo and A. Jaffe, "China and Long-Range Asian Energy Security," James A. Baker III Institute for Public Policy, Rice University, April 1999.

7. For example, Prime Minister A. B. Vajpayee's letter to President Bill Clinton after the May 1998 Pokhran nuclear tests identified China as a cause of India's security anxieties.

8. M. Borrus and S. S. Cohen, "Building China's Information Technology Industry," *Asian Survey* 38, no. 11 (November 1998).

9. "India, China Sign MoU on IT Tie-up," *Hindu,* 17 July 2000. The MoU was signed by visiting information technology minister Pramod Mahajan and his Chinese counterpart, Wu Jichuan, in Beijing. China has set aside special immigration quotas for Indian software engineers.

10. Author's conversation with Hon. M. M. Joshi on 6 June 2000.

11. Vijay Deshpande, presentation on "China-India Info-Tech Comparisons," Asia Society/Confederation of Indian Industry Seminar, Bangalore, India, 19 July 2001.

12. S. Mansingh and C. V. Ranganathan, "Approaches to State Sovereignty," in *Crossing a Bridge of Dreams: Fifty Years of India, China,* ed. G. P. Deshpande and Alka Acharya (Delhi: Tulika, 2001), 446–65.

13. Ibid., 464–65.

14. See, for example, the India and China chapters in M. Brown, ed., *Government Policies and Ethnic Relations in Asia and the Pacific* (Cambridge, Mass.: MIT Press, 1998).

15. The Indian home affairs minister L. K. Advani told the author in August 2000 that he had invited Chinese intelligence officials to visit Srinagar to meet captured Uighurs fighting on behalf of Kashmiris.

16. R. Kadian, *Tibet, India, and China: Critical Choices, Uncertain Future* (New Delhi: Vision, 2001), 175.

17. See "China Technology" cover story, *Far Eastern Economic Review,* 11 March 1999, 10–14.

18. Jawaharlal Nehru, *India's Foreign Policy: Selected Speeches 1946–64* (New Delhi, 1961), 376.

19. See, for example, J. Clad and J. Clarke, *After the Crusade: American Foreign Policy in the Post-Superpower Era* (New York: Madison Books, 1995).

9

Quiet Competition and the Future of Sino-Indian Relations

Mark W. Frazier

Predicting the course that relations between China and India will take over the next ten to twenty years is a hazardous endeavor, given the rapid economic growth and gains in geopolitical standing that have accrued to both states over the past decade. It is clear that the leaders of China and India have placed greater importance on stable relations with each other than was the case during much of the Cold War. However, any analysis of their future relationship must take into account a number of structural and historical conditions. Suppose that one concealed the identity of the two states in question and asked an international relations specialist to project the relative likelihood of their cooperation or conflict in the future, given the following conditions: two neighboring states have very large populations, growing economies, and expanding military capabilities; they went to war forty years ago over a still unresolved border dispute; they conduct a negligible amount of trade with one another; they have fundamentally different forms of government and cultural traditions; one state has delivered conventional weapons and nuclear technology to the other state's long-standing rival and security threat; and finally, one state recently undertook nuclear weapon tests and now seeks a credible, if minimal, deterrent to counter the other's advantage in nuclear weapons and delivery systems. Our analyst might be forgiven for arriving at a pessimistic outlook for future relations between the two countries so described. However, although the conditions listed do capture something of the natural rivalry that exists between China and India, I will argue in this chapter that it would be wrong to conclude from these factors that their future relationship will necessarily be marked by competition and conflict.

I will suggest in the analysis that follows that *because* so many sources of dispute exist between China and India, both sides have come to recognize the need to prevent these tensions from leading to a costly, overt rivalry. The prevailing pattern in Sino-Indian relations therefore can be characterized as one of quiet competition. By this I mean that mitigating factors dampen or mute a potentially antagonistic relationship between two states with past tensions, a lack of mutual trust, and competition over resources and influence outside their existing spheres. Foremost among these mitigating factors are internal priorities and concerns. For the short to medium term (three to ten years), leaders of both countries have staked a great deal on politically sensitive structural reforms and greater integration with the global economy. Moreover, Chinese and Indian authorities may encounter internal security challenges arising from the aspirations of ethnic and religious minorities for greater autonomy. Preoccupation with these and other internal concerns, of course, does not preclude a competitive or even hostile relationship with another state, but it raises considerably the costs of having external rivalries.

Given the existence of quiet competition in Sino-Indian relations, the next logical step in assessing the future is to ask how durable this muted or latent competition will be, and what factors will drive relations between Beijing and New Delhi in more cooperative or openly competitive directions. In the following sections I address five variables that will influence the Sino-Indian rivalry and surmise how changes in them will alter future relations between China and India. The variables are (1) each state's nuclear weapon strategy and doctrine; (2) their respective relations with the United States; (3) their respective relations with Pakistan; (4) their efforts at structural reforms and integration with the global economy; and (5) their domestic political structures, specifically foreign policy–making institutions, and the general ability of their governments to cope with internal security challenges. Based on this discussion, I turn to three possible scenarios that could develop in Sino-Indian relations: deepening competition leading to open rivalry, a turn toward cooperation, and continued quiet competition. Which scenario eventually emerges depends largely on the five trends analyzed in the sections that follow.

Nuclear Weapons and the Future of Minimum Deterrence

Although some have argued that India's pursuit of nuclear weapons introduces an extreme worst-case scenario into the range of possible outcomes in Sino-Indian relations—a nuclear exchange between Beijing and New Delhi—careful analysis suggests otherwise. There is very little chance of a nuclear arms race between China and India because their strategic doctrines, or rationales for possessing nuclear arms and conditions under which they would be used, differ considerably from the doctrines held by the Soviet Union and the United States during their Cold War nuclear rivalry. China and India, for the present time and the foreseeable future, hold quite similar assumptions about the deployment and use of nuclear weapons.[1] Specifically, both states regard their possession of nuclear weapons as a necessary deterrent to potential adversaries who might use them first. Security planners in China and India do not seek to have a rapid retaliatory capability, but an assured one. In essence, both states have pursued nuclear weapons in order to avoid being subject to nuclear threats or "blackmail" from adversaries. This minimum-deterrent posture stands in contrast to doctrines held by the Cold War superpowers, in which nuclear weapons factored into battlefield contingencies or other extensions of conventional warfare. Skeptics are right to ask whether the no-first-use pledges and other assurances on the part of China and India would be cast aside in the midst of an invasion or an international crisis.[2] Nuclear doctrine can also be revised in response to altered perceptions of threat. However, it is difficult to substantiate the claim that China and India are, as nuclear states and potential competitors, somehow inevitably locked into an escalating arms race.

The desire for strategic autonomy—the ideal of independence in foreign policy and nonalignment in great-power politics—has been especially important as a tradition in both Indian and Chinese foreign policy thinking. The pursuit of such autonomy arises in part from each nation's historical experiences and how contemporary elites interpret past instances of foreign domination. Leaders of both states are therefore acutely sensitive to how international regimes can constrain or limit foreign policy autonomy. Possession of nuclear weapons fulfills the need for strategic autonomy by offering an assurance that no rival can threaten the worst imaginable attack without knowing that it would suffer a retaliatory response.[3]

In part because of concerns about strategic autonomy, India was especially sensitive to efforts beginning in 1996 by the United States, in concert with China, to shore up the international nuclear nonproliferation regime by compelling India to join the Comprehensive Test Ban Treaty (CTBT).[4] From the Indian perspective, China had conveniently switched horses in 1996 when it agreed to sign the CTBT after rounding out its deterrent capabilities with nuclear tests of its own between 1994 and mid-1996. India, in this analysis, had to thwart a nuclear nonproliferation regime led by nuclear weapon states that wished to exclude India from their ranks. Such an outcome would, in India's view, erode its highly prized foreign policy autonomy by forcing it to align with one of the nuclear weapon states as a hedge against threats from another.

In this light, it is worth considering the changes in Sino-Indian relations that followed India's Pokhran II nuclear tests in May 1998. Despite the initial and predictable souring of Sino-Indian relations after Indian leaders more or less singled out China as the principal threat to Indian security and the rationale for India's pursuit of nuclear weapons, Sino-Indian relations recovered rather quickly. One could argue that the warming of ties after 1999 would have occurred sooner had India's nuclear tests not taken place. Yet it is also true that Pokhran II put Chinese as well as American officials on notice that India's security interests were not being adequately addressed. In either case, it is difficult to dispute the claim that all parties had to regard the Sino-Indian relationship with greater seriousness after May 1998.

The maintenance of a minimum nuclear deterrent by China and India clearly raises the stakes in a naturally competitive relationship. However, by virtue of this fact, a minimum nuclear deterrent could also keep a competitive relationship from evolving toward a hostile one. On balance, I would argue that the flurry of diplomatic activity between New Delhi and Beijing that began in 1999 and has continued since then would not have transpired without the incentive to engage in "damage control" in the wake of Pokhran II. From this analysis flow two crucial questions for the future of Sino-Indian relations in the coming decades. First, how will each state respond to the other's advances in nuclear weapon delivery systems necessary for a minimum deterrent? Second, under what conditions would

China or India (or both) move away from a minimum nuclear deterrent toward potentially more destabilizing doctrines that called for swifter, larger responses or for the tactical use of nuclear weapons in battlefield situations?

The first question will emerge in concrete form as India proceeds in the coming years with the fulfillment of its goal of an actual minimum deterrent. Unlike China, India does not maintain nuclear weapons readily deliverable on missiles or from bombers. India's nuclear arsenal is, as Ashley Tellis has termed it, a "force in being," meaning the various components—warheads, missiles, etc.—are dispersed but capable of assembly in a relatively short period of time.[5] If India's long-standing security goal has been to achieve a hedge against nuclear blackmail, then India has little option but to complete this quest for strategic autonomy by "weaponizing," or at least demonstrating that it possesses nuclear warheads that can readily be paired with delivery systems in order to deter an attack.

The second critical question regards changes in doctrine. If the current rationale for possessing nuclear weapons is to thwart the use or threatened use of nuclear weapons against India and China in the first place, what factors would push Indian and Chinese strategic planners to broaden the range of conditions under which nuclear weapons could be deployed and eventually used? Shifts in doctrine are difficult to predict—they could arise from domestic political transformations as new elites redefine security interests and defense strategies, but such political realignments are also difficult to forecast. However, for the next decade at least, any changes in nuclear doctrine by India and China are more likely to arise in response to external influences such as a shift in American strategy and doctrine.[6]

China's modernization of its nuclear forces is closely tied to perceptions of American deployment of its nuclear arsenal and of the U.S. pursuit of national missile defense (NMD). The construction of American NMD could have a lasting effect on the security equation in Asia and on India-China relations. On balance, American pursuit of NMD appears inimical to Chinese interests, and in turn to Indian interests, in preventing an adversary from credibly threatening to use nuclear weapons during a conventional war or other security crisis. New Delhi, Beijing, and Moscow in 2001 all evinced subtle shifts in their positions on American NMD. These adjustments, if they do indeed signal a willingness to accept some form of U.S. missile defense, suggest that NMD will have a more complicated effect on Asian security, and on Sino-Indian relations, than the predicted billiard-ball reaction of escalating nuclear arms races as China, then India, and then

Pakistan each reacts to a rival's changed deterrent capabilities.[7] Russia, India, and China could find acceptable some installation of an American missile defense system in exchange for certain security-enhancing benefits that would accrue to each. For example, the Indian government's carefully worded statement in May 2001 indicated that acceptance, or even support, of American NMD could be forthcoming provided that NMD is installed in the context of a reduction in the U.S. nuclear missile stockpile.[8] India's position on American NMD could also be linked to U.S. acceptance of India's ability to conduct missile tests and other measures to maintain its nuclear deterrent. Given the significance India attaches to foreign policy autonomy, however, it will not be inclined to accept a role that rigidly places it in the cogs of American strategic planning vis-à-vis China.

China's stance on American NMD is also complex and evolving. Chinese officials have consistently opposed NMD as a potential threat to its nuclear deterrent, and have stridently objected to regional deployment of a missile defense in Asia. However, the Chinese position showed some flexibility in 2001, when officials suggested the possibility of engaging in discussions with U.S. counterparts over America's intentions for NMD. For example, China's leading arms control negotiator, Sha Zukang, once warned that China's participation in various international regimes could be terminated if the United States built a national missile defense system.[9] Within a year, in May 2001, he held a press conference in which he sent a subtly worded message that there may in fact be room for compromise on NMD. Sha is well known to "shoot from the hip" in his public utterances, yet several Chinese analysts asserted that Sha would not speak publicly without approval first from the uppermost ranks of China's foreign policy elite, such as the Foreign Affairs Leadership Group of the Chinese Communist Party (CCP).[10] Whatever the case, any acceptance of American NMD on the part of China will have to come with substantial payoffs.

In the final analysis, how American NMD influences future relations between India and China will depend on how U.S. officials present their position to security planners in Beijing and New Delhi. If American officials manage to persuade their Chinese counterparts that NMD will not undermine China's deterrent capabilities, then ceteris paribus NMD will have little effect on Sino-Indian relations. However, if China were to conclude that America's pursuit of NMD does indeed undermine China's deterrent capability, Beijing could respond by accelerating its development of long-range ballistic missiles, by pursuing technologies that would neutralize the new American missile defenses, and possibly by delivering these and other technologies to other states. India's deterrent could be undermined if China resumed or continued the transfer of nuclear weapon materials and technology to Pakistan. Thus, regardless of whether NMD proves technically viable in the end as an effective missile shield for the United States, the pursuit of NMD over the next ten to twenty years will almost certainly trigger anticipatory moves by Chinese defense planners to upgrade Beijing's nuclear force structure in an effort to overcome a U.S. missile defense. The impact on Sino-Indian relations of China's response to NMD specifically depends on New Delhi's reaction to an enhanced Chinese nuclear force structure; but it is difficult to argue that India would refrain from accelerating the development of its nuclear forces to match advances in China's arsenals.

In terms of modernizing conventional forces, India and China will continue to move ahead with indigenous weapons programs while relying on Russia as a vital source for the expansion of their military capabilities, especially for attack aircraft and naval vessels. Russia—and its uncertain future status as an Asian power—remains an important variable in India's interpretation of its need to balance China. A stronger Russia serves India as a useful counterweight to China's expanding power. Notwithstanding declarations of Sino-Russian cooperation and considerable arms sales to China, Moscow has sufficient reasons to weigh in with India in efforts to manage the expansion of Chinese power in coming years. As Rajan Menon notes, "One certainty is that Russia will maintain the Soviet-era alignment with India, not only for its intrinsic benefits (economic cooperation and arms sales) but also as part of a broader strategy of balancing China."[11]

Thus, the pursuit and maintenance of a minimum nuclear deterrent and defense modernization more broadly will grant China and India a measure of strategic autonomy and fulfill their preferences for maximum flexibility in foreign policy. However, as illustrated by the issue of American NMD, relations between China and India will be heavily influenced by their respective relations with the United States.

The United States as a Pivot

Despite diplomatic proclamations during state visits, and on other occasions that offer Chinese and Indian leaders the opportunity to enumerate areas of mutual interest, future relations between the two states will remain firmly embedded within a triangle formed with the United States. In this triangulation, the United States maintains complicated but generally stable ties with Beijing and enjoys a rapidly improving relationship with New Delhi, more or less unencumbered by considerations of how its relations with one affect its relations with the other. Both China and India have much to gain from positive relations with the United States, such as access to U.S. markets and investment capital along with the security benefits that come with being on good terms with the world's only superpower. Put another way, the United States stands in a pivotal position in the Sino-Indian-U.S. triangle.

The pursuit of benefits that derive from positive relations with Washington need not entail a zero-sum calculus, but here the problem of a quietly competitive relationship has in the past generated a certain level of uneasiness whenever the United States appears to be favoring the interests of one state over the other. Depending on the policy area and the context, U.S. bilateral cooperation with India in the 1990s at times created suspicion among Chinese leaders about possible U.S. intentions to contain China. Likewise, Sino-American cooperation has raised anxieties among Indian policy makers about the emergence of China. Their concerns have centered on the possibility that the United States has decided to sacrifice Indian interests in its own quest for stable Sino-American ties. For example, a number of analysts have noted that Sino-American cooperation on nuclear nonproliferation agendas in the mid-1990s that sought to block India from joining the ranks of nuclear weapon states alarmed India's foreign policy–making community to such an extent that India felt compelled to conduct nuclear tests as a response.[12] The existence of such a triangle raises two crucial questions in assessing future relations between India and China: How will the United States, in its bilateral relations with China and India, influence Sino-Indian relations in the years ahead? Furthermore, is it possible for Sino-Indian relations to develop independently of concerns about one another's ties with the United States?

The issues that will challenge Sino-American relations in the future are far too complex and multifaceted to translate into zero-sum gains (or losses) for India. Although many in the Indian foreign policy–making community may at times feel slighted by U.S. attention to China on a wide array of issues, it is difficult to conclude that U.S. diplomatic efforts to halt the proliferation of missile and nuclear materials, to bring China into the World Trade Organization, and otherwise to integrate China into international regimes somehow come at the expense of Indian interests. Still, it is true that the emergence of strongly negative relations between the United

States and China would give India the opportunity to enhance its cooperation with the United States on several fronts, possibly involving an alliance relationship. Some assessments note that India could become the pivotal state in the triangle if a sustained period of rivalry were to emerge between the United States and China. For example, in the "India card" scenario offered by Mohan Malik, India "might come to occupy the same place in the U.S. security calculus that China had during the U.S.-Soviet Cold War years from 1971 to 1989."[13]

On this note, it is instructive to assess an alternative and quite different Indian response to some future Sino-American confrontation. Indian leaders, in keeping with the preference for nonalignment, could choose to adopt a nonaligned position. Instead, India might undertake cooperative, multilateral approaches with Japan, Russia, and the Association of Southeast Asian Nations (ASEAN) to prevent a Sino-American confrontation from worsening. Other states in Asia have obvious, immediate interests in preventing Sino-American tensions that would, at a minimum, imperil their economies by reducing trade and investment flows. Whereas Japan and other U.S. allies in Southeast Asia would find it difficult not to support the United States in a conflict with China, India would have the option at least of taking a more flexible position. Only a dramatic decline in the security environment in Asia or a fundamental reorientation in Chinese foreign policy, in which India felt genuinely threatened by Chinese intentions, would lead India into an alliance with the United States.

The nature and tenor of U.S.-Indian relations will be in many respects a more direct influence on the prospects for Sino-Indian relations. Unlike U.S.-China relations, wherein the issue of India's emergence is a secondary priority at best, security discussions between Washington and New Delhi will continue to center on China and its intentions. India and the United States share a number of strategic and economic interests, including counterterrorism, the security of sea-lanes in the Indian Ocean, and the overall stability of Asia. None of these is inimical to Chinese goals, but it is the manner in which the United States and India cooperate to pursue these interests that will shape the response of Chinese leaders. Broadly speaking, U.S.-Indian cooperation will not pose a security threat to China. It is only when the respective leaders characterize the U.S.-Indian relationship as a strategic device to counter the emergence of Chinese power that Chinese analysts will grow concerned about India. Talk of the "China threat" among some circles in New Delhi and Washington will only confirm the suspicions of those in Beijing who are already wary of U.S. intentions in South Asia and elsewhere around China's periphery.

However, U.S.-Indian cooperation is not necessarily a given, despite the fact that Prime Minister Atal Behari Vajpayee once remarked that the two are "natural allies."[14] As Kanti Bajpai has observed, having shared interests does not necessarily translate into the United States and India having shared perspectives on how to achieve them. One source of past difficulties in U.S.-Indian relations has been the fact that the existence of numerous shared interests failed to translate into any significant results—that, despite so many similar goals, cooperation seemed to elude the two parties.[15] This persistent feature in U.S.-India relations is not likely to recede quickly in the near future. In relative terms, U.S. relations with New Delhi are regarded as low-maintenance, while the hazards involved in U.S.-China relations make them a decidedly high-maintenance affair. Somewhat paradoxically, the state with which the United States enjoys a wider array of shared interests receives less diplomatic attention than the state with which it has some fundamental areas of difference. Short of a major U.S. withdrawal from Asia, a highly unlikely prospect over the next two decades, there is little reason to believe that Sino-Indian relations can break out or exist independently of the Sino-Indian-U.S. triangle.

The Pakistan Factor

The future of Sino-Indian relations must also be assessed in the context of Pakistan. Here the uncertainties surrounding the future of the government of Pervez Musharraf, and the survivability of the Pakistani state more broadly, cloud the analysis, but we can begin with a few propositions.

First, the elevated geopolitical importance of Pakistan by virtue of U.S.-led counterterrorist efforts bodes well for future Sino-Indian relations. China, India, and the United States have substantial, pressing interests in curbing terrorist activity in Central Asia, and American involvement with and pressure on Pakistan can be viewed by India and China positively in this regard. One of the gravest outcomes for regional security would be for Pakistan to sink into a protracted civil war involving pro-government troops against fundamentalist Islamic rebels, possibly supported by breakaway units of the Pakistani military and possibly vying for control of Pakistan's nuclear weapon facilities. This is a scenario that the United

States, India, China, and every other power in the region have a common interest in preventing. While a state failure in Pakistan or a war between Pakistan and India would require astute diplomacy from Beijing and New Delhi to prevent a downturn in Sino-Indian relations, such events would not inevitably bring China and India into competitive or conflictual stances. A political crisis in Pakistan therefore would compel India, the United States, and possibly China as well to coordinate their responses to prevent a civil war and the refugee flows that would surely ensue.

A second proposition is that the threat of armed hostilities between India and Pakistan will linger as long as Musharraf and the Pakistani military remain in power. For future Sino-Indian relations this means that the question of Chinese support for Pakistan—diplomatically, financially, militarily, or combinations thereof—during an Indo-Pakistani conflict will weigh heavily in the defense plans of Islamabad and New Delhi. However, it would take a major shift in foreign policy priorities for China to determine that its national interests dictated getting enmeshed in an Indo-Pakistani conflict. Even when China offered military aid and diplomatic support in conflicts between India and Pakistan in 1965 and 1971, it stopped short of actual armed intervention on the side of Pakistan. (China's threat to intervene militarily in 1965 did compel India to reach agreement with Pakistan to cease hostilities.) More recently, during armed clashes in 1999 between Pakistani and Indian forces in the Kargil region of Kashmir, China not only declined to intervene but also offered virtually no public diplomatic support to Pakistan.

In bald-faced realpolitik terms, a resumption of hostilities between India and Pakistan would serve no purpose from China's perspective. Given current asymmetries between India and Pakistan, such a conflict would most likely result in a more powerful, dominant India shorn of the threat from its long-standing rival. As one Indian security official also noted, China realizes that if war broke out between India and Pakistan, this would only mean more American involvement in the region, which China would not necessarily welcome.[16] From a purely self-interested perspective, therefore, China on balance would prefer not to see another Indo-Pakistani conflict. China and the United States could leverage their support for Pakistan to compel Islamabad to be the first to stand down should Indian and Pakistani hostilities appear imminent. Depending on how future crises are handled, Chinese efforts to restrain Pakistan could go a long way in demonstrating to India that Beijing no longer views Pakistan as a strategic counterweight to India.

In a worst-case scenario in which state failure in Pakistan and an Indo-Pakistani war occurred sequentially, China would likely seek to participate in a multilateral (and U.S.-led) effort to end the hostilities. Although Chinese participation in such an enterprise would raise suspicions among Indian foreign policy makers, Chinese involvement in conflict resolution or relief efforts would go far to undermine Indian assumptions that China consistently sides with Pakistan in its disputes with India. On the other hand, any unilateral Chinese responses that favored Pakistan in an armed conflict with India, or that established a client regime of Beijing in the event of a state failure, would place strong and potentially unsustainable pressures on Sino-Indian relations and lead to long-term conflictual relations. Currently, however, Beijing's interests lie in steering clear of such an outcome, given the high costs of propping up a Pakistani regime at war with India.

All that said, cooperative Sino-Indian relations will remain elusive until leaders reach some accommodation over the nature and substance of China's relationship with Pakistan. India has pursued improved relations with China for more than a decade without any assurances that Beijing would curb its military and diplomatic support of Pakistan; however, the Sino-Pakistani friendship will continue to raise doubts among policy makers in New Delhi. Sino-Indian relations will also be harmed should any new evidence emerge that China has delivered or continues to provide Pakistan with critical technology for the production of nuclear weapons. However, China's relations with Pakistan and other South Asian states will be less directly linked to Sino-Indian relations than was the case in past decades. China, for its part, has modified its stance of offering public support for the Pakistani position on the status of Kashmir. The prospects are thus significantly diminished from what they were in the past that Pakistan's relations with China will inevitably harm relations between China and India.

My analysis thus far suggests that as a result of their nuclear weapon programs, their relations with the United States, and their relations with Pakistan, China and India will keep their natural competition within manageable boundaries and avoid an open rivalry. Yet the discussion has assumed up to now that both China and India can maintain past rates of economic growth and overcome a number of short-term challenges associated with structural reforms. How they cope with these and other challenges that arise from being the world's two most populous states will determine a great deal about whether foreign policy autonomy, nuclear deterrents, and flexible relations with major powers can be maintained over the long term.

Even if India gains a robust nuclear deterrent, the payoffs would certainly be lessened if its economy were enfeebled at the same time. As one commentator at a workshop in New Delhi in 2001 so trenchantly put it, without sustained economic growth India could become "a Bangladesh with strategic autonomy."[17]

Economic Growth and Relative Gains

The current leaders of China and India have determined that they can achieve economic growth and enhanced power most effectively within a peaceful, stable international environment. Most economic growth forecasts predict 5–6 percent annual gross domestic product (GDP) expansion in India over the next five years and 6–7 percent per year for China. If sustained for the next ten to twenty years, these growth rates would have significant implications for these countries' positions as regional powers in Asia. Competition for resources and influence in Central and Southeast Asia, well under way by the 1990s, would intensify. Indian and Chinese navies would have the ability to patrol the shipping lanes in the Indian Ocean and the South China Sea with greater frequency. However, the current focus on expanded economic growth also means that India and China are willing to put aside the resolution of bilateral problems for a decade or so, when each assumes that its enhanced economic and political clout will translate into a better bargaining position. In this respect, the paramount goal of pursuing economic expansion while managing the effects of globalization suggests that India and China will avoid foreign policy entanglements that might undermine prospects for continued growth in their economies.

China over the past two decades has adopted a strategy that places economic growth as a central priority, and in many respects this priority governs the conduct of China's international relations. The strategy is designed to buy time for China to amass economic and military power so that it can, by 2015 or so, use this power to resolve outstanding disputes with its neighbors and, most important, those with the United States.[18] While it is commonplace for states to rely on economic expansion as a driver of national power and overall capabilities, in China's case the need for economic expansion and export markets transformed its foreign policy and overall strategy beginning in the late 1970s. In the future, a more economically powerful China will nonetheless be a more interdependent

China, constrained from acting in ways inimical to its continued economic growth. In addition, China faces a series of critical structural reforms in the coming decade, reforms that will be pushed from the outside in some respects by China's entry into the World Trade Organization (WTO). Resolving the massive accumulation of bad loans in the banking sector, establishing a viable social safety net, and attending to widening disparities in income will be more than enough to keep Beijing's leaders preoccupied over the next decade. The consequence of all this for China's relations with India is that, barring the important possibility of competition for energy resources, India's own economic strides will not arouse concerns among Chinese foreign policy makers.

In India, a general consensus exists on the need for "second-generation" reforms such as labor legislation and privatization, but some analysts and many business professionals are skeptical that these reforms will make sufficient headway because of the multiplicity of veto points in India's federalist democracy. Still, the relative continuity of commitment to reforms despite changing governments in the 1990s suggests that future Indian governments will continue to move away from the statist and socialist economic policies of the past. The other substantive debate over the future of the Indian economy relates to the costs of the nuclear weapon program. Liberal-minded analysts assert that India's global power will derive from its economic performance and attractiveness to foreign investors, and they caution that advancing its nuclear weapon capabilities will come at too high a cost. As Brahma Chellaney has put it, "Without economic power, India can have no security, even with nuclear weapons."[19] Others, generally security analysts, assert that there is no such trade-off between India's emergence as an economic and a nuclear power; moreover, economic expansion and security enhancement must move ahead at the same time.

The Indian and Chinese economies now have extensive linkages to foreign markets and sources of investment capital, but these linkages have yet to extend to one another. Although bilateral trade between India and China has expanded rapidly in recent years, it still amounts to only $3 billion to $4 billion annually, including an estimated $1 billion in smuggled goods that change hands.[20] The reduction in Indian tariff and nontariff barriers in the 1990s brought a surge in Chinese imports of electronics, apparel, toys, and other consumer goods at prices that prompted many in the Indian business community to file dumping charges. Of the ninety-three antidumping cases under investigation by the Indian government in 2001, almost half were directed at Chinese imports.[21] This is a pattern that is likely to continue as both India and China use safeguard measures to respond to import surges from one another.

Even in the area of information technology, which officials routinely cite as an area of future cooperation between India and China, there are signs of competition on the horizon. While the establishment of various training programs in respective technology centers (Shanghai, Shenzhen, Beijing, Bangalore) holds some promise for cooperative arrangements such as joint bidding on international projects by Indian software developers and Chinese hardware manufacturers, China will not cede its domestic software market to Indian firms. In fact, the Chinese government has developed industrial policies to promote the growth of China as a center for software development, aiming to narrow the vast gap in exports of software services between India and China. In 2000, China's exports of software services stood at a negligible $130 million, whereas India's were $5.7 billion. There is good reason to predict that China will quickly expand its software services sector. Not only is China's average hourly cost for source coding half that of India's, but China represents the most important future market for many firms, a compelling reason in its own right for investors to choose China over India. This fact is not lost on India's Manufacturers' Association for Information Technology, which in 2001 warned its members of China's potential emergence as a rival in software services.[22] The continued growth in China's software services exports will be constrained by a scarcity of English-trained engineers, ongoing disputes over the Chinese government's enforcement of laws related to intellectual property, and compliance with WTO standards for intellectual property. Still, many business analysts predict that the draw of China's market will offset these and other concerns. As the chief financial officer of a Beijing software firm noted in 2001, "Within ten years, China will be far bigger than India as a software exporter. That's because we have a huge domestic market for high-tech products—unlike India—and whoever comes from a large market base will naturally have a powerful export ability."[23]

Despite the possible exception of software services, China and India will not compete directly for foreign investment, given the vast size of both markets and their uneven pace of opening different sectors. Global corporations do not face the choice of investing in either India or China, but generally the question is how much to invest in each, and when. Nor will India or China view the other country's rising levels of foreign direct investment (FDI) with much apprehension about relative gains, though some Indian businesspersons and policy makers regard the FDI figures for China with a combination of awe and bemusement. In this respect, the often-cited gap in FDI—$46.8 billion in inflows to China versus $3.4 billion to India in 2001—carries symbolic weight but does not portend competition between the two economies for inflows. The FDI gap will probably remain for some time, even if Indian financial authorities at the central and state levels lift various restrictions and further liberalize foreign investment procedures.

The two states are likely to find avenues of cooperation as negotiations evolve in the WTO's Doha round. Both India and China have been more successful to date than many other developing nations in gaining benefits from integration with the global economy, and in that sense they have divergent interests from other developing nations afflicted by various financial and monetary crises. But China and India may find several opportunities to lead developing countries in opposing moves by the United States and the European Union to introduce labor and environmental standards into future multilateral trade talks. China and India might also cooperate to fashion a developing country position on patents and other intellectual property issues.

In sum, the political challenges of coping with structural reforms and the imperative of sustaining growth in India's and China's increasingly open economies bode well for keeping Sino-Indian relations within their current bounds. While there may be future instances of economic competition in some sectors and occasional trade disputes between the two countries, the Chinese and Indian economies are sufficiently segmented to prevent their economic growth from generating a rivalry.

Domestic Factors

The effect of future changes in domestic political institutions within China and India on their bilateral relationship will be indirect at best. Still, it is worth considering how domestic politics and institutions in both states might affect long-standing problems in their relationship such as the border dispute, nuclear weapons deployment, or Sino-Pakistani relations. For example, will China's "fourth generation" of leaders seek to change China's basic orientation toward India? How might substantial political reforms in China influence its views of and diplomacy toward India? How would a stridently nationalistic Chinese government or an aggressively Hindu-nationalist India respond to bilateral problems in Sino-Indian relations? Given that some have predicted that governance crises of various sorts will occur in India and China in the future, which of these might seriously destabilize Sino-Indian relations? Because so much would depend on externalities—for example, the circumstances surrounding a transformation in the political landscape, and the preferences of individual leaders who emerge in the future—it is better to respond to these questions with a few general points rather than to idly speculate based on dozens of contingencies.

First, the new generation of CCP leaders faces the challenge of building relations with China's military authorities and working within the complicated structure of civil-military relations in China. This is significant for Sino-Indian relations because experts have identified the People's Liberation Army (PLA) as far more hawkish in its orientation toward India and more suspicious of India's foreign policy objectives than are civilian policy makers.[24] Even though in theory China's military is subservient to the Chinese Communist Party and linked to it through the party's Central Military Commission, each new leader of China has had to cultivate close ties with the PLA. The latter also has substantial weight within the foreign policy–making process, and at times can be at odds with the civilians in the Ministry of Foreign Affairs. Although bureaucratic competition in the foreign policy–making process is neither new nor unique to China, the leadership transition would appear to raise the bargaining position of China's military for the short term at least, and this may result in a tougher line in policy toward India.

Second, India is undergoing an important change in civil-military relations. The long-standing civilian controls over the military in India have been reformed, and if these reforms succeed, they will permit greater involvement of senior officers in the defense policy–making process. Before, military policy had been under the control of civilian ministries and ultimately the Parliament. The recent reforms imply that India's posture toward China will reflect a greater balance of military and civilian perspectives. To date, the Indian military has exerted a moderating influence on foreign policy toward China, in contrast to the "China threat" perspectives found among some elements of the Bharatiya Janata Party and its coalition partners. In the late 1990s, the office of the prime minister and its inner-cabinet security committees, including a recently established National Security Advisory Board, sought broader coordination and control of the service branches through the integration of personnel, budgets, and operations. Based on the findings of recent government commissions and reports, the Indian government in 2001 began to integrate formally the armed services and to establish a legally bound consultative role in policy making for senior officers. A Joint Strategic Forces Command to manage nuclear weapon systems was established in late 2001. The integration of the top ranks of India's armed forces should in principle increase their effectiveness by enhancing their ability to coordinate patrols of strategically important regions and sea-lanes.[25] Given that Chinese naval vessels are also likely to operate in some of those same sea-lanes, improving coordination systems in the Indian military is a positive step that will lessen the chances of accidental conflicts.

Third, in the remotely possible event that political reforms bring competitive elections to China in the next twenty years, it is not likely that these leaders would be any less sensitive about long-standing core issues in Chinese foreign policy such as sovereignty and defense modernization. From a security standpoint, democratically elected leaders of China might be more transparent in their handling of defense budgets and expenditures, but it is not likely that China would abandon its defense modernization program, including its nuclear dimension. A democratically elected leader of China would have to move very cautiously in negotiating a solution to the border dispute with India, given the potential for backlash among any number of constituencies. In short, some of the same concerns that exist today in China's relations with its Asian neighbors would persist under a China whose rulers were chosen in competitive elections.[26]

Finally, it should be noted that the future of Sino-Indian relations will be indirectly but significantly influenced by the myriad internal governance problems that both encounter as "soft states." Health crises such as HIV/AIDS and the emergence of infectious diseases such as severe acute respiratory syndrome (SARS), environmental catastrophes such as water shortages, and various forms of social unrest, including separatist movements, sectarian conflict, and tax riots—all will pose major governance challenges to future leaders of China and India. How such challenges will play in the respective foreign policies of China and India, and in their bilateral relationship more specifically, is difficult to ascertain. At a minimum, we can say that if one of these states encounters broad and sustained unrest resulting from a failure to address such problems, then significant advantages in relative power would accrue to the other state. All of these internal security issues would exert distant and largely indirect effects on Sino-Indian relations, with one notable exception: the status of Tibet and movements for Tibetan autonomy.

A Tibetan uprising would involve Sino-Indian relations for obvious geographic reasons and because the Tibetan exile community, including the Dalai Lama, is based in Dharamsala, India. However, it is less the activities of Tibetan independence advocates than the inevitable passing of the current Dalai Lama that stands as the most likely issue to propel Tibet back into the forefront of Sino-Indian relations. The succession politics that are sure to follow over the selection of the next Dalai Lama could have broader ramifications for Sino-Indian relations. The Tibetan exile community is said to be increasingly restless and factionalized. Once the spiritual leader of the Tibetan exiles passes from the scene, different factions will vie to install a new Dalai Lama of their liking.[27] Among these factions are some who might pursue measures to support and foment selective violence against Chinese security forces across the border. The government of India could find itself under heightened diplomatic pressure from Beijing if a dispute were to ensue over the selection of the next Dalai Lama or if the Chinese demanded the extradition of certain Tibetan exiles. Indian interests would also be directly involved should a security crisis emerge in Tibet. At a minimum, there would be a substantial flow of refugees across the Nepalese and Indian borders, forcing India into a position that could easily raise the ire of the Chinese leadership.

Chinese and Indian officials are well aware of the internal security challenges that each state faces and the risks of large-scale violence. A governing crisis could be triggered either by an overt challenge, such as a separatist movement, or by the failure to alleviate poverty in regions that continue to fall behind prosperous regions in each country. However, even if a political or economic crisis were to pose threats to the future of governments in either India or China, security managers would be compelled to turn their attention to internal stability, not necessarily to engage in adventurous foreign policy actions. Although saber-rattling and actual conflict would be an option to divert attention from domestic problems, the chances are remote that a Chinese or Indian government beset with a domestic crisis would select a trans-Himalayan conflict—with all the geopolitical consequences and risks that would involve—as the battleground on which to rally domestic populations. If either government were to choose a wartime mobilization to shift attention away from a domestic crisis, they would surely engage a smaller, less consequential rival.

Scenarios

Given that China and India have both placed great importance on economic expansion and global linkages as the primary means to achieve greater security over the next twenty years, it will be the pace and magnitude of each state's economic growth—and how this growth is converted into military capabilities—that will serve as the main influence on the trajectory of Sino-Indian relations. We should be cautious in using current rates of economic growth to project future differences in economic size and overall power. Still, the variation in economic growth between India and China in the 1990s has already deeply influenced the strategic orientations of both states toward one another. Consideration of whether the current gaps in the size of their economies—in foreign investment, trade, and other measures now favoring China—will narrow, widen, or remain roughly the same can serve as a useful starting point to explore three possible futures in Sino-Indian relations.

Deepening Competition

Asymmetric growth in the Chinese and Indian economies could lead to an openly competitive relationship in several ways. For example, one possibility is that China's structural reforms eventually succeed in bringing about renewed, sustainable economic growth that the CCP translates into newfound legitimacy and a modernized military, while India's reforms bring slower growth and less certain advances in defensive capabilities. As this gap widens, the probability increases that India will turn to outside powers such as the United States as a hedge against a potentially assertive China in any number of areas where Chinese and Indian interests are at odds. At one extreme, India's leaders would abandon the pursuit of an independent foreign policy and seek out security alliances with the United States, Russia, or others. At a minimum, a stagnant or slow-growth Indian economy will create anxieties about China's relative power and will encourage India to seek collective security arrangements with those of China's neighbors who also feel anxious about China's rise, such as Japan.

Another possible trajectory is for Sino-Indian competition to deepen if China suffers a sustained downturn in economic performance, while India becomes the next economic giant of Asia and then translates its economic gains into a rapid expansion of conventional and nuclear forces. Under these conditions, India could become more assertive in challenging China's diplomatic ties with India's neighbors, its naval patrols in the Indian Ocean, its claims to the western sector of the Himalayan border, and its pursuit of energy resources in Central Asia. This possibility appears, from the perspective of early 2003, as distinctly remote given China's continued economic expansion. It would take a seismic shift in the Asian economic environment for India to replace China as the world's export powerhouse and leading recipient of foreign direct investment. On this note, however, it would be wise to recall that few people envisioned in the early 1990s that Japan would stagnate for as long as it has and that China would emerge by the end of the decade as an economic competitor in the eyes of many Japanese.

The far more probable economic scenario remains, however, that China's growth will continue to outpace that of India. This sense of lagging behind China will prod Indian leaders to push ahead with reforms and to seek deeper ties with China's neighbors in East Asia. In many respects, India's "Look East" policy of developing economic and military cooperation with states in Southeast Asia and with Japan is a harbinger of how India will respond to China's increasing power and influence.

A Turn toward Cooperation

Several possibilities exist in which the quietly competitive relationship moves toward cooperation. The most obvious of these, from a balance-of-power perspective, is that Sino-Indian cooperation emerges from these countries' shared interest in balancing against an overly assertive United States. India and China could find reason to develop long-term cooperation based on their shared opposition to U.S. military interventions, particularly in cases that involve disputes over the autonomy of ethnic groups, as occurred with the Yugoslavia campaign in 1999. While the American-led war on international terrorism beginning in 2001 opened several avenues of cooperation for Washington, Beijing, and New Delhi to combat terrorist threats, subsequent American campaigns waged in the name of counterterrorism, such as the conflict in Iraq in 2003, will continue to place India and China at odds with U.S. policy. Furthermore, substantial differences will arise over the manner in which Beijing, New Delhi, and Washington define and pursue organizations that each labels as threats to national security. Here India and China will be in concert over the sovereign right of states to use force internally against groups that they deem to be security threats, and both will resist American calls for dialogue and restraint. Still, the shared preference for a restrained use of American power that avoids infringements of state sovereignty will not be sufficient to serve as the basis for sustained Sino-Indian cooperation. Because of the importance of the American market to their economic strategies, both states need good relations with the United States and would be sacrificing a great deal should they cooperate overtly in an anti-U.S. coalition.

Sino-Indian relations could also move in the direction of long-term cooperation if India, having fallen so far behind China in relative power terms, chose to cope with the rise of China by aligning itself with its northern neighbor. Under this scenario, Indian leaders would determine that the benefits of bandwagoning with China outweighed those of trying to rely on multilateral security arrangements or on alliances with major powers such as the United States. This represents a possible but remote outcome for obvious reasons. It would mean that Indian leaders would acquiesce to Chinese leadership in Southeast Asia, Central Asia, and even the Indian Ocean. Barring a sequence of catastrophes that weakened India severely, it is difficult to see how India would accept Chinese leadership in Asia without first challenging it by overtly aligning with the United States or Russia to balance Chinese power.

Some might argue that the current pursuit by China and India of economic growth and international linkages through trade and investment holds promise for substantial mutual gains in security that would lessen, if not eliminate, the sources of latent Sino-Indian competition. As the leaders of both states deepen engagement in various international organizations and multilateral forums, sufficient trust will be achieved to address issues such as the disputed border and China's relations with Pakistan. For this scenario to come to fruition, however, the economic benefits of global linkages have to trump concerns about relative gains of rival states, and concerns about advances in defensive capabilities. Few if any neighbors of China, especially India, will pin their security calculations to the belief that Chinese leaders will refrain from exercising power or from using force to resolve a dispute because the economic costs are too high. The pursuit of economic expansion and further linkages with the global economy have dampened Sino-Indian competition for now, but these economic benefits are not sufficient to induce a period of long-term cooperation between the two states.

Continued Quiet Competition

Of all the scenarios and variations of them considered here, the one with the highest probability is that the quiet competition between China and India will continue over the next twenty years. This prediction offers a mixture of optimism and concern. First, given their current strategies of accumulating power through economic growth and international linkages, neither India nor China stands to benefit from an open rivalry. India, for its part, has benefited from the current environment in which it is gradually gaining acceptance from the United States and others as an important power with interests and influence beyond its region. Given the importance of retaining its foreign policy autonomy, India will be reluctant to stake its future on an exclusive alliance with the United States. Instead, India will develop multifaceted, flexible security relationships that also involve Japan, Russia, and ASEAN. The underlying purpose of Indian strategy is thus to signal to China that India can become part of an anti-Chinese coalition should China take stances that threaten the security of its neighbors. Preserving a stable security environment conducive to expanded trade and investment, while also preparing for a more powerful and potentially assertive China, are cornerstones of an Indian strategy that had clearly emerged by the late 1990s. India's strategic orientation, though it accepts the possibility of renewed tensions between China and India, will not necessarily lead to renewed competition between the two.

China, on the other hand, will continue to view India as a significant regional power but a decidedly second-tier global power. This perception of India as a developing but fundamentally constrained power with an unstable democracy and irresolvable socioreligious cleavages is one source of the natural rivalry between India and China. That perception will not recede for many years. China will continue to frame its relations with India in terms of its desire to have good relations with all its neighbors, including expanding economic relations and cooperation on issues of mutual interest. This stance ironically fuels Indian suspicions, because China's relations with Pakistan have obviously undermined Indian security in the past. The improvement in Sino-Indian relations in the 1990s, in fact, came with the tacit acceptance that India would not make China's relations with Pakistan an issue or an obstacle to better Sino-Indian relations.

This seemingly benign scenario of continued quiet competition nevertheless requires a certain degree of caution. Numerous important and unresolved issues will loom in the background of Sino-Indian relations and fuel their natural rivalry. Many of these have been mentioned in this chapter and discussed in greater detail by other contributors to this volume. They include the question of China's transfers of nuclear and missile technology to Pakistan, the long-standing border dispute, and uncertainties regarding nuclear weapon programs. Any of these issues could push Sino-Indian relations into overtly competitive or even hostile stances. They will remain in the background because Chinese and Indian leaders lack the incentives and the political will to address these problem areas. As a result, these leaders will dodge the difficult issues in the relationship. They will postpone any resolution of these issues for the next generation, and they will make sure that these problems do not become sources of open rivalry and disputes. An Indian security official offered a revealing assessment that nicely sums up the conclusion here regarding the future of Sino-Indian relations: "There will always be a sense of rivalry between China and India. It hasn't gone away regardless of how many centuries we go back. But in ten to fifteen years this rivalry will not degenerate into anything. We don't want it, and they don't want it."[28]

Notes

1. Ashley J. Tellis, "India's Emerging Nuclear Doctrine: Exemplifying Lessons of the Nuclear Revolution," *NBR Analysis* 12, no. 2 (May 2001): 68–69.
2. See, for example, Garver's discussion of circumstances under which China's no-first-use pledges might break down. John W. Garver, *Protracted Contest: Sino-Indian Rivalry in the Twentieth Century* (Seattle: University of Washington Press, 2001), 340.
3. Tellis, "India's Emerging Nuclear Doctrine," 31.
4. Garver, *Protracted Contest,* 353–64.
5. Ashley J. Tellis, *India's Emerging Nuclear Posture: Between Recessed Deterrent and Ready Arsenal* (Santa Monica, Calif.: RAND, 2001).
6. Alastair Iain Johnston, "China's New 'Old Thinking': The Concept of Limited Deterrence," *International Security* 20, no. 3 (Winter 1995–96): 5–42.
7. Such concerns were voiced in a U.S. National Intelligence Estimate during the Clinton administration, in which the authors noted how American NMD could lead to a nuclear arms race in East and South Asia. See Judith Miller and James Risen, "A Nuclear War Feared Possible over Kashmir," *New York Times,* 8 August 2000 (accessed via LexisNexis Academic).
8. Pamela Constable, "Missile Defense Plan Is Uniting U.S., India; Americans Hint at Possibly Lifting Sanctions," *Washington Post,* 20 May 2001, A21.
9. John Pomfret, "China Threatens Arms Control Collapse," *Washington Post,* 14 July 2000, A1.
10. Conversations with foreign policy analysts and advisors in Beijing and Shanghai, July 2001.
11. Rajan Menon, "Russia," in *Strategic Asia 2001–02: Power and Purpose,* ed. Richard J. Ellings and Aaron L. Friedberg (Seattle: National Bureau of Asian Research, 2001), 206.
12. Garver, *Protracted Contest,* 361–64; Mohan Malik, "Nuclear Proliferation in Asia: The China Factor," *Australian Journal of International Affairs* 53, no. 1 (1999): 31–41.

13. Malik, "Nuclear Proliferation in Asia," 39–40.

14. C. Raja Mohan, "PM Wants Indo-U.S. Ties on an Equal Footing," *Hindu,* 29 September 1998 (accessed via LexisNexis Academic).

15. Kanti Bajpai, "India-U.S. Foreign Policy Concerns: Cooperation and Conflict," in *Engaging India: U.S. Strategic Relations with the World's Largest Democracy,* ed. Gary K. Bertsch, Seema Gahlaut, and Anupam Srivastava (New York and London: Routledge, 1999), 209.

16. Interview, New Delhi, 18 July 2001.

17. Workshop commentator, New Delhi, 16 July 2001.

18. Michael D. Swaine and Ashley J. Tellis, *Interpreting China's Grand Strategy: Past, Present, and Future* (Washington, D.C.: RAND, 2000), 97–150.

19. Brahma Chellaney, "India's Nuclear Planning, Force Structure, Doctrine and Arms Control Posture," *Australian Journal of International Affairs* 53, no. 1 (1999): 68.

20. Briefing from official source, Beijing, 11 July 2001.

21. "India: Export Growth Dips Due to Global Economic Slowdown," *Hindu,* 3 August 2001 (accessed via LexisNexis Academic).

22. Allen T. Cheng, "Code Red," *Asiaweek,* 27 July 2001, available at www.asiaweek.com/asiaweek/technology/article/0,8707,168248,00.html.

23. Ibid.

24. Ming Zhang, *China's Changing Nuclear Posture: Reactions to the South Asian Nuclear Tests* (Washington D.C.: Carnegie Endowment for International Peace, 1999), 28–30.

25. "India: Tri-service Integrated Command in Place," *Hindu,* 30 September 2001 (accessed via LexisNexis Academic).

26. David Bachman makes a similar prediction. See David Bachman, "China's Democratization: What Difference Would It Make for U.S.-China Relations?" in *What if China Doesn't Democratize? Implications for War and Peace,* ed. Edward Friedman and Barrett L. McCormick (Armonk N.Y.: M.E. Sharpe, 2000), 195–223.

27. Barry Bearak, "Lama's Escape Inflames Buddhist Rivalry," *New York Times,* 3 February 2000 (accesed via LexisNexis Academic).

28. Interview, New Delhi, 18 July 2001.

Part III

Implications for the United States

10

The Evolution of the Strategic Triangle: China, India, and the United States

Harry Harding

The concept of a strategic triangle has become familiar to analysts of international affairs. It refers to a situation in which three major powers are sufficiently important to each other that a change in the relationship between any two of them has a significant impact on the interests of the third. The greater that impact, actual or potential, the greater is the significance of the triangular relationship.

During the Cold War, the most important strategic triangle was the relationship among the Soviet Union, the United States, and China. The collapse of the alliance between Moscow and Beijing in the late 1950s and 1960s caused a fundamental change in the relations among these three nations. At first, Beijing adopted a "dual adversary" policy toward both superpowers, but it eventually concluded that the threat from the Soviet Union was too great to confront alone. The Nixon administration was quick to see that an accommodation between the United States and China would change the global balance of power decisively in favor of the United States.

Richard Nixon's initial objective was to use rapprochement with China to promote détente with Moscow so that, in Henry Kissinger's memorable phrase, the United States could "drink its vodka and have its maotai too." Later, Moscow's invasion of Afghanistan and the Vietnamese intervention in Cambodia brought the United States and China even closer. A triangle that had once featured a Sino-Soviet alliance against the United States had evolved into a Sino-American alignment to contain the Soviet Union.

In the post–Cold War era, other triangular relationships have emerged. In Asia, the most familiar is that among China, Japan, and the United States. The future shape of that triangle remains uncertain. Will it be a concert of powers, in which the three great nations share enough common values and common interests to work together to promote peace and prosperity in the Asia-Pacific region? Will it be a firm alliance of two against one—an alignment in which the United States and Japan work together to contain the expansion of Chinese power? Will it be a balance of power, in which Japan tries to mediate a "new Cold War" between China and the United States? Conversely, will the United States attempt to mediate an emerging rivalry between China and Japan in Asia? Or will the triangle be highly fluid, with each pair of countries working together on some issues, but finding themselves in disagreement on others, without forming any firm or enduring alignment?

These examples suggest the fascinating complexity of triangular relationships in international affairs. Triangles can take many forms, depending on the relative power and interests of the three countries involved: all working together, two-against-one, all-against-all, one mediating the conflict between the other two, and several other possibilities. Some triangular patterns are more stable than others. Alliances of two-against-one can be fairly enduring. So can concerts of powers, linking all three nations together in common endeavors. By contrast, the all-against-all pattern is unstable, since there will be great incentives for two to ally against the third, at least temporarily. And perhaps the most unstable of all is the so-called "romantic triangle," in which one player tries to have positive relations with two rivals, benefiting from their jealousy.

Although the most familiar "strategic triangles" in the contemporary era have been the Sino-Soviet-American triangle of the 1970s and 1980s and the Sino-Japanese-American triangle of the 1990s and today, another triangle deserves our attention: that among China, India, and the United States. This chapter explores the dynamics of that triangle—past, present, and future. Its principal conclusions can be simply stated:

- The three countries have always formed a strategic triangle, ever since India became independent, China became communist, and America decided to become a permanent player in the Asian balance of power—all in the late 1940s. From that time onward, each country's policy toward one has to some degree been influenced by its relations with the other.
- However, the triangle was, until recently, a secondary pattern in international affairs, largely because of the relative weakness of India. Neither China nor the United States has usually seen India as a card that can be effectively played against the other. Both Washington and Beijing have seen other countries—especially the Soviet Union and Japan—as far more central to their security.
- Nor has the triangle ever crystallized into a firm alignment of two against one. Although there were tendencies toward an alignment of India and the United States against China in the early 1960s, and an alignment of China and the United States against India in the mid-1970s, in no case has such an alignment ever formed for long. Instead, the relationship among the three has been relatively fluid.
- With the rise of Chinese and Indian power in the twenty-first century, the U.S.-China-India triangle will likely become more important. All three countries will become increasingly aware of the security challenges and opportunities that the others may present. They will therefore be more concerned about the contours of the triangular relationship and will seek to mold the triangle into patterns that favor their interests.
- It is not yet clear what form the U.S.-China-India triangle will take in the coming years. Some analysts speculate about a U.S.-India alignment against a rising China; others about a China-India alignment about an overbearing America; still others about a growing community of interests among the three. While none of these three outcomes can be ruled out, the most likely pattern for the foreseeable future is a complex and shifting triangular relationship in which the three countries share common and divergent interests. Each country will try to form partnerships with the others where their interests coincide, mobilize the support of one against unacceptable initiatives by the other, and prevent the other two from forming an alignment against it.

The Triangle during the Cold War

A review of the triangular relationship among China, India, and the United States during the Cold War reveals the ways in which the three defined their bilateral relationships with an eye to the other. It also shows that the linkages among the three changed relatively frequently, without ever leading to enduring alignments of any two against the other.[1]

The Early and Mid-1950s: A Sino-Indian Alignment against the United States?

More than any subsequent period, the early years of the Cold War saw a reasonably close relationship between India and China, and a strained or hostile relationship between the two of them and the United States. In large part, this reflected the common anticolonial heritage of the two countries, as well as their common desire to avoid an antagonistic relationship.

Of the two, India played the more active role in promoting a partnership between India and China. From the beginning, Prime Minister Jawaharlal Nehru tried to show his sympathy toward China as a fellow Asian nation, newly freed from imperial rule, that sought to play an independent role on the international stage. To that end, India attempted to serve as a mediator between Beijing and Washington during the early months of the Korean War, conveying Chinese warnings against an American invasion of the North. New Delhi recognized Beijing as the new government of China in 1949, broke relations with the Nationalists on Taiwan, supported UN membership for the People's Republic of China, opposed the U.S. intervention in the Taiwan Strait in 1950, and refused to sign the peace treaty with Japan in 1951.

India also sought to accommodate China on crucial bilateral issues. Most important, in the Sino-Indian treaty of 1954 New Delhi accepted Chinese sovereignty over Tibet and renounced any special privileges in Tibet that it might have claimed to have inherited from the British. John Garver has described this strategy of accommodating China on Tibet and supporting Beijing internationally as a deliberate policy of appeasement, so as to minimize any potential Chinese threat to India and to maximize India's influence in international affairs.[2]

For a time, China responded sympathetically to the Indian overtures. For the first seven or eight years of communist rule, faced with the containment policy of the United States abroad and with the challenge of consolidating power at home, Beijing adopted a relatively moderate course in its foreign policy. In addition to forging alliances with the communist bloc, it promoted friendly ties with newly independent countries in the developing world such as India. Although the governments of these countries were not communist, they were seen as sharing a common anticolonial heritage with China, and therefore as potential partners in a "united front" against the West.

For its part, the United States looked with disfavor on both China and India during the early 1950s, although it was far more hostile to the former than the latter. Washington saw China as its principal adversary in Asia—more so than the Soviet Union, which at this point had few strategic resources in the region. This perception was validated in American eyes when China intervened in the Korean War in late 1950, supported the Viet Minh in their struggle against the French in the early 1950s, and attacked offshore islands controlled by Taiwan in 1954–55. The United States responded by creating a network of alliances and bases in the Western Pacific—with Japan, South Korea, the Philippines, Thailand, Australia, and New Zealand—that were aimed at containing the rise of Chinese power.

And although the United States did not see India as an adversary, its policy of neutrality and nonalignment during the Cold War was viewed, at least by Secretary of State John Foster Dulles, as nothing short of immoral. Moreover, in its enthusiasm for creating security relationships to contain China and the Soviet Union, the United States established an alliance with India's archrival, Pakistan, and sold arms to that country. It also supported Pakistan's position on Kashmir after the partition of that region in the 1947 war, favoring a plebiscite in all of Kashmir, including the part controlled by India. Thus, the United States adopted positions on issues crucial to Indian security that New Delhi could reasonably see as antagonistic.

All of this might have encouraged New Delhi and Beijing to find common cause against the United States, and there was indeed a brief period of India-China solidarity in the mid-1950s. Bilaterally, this era of good feeling was embodied in the slogan "Hindi-Chini bhai-bhai" ("Indians and Chinese are brothers") and in the exchange of high-level visits by Indian and Chinese leaders. Multilaterally, it was reflected in their common efforts to mobilize the newly independent nations of the Third World into a nonaligned force in international affairs, through such avenues as the Bandung Conference of 1955.

However, this partnership between India and China did not crystallize into an anti-American alignment. For one thing, despite the American alliance with Pakistan and Washington's support for Pakistan's position on

Kashmir, the United States did not allow India-U.S. relations to degenerate into hostility. Dulles's contempt for India's neutrality was not shared by President Dwight D. Eisenhower, who perceived its advantages. India's policy of nonalignment deprived the Soviet Union of an ally, in contrast to China, which, despite Beijing's independent leanings, was formally allied with Moscow. At the same time, India's neutral position did not place any particular strategic burden on the United States, unlike America's alliances with smaller countries in Asia, such as South Vietnam and Taiwan, which required security commitments and military assistance. The Eisenhower administration therefore never wrote India off altogether. Indeed, it provided significant economic aid to India throughout the 1950s.

In addition, the positive bilateral relationship between India and China was neither close nor enduring. Beijing always saw noncommunist nations like India as wavering and unreliable partners in a united front against the West. In part, this reflected a classic Marxist class analysis of international affairs: the leaders of noncommunist nations in the Third World represented the "national bourgeoisie," with whom cooperation could only be undertaken on a tactical and temporary basis. When Mao Zedong's policy toward his own national bourgeoisie changed in the mid-1950s with the nationalization of Chinese industry and commerce, it was almost inevitable that Chinese foreign policy would change accordingly.

Moreover, even if Beijing had eschewed an ideological approach to its foreign policy, there were clear differences in national interest between India and China. Genuinely committed to nonalignment, India was reluctant to be drawn into an anti-Western partnership with China—a country that, after all, was still allied with the Soviet Union. Moreover, there was a structural rivalry between the two, in that both sought to play the leadership role with regard to the newly independent nations of Asia. And by the middle of the 1950s, New Delhi had become aware that, despite its own accommodating attitude toward China's position in Tibet, Beijing maintained extensive territorial claims along the India-China border. This, too, soon became a major irritant in their bilateral relations.

In short, despite the possibility that the two great developing states of Asia would find common ground against the West, the triangular relationship among India, the United States, and China never culminated in an alignment of two against one in the early 1950s. American policy toward India was never so hostile, nor the mutual trust between China and India sufficiently great, to permit India and China to forge a partnership against the United States.

The Late 1950s and 1960s: An India-U.S. Alignment against China?

Any possibility of an alignment of India and China against the United States was eliminated by the outbreak of open hostility between the two countries over the situation along their common border. In 1959, and again in 1962, the territorial dispute between China and India exploded into war. The border war of 1959 occurred in the context of the Chinese imposition of communist policies in Tibet, the flight of the Dalai Lama out of Tibet, and the establishment of his Tibetan government-in-exile in India. In 1962, an even larger war saw the Chinese conquest of the entire North East Frontier area of India, the humiliation of the Indian army charged with defending it, and then unilateral Chinese withdrawal to what Beijing considered to have been the line of control before the war began.

The dramatic deterioration of Sino-Indian relations into open conflict, together with the continued strategic confrontation between China and the United States, might have been expected to drive India and the United States together. And, indeed, the two countries considered a major redefinition of their relations in the late 1950s and early 1960s. In 1959, Eisenhower was the first sitting American president to visit India, where he endorsed New Delhi's position on border issues. In 1962, at the height of the second Sino-Indian border war, President John F. Kennedy sent the U.S. Navy into the Bay of Bengal to show American support for India, and Nehru appealed to the United States for military aid. American economic aid to India was increased to unprecedented levels.

However, even the China-India border conflict was not enough to forge a close alignment between India and the United States. For one thing, the 1962 war came quickly to an end and was followed by a unilateral Chinese withdrawal from the territory in northeast India that it had successfully invaded. With the immediate Chinese threat to Indian security reduced, India had a less immediate need for a strategic relationship with the United States. And the Americans maintained their previous conclusion that an alliance with India would present far more costs and risks to the United States than benefits.

Moreover, the American alliance with Pakistan remained an obstacle to a closer U.S.-India relationship. Although a few American officials wanted to "ditch Pakistan" and form a new alignment with India, the Kennedy and Johnson administrations were unwilling to do so.[3] Not only was there sympathy for Pakistan as a faithful ally of the United States—an image assiduously cultivated by Pakistani leaders—but there was also an emerging concern that, if the United States were to abandon Pakistan, it would drive Pakistan further into the arms of China, which was keen to find a counterweight against its rival in India. Thus, despite its flirtation with New Delhi over the possibility of a security relationship with India, the United States reserved its most sophisticated arms for Pakistan, not for India; and it continued to support the Pakistani position on Kashmir, not the Indian.

The U.S. alliance with Pakistan was sorely tested by the India-Pakistan war of 1965, given that the conflict began with Pakistani infiltration into Indian-controlled Kashmir. Despite its alliance with Pakistan, the United States took a neutral position in that conflict and suspended U.S. arms sales to both countries. However, this was not enough to mollify India. New Delhi had hoped that what it regarded as clear evidence of Pakistani aggression would produce an even more favorable American reaction—an end to the military alliance with Pakistan, or at least a modification of the American position on Kashmir. The even-handed American response to the war, in the context of its continued alliance with Pakistan, could not bring the United States that much closer to India.

There were other barriers to a significant breakthrough in India-U.S. relations during this period. One was the Indian seizure of Goa, the Portuguese colony along the west coast of India that was the last outpost of Western colonialism on the subcontinent. This not only was an assault on the interests of one of America's NATO allies, but it also exacerbated concerns that India was trying to establish hegemony over South Asia. This provided a further rationale for the United States to maintain, rather than terminate, its alliance with Pakistan.

Nor did India accommodate the American positions on other major international issues. New Delhi not only failed to support the American intervention in Vietnam but also became one of its most vocal critics. India opposed the nuclear Nonproliferation Treaty as an attempt by the Soviet Union and the United States to preserve their nuclear monopoly and prevent countries like India from acquiring equal status as nuclear powers. In doing so, India managed to oppose, at one and the same time, American initiatives to contain communism and to promote détente with the Soviet Union.

Finally, Washington and New Delhi had serious disputes over Indian domestic policy. Even as the United States increased its economic assistance to India in the 1960s, the Johnson administration simultaneously imposed far more extensive and intrusive conditions on that aid than had any of its predecessors. Lyndon B. Johnson attempted to micromanage

India's agricultural policy and forced India to accept a devaluation of its currency. Whatever the wisdom of the American position on these issues, it caused widespread resentment in India.

Thus, the Sino-Indian border conflict did not drive India into the arms of the United States. The United States still did not see India as a effective counterweight against China, but rather as a potential drain on American strategic resources. The United States could rely on its alliances with Japan, South Korea, Australia, New Zealand, and the members of the Southeast Asian Treaty Organization (SEATO); it did not need India to contain China. Unlike America's allies, India continued to take contrary positions on crucial international issues, such as Vietnam and nonproliferation. And a strategic alignment with India might imply an American commitment to Indian security against China that the United States would not want to fulfill.

Nor could India count on the United States as a reliable strategic partner. The American alliance with Pakistan meant that, no matter how hostile U.S.-China relations became, the United States could not be expected to provide its most advanced arms to India, or to significantly change its position in the India-Pakistan rivalry. That, in turn, implied that Washington would be constrained in its ability to provide India with unstinting support in a confrontation with China. Moreover, India's willingness to form a security partnership with the United States was still limited by the Nehruvian commitment to nonalignment in international affairs.

The 1970s: A Sino-American Alignment against India?

The 1970s were a period of significant realignment in international affairs—the most significant since the emergence of confrontation between the United States and the Soviet Union after the end of World War II. The underlying contradiction between the two superpowers remained unresolved, and in that sense the basic Cold War structure remained intact. But the alignments within each bloc underwent significant change.

First, the shift in relative power between the United States and the USSR, with the rise of Soviet military power in Asia and the weakening of the U.S. position due to the Vietnam War, encouraged a fundamental shift in China's position, from the dual adversary policy of the 1960s toward an alignment with the United States. This dramatic change in China's position in the original "strategic triangle" was highlighted by the visits that first Henry Kissinger and then Richard Nixon made to Beijing in 1971 and 1972.

As Sino-Soviet relations deteriorated and Sino-American relations improved, the Soviet Union identified India as a key strategic partner. The Soviet Union did not have other reliable allies in Asia on which it could count in a confrontation with either China or the United States. The United States had a powerful network of alliances in the region; the Soviet Union had only Mongolia, for at this point North Vietnam and North Korea were at best neutral in the Sino-Soviet split. Thus, Moscow needed New Delhi far more than Washington ever had. And, unencumbered by a strategic relationship with any of India's neighbors comparable to the U.S. alliance with Pakistan, it was willing to provide India with advanced military equipment to a degree the United States had not been.

India, under Indira Gandhi, was prepared to reciprocate, signing a treaty of peace and friendship with the Soviet Union in 1971, just after the Kissinger visit to China. This was part of a far broader redefinition of Indian foreign policy that was taking place at the same time. Not only was Mrs. Gandhi now willing to abandon what was now regarded as the overly idealistic principle of nonalignment in foreign affairs. She was also willing to assert and pursue the realist objective of attaining a dominant position in the balance of power in the South Asian region.

As India and the Soviet Union moved into a close alignment, the United States reaffirmed its alliance with Pakistan, both as a counterweight against Moscow's efforts to increase its position in South Asia and as a barrier to Indian efforts to achieve dominance in that region. By the mid-1970s, the United States was willing to resume the arms sales to Pakistan that it had suspended during the Indo-Pakistani war of 1965. Moreover, the United States was now prepared to welcome Pakistan's growing military ties with China, which Beijing carefully justified not just as counterbalancing India, but also as containing the expansion of Soviet influence in Central Asia. It was in this context that China began to support Pakistan's nuclear weapon program.[4]

As U.S.-Pakistani ties improved, U.S. relations with India deteriorated further. From the American perspective, the India-Soviet treaty of 1971 ended any Indian pretense at nonalignment and placed New Delhi fully in the Soviet camp. The internal state of emergency declared by Prime Minister Indira Gandhi in 1975 eliminated any lingering sense that India and the United States were bound together by a shared commitment to democracy. India's first nuclear tests in 1974, although nominally tests of a "peaceful nuclear explosive," showed that New Delhi not only opposed the spirit of the nonproliferation treaty but was willing to act in defiance of its terms.

The strained personal relations between Mrs. Gandhi and Richard Nixon only exacerbated the worsening of U.S.-Indian ties.

Together, these developments added up to a potential confrontation between U.S.-China-Pakistan alignment, on the one hand, and an India-USSR alignment, on the other. This tendency toward polarization appeared first during the third India-Pakistan war, that of 1971, in which India supported the secession of East Pakistan and the establishment of the independent state of Bangladesh. China and the United States could do little to prevent the dismemberment of Pakistan—indeed, China rejected a direct request from Pakistan that it launch a diversionary action along the Sino-Indian border, even though the United States sent an aircraft carrier battle group into the Bay of Bengal in a fruitless display of force. But they could, and did, send clear signals that they would jointly oppose a further Indian assault on West Pakistan. Later in the decade, the United States, China, and Pakistan all worked together to oppose the Soviet intervention in Afghanistan, an action that New Delhi was initially careful not to oppose.

Even here, however, the trends never crystallized into two antagonistic alignments. Washington realized, in the 1970s as in the early 1950s, that India was simply too important for the United States to abandon. Indeed, President Jimmy Carter's national security adviser, Zbigniew Brzezinski, saw India as one of the major emerging regional powers (along with countries such as Nigeria and Brazil) with which the United States should have closer relations. At the same time, Washington showed increasing concern about the military cooperation between China and Pakistan, especially as it involved not just the transfer of conventional weapons, but also Chinese assistance in building nuclear weapons and strategic missile systems.

Conversely, with the end of the Maoist era and the inauguration of economic reform, China adopted a more omnidirectional foreign policy, which featured an attempt to reduce tensions with India and the Soviet Union even while maintaining a close political and strategic relationship with Pakistan. In 1978, China and India resumed high-level diplomatic dialogue for the first time since the border war; by 1982, China had announced an "independent foreign policy," implying that it would no longer seek to align with the United States against the Soviet Union.

In short, although India formed and maintained a close security relationship with the Soviet Union, involving the import of significant quantities of arms from Moscow, the other bilateral relationships remained more complex. Both Washington and Beijing kept their channels of communication with India open; neither desired a complete break with New Delhi.

The Triangle after the Cold War

As the Cold War wound down and then came to an end, the triangular relationship among China, India, and the United States remained fluid. At various times, there has been speculation about the possibility of an alignment of two of them against the third. As during the Cold War, each of the logically possible alignments seemed conceivable at one point or another: the United States and China against India; India and the United States against China; and even China and India against the United States.

However, none of those alignments has ever been consummated. Instead, all three countries have worked toward more cooperative relationships with each other, although sometimes with interruptions and always within limits. China has sought better relations with India, first to break up any possible encirclement by the Soviet Union and more recently to prevent India from forging a close relationship with the United States. As the Soviet Union weakened and then collapsed, India had to restructure its own international relationships, reducing tensions with China and building ties with the United States. And the United States increasingly sees India, as well as China, as a major Asian power with whom cooperative ties would be beneficial. Let us consider each of these bilateral relationships, and then turn to the possibility of an alignment of any two of the countries against the third.

The Bilateral Relationships among the Three

As just noted, there have been significant improvements in China-India relations over the last fifteen years, beginning with Prime Minister Rajiv Gandhi's visit to China in 1988. Both countries have seen the advantage of reducing tensions and building bilateral political and economic ties, and have succeeded in doing so to some degree. For example, they have expanded their economic relationship, albeit from a very low base and despite growing concerns in India that China will benefit disproportionately from its ability to penetrate India's domestic market with low-cost consumer goods. As Sumit Ganguly has shown in chapter 4 of this volume, they have installed confidence-building measures along their border and have made some small progress in demarcating the line of control in the middle sector, although they have not made any progress toward settling the underlying territorial disputes. Finally, there has been some change in China's stand on Kashmir, from its earlier support for Pakistan's position to a more neutral stance.

These limited improvements in bilateral India-China relations have been accompanied, however, by an increasing sense of rivalry on the broader regional stage. However much the Chinese may have distanced themselves from Pakistan on the issue of Kashmir, they have not abandoned their broader military and political relationship with Islamabad, which Beijing describes as an "all-weather friendship." Furthermore, many Indians believe that China has simultaneously been trying to build up its strategic ties with Myanmar and more recently with Bangladesh. Indian analysts have concluded that China is thereby aiming to counterbalance India on two fronts, both east and west, rather than just one. This, in turn, has been seen as part of a broader Chinese strategy of trying to tie India down in South Asia and to prevent it from playing a more active role in either Southeast Asia or Asia more generally, so that China could become the leading power in the region.

Even more dramatic changes have occurred in U.S.-India relations. The economic relationship between the two countries has developed rapidly. The size of the Indian economy has attracted growing interest on the part of American business, facilitated by the increasing number of Indian entrepreneurs, including many in high-tech sectors, now resident in the United States. India has engaged in a gradual program of economic reform, in part to keep up with the rapid economic growth of China. India's increasing openness to foreign trade and investment has also facilitated the expansion of economic ties with the United States.

There has also been a notable expansion of political and security ties between the United States and India. With the collapse of the Soviet Union, India sought to establish warmer political relations with Washington, even though it continued to buy the bulk of its imported arms from Russia. At the same time, the United States was eager to gain Indian cooperation for its deployments in the Indian Ocean and in the Persian Gulf. Both sides saw the advantage in expanding their security relationship in the context of the rise of Chinese economic and military power. This closer relationship was symbolized by the exchange of visits between U.S. President Bill Clinton and Indian Prime Minister Atal Behari Vajpayee in 2000, during which the two leaders spoke of forming a "natural partnership" and a "qualitatively new relationship." The two countries have subsequently expanded their military cooperation to include joint exercises, arms sales, and technology transfers.

At the same time as it was developing its new relationship with India, the United States was attenuating somewhat its ties with Pakistan. No longer was the United States constrained in this regard by a need to use Pakistan as a vehicle for improving relations with China, as had been the case in the early 1970s, or for containing Soviet expansion into Central Asia later in the decade. In 1990, the first Bush administration halted American arms sales to Pakistan on the grounds that it could no longer certify that Pakistan had not developed nuclear weapons. And throughout the 1990s, Washington showed increasing concern about Pakistan's nuclear weapon and missile programs, its increasingly Islamist orientation, and its refusal to support the American presence in the Persian Gulf. Although Washington did not engineer the decline in U.S.-Pakistani relations in order to improve its ties with India, the growing distance between the two countries certainly facilitated the improvement of U.S.-Indian relations. After all, India had always regarded the U.S.-Pakistani alliance as a major deterrent to closer security relations with the United States.

The terrorist attacks of September 11, 2001, halted the erosion in U.S.-Pakistani ties. Pakistan's willingness to cooperate with the United States in the war against the Taliban regime in Afghanistan, and in attempting to suppress Al Qaeda operations in Pakistani territory, revitalized the military alliance between the two countries. The United States promptly removed the sanctions that it had imposed against Pakistan's nuclear weapon program, despite some evidence that Pakistan was continuing to cooperate with North Korea in the development of nuclear weapons and the missile systems that could deliver them. This resurgence of the U.S.-Pakistan relationship has worried and irritated Indians, but does not seem to have obstructed the improvement of U.S.-Indian security ties. This is largely because the U.S.-Pakistan alliance no longer places clear limits on the level of American security cooperation with India, as had been the case in the past.

Of the three sides of the triangle, the U.S.-China relationship has been the most turbulent, at least since the Tiananmen Square incident of 1989. For much of the 1990s, Americans were preoccupied with violations of human rights in China and with China's growing trade surplus with the United States. Later in the decade, they also became concerned about the growth of China's military power and the possibility that it might be used to threaten Taiwan or even challenge the preeminent American position in the

Western Pacific. The Chinese, too, had their own apprehensions: that Taiwan was drifting way from unification with China and toward more formal independence; that Americans were sympathetic to Taiwanese independence; and that more generally the United States sought to obstruct the rise of Chinese national power through a policy that some Chinese regarded as the containment, subversion, and fragmentation of their country. The emergence of skepticism and mistrust in both countries became apparent in the angry Chinese response to the accidental American bombing of the Chinese embassy in Belgrade in 1999 and in the equally angry American response to the collision between a U.S. Navy surveillance plane and a Chinese fighter jet in 2001.

However, both the Chinese and American governments have sought to maintain a stable relationship. Despite the Clinton administration's early concern about human rights in China, and the second Bush administration's early apprehension about China's emergence as a "strategic competitor" and possible strategic rival of the United States, both administrations ultimately saw the desirability of working toward a cooperative relationship with Beijing. Similarly, impressed by the preeminent American position both globally and regionally, convinced of the need for access to the American market, and preoccupied with maintaining domestic stability, Beijing reached the same conclusion. The growing economic ties between the two countries have increased both governments' incentive to maintain stable political relations. And the terrorist attacks of September 11 and the North Korean nuclear weapon program have, at least so far, been powerful common interests bringing Washington and Beijing closer together.

The Shape of the Triangle

The overall pattern of the 1980s and 1990s, then, has involved dramatic improvements in U.S.-India ties, a reduction of tension in bilateral India-China relations, and a U.S.-China relationship that, although turbulent, remains stable. This has worked against the creation of a firm alignment of any two of these three countries against the third. Although each conceivable alignment has been discussed, and one of them was formed briefly, as yet none of them has become a lasting feature of the strategic triangle.

Early in the post–Cold War era, when U.S.-China relations were still suffering from the aftermath of the Tiananmen Square incident and before U.S.-Indian relations had improved, India and China discussed the possibility of working together to resist the consolidation of American global hegemony, possibly as part of a broader China-India-Russia alignment (as was suggested in 1999 by Russian Foreign Minister Yevgeny Primakov). Chinese and Indian leaders expressed general agreement on the desirability of new international political and economic orders, organized around the concepts of promoting multipolarity, opposing hegemony, and promoting the rights of developing countries.[5]

But the prospective alignment of China and India as two developing countries suffered the same fate in the 1990s as it had in the 1950s. The common interests in a multipolar world were not sufficient to overcome their bilateral problems or their sense of rivalry in Asia. Nor, at the end of the day, was either country willing to declare itself in opposition to the United States, on whose markets and technology both depended.

Another possible alignment, and one that formed briefly in the late 1990s, was between the United States and China against India. As Susan Shirk shows in chapter 3, the Indian nuclear tests of 1998 came at a time when both Washington and Beijing were looking for a new strategic rationale for their relationship, to replace the common opposition to Soviet expansion that had brought them together in the 1970s. At that time transnational issues, such as terrorism, did not seem as compelling as they would only a few years later. Instead, the two countries seized upon their common concern with India's nuclear weapon program—and the subsequent Pakistani weapons tests—as a useful, and perhaps necessary, way of overcoming their differences over Taiwan, human rights, and trade. The joint U.S.-China statement on South Asia, issued at the time of the Clinton visit to Beijing in June 1998, symbolized this apparent alignment.

However, Beijing's and Washington's continuing interest in improving their respective ties with New Delhi ultimately overwhelmed their interest in using the South Asian nuclear tests as a way of solidifying their ties with each other. Both China and the United States soon returned to more normal relationships with India, lifting most economic sanctions, muting their criticism of India's nuclear program, and restoring normal diplomatic dialogue with New Delhi.

Finally, the third possible alignment has been that of the United States and India against a rising China. This possibility was implied by Indian Prime Minister Vajpayee in the late 1990s and early 2000s, when he invoked the security threat from China as the principal rationale for India's nuclear weapon tests of 1998 and appealed for American understanding, if not support, for India's actions. As Steven Hoffmann has noted in chapter 2, conservative Indian security analysts went further, saying that the United

States also faced a growing security threat from Beijing, and that New Delhi and Washington should work together to counter it. Some American analysts have also been attracted by the idea of bringing India into a multilateral alignment aimed at containing China.[6]

So far, however, neither India nor the United States has been willing to create such an overtly anti-Chinese alignment. Neither wants to sacrifice the improvements in their bilateral relationships with China that have occurred over the last decade. Neither wants to run the risks that a confrontational relationship with Beijing would entail. Neither is so immediately threatened by the rise of Chinese power as to see the need for a strategic partnership to counter it. Although an Indian-American alignment against China remains a possibility and might emerge in response to aggressive Chinese behavior in Asia, it is not the preference of either country. Both India and the United States are eager to develop their strategic relationship, but not to declare China to be their common adversary.

Looking Ahead

For the last fifty years, in short, India-China relations have never been close. The main pattern has been Sino-Indian rivalry, with the tensions between them rising and falling: very high in the late 1950s and early 1960s as a result of the Tibetan uprising and the border war; quite high again in the 1970s, when India assisted the dismemberment of China's ally, Pakistan; and relatively low in the 1980s and 1990s, as a result of the moderation of Chinese foreign policy in the reform era and India's desire for reduced tensions as the Soviet Union crumbled and fell. The two countries have occasionally sought to identify their common interest, as developing countries, in opposing the hegemony of the United States and in promoting a more equitable international order. But that apparent common interest has never brought the two close together for long.

However, the Sino-Indian rivalry has not brought the United States into a clear alignment with one against the other in the way that the collapse of Sino-Soviet relations in the 1960s ultimately brought about a China-U.S. alignment against Moscow. An American partnership with one country against the other appeared most conceivable at four points in time: a U.S.-India alignment against China in the early 1960s and again in early in the 2000s, and a U.S.-China alignment against India in the 1970s and again late in the 1990s. But none of these incipient alignments has proved lasting.

Each of the repeated failures of the U.S.-China-India triangle to result in an alignment of two against one has obviously had its own particular explanation. But there are some important common denominators as well. Perhaps most important, from the American perspective, India was never a significant enough problem to warrant an alignment with China against it; nor was India ever a powerful enough partner to warrant a U.S.-India alignment against China. This reflected a long-standing asymmetry in American perceptions of India and China. The United States saw China as a global power, but viewed India as a subregional actor. In Washington's eyes, China was the counterpart of the Soviet Union in a global strategic triangle, whereas India was the counterpart of Pakistan in the smaller strategic setting of South Asia. In some ways, the larger strategic triangle existed but the United States did not perceive it.

But what about the future? The analysis in this volume suggests that that the triangular relationship may become more salient in the coming decades as the national power of India and China increases and as South Asia and East Asia are gradually integrated into a single region. However, the relationship among the three powers will probably remain fluid, without ever crystallizing into an enduring alignment of two against one.

India and China as Rising Powers

Both India and China are rising powers, aiming to enlarge their influence both regionally and globally. But, as T. N. Srinivasan shows in chapter 7, each faces major domestic uncertainties that may limit its ability to achieve the major-power status it seeks.

India has deep ethnic, linguistic, caste, and regional cleavages. The country has found it difficult to break decisively away from its socialist legacy in economic policy and to find more effective ways of mobilizing its vast human and material resources to build a more advanced economy. And yet India has the advantage of effective political institutions, including a free press, a vibrant civil society, the rule of law, and strong democratic traditions. None of these institutions is perfect, and some Indians regard them as obstacles to the undertaking of painful economic reforms. But they provide India with a safety valve so that the country can absorb and respond to the contradictions of a society in flux.

China's situation is in some ways the opposite of India's. China has made far more impressive progress than India in renouncing many of its past economic policies, adopting market-oriented, outward-looking reforms, and creating a steadily growing place for private ownership. But China's political institutions have lagged behind the pace of economic change. Despite some progress toward political reform, Chinese citizens do not enjoy same degree of press freedoms, civil liberties, and legal guarantees as Indians do. Although China's leaders speak in general terms about the need for some kind of democracy, its political institutions are not as responsive as India's. Moreover, like India, China is also rent by ethnic, class, and regional cleavages, which are likely to become wider rather than narrower during the course of its economic development.

Whereas the principal danger facing India is economic stagnation exacerbated by political gridlock, the principal danger confronting China is a political explosion should economic progress stall. Still, while keeping in mind that neither country's future course is clear, the odds are that both China and India are on their way to acquiring major-power status. Each is of a size and self-confidence to have a global view, as well as to carry great weight in their respective regions. Their economies will have growing significance as suppliers of both exports and investment capital, and their domestic markets will be of increasing interest to both exporters and investors.

At the same time as China and India are rising in importance, the map of Asia is being redrawn to include them both. In the not-too-distant past, Asia was widely seen as divided into three relatively distinct subregions: East and Northeast Asia (Russia, China, Mongolia, Korea, Japan); Southeast Asia (Vietnam, Cambodia, Laos, Thailand, Malaysia, Singapore, Indonesia, the Philippines, and Myanmar); and South Asia (India, Pakistan, Bangladesh, Sri Lanka, and the Himalayan states). This mental map of the area was not unreasonable: the cultural and historical differences among these regions were sufficiently great, the economic ties among them sufficiently small, and the regional institutions linking them sufficiently weak that they were indeed quite separate.

The end of autarkic development strategies and the rapid growth of trade and investment flows have broken down this sense of mutual isolation. Southeast Asia is now a major trading partner of East and Northeast Asia. South Asia, too, is expanding its economic ties with Southeast Asia, China, Korea, and Japan. Increasingly, all of Asia is being knit together into a single interdependent economy. And the creation of pan-Asian institutions—first the Asian Development Bank (ADB) in the 1960s, then the

Asia-Pacific Economic Cooperation forum (APEC) in the 1980s, and then the ASEAN Regional Forum (ARF) on security in the 1990s—has reinforced the sense of a single region with a common identity.

Located in the heart of East Asia, China has been part of this process, especially since it began its program of reform and opening in the late 1970s and early 1980s. China joined the Asian Development Bank in 1986, joined APEC in 1991, and was a founding member of the ASEAN Regional Forum in 1994. More recently, China has participated with Japan, South Korea, and ASEAN in forming the ASEAN Plus Three group, which has discussed first international financial matters and now regional political issues. There are also plans to create a free-trade area between China and ASEAN, a so-called ASEAN-plus-one arrangement.

India was at first peripheral to this process, for it was not seen to be part of the same region as Southeast or Northeast Asia. But the concept of "Asia" is expanding once again, so as to incorporate India and, perhaps, the rest of South Asia. India is not yet a part of APEC. But it was one of the founding members of the Asian Development Bank in 1966, and joined the ASEAN Regional Forum in 1996. For both economic and security reasons it is expanding its bilateral links with various Southeast Asian countries, as well as with China and Japan. ASEAN and India will soon hold their own regular dialogue, corresponding to the ASEAN Plus Three grouping that links ASEAN with East and Northeast Asia.

As the boundaries of Asia are redrawn to include South Asia, the relationship between China and India will become an increasingly important feature of the international relations of the Asia-Pacific region, on a par with the relations between China and Russia, Russia and Japan, China and Japan, and other pairs of major powers. This is especially true in the area of proliferation. India's strategic program is in part a response to China's. India wishes to avoid a situation in which its border dispute with China, or its conflict with Pakistan, is conducted under the shadow of a Chinese nuclear capability against which India has no deterrent. In addition, India invokes a security threat from China as a rationale for its nuclear weapon and missile programs.

The reverse causal relationship is somewhat weaker. As George Perkovich points out in chapter 6, China's strategic weapons program has thus far been driven primarily by its desire for a credible deterrent against the United States. And Beijing may well assume that a deterrent that is sufficient to deal with the United States will be more than sufficient to cope with India's far weaker nuclear arsenal. However, at least some of China's strategic cooperation with Pakistan—its provision of nuclear and missile technology—was the result of Beijing's desire to provide a counterweight to India along India's western border.

Similarly, the two countries' policies toward South and Southeast Asia are to some degree linked to a quiet rivalry between them. Although China seems willing to acknowledge—although not necessarily to welcome—New Delhi's dominant role in much of South Asia, it has sought to ensure Pakistan's security so as to maintain a counterweight against India. Accordingly, China has provided assistance first to Pakistan's nuclear program, and later to its missile programs. Some analysts also believe that China's growing political and military relations with Myanmar and Bangladesh are aimed at providing a second counterweight on India's eastern border.

Conversely, India is showing a growing interest in expanding its ties with Southeast Asia, especially with Vietnam. While there is a clear economic rationale for this effort, to a degree it is also being driven by New Delhi's desire, at a minimum, to prevent Southeast Asia from becoming an exclusive Chinese sphere of influence and, at a maximum, to produce a Southeast Asian counterweight against China comparable to China's Pakistani counterweight against India.

As Ashley Tellis suggests in chapter 5 of this volume, China appears reluctant to see India join regional institutions. As noted earlier, India was able to join the Asian Development Bank in the 1960s because that organization, following the lead of such United Nations organizations as the Economic Commission for Asia and the Far East (ECAFE), has always viewed South Asia, Southeast Asia, and East and Northeast Asia as being parts of a single region. It has also been able to join the ASEAN Regional Forum on security, because its relevance to the security problems of Asia was undeniable. But China has been trying, so far successfully, to resist the expansion of East Asian economic organizations to include India or any other South Asian nation. Thus, New Delhi has not yet been able to participate in either APEC or the Asia-Europe Meeting (ASEM).

To be sure, the India-China relationship is not the only cause of the two countries' policies in these areas. The Indian nuclear and missile programs are not just aimed at China but are part of India's claim to be a major regional and global power. China's relationship with Pakistan is increasingly aimed at maintaining influence in Central Asia as well as preserving a favorable balance of power in South Asia. To a degree, its arms sales to Islamabad are also a convenient bargaining chip to use against American arms sales to Taiwan. But, although each country's foreign policies are shaped by many factors, their competitive relationship is already one driver, and it is one that is likely to become more prominent as their national power grows.

The Future of China-India Relations

As the contributors to this volume have shown, except for a brief period in the early 1950s the India-China relationship has been essentially competitive, with open conflict during the border clashes of 1959 and the border war of 1962. Looking ahead, we can forecast a complex relationship that will include elements of cooperation, competition, and possibly even conflict.

In the realm of security, the possibility of direct conflict exists, not only because of the disputed border but also if there were significant instability in Pakistan, Tibet, Myanmar, or any other area in which both India and China have an interest. Each country will also continue to design and deploy its military forces in large part with an eye to the other. However, in the near term the two countries wish to avoid conflict, as shown by their effort to install confidence-building measures along their border and to expand their political and military dialogue. China does not want a confrontation with India to drive New Delhi into a close strategic alignment with the United States. Nor is India certain that it could rely on American, let alone Russian, backing in the event of a confrontation with China.

As two large developing countries with a common anticolonial background, India and China hold common perspectives—and sometimes take coordinated positions—on a variety of international issues. Their common status as developing economies may lead them to take similar positions on international trade issues, sharing opposition to the inclusion of labor and environmental standards in international trade agreements. Their similar experiences with Western colonialism and imperialism may imply similar stands on questions of sovereignty, with a shared skepticism about unilateral humanitarian intervention and about the use of economic sanctions to promote human rights. Their common concern with enhancing their international power and status may give them a shared interest in forging a world that is more multipolar than unipolar. Increasingly, too, they may have similar views on the need to ensure the flow of energy resources from Central Asia and the Middle East.

However, neither country is entirely comfortable with the rise of the other. They may therefore compete for influence in Central and Southeast

Asia, and for leadership positions in international organizations such as the United Nations and various regional organizations. They may also compete for the favor of the United States, each one attempting to draw Washington into an alignment—at least temporarily—against the other.

Finally, the geographical barriers between the two countries, and their roughly similar levels of development, do not suggest extensive commercial ties between them. Indeed they will increasingly compete with one another economically, although the extent to which this is so will depend on India's ability to undertake meaningful economic reforms and on China's ability to keep ahead of India in many areas of export. However, as James Clad suggests in chapter 8, the two economies may enjoy certain complementarities in the area of information technology that could lead to strategic partnerships between Chinese and Indian firms.

This blend of common, competitive, and conflicting interests makes it possible to envision a variety of futures for India-China relations, many of which have been explored by Mark Frazier in chapter 9. However, the most likely scenario is that of a competitive relationship, unbuffered by extensive economic ties but without a significant possibility of armed conflict.

Implications and Recommendations

What are the consequences of these developments for the United States? The analysis in this volume suggests three implications that both the American public and American policy makers should consider.

First, the United States must regard both India and China as rising Asian powers. It should increasingly treat India on a par with China as a major regional power with global aspirations, rather than regarding it simply as Pakistan's counterpart in a South Asian balance of power. This is not to say that the United States can now ignore Pakistan. In the war against terrorism, in the effort to stabilize Central Asia, and in the struggle against proliferation of weapons of mass destruction, Pakistan presents a complex mixture of challenges and opportunities to the United States. But the United States needs to complement its traditional focus on the subcontinental triangle that links the United States, Pakistan, and India with greater attention to the larger Asian triangle that connects the United States, India, and China.

This understanding will require less change in the American approach to China than in its approach to India. China's importance has long been understood in the United States—indeed, it has perhaps occasionally been exaggerated. China is the world's most populous country, with a high and sustained rate of economic growth, permanent membership on the UN Security Council, growing military capabilities, and a will to be acknowledged as a major regional and global power. As such, China deserves a prominent place in American calculations. Moreover, with the exception of the period immediately following the Tiananmen crisis of 1989, it has generally received it.

By contrast, India's importance has tended to be understated until recently. Americans have generally seen India on a par with Pakistan rather than with China. But India, too, is on the move. Its population will exceed China's in a few decades. India has enormous economic potential, although its economy is still constrained by interventionist domestic policies and protectionist polices toward foreign trade and investment. India has nuclear capabilities, a large army, and a blue-water navy. It is the key power in South Asia, is an emerging power in East Asia, and shows the desire to play a major role globally.

Accordingly, India should receive more attention in American foreign policy making than has generally been the case in the past. Both the George W. Bush administration and its predecessor, the Clinton administration, have moved in this direction, showing clear indications that India is now regarded as a major power with which frequent strategic dialogue is essential.

Second, the United States should also view Asia increasingly as a single region in which the India-China relationship will play a major role. This will require a significant reconceptualization and reorganization of the way in which the United States looks at the region, and a reorganization of the ways in which Washington deals with it.

The academic community, for example, has long separated the study of South Asia from the study of East Asia. If not studied entirely on its own terms, South Asia was more likely to be linked with Southeast Asia—understandable given the historic and cultural links between the two regions, but increasingly anachronistic given the growing economic and political integration of the region as a whole. Universities and research organizations must increasingly connect the study of South Asia, Southeast Asia, and East and Northeast Asia into single centers and programs, examining the ways in which the situation in one part of Asia increasingly affects developments in others.

The U.S. government will also have to reorganize itself in ways that acknowledge the interconnections within the region. Interestingly, in the Defense Department responsibility for all of Asia—from Northeast Asia through Southeast Asia to South Asia—has traditionally been assigned to the Pacific Command in Honolulu. Elsewhere in the government, however, different parts of Asia have been placed under different agencies. During most of the Cold War, South Asia was seen as linked more closely to the Middle East than to East Asia; it was assigned to the units responsible for Near Eastern affairs in both the Department of State and the National Security Council. Then, to give the situation in South Asia more attention, a separate South Asian Bureau was created in the State Department in the early 1990s.

Washington is gradually recognizing these new regional boundaries and is reorganizing itself accordingly. The Bush administration has merged the staff members responsible for South Asia in the National Security Council (NSC) together with those responsible for East and Southeast Asia. It may be time to undertake a comparable reorganization in the State Department as well.

Third, and most important, the United States needs to think carefully about the future of the strategic triangle among China, India, and the United States and about America's posture within it. Given the differences between the United States and China and between China and India, it would be naive to think that the three powers can all maintain highly cooperative relations, forming a concert of powers. At the same time, it would be unwise to view India as a partner in a firm strategic alignment with China.

As noted earlier, some analysts in both India and the United States have advocated a strategic alignment between the United States and India to contain China. In essence, their argument is that China is a growing authoritarian state with uncertain ambitions in Asia that is likely to become a strategic competitor of the United States. India, by contrast, is a democratic state whose ambitions in the region do not conflict fundamentally with America's. India can become a natural partner—even an ally—of the United States. Because China's rise poses a threat to both India and America, these analysts say, it is appropriate for the two countries to form a counterweight against China, just as the United States and China formed an alignment against the Soviet Union in the 1970s and 1980s.

But, at present, such an approach would be not be the best strategy for the United States. For one thing, we should not presume a confrontational relationship between the United States and China. Despite the many differences between the two on issues ranging from Taiwan to human rights to trade, and despite each country's mistrust regarding the other's longer-term strategic orientation, there are also many common interests between the United States and China, as the September 11 tragedy shows. Whatever the rhetoric during the 2000 election campaign, the George W. Bush administration has made clear that it would prefer to see a cooperative relationship than a conflictual one. The Chinese government has responded in kind. This implies that an antagonistic relationship between the United States and China is not inevitable.

Nor should one assume a confrontational relationship between India and China. The two countries are likely to have a competitive relationship, focused increasingly on the expansion of economic and political influence into Southeast Asia. But competition does not necessarily imply open hostility. In fact, both New Delhi and Beijing have been trying to improve their bilateral relations, in the common understanding that a confrontational relationship would not be in the interest of either country.

The history of the triangle implies, in fact, that it is highly unlikely that either the Indian or the American governments will seek an anti-China alignment, unless Beijing's policy toward both of them becomes far more hostile and uncompromising than it is at present. In the absence of such an uncompromising Chinese posture, a U.S.-India alignment would unwisely lock both countries into antagonistic relationships with China that would not be in either nation's interest. It might imply an American commitment to Indian security that it would be expensive for the United States to meet. Conversely, it might imply an Indian reliance on American backing that India would not want.

The analysis in this volume suggests instead that the United States should pursue better relations with both countries, in the expectation that it will cooperate with India on some issues, with China on some issues, and with both countries on still others. On some questions the United States may find that both China and India take positions that differ from America's.

On economic issues, for example, the United States has an interest in opening the huge markets of India and China to U.S. exports and investment. In principle, both the Chinese and Indian governments agree, having acknowledged the importance of market forces and deeper integration into the world economy to their economic development strategies. But there will still be significant differences between the United States and both India and China over economic issues. In the case of China, the United States will probably experience frustration at the slow and incomplete Chinese implementation of its obligations as a member of the WTO, especially if the American economy slows and if the U.S. trade deficit with China increases.

In the case of India, the United States will face the problem of encouraging painful economic reforms and market-opening measures in a country that is already in the WTO. The United States may also find that China and India, like many other developing countries, are skeptical about the American agenda for a new round of WTO negotiations, particularly if the United States seeks to lower barriers to investment or to add labor and environmental standards to trade negotiations.

Similarly, in the realm of security, India and China increasingly support international nonproliferation norms, just as does the United States. However, they both can be expected to differ with the United States in significant ways. Both countries are intent on developing credible but limited nuclear deterrents. China is already deploying both intercontinental ballistic missiles (ICBMs) and submarine-launched missiles capable of targeting the United States, and India may do so in the foreseeable future. At worst, these strategic programs may threaten America's own security; at a minimum, they run counter to the U.S. preference to restrict vertical proliferation by established nuclear powers.

Conversely, both India and China will feel challenged by American efforts to deploy ballistic missile defense (BMD). An American BMD program will directly threaten Chinese security interests by reducing the credibility of Beijing's deterrent against the United States. It may also threaten Indian interests as well, not so much because an American BMD will erode the credibility of India's deterrent, but because it will most likely lead to increased Chinese strategic deployments that will be of concern to New Delhi.

The United States also has an interest in preventing horizontal proliferation—the spread of weapons of mass destruction from one state to another. India has not followed policies of horizontal proliferation that are of concern to the United States. China, however, has—especially with regard to Pakistan. The development and expansion of India's nuclear deterrent and conventional capabilities may encourage China to continue its assistance to Pakistan so as to maintain a more favorable balance in South Asia. This risk will be greater if there is no improvement in either India-Pakistan or China-India relations.

Finally, the United States has major human rights complaints about China, but lesser concerns with India as well. In China, most of the issues have involved the nondemocratic nature of the regime: the suppression of views that challenge the leading role of the Chinese Communist Party, the suppression of independent political parties and trade unions, the controls over the press. In addition, however, China is a multiethnic nation, and minorities (especially Tibetan and Uighur) have been targets of repression. So, too, have been religious organizations (whether Buddhist, Christian, or Islamic) that are independent of the party.

As a democracy, India poses far fewer human rights concerns for the United States, but they are not altogether absent. One issue has been the treatment of the local population in Kashmir, elements of which are charged by India with fomenting terrorism. Another issue is the continuing de facto discrimination against lower castes in Indian society. The rise of Hindu nationalism in India, some of it government-sponsored, may lead to increasing ethnic tensions across the country that could also raise human rights issues.

As already indicated, both China and India are skeptical of international human rights regimes that would target their own abuses. In the case of China, this is regularly evident at the annual meetings of the United Nations Committee on Human Rights. In the case of India, it became apparent at the recent UN conference on racism in Durban, at which India resisted including its caste system in discussions of racial discrimination. Human rights may therefore be an issue on which the United States may encounter common opposition from both India and China.

It remains to be seen how September 11 will affect this aspect of American foreign policy. It is possible that the United States will be more tolerant of the suppression of separatist groups in Kashmir, if they can be credibly and fairly accused of terrorism. It is also possible that, in the aftermath of the crisis, the United States will place somewhat lesser emphasis on human rights matters relative to security questions. Still, it is likely that human rights will retain an important role in American foreign policy, and the issue will introduce occasional tensions into our relations with both China and India.

Thus, the three countries in this new strategic triangle have both common and divergent interests. Although there may be continued talk of "partnerships" or "alignments" on all sides of the triangle, and although each pair of countries will find common ground on particular issues, overall the relationships among them are likely to remain fluid:

- At times India and the United States will find common ground against China, especially if the expansion of Chinese influence in Asia seems to be directed at excluding them from any part of the region, or if it threatens the security of countries friendly to India or to the United States.

- At times the United States and China may find common ground against India, especially if India violates nonproliferation norms in its quest for nuclear status, or poses a threat to the security of Pakistan or of any other neighbor.
- At times India and China will find common ground against the United States, particularly if the United States tries to exclude them from the global status they both seek, or if the United States adopts policies that are seen as excessively unilateral or interventionist. A continued American presence in Central Asia, in the aftermath of September 11, could conceivably be of concern to both Beijing and New Delhi.
- At times all three may work together to pursue common interests, especially in the realm of transnational problems such as terrorism, in maintaining stability in Central Asia and the Persian Gulf, and in promoting global prosperity and openness.

The future relationship among the three countries may occasionally resemble a romantic triangle, in which one tries to benefit from the tensions between the other two. The two countries that might plausibly seek the pivotal position in such a triangle would be the United States and India. If there is a downturn in the India-China relationship, then both Beijing and New Delhi might compete for preferred treatment from the United States. To modify the quotation from Henry Kissinger cited at the beginning of this chapter, this would enable the United States to enjoy its Indian curry and its Peking duck in the same meal. But it is also possible that New Delhi might strive for the same situation. If India can improve its relationship with China and if Washington's ties with Beijing should later deteriorate, then India might try to manipulate the U.S.-China rivalry to its own advantage.

However, as already noted, a romantic triangle is inherently unstable. The country occupying the pivotal position may indeed benefit if the tensions between the other two remain moderate. But if the relationship between the others deteriorates further—from tension to rivalry to confrontation—then the country that once occupied the pivotal position may be under irresistible pressure to choose between them.

Although the United States may therefore benefit from a moderate degree of competition between India and China, it would find little advantage from a confrontational relationship between them. Indeed, the United States has an interest in supporting continued improvements in India-China relations. In particular, it would be desirable for the two countries to develop confidence-building measures along their disputed border, working toward an eventual territorial settlement. It is also in the U.S. interest that they maintain frequent official and unofficial dialogue, and that they promote their economic and cultural ties. The prospect that these interactions would produce a close Sino-Indian relationship, defined in opposition to American interests, is remote. Even as Sino-Indian relations improve, the United States will probably enjoy better relations with both India and China than they have with each other.

The shape of this new strategic triangle, as measured by the relative warmth of its three sides, will most likely vary over time, depending on the relative salience of different international issues at any given moment and on the policies adopted by Beijing and New Delhi. It is unlikely that the triangle will sufficiently shift to form an enduring alignment of two against one. If it did, given the relative power of the three countries, it is most likely that the alignment would pit India and the United States against a more assertive China. But such an arrangement is not in the American interest. Rather, Americans should prefer a triangle in which the United States can work together with both India and China to advance common interests.

Notes

1. This historical overview draws heavily on several major works on U.S.-India and India-China relations over the last fifty years, including Dennis Kux, *India and the United States: Estranged Democracies, 1941–1991* (Washington, D.C.: National Defense University Press, 1993); Satu P. Limaye, *U.S.-Indian Relations: The Pursuit of Accommodation* (Boulder, Colo.: Westview Press, 1993); and John W. Garver, *Protracted Contest: Sino-Indian Rivalry in the Twentieth Century* (Seattle: University of Washington Press, 2001). On U.S.-China relations, see Harry Harding, *A Fragile Relationship: The United States and China since 1972* (Washington, D.C.: Brookings Institution Press, 1992); and David M. Lampton, *Same Bed, Different Dreams* (Stanford: Stanford University Press, 2001).
2. Garver, *Protracted Contest,* 29.
3. Kux, *Estranged Democracies,* 182.
4. The contributors to this volume offer somewhat different explanations of China's cooperation with Pakistan's nuclear weapon program. In particular, they differ over the relative weight that should be assigned to China's desire to counterbalance India and its desire to counterbalance the Soviet Union.
5. See John W. Garver, "The China-India-U.S. Triangle: Strategic Relations in the Post–Cold War Era," *NBR Analysis* 13, no. 5 (October 2002): 13–16.
6. Ibid., 52–53.

Contributors

James Clad handles Middle Eastern affairs with special reference to Iraq at the Overseas Private Investment Corporation in Washington, D.C. Previously he was professor of South and Southeast Asian studies at Georgetown University's School of Foreign Service, director for Asia Pacific energy at Cambridge Energy Research Associates, and South Asia correspondent for the *Far Eastern Economic Review.*

Francine R. Frankel is founding director of the Center for the Advanced Study of India and the Madan Lal Sobti Professor for the Study of Contemporary India and professor of political science at the University of Pennsylvania. Her book *India's Political Economy, The Gradual Revolution 1947–77* was translated into Chinese and published by the Chinese Academy of Social Sciences; a second, updated edition is expected to be published in 2004. She has organized major collaborative research projects and is an editor and contributor of *Transforming India, Social and Political*

Dynamics of Democracy, and a contributor and co-editor (with M.S.A. Rao) of the two-volume work *Dominance and State Power, Decline of a Social Order.* Currently, she is at work on the formative period in Indo-U.S. relations, based on original archival documents.

Mark W. Frazier is an assistant professor of government and the Henry Luce Assistant Professor in the Political Economy of East Asia at Lawrence University. He is the author of "China-India Relations since Pokhran II: Assessing Sources of Conflict and Cooperation," published in *AccessAsia Review.* Currently he is working on a study of how central and local governments implement labor legislation and labor market reforms in China and India. He is the author *The Making of the Chinese Industrial Workplace: State, Revolution, and Labor Management.*

Sumit Ganguly is director of the India Studies Program at Indiana University in Bloomington and the Rabindranath Tagore Chair in Indian Culture and Civilization and former professor of Asian studies and government at the University of Texas at Austin. A specialist on South Asian regional security issues, Ganguly has published widely in a range of professional journals. He is also the founding editor of *India Review,* the only refereed, quarterly, social science journal devoted to the study of contemporary India. Ganguly serves on the editorial boards of *Asian Affairs, Asian Survey, Current History,* and the *Journal of Strategic Studies.* He is a member of the Council on Foreign Relations in New York and the International Institute of Strategic Studies in London. His most recent book is *Conflict Unending: India-Pakistan Tensions since 1947.*

Harry Harding is dean of the Elliott School of International Affairs and professor of international affairs and political science at George Washington University. He serves on the boards of the Asia Foundation, the National Committee on U.S.-China Relations, and the Atlantic Council. He has previously been a member of the U.S.-PRC Joint Commission on Scientific and Technological Cooperation and the Defense Policy Board, and president of the Association of Professional Schools of International Affairs. A specialist on U.S. relations with Asia, his most recent book is *A Fragile Relationship: The United States and China Since 1972.*

Steven A. Hoffmann is the Joseph C. Palamountain Chair in Government at Skidmore College. He is the author of numerous publications covering

Indian politics, India-China relations, and India-U.S. relations, including *India and the China Crisis.* He was a Public Policy Scholar in the Asia Program at the Woodrow Wilson International Center for Scholars, and has lectured widely in India, Israel, and the United States.

George Perkovich is vice president for studies at the Carnegie Endowment for International Peace. He is the author of *India's Nuclear Bomb,* an award-winning history of India's nuclear weapons program and decision-making process. He has published many scholarly and popular press articles on international security issues. His current work addresses questions of fairness and equity in the international system, including the World Trade Organization and other nonsecurity regimes and institutions.

Susan L. Shirk is a professor in the Graduate School of International Relations and Pacific Studies at the University of California at San Diego and research director of the University of California system-wide Institute on Global Conflict and Cooperation. She served as U.S. deputy assistant secretary of state in the Bureau of East Asia and Pacific Affairs, with responsibility for the People's Republic of China, Taiwan, Hong Kong, and Mongolia. Shirk is the author of *How China Opened Its Door: The Political Success of the PRC's Foreign Trade and Investment Reforms; The Political Logic of Economic Reform in China;* and *Competitive Comrades: Career Incentives and Student Strategies in China.*

T. N. Srinivasan is the Samuel C. Park, Jr., Professor of Economics at Yale University. Formerly a professor and later research professor at the Indian Statistical Institute, Delhi, he has taught at numerous universities in the United States. His research interests include international trade, development, agricultural economics, and microeconomic theory. He recently authored *Reintegrating India with the World Economy* with Suresh D. Tendulkar and edited *Trade, Finance, and Investment in South Asia.* Srinivasan is a fellow of the American Philosophical Society, the Econometric Society, and the American Academy of Arts and Sciences, and a foreign associate of the National Academy of Sciences.

Ashley J. Tellis is a senior associate at the Carnegie Endowment for International Peace in Washington, D.C., and former senior adviser to the ambassador at the Embassy of the United States in New Delhi, India. Previously, Tellis served on the National Security Council staff as special assistant to the president and senior director, Strategic Planning and Southwest Asia. Prior to joining the State Department, he was a senior policy analyst at RAND, Washington, D.C., and professor of policy analysis at the RAND Graduate School. His research interests include international relations theory, military strategy, and proliferation issues, South Asian politics, and U.S.-Asian security relations. He is the author of *India's Emerging Nuclear Posture* and co-author (with Michael Swaine) of *Interpreting China's Grand Strategy: Past, Present, and Future,* as well as numerous monographs and articles on various dimensions of Asian security.

Index

Note: Page numbers followed by *n, f,* or *t* refer to notes, figures, or tables.